D0984368

THE EARLY PLAYS

OF

Mikhail Bulgakov

THE EARLY PLAYS

OF

Mikhail Bulgakov

Edited by Ellendea Proffer

TRANSLATED BY

Carl R. Proffer AND *Ellendea Proffer*

INDIANA UNIVERSITY PRESS

BLOOMINGTON / LONDON

*For performance rights contact Indiana University Press
or Ann Elmo Agency, New York.*

*Published in Canada by Fitzhenry & Whiteside Limited,
Don Mills, Ontario*

Library of Congress catalog card number: 70-166117

ISBN: 0-253-11885-9

Manufactured in the United States of America

To the memory of

ELENA SERGEEVNA BULGAKOVA

Contents

PREFACE

THIS VOLUME CONTAINS FIVE PLAYS BY MIKHAIL BULGAKOV, the first five plays written in his maturity—1925–1930.[1] Two of these, *Zoya's Apartment* and *The Crimson Island,* have never been published in the Soviet Union. Half of the Russian text of *The Crimson Island* has been published in an émigré journal, as has an early version of *Zoya's Apartment.* Our translation of the final text of *Zoya's Apartment* was recently published in the scholarly journal *Canadian Slavic Studies* (summer 1970). The complete text of *The Crimson Island* appears here for the first time in translation. Bulgakov's finest play, *A Cabal of Hypocrites,* is also translated here for the first time into English.

Bulgakov wrote five other major plays: *Adam and Eve, Bliss, Ivan Vasilievich, Last Days,* and *Batum.* Translations of these plays will comprise a planned second volume.

Since Bulgakov's life is poorly known even in the U.S.S.R., and errors of fact are common even in published sources, especially in the West, the introduction to this volume is a chronological account of his life. It is based on disparate published sources, checked against archival materials and interviews with his widow and friends. While most readers will probably have some familiarity with Soviet literature, I have tried to give explanations which will keep the general reader from being totally bewildered. With a few exceptions I have avoided scholarly apparatus, thinking that this belongs in a full-length study of Bulgakov's career. For all Russian sources the reader is referred to E. Proffer, "The Major Works of Mikhail Bulgakov," Ph.D. dissertation, Indiana University, 1970.

1. Bulgakov began *The Days of the Turbins,* then entitled *White Guard,* in 1925. Although some changes were made during the years 1931–36, Bulgakov completed *A Cabal of Hypocrites* in 1930.

I have also provided an introduction to each play. These sections provide information on the history of the works and brief critical commentaries.

All footnotes within the translations belong to the editor. They explain historical allusions not covered in the introductions and identify literary allusions and songs wherever possible.

The translations of published plays are made from the texts in Mikhail Bulgakov, *P'esy* (Moscow, 1962).

I wish to thank Steve Soudakov and Vladimir Ushakow for their generous help with problems of translation and Assya Humesky for her assistance in identifying Russian songs.

E. P.

November 24, 1970
Ann Arbor

INTRODUCTION

MIKHAIL BULGAKOV: 1891–1940

MIKHAIL BULGAKOV was the rare literary phenomenon, a writer who wrote both plays and novels successfully. As a result of the literary cold war, Bulgakov has been regarded as a playwright in the Soviet Union, but as a novelist in the West. Until the publication of *The Master and Margarita* Bulgakov was generally ignored in the West, despite the fact that he had written one of the most popular plays ever produced by the Moscow Art Theater (*The Days of the Turbins*), not to mention many other plays, stories, and a fine novel entitled *White Guard*. *The Master and Margarita* brought him to prominence, but Bulgakov had been there all along. And although it is rather late, the time has come to acquaint the Western reader with the best Russian playwright of the Soviet period.

Once, when asked whether he preferred narrative or dramatic forms, Bulgakov replied that he needed them both, just as a pianist needs both his left and right hand. As a result, throughout his literary career plays alternated with prose fiction. But in spite of this balance, Bulgakov was avowedly a man of the theater and had no desire to belong to Moscow literary circles. Most of his friends were connected with the theater—playwrights, actors, theatrical designers, and directors. This was the world he seemed destined for from childhood.

Born in Kiev in 1891, Bulgakov was already preparing himself for the theater when he sat around bonfires and told his fellow students stories in which he imitated all of the characters' voices. These stories were complexly plotted, full of mystifications and sudden twists. But this inventive storyteller chose to go into medicine when he enrolled in the University of Kiev, and specialized in venereology rather than in literature. During his university years Bulgakov took part in amateur theatricals, but it was not until after the Revolution that he deserted medicine for literature.

Bulgakov wrote his first plays for a small theater in the Caucasian city of Vladikavkaz, where he found himself in 1920, one of the last years of the Civil War. The plays were very popular, but he was not at all satisfied with his provincial success.

> I recall that about a year ago I wrote you that I had begun to be printed in the newspapers. My feuilletons appeared in many Caucasian newspapers. That summer I continually appeared at public programs with my stories and lectures. Then my plays were done on the stage. First the one-act humoresque *Self-defense*, then the hastily written four-act drama *The Brothers Turbin*.
>
> They hollered "author!" in the theater, and they clapped and clapped. . . . When they called me out after the second act I came out with a dull feeling. . . . I looked dully at the made-up faces of the actors, at the thundering audience. And I thought: "Why, my dream has been realized, but in such an ugly way: instead of the Moscow stage—a provincial stage; instead of the drama about Alexei Turbin which I had cherished—a hastily done, immature thing. . . ."
>
> I am working sedulously. I am writing a novel—the only carefully thought out thing of this whole time here.[1]

From this it can be seen that at twenty-nine Bulgakov was both highly critical of himself and very ambitious. The novel referred to was to become Bulgakov's *White Guard*. The theater put on four of Bulgakov's plays—the two which he mentions, *The Paris Communards*, and *The Sons of the Mulla*. Bulgakov later said he hoped all copies of the plays were destroyed.

In the fall of 1921 Bulgakov moved to Moscow—a Moscow which was struggling with hunger, lack of heating, and an improbable amount of snow. His Moscow career began with a series of hack jobs, repugnant to him, but necessary for survival. At a time when he was trying to write the novel *White Guard* he was forced to produce feuilletons in enormous quantities. In three years he worked for newspapers and magazines with such revolutionary titles as *Red Panorama, Red Magazine for All, Red Newspaper, Red Pepper, On*

Watch, and *The Megaphone.* Most of his work appeared in the newspapers *The Whistle* and *On the Eve.* Through long and resentful acquaintance he grew to hate newspaper work and editors. In his autobiography he wrote:

> At the end of the year I came to Moscow without money, without belongings, to remain there forever. I underwent long torture in Moscow; in order to support myself I served as a reporter and feuilletonist for the newspapers, and I came to hate these jobs, which have no honors. At the same time I learned to hate editors, I hate them now, and I will hate them all the rest of my life.

E. Mindlin, a co-worker of Bulgakov in the editorial room of *On the Eve,* in Moscow, recalls that Bulgakov was very popular with readers in Berlin, and that Alexei Tolstoy, editor of the paper's literary supplement, was constantly asking for more Bulgakov stories. Unlike his younger colleagues who affected a bohemian-proletarian disorder in appearance, Bulgakov ignored the fashion of the Civil War period and the era of the New Economic Policy.

> Everything about Bulgakov—things we couldn't get like the dazzlingly fresh collars, hard as plaster-of-Paris, and the carefully knotted tie, a suit that was not modish but finely tailored, the pressed crease in the trousers, the special forms of address to his interlocutors and the appending of old-fashioned particles like the ending "-s" ["sir"], as in "if you please, sir" or "as you wish, sir," the kissing of women's hands, and the almost regal ceremony of his bows—absolutely everything made him stand out in our society and environment. And also, of course, the long fur coat, in which he came, full of dignity, to the editorial office, invariably holding his hands inside the sleeves!

Gradually Bulgakov's feuilletons grew into short stories, and in 1923 his first important work came in the May issue of the journal *Russia.* "Notes on the Cuffs" is a comic retelling of Bulgakov's first days in Moscow; another part of the same work recalls his life in the Caucasus. In 1924 "Diaboliad," the longest story he had yet written, was published in the literary almanac *The Depths,* and in October of the same year he wrote his first really famous story "The Fatal Eggs," which appeared in another issue of the same almanac in 1925. A novella called *Heart of a Dog* was written in the first months of

1925, but rejected by *The Depths*. Nineteen-twenty-five was a year of great events for Bulgakov. His first collection of stories, *Diaboliad*, was published that year, and the first two parts of *White Guard* were published in the journal *Russia*—which the authorities closed down partly as a result of the novel. But for Bulgakov all of these events were eclipsed by an invitation from the Moscow Art Theater (MXAT) to turn the novel *White Guard* into a play.

By a strange coincidence, Bulgakov had already begun to make a play of the novel. Happily he worked on the play for MXAT and between June and September he finished what he labeled the "latest typed copy."[2] After much rewriting, in which Ilya Sudakov, Pavel Markov, and Stanislavsky participated, the play was put into rehearsal in February of 1926. In July Stanislavsky ordered a 1,000-ruble advance paid to Bulgakov, and this changed Bulgakov's life. No longer did he have to grind out feuilletons each day—he could enjoy the luxury of working on his own projects.

By September 26 the theater received permission to put on the play, and a public rehearsal was held on the morning of October 2, 1926. At the rehearsal were some members of the Central Repertory Committee *(Glavrepertkom)*[3]—V. Blyum, A. Orlinsky, and Lunacharsky. Several Party members were also in the audience—they left in protest before the play was over. The same evening at the Communist Academy there was a public discussion of "Theater Politics of Soviet Power" with Lunacharsky, Orlinsky, the poet Vladimir Mayakovsky, and others taking part. The specific topic was discussed, but everyone was much more interested in discussing *The Days of the Turbins* (as the play had been renamed over Bulgakov's objections) and its obvious unsuitability for the Soviet stage. The anti-Bulgakov faction was so outspoken in its censure of the play that the directorate of the theater decided not to invite Bulgakov to the première!

After the opening all of the critics reviewed the play negatively, each giving a different explanation of what was wrong with it. The left-wing Russian Association of Proletarian Writers' feeling toward the fellow-travelers, Mayakovsky's personal enmity,[4] and Bulgakov's uncompromising attitude—all of these things could be blamed, but the most obvious reason for the attacks is that *The Days of the Tur-*

bins was the first play to depict the Whites simply as human beings, rather than as fiendish enemies. There were faults in the play, mainly because Bulgakov's collaborators insisted on certain changes—the absolutely false ending, for example, was suggested by Stanislavsky. But artistic faults were not what interested these critics. Bulgakov was a symbol, and to attack him was to attack the "internal émigrés."

Few writers could have endured the reviews Bulgakov received. For example: "Of course, there is no play here at all—and the author and the theater most clearly give away the artistic insignificance of the 'play' by their pitiful wandering from one title to another." There were even more abusive reviews—ones in which Alexei Turbin was referred to as a "son of a bitch." There was a whole series of open public meetings devoted to the "Trial of *White Guard*." Literary professionals who were well versed in contemporary literature and literary politics, men who had read *White Guard* and Bulgakov's other works saw their chance to squash this arrogant intellectual who did not follow the new literary fashions. The attacks on "Bulgakovism" became self-generating—some of the critics made careers out of attacking him. But because of the reaction of audiences to the play Bulgakov became famous, and despite the attacks, somehow fashionable. The play was the greatest success the Moscow Art Theater had in the era after the Revolution; and this more than made up for the reviews.

Because of this success, Bulgakov could more or less write what he wanted, and in these years (1926–1929) the theater became his life. No playwright in the history of Russian drama, with the exception of Ostrovsky, was so deeply involved with all aspects of theater life. From 1925 Bulgakov was a playwright, an adaptor, a director, and even an actor. Part of the great audience success that *The Days of the Turbins* had was due to Bulgakov's personal direction of the actors. He was a writer who could act out all of his characters from the pose of the body to the pattern of intonation. He himself played a role in the *Pickwick Club*. The close friends who came to his apartment were theater people—the set designer Pavel Vilyams, and fellow dramatists Nikolai Erdman, Alexei Fayko, and Sergei Ermolinsky.[5]

In spite of the continued attacks on his work in the press by such Party-oriented keepers of the faith as critics Leopold Averbakh and V. Blyum, Bulgakov continued to be very productive—though unpublished. In 1928 he began the story entitled first "The Black Magician," then "The Consultant with a Hoof," which would evolve into the novel *The Master and Margarita;* and he had three plays running: *The Days of the Turbins* at the Moscow Art Theater, *Zoya's Apartment* (written and premièred in 1926) at the Vakhtangov Theater, and *The Crimson Island* (written in 1927) at the Kamerny Theater. The critics hated him, but the public begged for tickets.

In 1928 Bulgakov finished another play—the controversial *Flight* which he had begun in 1926. Despite the praise of Gorky and others, the play was not passed by the Central Repertory Committee. Stalin thought the play was "dangerous" and also expressed dislike for *The Crimson Island* (premièred at the end of 1928). Bulgakov refused to rewrite *Flight,* and perhaps this more than anything else irritated both the critics and Stalin. One fact is clear: after March of 1929 all of Bulgakov's plays were banned from the stage. None had yet been published. People started to avoid him, his name suddenly disappeared from the newspapers, and the open discussions stopped— since his works were no longer played or published, it was superfluous to attack him.

It was one of the most difficult times of his life, and as Ermolinsky writes in his memoirs, precisely then Bulgakov showed the firmness of his character in allowing no compromises. Eight months after *The Days of the Turbins* was banned, Bulgakov started work on a new play entitled *A Cabal of Hypocrites.* It is not strange that the play shows a Molière who is crushed by a secret society and a despotic king. Nor is it incomprehensible why the banning of *Tartuffe* is presented as the final blow which broke Molière.

In this year of despair Bulgakov met Elena Sergeevna Shilovskaya, the woman who was to become his third wife. Little is known about his first wife, and he was no longer with her when he moved to Moscow; presumably he was married in Kiev after finishing his medical practice in the provinces. His second wife was Lyubov Evgenievna Belozerskaya, to whom he dedicated *White Guard.*

At the time Elena Sergeevna was married and had two sons. To Bulgakov's already considerable list of miseries was added another. Since his career appeared to be ruined and since the happiness of so many people was involved he and Elena Sergeevna decided that it was best for all concerned if they stopped seeing each other. This decision coincided with the banning of *Days*. At the most difficult time, Bulgakov was alone.

Sometime between February and early March of 1930 Bulgakov's play *A Cabal of Hypocrites* was rejected by the censorship. It was after this final blow, when he was unable to work, unable to see the one person he loved, fearing that his friends might face future problems because of association with him, that Bulgakov burned the drafts of *The Master and Margarita,* a novel entitled *Theater,* and a comedy.

On March 28, 1930 he wrote a letter to the Soviet government, in effect to Stalin. His usual proud, uncompromising spirit shines through the letter, as does his desperation. Nineteen-thirty was not as bad a year as those to come, but it is inconceivable that any writer would have admitted at that time, as Bulgakov did, to "deep skepticism in regard to the revolutionary process taking place in my backward country, and putting my much beloved 'Great Evolution' in opposition to it," not to mention saying that basic to his works was the idea that the intelligentsia represented the best in Soviet society. At a time when constructionist novels which glorified the common man were being ordered, Bulgakov declared that he described in black and mystical colors the "senseless, ugly features of our life . . . the depiction of the terrible traits of my people, those traits which long before the revolution caused the deepest sufferings of my teacher, Saltykov-Shchedrin." Bulgakov described how friends advised him to write a letter of repentance, repudiating his previous works, promising to be a writer who was totally dedicated to Soviet power. But, he wrote, he could not do it—just as he could not write a "Communist play": "But I would scarcely be able to present myself to the government in the proper light—having written a mendacious letter which would be a sloppy and naive political curvet." Taking an offensive position where one would expect a defensive one, Bulgakov goes on to catalogue the bad reviews he received[6] and then proceeds to denigrate the Central Repertory Committee which "is ruining the Soviet dramaturgy and will ruin it." When he finally came to the main point—asking for permission to leave the country, the request was so phrased as to be almost a demand: "I request the government of the U.S.S.R. to order me to leave the borders of the U.S.S.R. immediately." But the next paragraph implied that if he could "be of use" to the Soviet government, he would not want to leave: "I appeal to the humanity of Soviet power and ask that I, a writer who cannot be useful in his fatherland, be released magnanimously to freedom." Bulgakov then listed what jobs he would take if the authorities see fit not to let him leave—he would be a director and if not that an extra, and if not that a stagehand: "If this too is impossible, I request the Soviet government to do with me as it sees fit, but to do *something,* because at this time I— a playwright, author of five plays well known in the U.S.S.R. and abroad—am faced with poverty, the street, and perishing." It is only in these last paragraphs that the tone of indignation gave way to one of controlled desperation.

It seems clear that Bulgakov (who could have emigrated when his brothers did) had no real desire to emigrate. The tone of the letter is that of a man who has been deeply offended, who wants justice, and who wants to put his case as strongly as possible. Although one cannot doubt that the letter is an absolutely sincere description of Bulgakov's feelings, it is also a masterpiece of dramatic expression. How could anyone not respond to such honesty, such refusal to grovel? Of course, Bulgakov and all of his friends fully expected that Stalin would either not respond, or that he would make Bulgakov's life even more miserable. But one of Stalin's chief characteristics was the desire to seem unpredictable. Perhaps the fact that Bulgakov had not yielded to any of the pressures to become a "Socialist" writer impressed him in some way—he could not have encountered many Bulgakovs in his own circle. Whatever the reason, Stalin did react unexpectedly. He telephoned Bulgakov on April 18—twenty-one days after the letter was sent. Those twenty-one days must have been incredibly difficult for Bulgakov. The conversation between despot and artist was recorded in Elena Sergeevna Bulgakova's diary:

S. We have received your letter. And read it with our comrades. You will have a pleasing answer. Perhaps we really should let you go abroad. What is it, have we bored you very much?

B. I have thought very much recently about whether a Russian writer can live outside his Motherland, and it seems to me that he cannot.

S. You're right. I don't think so either. Where do you want to work? At the Art Theater?

B. Yes, I would like to. But I asked about it—they refused me.

S. Well you submit a request there. It seems to me that they will agree. . . .

In *Days of the Turbins,* when Shervinsky finally decides to stay in Russia, the German General says approvingly: "Right, Lieutenant. One should never abandon one's homeland. *Heimat ist Heimat.*"

One can see various sides of Bulgakov's personality in the letter to the Soviet government. Visible is the son of the theology professor who inculcated in his eldest son a stern, uncompromising attitude toward truth and honor, who believed that one can clearly discriminate between right and wrong, and who, like Yeshua in *The Master and Margarita,* believed that "to tell the truth is easy and pleasant." One can also hear the self-assured member of the intelligentsia, who refers to himself as a "bourgeois dramatist"—a man who knows who he is and who is not about to declare that the uneducated are better than he is, no matter how political fashions change. Also present is the artist who believes in himself and in his talent, and who bitterly resents the attacks on his work. Finally, there is the citizen who, loving his country, must tell the truth about what is wrong with it, if it is to survive.[7] All through the letter the emphasis is on the idea that Bulgakov is—and wants to be—"objective"; he states that in his plays he makes "great efforts to stand above the Reds and the Whites."

The letter caused yet another change of fortune. In September Bulgakov joined the staff of MXAT. Stanislavsky expressed happiness about the appointment of Bulgakov as an assistant director and literary consultant, and said he had great hopes for him as a director, because Bulgakov had been responsible for much of the directing of *Days of the Turbins.*

The stage version of *Dead Souls*—which Bulgakov had begun work on in May 1930—was his first assignment for the Moscow Art Theater.[8] With it he became an adapter instead of a creator—apart from the dramatization of *Dead Souls,* he worked on film scripts for *Dead Souls, The Inspector General, Anna Karenina,* and *War and Peace.* As his forty-first birthday approached, he wrote to Popov complaining about this kind of work and saying that a dramatization of the *Brockhaus-Efron Encyclopedia* would probably be next. He did little writing on his own—the science fiction comedy *Adam and Eve*[9] and some work on *The Master and Margarita* which he had begun again. Bulgakov's situation was far more endurable than it had been before the letter to Stalin, but he was still weighed down by personal problems and lack of time for creative work. In 1932, suddenly and inexplicably, his life changed again. Stalin appears to have intervened once more, and Bulgakov wrote to his friend Ermolinsky:

> In the middle of January, 1932 as a result of reasons which are unknown to me and into an examination of which I cannot enter, the government of the U.S.S.R. sent MXAT a remarkable directive to revive the play *The Days of the Turbins.* For the author of this play this means that he, the author, has been given back part of his life.

This event changed everything from Bulgakov's work at the theater to his personal life. He married Elena Sergeevna Shilovskaya and became the guardian of her five-year-old son in 1932, the year of the rebirth of *The Days of the Turbins.*

Bulgakov moved from the noisy apartment on Great Pirogovskaya Street to one on Furmanov Lane. Instead of bohemian disorder, he was surrounded by comfortable and tasteful furnishings. One of his friends described how worried he was when he first met Bulgakov's wife and saw the new apartment—everything was lovely and orderly, the table was set with beautiful dishes and good food, and as he was thinking "My indefatigable and bold Bulgakov is lost— he's gone bourgeois," Bulgakov appeared in his same old lilac bathrobe and dirty nightcap. He had changed, but for the better. Gone was the extreme tension of the previous months. Never again would he have to suffer alone; his wife's faith in Bulgakov's talent was as unshakable and powerful as Margarita's, and in the middle of the nightmare that was Moscow in the 1930's they managed to be happy together.

SOMEHOW it always surprised his friends that Bulgakov could do all of his "bread-and-butter" projects and still find time to write his own works. From 1932 to his death he wrote prolifically: a biography of Molière, the adaptation of *Dead Souls,* a translation of *L'Avare,* a reworking of *Le Bourgeois gentilhomme* called *Half-mad Jourdain,* three scenarios, four libretti, five plays—*Bliss* (1934), *Ivan Vasilievich* (1935), *Last Days* (1935), *Don Quixote* (1938), and *Batum* (1938)—and the *Theatrical Novel.* Of course, *The Master and Margarita* was also completed and it was the work which dominated his imagination for twelve years. As he wrote in a letter to Popov on June 26, 1934: "I am adapting *Dead Souls* for the screen and I'll bring the completed thing with me. Then the fuss with *Bliss* will start. Oh, so much work I have to do! But through my head wander my Margarita and the cat and the magic flights. . . ."

That he got so much work done seems even more unusual when one considers that he was not at all methodical in his writing; bursts of energy would be followed by exhaustion or sheer inactivity. When he was writing "for himself" he would often close the study curtains and light candles so that he could concentrate on the sight and sound of his work. When dictating to his wife, he would sometimes stand looking out the window, and it was clear to her by the way he corrected himself that he actually saw what he was describing, and that it was a matter of describing it accurately. When he was not writing, he would rummage through his books. Generally, he did not like poetry, except for Pushkin—"but Pushkin is not poetry," he would say.[10] His favorite writers remained Gogol, Saltykov-Shchedrin, and the nineteenth-century dramatist Sukhovo-Kobylin—and of course Molière. (He told his wife that when he died, the first person he would go to see in the next world was Molière.) But the kinds of books he really loved and read most avidly were old reference works, dictionaries, biographies, grammars, old magazines and newspapers.

When he was not working he would often go to drugstores and

buy medicines. He also enjoyed visiting his friends when they were sick and acting as doctor. But his favorite relaxation was exchanging stories with his friends in the evening—just as he had done on the Dnieper when a schoolboy. One of his friends recalls how Bulgakov would sit on the couch, one leg under him, chin propped on hand, creating hilarious stories. The stories did not depend on word-play or caricatures of acquaintances; rather they were flights of fantasy in which comic characters lived—characters that seemed real to the listeners. His stories were so funny that often his listeners ended up on the rug laughing hysterically. On occasion Bulgakov lived the stories instead of telling them. Once, when visiting the writer Paustovsky, he pretended to be a rather stupid German, a former prisoner of war, for the benefit of Paustovsky's guests—people whom he did not know in the slightest. As he notes in his memoirs, Paustovsky was both amused and impressed:

> Then I first understood all the power of Bulgakov's reembodiement (*perevoploščenie*). At the table, giggling stupidly, sat a blond little German with dull, empty eyes. Even his hands got sweaty. Everyone was speaking Russian, and of course, he didn't know a word of the language. But he apparently wanted very much to take part in the conversation, and he wrinkled his brow and muttered, trying desperately to recall some one Russian word he knew.
>
> At last the light came. The word was found. A plate of ham was put on the table. Bulgakov plunged his fork into the ham and cried ecstatically, "Peeg, peeg!" and dissolved in squeaky, triumphant laughter. None of the guests who did not know Bulgakov had the slightest doubt that a young German was sitting before them—and an utter idiot besides. This charade lasted several hours until Bulgakov got bored with it, and suddenly in purist Russian he sang the first line of *Eugene Onegin:* "My uncle has most honest principles."

Bulgakov's private theatricals were the only ones he was involved in after he left MXAT and went to work at the Bolshoi Theater in 1936. This departure resulted from the way Stanislavsky and Gorchakov mishandled his play *A Cabal of Hypocrites*—and its forced removal from the repertory after only a few performances in February and March 1936.[11] He kept up his ties with the Art Theater, but felt that he was a "service author" at MXAT, and could no longer endure the battles over rewriting. It is no coincidence that at this time Bulgakov began to write a mordant lampoon on Stanislavsky and MXAT—his *Theatrical Novel.*

Bulgakov, who had grown up an opera-lover in a family of opera-lovers, felt at home at the Bolshoi. When composing libretti *(Minin and Pozharsky, The Black Sea, Peter the Great,* and *Rachel)*[12] he would imagine himself the composer, singer, or director; and he would sing the arias, accompanying himself on the piano. At other times he would pretend to conduct the orchestra. His love for opera was almost as great as his love for the theater. He often went to *Aida* by himself, saying he was entranced by the outdated, slow-moving production and the second-rate singers—he claimed there was a sort of poetry in this very inertia, this monotony. Nostalgically he loved old-fashioned theaters and abhorred the new modern style —even though many of his plays were experimental and could not have been staged in the old theaters.

In 1937 Bulgakov suddenly put aside the book he had been working on, the half-completed *Theatrical Novel.* He had diagnosed the early symptoms of neurosclerosis in himself and decided that he must work seriously on the novel he considered his major work—*The Master and Margarita.* At the same time he had to continue more "practical" projects. He did not tell his friends about his illness, but kept on as usual. In 1938 he wrote two plays—one an adaptation of *Don Quixote* for the stage (completed in December), the other a play about the young Stalin—*Batum* (also dated 1938). *Batum* deals with the revolutionary movement in the Caucasus. Stalin is portrayed without a halo and under a different name. The play is favorable to Stalin—or, rather, to the young mountaineer-revolutionary. Since Bulgakov knew that he was dying there is no question of trying to curry favor—something hardly typical of him at any time. He might have written the play as a type of protection for his wife, but it seems much more likely that Stalin, a despot, fascinated him—just as Pilate, Louis XIV, and Nicholas I had. In any case the actor Khmelev was all ready to play the main role, but Stalin said: "All children and all young people are alike. There is no need to put on a play about the young Stalin."[13]

Bulgakov's illness progressed, and his friends still did not know.

When he began to be afraid to go anywhere alone, when his ordinarily intense introspection increased to the point of suffocation, when he started wearing dark glasses all the time and staying in the house as much as possible, his friends realized that he was very sick—but they had no idea that he was coming to terms with what he knew was a rapidly approaching death. Instead they assumed that he was passing through some nervous crisis. There had always been certain strange aspects to his personality—for example, he always washed his hands after touching dogs. When his intimates made fun of his fastidiousness, Ermolinsky records, Bulgakov would defend himself: "Every man should be a doctor in the sense that he disarms all invisible enemies which threaten his life. If I were the Chief of Police I would cancel the passport and replace it with an obligatory presenting of a urinanalysis." Bulgakov's years of looking at the world under the microscope had left a permanent mark on him.

He had greater worries. He made no pretense of humility about his work, and he considered himself a "master." He had always worried greatly about the honor of his literary name, and he never forgot or forgave his literary enemies. No longer could his friends joke with him about his excessive sensitivity to criticism and his role as a "knight of art." Some of his fears at this time were those of almost every Soviet writer in the late thirties. Ermolinsky quotes Bulgakov as saying: "I cannot get used to it, but it's time to. I am frightened, always frightened by every manifestation of mistrust toward myself or when I run up against suspicious captiousness about every word I write. But maybe I am not the only one who has this misfortune." Bulgakov, although no longer a part of the official literary world, followed the fortunes of his acquaintances. He saw many writers being destroyed, and an equal number being turned into servants of the regime. He judged the latter harshly—he was against compromise, even compromise for survival. It was a very difficult period—difficult even for honorable people to avoid some kind of compromise. Writers refused to recognize those who were in trouble, people avoided suspicious acquaintances, friend reported on friend. Bulgakov managed to find his way through this maze of hypocrisy and betrayal without once compromising his integrity. In

Moscow even those who actively disliked him for his ironic and aristocratic manner admit that there was never anything to reproach him for.[14]

In September of 1939 Bulgakov and his wife went to Leningrad to enjoy a change of scene after having worked unusually hard that summer. In Leningrad his illness suddenly took a turn for the worse. The doctors diagnosed hypertension and the onset of uremia. Bulgakov, however, knew it would develop into sclerosis of the kidneys. What was happening to him was a repetition of what had happened to his father. The fact that the doctors had finally confirmed his own diagnosis seemed somehow to calm Bulgakov. Now the secret was out, and he could talk about it to his friends. On his first day back from Leningrad he very calmly told Ermolinsky how the disease would progress. He predicted the number of days each stage would last and how many months he had left. Ermolinsky did not believe him at first, but then the stages began to develop exactly as Bulgakov had predicted.

In September Bulgakov went blind. For the next seven months he had to dictate corrections in *The Master and Margarita*. At first his friends would come, pull a table up to his bed, drink and talk with him, but he soon grew too weak for such gatherings. His mental state is suggested by the remark he made to Ermolinsky to the effect that Nietszche was a fool for having said that if one is not successful in life, one will be successful in death. In February his condition worsened, but Bulgakov (who had said that one should continue to work up until the last moment of consciousness) continued to dictate changes to his wife, and added the epilogue to the novel after the manuscript was bound. Thus the work he considered his masterpiece was finished before his death.

Bulgakov died on March 10. That night his close friend Nikolai Erdman, who had been forbidden to enter Moscow, came secretly from Vyshny Volochok, spent two hours in the apartment, and then left without having said a word.

There were many people at the funeral, but very few of them were writers. Bulgakov died as he had lived, among people of the theater.

NOTES

1. From a letter to his cousin, K. R. Bulgakov, February 1, 1921.

2. M. Bulgakov, *Belaja gvardija,* p'esa v 5'ti aktax. Lenin Library *Otdel Rukopisej* (M10837/No. 1).

3. *Glavrepertkom* had the job of censoring, banning, or passing all plays. Lunacharsky, who was Commissar of Education (and wrote plays himself), was the most powerful—and tolerant—of this group.

4. Mayakovsky's hostility goes back to the early twenties. Valentin Kataev describes the first acrimonious meeting of Mayakovsky and Bulgakov in his *Grass of Oblivion.* Mayakovsky attacked Bulgakov in print for "The Fatal Eggs." Later a long but veiled polemic went on between the two writers. Mayakovsky sneered at Bulgakov in his poem "The Face of the Class Enemy" (1928), and his play *The Bathhouse* is partly a polemic against *The Crimson Island.* Bulgakov's plays *Adam and Eve* and *Bliss* are answers to certain themes and motifs in Mayakovsky's *The Bedbug* and *The Bathhouse.*

5. Nikolai Erdman's most famous play *The Warrant* had appeared in 1925. Alexei Fayko's *Evgraf, the Adventure-Seeker* was put on in 1926. Sergei Ermolinsky later wrote important memoirs on Bulgakov.

6. During the years of his "public life" Bulgakov kept albums in which he pasted reviews of his works. By 1930, he said, he had 301 reviews: 3 good ones and 298 which were "hostile and abusive."

7. Bulgakov impressed those who read the letter at his apartment— among them Evgeny Zamyatin. In June of 1931, Zamyatin himself wrote a letter to Stalin, and he came to read Bulgakov's letter first. Of course, the cases were not identical; Zamyatin, unlike Bulgakov, had been on the side of the Revolution—he had no White Guard stigma. On the other hand he had written the heretical novel *We,* and he was often attacked with Bulgakov.

8. M. Bulgakov, *Zapisnaja kniga 1929–30,* Lenin Library *Otdel Rukopisej* (M10837/ No. 5, p. 19). Bulgakov notes: "the beginning of work: 17 V 1930."

9. Written in 1931, the play has only been published in English. It deals with a catastrophic world war which, prophetically, resembles World War II and the bombing of Hiroshima. Adam and Eve are newly-weds who, along with the opportunistic writer Ponchik-Nepobeda and a few others, are saved by a ray invented by a pacifist academician.

10. During Bulgakov's stay in the Caucasus he met the great poet

Osip Mandelstam, and was impressed when he read his poetry for the first time. Later he lived in the same building as Mandelstam and Mandelstam's close friend Anna Akhmatova. Akhmatova became a close friend of the Bulgakovs and wrote a touching poem on Bulgakov's death. In the latter part of his life Bulgakov also met Boris Pasternak and valued his poetry highly.

11. This is discussed in detail below, in the introduction to *A Cabal of Hypocrites*.

12. *The Black Sea* (1936) is based heavily on motifs from *Flight,* combined with a new hero, Commander of the Front Mikhailov, whose protoype was General Frunze. *Rachel* (a one-act opera by Glière) is based on Maupassant's "Mademoiselle Fifi." The other two operas are on Russian historical subjects.

13. This is quoted in V. Petelin, "M. A. Bulgakov i *Dni Turbinyx,*" *Ogonek,* No. 11 (March, 1969), p. 28. Although there is serious question about its authenticity, he also quotes this entry from Elena Sergeevna Bulgakova's diary: "July 3, 1939. Yesterday morning Khmelev's phone-call, asks to hear the play. An excited, joyful tone—again a play by M. A. in the theater! In the evening at our place—Khmelev, Kalishyan [Director of MXAT], Olga [Boshkanskaya, an actress]. Misha [Bulgakov] read several scenes. Then dinner and sitting around for a long time after. Conversations about the play, MXAT, the system. The sun was already rising when they went home." Another version of this story holds that Stalin never read the play, that members of the Politburo rejected it after a private reading at MXAT.

14. A recollection of Nadezhda Mandelstam is suggestive. She notes that when her husband was arrested and exiled for a poem against Stalin "Akhmatova went to the Bulgakovs and returned very touched by the reaction of Elena Sergeevna, Bulgakov's wife, who burst into tears when she heard about our exile and gave us everything she had." Nadezhda Mandelstam, *Hope Against Hope* (New York, 1970), p. 39.

THE EARLY PLAYS

OF

Mikhail Bulgakov

THE DAYS
OF THE TURBINS

A PLAY IN FOUR ACTS

INTRODUCTION

WHEN *White Guard* APPEARED as a novel in 1925, MXAT was searching for new plays—or works which could be made into plays—with which to satisfy the demands of the Party for "Soviet" theater. One of the readers of the journal *Russia,* a certain Vershilov, read the first part of *White Guard* and went to Pavel Markov, head of MXAT's literary section. Markov became interested, and Bulgakov was asked to come to the theater in order to discuss the possibilities of making the novel into a play. Bulgakov did so gladly, because as it happened he had already started turning the work into a play on his own. What happened then is not clear. One imagines that events were somewhat reminiscent of Maksudov's entry into the theater in *Theatrical Novel.* At any rate it is known that both Pavel Markov and Ilya Sudakov "helped" Bulgakov turn his novel into a play. Markov says: "The theater began to work lovingly and passionately with the writer on the deepening and perfecting [*nad uglubleniem i usoveršenstvovaniem*] of the dramatization." Actually, they helped him shorten the play he had already written and change certain political references *(uglublenie).*[1]

In his first version Bulgakov was clearly trying to retain the epic feeling of the novel—all sides of the Revolution were to be seen. The play was supposed to be episodic, but Bulgakov was encouraged to write a classically tight play—which did not at all serve his original intention, and which, as he sarcastically suggested, was geared to the trolley schedule in Moscow. The first completed version of the play contained thirteen scenes and was entitled *White Guard.*[2] The theater forced Bulgakov to change the provocative title and to cut the script to seven scenes (one of which is omitted in the current MXAT production). Obviously an enormous amount of work was done on the play, but in most cases it is impossible to say which changes were

Bulgakov's and which were Markov's and Sudakov's.[3] Further muddying the waters is the fact Stanislavsky made changes while the play was in rehearsal,[4] and subsequent productions have added their own touches. All of these accretions make dealing with the play extremely difficult. Certain things in the play are flagrantly un-Bulgakovian. For example, the last scene in which the heroes solemnly listen to the "International" seems hardly in keeping with Bulgakov's usual good taste and avoidance of what can be best labeled hackneyed ideological theatrics.[5]

There were more tensions involved in the production of *Days of the Turbins* than one can see on the surface. Most of the characters in the play are young, which meant that the older, established actors were left out of the production of a play in which they all wanted to have parts. Stanislavsky reportedly had very little to do with the production, making a grand entrance rather late in the course of rehearsals, dictating changes that were at times completely capricious.[6] The young actors of MXAT who had never before had a chance to shine were rehearsed by Sudakov and Bulgakov himself. Since these actors had grown up during the Revolution, Civil War, and Soviet power, they had little notion of how prerevolutionary aristocrats behaved. Bulgakov, although he liked the director, did not consider him to be first-rate, and therefore took many of the directing duties on himself, showing the actors exactly what he wanted, and spending long hours rehearsing with them. The young actors did him proud, and Bulgakov was delighted with the production.

The play's première on October 5, 1926 brought decidedly negative reviews and one of the greatest controversies in the history of the Soviet theater began. The hostility of many critics is well documented, but the play was a success. One spectator, himself connected with MXAT later, remembers that at the second performance, which he attended, no one left his seat during the intermissions. This was unheard of—the audience stayed, discussing the play in whispers. A well-known theater scholar, and a Party member, felt completely dumbfounded and fascinated at one of the first performances. As a young man whose family was deeply involved in revolutionary activities, it had never even entered his head that the

Whites had any human traits. *Days of the Turbins,* he said, was the first thing to make him see the Revolution differently—after that he could not see the Whites as unredeemed monsters.

T HE historical background of the play is extremely complicated, and in order to understand why the Turbins are against all of the political groups it is necessary to know something of the political situation in Kiev from December 1918 to February 1919.

After the Revolution began, Ukrainian nationalists turned to the Rada, the governmental body whose chief leaders were Hrushevsky, Vinnichenko, and the adventurer Petlyura. The Rada, which was overthrown in February of 1918 when Soviet armies entered Kiev, went to the Germans for help—despite the fact that foreigners were anything but popular with the Ukrainian masses. Three weeks later the Soviets were overthrown by the German army. The Rada returned, with Petlyura again one of its leaders. But German support did not sit well with the people, and the Germans themselves felt that since the Rada was not popular it could be replaced by a government which would be even more responsive to German desires—namely the government of the Hetman Skoropadsky. The Rada, although unable to cope with the lure of Bolshevism for the masses, at least intended social reform; the Skoropadsky government was totally uninterested in any such reforms, and was frankly reactionary—so it could offer nothing either to nationalists or leftists. It was a government for the wealthy landowners and the German army.

Skoropadsky reigned until the German collapse in November 1918. His flight figures prominently in both *White Guard* and *The Days of the Turbins,* which begin at this time. Remnants of the former Rada once again established themselves in Kiev, as the "Ukrainian Directorate," and Petlyura, rapidly taking on the appearance of a would-be dictator, was commander-in-chief. In February of 1919, only a few months after regaining control, the Rada was again deposed by the Soviet armies. This is the point at which both the novel and the play end. However, it is important that the Soviet forces were in control only for a short while—a fact which changes the interpretation of the novel and the play considerably and renders the end of the play inaccurate, in that it implies that the Bolsheviks had come to stay.

In 1919 Kiev was again occupied by Petlyura and by Denikin's White forces. In December 1919 the Red Army came back again. Petlyura then went to Poland for help, and sold out the nationalists by agreeing to abandon claims to East Galicia in exchange for the rule of the Ukraine as a Polish satellite. The Polish army occupied Kiev from May to June of 1920, at which time the Soviet army again took Kiev and finally put an end to the bewildering changes of government.

As with many Soviet plays and novels, establishing a definitive text is difficult. Existing translations differ in the texts used. This translation is made from the version published in the Soviet Union, and this was apparently made from the script used at MXAT beginning in 1929. (The play was banned in January 1929.) Only access to the MXAT archives and Bulgakov's papers could solve these problems with certainty, but two things are clear: this text is not the one used at the première, and the text used at the première is not the one Bulgakov would have liked to use.

NOTES

1. For example, in the original "Trotsky" was usually used (as a metonymy) instead of "Bolsheviks" in the political speeches.

2. M. Bulgakov, *Belaja gvardija*. P'esa v 5-ti aktax. Lenin Library Otdel Rukopisej [Fond 562/ Ed. xran. 3]. On the last page, after the final curtain, Bulgakov dated this text: "June-September 1925/ Moscow" (p. 139).

3. Sudakov notes that in the original text Alexei Turbin was still a doctor and the role of Colonel Malyshev was separate: "I persuaded M. A. Bulgakov to join these two roles into one, in the interest of compactness in the play." I. Sudakov, "Rannie role N. P. Xmeleva," *Ežegodnik MXAT* 1945 (M. 1948), II, 38. The final Alexei Turbin is a blend

of three characters—Dr. Alexei Turbin, Colonel Nai-Turs, and Colonel Malyshev.

4. According to Gorchakov, the striking scene with Alexei's nightmare "disappeared from the play at the insistence of Stanislavsky." N. Gorčakov, *Režisserskie uroki Stanislavskogo* (M., 1951), p. 317.

5. The original ending was quite different. Judging by Gorchakov's remarks, Stanislavsky is responsible for the "positive" ending.

6. During Stanislavsky's lifetime his name did not appear on any of the posters or programs connected with the play. Ilya Sudakov was listed as the director. After his death the vague formula "artistic guide of the production" was used to indicate Stanislavsky's role in *Days*.

Cast of Characters

Turbin, Alexei Vasilievich, an artillery Colonel, 30 years old.

Turbin, Nikolai, his brother, 18 years old.

Talberg, Elena Vasilievna, their sister, 24 years old.

Talberg, Vladimir Robertovich, a General Staff Colonel, her husband, 38 years old.

Myshlaevsky, Viktor Viktorovich, a Captain Second Grade in the artillery, 38 years old.

Shervinsky, Leonid Yurievich, a Lieutenant, the Hetman's personal aide-de-camp.

Studzinsky, Alexander Bronislavovich, a Captain, 29 years old.

Lariosik, a cousin from Zhitomir, 21 years old.

The Hetman of the entire Ukraine.

Bolbotun, Commander of Petlyura's First Cavalry Division.

Galanba, a Cossack Lieutenant for Petlyura, a former Uhlan Captain.

Hurricane.

Kirpaty.

Von Schratt, a German General.

Von Dust, a German Major.

A German Army Doctor.

A Deserter from the Sech.

A Man with a basket.

A Lackey.

Maxim, caretaker of the high school, 60 years old.

A Gaidamak Telephone Operator.

FIRST OFFICER.
SECOND OFFICER.
THIRD OFFICER.
FIRST CADET.
SECOND CADET.
THIRD CADET.
CADETS AND GAIDAMAKS.

The first, second, and third acts take place in the winter of 1918, the fourth act in the beginning of 1919. The scene is the city of Kiev.

ACT I

SCENE ONE

THE TURBINS' APARTMENT. *Evening. A fire in the fireplace. As the curtain opens, a clock strikes nine and softly plays a Boccherini minuet.* ALEXEI *is bent over some papers.*

NIKOLKA (*plays a guitar and sings*).
      By the hour the news gets worse.
      Petlyura's coming to attack
      We loaded the machine guns
      We blasted the Petlyuruns.
      Machine guns agunnin'—ack-ack, ack-ack . . .
      Good guys they were—ack-ack, ack-ack . . .
      You saved us all—soldier boys!
ALEXEI. What the devil are you singing! Street songs? Sing something decent.
NIKOLKA. Why street songs? I composed it myself, Alyosha. (*He sings.*)
      Whether you sing or not
      Your voice is not so hot!
      There are some voices one hears . . .
      That would make a cockroach hold its ears . . .
ALEXEI. That applies precisely to *your* voice.
NIKOLKA. Alyosha, you've no reason to say that, honestly! I do have a voice—true, not like Shervinsky's, but still a pretty decent one. A dramatic voice—baritone most likely. Lenochka, hey Lenochka! What kind of voice do you think I have?
ELENA (*from her room*). Who? You? Absolutely none.
NIKOLKA. She's just upset, that's why she answers that way. But

nevertheless Alyosha, my voice teacher used to say to me, "Nikolai Vasilievich," he said, "in principle, you could sing in the opera, if it weren't for the Revolution."

ALEXEI. Your voice teacher is an ignoramus.

NIKOLKA. I knew it. A total unhinging of nerves in the Turbin house. My voice teacher's an ignoramus. I have no voice, (even though yesterday I still did) and general pessimism. (*He strums the strings.*) Although you know, Alyosha, I'm starting to worry myself. It's already nine o'clock and he said he'd arrive in the morning. Maybe something has happened to him?

ALEXEI. You talk more quietly. Understand?

NIKOLKA. It's a chore, oh Lord, to be the brother of a married sister.

ELENA (*from her room*). What time is it by the dining-room clock?

NIKOLKA. Uh . . . nine. Our clock's fast, Lenochka.

ELENA (*from her room*). Please don't make things up.

NIKOLKA. Uh-oh, she's upset. (*He sings.*) It's cloudy . . . Ah, how cloudy it all is! . . .

ALEXEI. Don't rip out my heart strings, please. Sing something cheerful.

NIKOLKA (*sings*).

> Say there, summer boys!
> Say there, summer girls!
> The season's already old . . .
> Hey, old song of mine! . . . The sweetest one! . . .
> Chug-a-lug a bottle
> Of good old Russian wine!! . . .
> The usual Russian caps
> And fancy riding boots,
> Here come the Guard's cadets . . .[1]

(*The electricity suddenly goes off. A military unit passes by the windows, singing a song.*)

ALEXEI. God knows what's going on! It goes out every other minute. Lenochka, bring some candles please.

ELENA (*from her room*). Yes! . . . All right! . . .

ALEXEI. Some unit has gone by.

---

1. A real cadet song.

Coming out carrying a candle, Elena *stops and listens. A distant cannon shot.*

NIKOLKA. That was close! It sounds like they're firing near Svyato-shino. I wonder what's happening there? Alyosha, why don't you send me to find out what's going on at headquarters. I'd like to ride over.

ALEXEI. Of course, all they need is you. Please sit at ease.

NIKOLKA. Yes sir, colonel, sir . . . Really, I want to . . . you know, because this inactivity . . . it's really shameful . . . People are fighting there . . . If only our division would be ready sooner.

ALEXEI. When I require your advice on the preparation of the division, I'll tell you. Understand?

NIKOLKA. I understand. Sorry, colonel, sir.

The lights flare up.

ELENA. Alyosha, where's my husband?

ALEXEI. He'll come, Lenochka.

ELENA. But what is this? He said he'd come in the morning, but it's nine o'clock right now, and he still isn't here. Maybe something has happened to him?

ALEXEI. Lenochka, of course that's impossible. You know yourself that the Germans are protecting the front on the west.

ELENA. But why isn't he here yet?

ALEXEI. Well, obviously, they have had to wait at every station stop.

NIKOLKA. Revolutionary traveling, Lenochka. You go an hour, you stop for two.

The doorbell.

Well, there he is, I told you so! (*He runs to open the door.*) Who is it?

MYSHLAEVSKY'S VOICE. Open up, for God's sake, right away.

NIKOLKA (*lets* Myshlaevsky *into the entrance hall*). Is that you, Vitenka?

MYSHLAEVSKY. Well of course it's me, may I be damned if it's not! Nikolka, take my rifle, please. This is all a hell of a mess.

ELENA. Viktor, where have you been?

MYSHLAEVSKY. The Red Inn district. Hang it carefully, Nikolka. There's a bottle of vodka in the pocket. Don't break it. Let me spend the night here Lenochka, I couldn't make it home, I'm absolutely frozen.

ELENA. Oh my God, of course! Go right to the fire.

They go toward the fireplace.

MYSHLAEVSKY. Oh ... oh ... oh ...

ALEXEI. What's wrong with them, couldn't they give you any felt boots?

MYSHLAEVSKY. Felt boots! They're such bastards! (*He rushes to the fire.*)

ELENA. Here's what we'll do: the bath water is heating right now, you undress him right away, and I'll get some underwear for him. (*She exits.*)

MYSHLAEVSKY. Pull them off, my boy, off, off, off ...

NIKOLKA. Just a second, just a second. (*He pulls off* Myshlaevsky's *boots.*)

MYSHLAEVSKY. Take it easy, brother, ooh, easy now! I'd like a drink of vodka, just a little bit of vodka.

ALEXEI. I'll get it right away.

NIKOLKA. Alyosha, his toes are frozen.

MYSHLAEVSKY. To hell with my toes, they're gone, that's obvious.

ALEXEI. What's wrong with you? They'll thaw out. Nikolka, rub his feet with vodka.

MYSHLAEVSKY. So, now I've let my feet be *wiped* with vodka. (*He drinks.*) Rub with your hands. It hurts! ... It hurts! ... Take it easy.

NIKOLKA. Oy—oy—oy! ... How the captain's frozen!

ELENA (*appears with a robe and slippers*). Get him to the bath right away. Here!

MYSHLAEVSKY. God preserve you, Lenochka. Give me some more vodka. (*He drinks.*)

Elena *exits.*

NIKOLKA. Well, are you warming up, captain?

MYSHLAEVSKY. It's a little better. (*He lights a cigarette.*)

NIKOLKA. Tell us, what's going on down by the Inn?

MYSHLAEVSKY. There's a storm at the Inn. That's what's there. And I'd send the storm, the freezing cold, the German bastards, and Petlyura straight to. . . .

ALEXEI. I don't understand, why did they send you off to the Inn?

MYSHLAEVSKY. Why the peasants are there at the Inn. Those same damned God-bearers out of the works of Mr. Dostoevsky.

NIKOLKA. What do you mean? In the newspapers it says the peasants are on the Hetman's side . . .

MYSHLAEVSKY. Why are you throwing newspapers at me, you cadet? I'd have all your newspaper scum hung on the nearest tree! Out scouting this morning I personally ran up against one old bird and I asked, "Where are your men?" It was like a ghost town. And he was kind of shortsighted and didn't see that I had officer's straps under my cloak hood, and he answers me, "They all done run off to Petlyura . . ."

NIKOLKA. Ay-yay-yay-yay-yay.

MYSHLAEVSKY. Precisely, "ay-yay-yay-yay-yay . . ." I took that God-bearing son of a bitch by the collar and said, "They all done run off to Petlyura?" Now I'm going to shoot you, you old . . . You'll learn from me how they run off to Petlyura. You'll run from me to the Kingdom of Heaven.

ALEXEI. How did you end up in town?

MYSHLAEVSKY. We were replaced today, glory to God! The infantry home guard came. I kicked up a fuss at headquarters on sentry duty. It was a pain! They sit there drinking cognac in their railroad car. I say to them, you, says I, are sitting with the Hetman in his palace, but artillery officers are booted out in the snow to exchange shots with the peasantry! They didn't know how to get rid of me. They said, we are ordering you, captain, to any artillery unit that fits your specialty. Go on into town. . . . Alyosha, take me into your unit.

ALEXEI. With pleasure. I wanted to call you myself. I'll give you the first battery.

MYSHLAEVSKY. My benefactor . . .

NIKOLKA. Hurrah! . . . We'll all be together. Studzinsky as senior officer . . . Wonderful! . . .

MYSHLAEVSKY. Where are you stationed?

NIKOLKA. We've taken over the Alexandrovsky High School. We can move out tomorrow or the day after.

MYSHLAEVSKY. Are you just sitting here waiting anxiously for Petlyura to bang you on the back of the head?

NIKOLKA. Well, we'll see who bangs whom!

ELENA (*appears with a huge towel*). Well, Viktor, get going, get going. Go wash up. Here's a towel.

MYSHLAEVSKY. Lovely Lena, allow me to embrace and kiss you for your trouble. What do you think, Lenochka, should I drink some more vodka now or later, right after supper?

ELENA. I think later, right after supper. Viktor! You didn't see my husband? He's missing.

MYSHLAEVSKY. What's the matter with you, Lenochka, he'll turn up. He'll come soon. (*He exits*).

An uninterrupted ring of the doorbell.

NIKOLKA. Well, there he is! (*He runs to the entrance hall.*)

ALEXEI. Lord, what kind of way is that to ring?

Nikolka *opens the door.* Lariosik *appears in the entrance hall carrying a suitcase and a bundle.*

LARIOSIK. Well, here I am. I did something to your doorbell.

NIKOLKA. You left the button jammed in. (*He runs out the door onto the stairs.*)

LARIOSIK. Oh, my God! Forgive me, for God's sake! (*He enters the room.*) Well, here I am. Hello, dear Elena Vasilievna, I recognized you right away from pictures. Mama asked me to give you her warmest regards.

The bell stops. Nikolka *enters.*

And equally to Alexei Vasilievich too.

ALEXEI. My respects.

LARIOSIK. Hello, Nikolai Vasilievich, I've heard so much about you. (*To everyone.*) I see you're surprised? Allow me to hand you this letter—it will explain everything to you. Mama told me that before I even took off my coat I should let you read the letter.

ELENA. What illegible handwriting!

LARIOSIK. Yes, it's terrible! Allow me, it'll be better if I read it myself. Mama has such handwriting that sometimes she'll write something and then afterwards not understand what it was she wrote. I have the same kind of handwriting. It's hereditary in our family. (*He reads.*) "Dear, dear Lenochka! I am sending you my boy just like relatives should; shelter and protect him, as you know how to. After all, you have such a huge apartment . . ." Mama loves and respects you very much, and Alexei Vasilievich equally. (*To* Nikolka.) And you too. (*He reads.*) "The little fellow is entering Kiev University. With his abilities . . ."—oh, this is just like mama! . . .—"it's impossible to sit in Zhitomir wasting time. I will send you the cost of his room and board regularly. I wouldn't want a little fellow who is accustomed to his family to live among strangers. But I'm in a great hurry, the hospital train is coming now—he'll tell you everything himself . . ." Hm . . . that's all.

ALEXEI. Allow me to inquire with whom I have the honor to be speaking?

LARIOSIK. What do you mean with whom? Don't you know me?

ALEXEI. Unfortunately, I haven't had the pleasure.

LARIOSIK. My God! And you, Elena Vasilievna?

NIKOLKA. I don't know either.

LARIOSIK. My God, this is really witchcraft! Why, Mama sent you a telegram which should have explained everything to you. Mama sent you a telegram sixty-three words long.

NIKOLKA. Sixty-three words! . . . Ay-ay-ay! . . .

ELENA. We didn't get any telegram.

LARIOSIK. You didn't get it? My God! Forgive me please. I thought you were expecting me, and right away, before I have my coat off . . . excuse me . . . I think I broke something too . . . I'm a terribly unlucky person!

ALEXEI. Be so good as to tell us what your name is.

LARIOSIK. Larion Larionovich Surzhanski.

ELENA. Is this Lariosik? Our cousin from Zhitomir?

LARIOSIK. Well, yes.

ELENA. And you . . . you've come to visit us?

LARIOSIK. Yes. But you see, I thought you were expecting me . . . forgive me, please, I've tracked up your floor . . . I thought you were expecting me, but if this is how things are, I'll go to some hotel . . .

ELENA. Where could you find a hotel nowadays? Wait, first of all you take off your coat.

ALEXEI. Why nobody's ordering you out, please take off your coat.

LARIOSIK. I'm sincerely obliged to you.

NIKOLKA. Over here, please. You can hang your coat in the entrance hall.

LARIOSIK. I'm sincerely obliged to you. What a fine apartment you have!

ELENA (*in a whisper*). Alyosha, what are we going to do with him. He's so nice. Let's put him in the library, the room is empty anyway.

ALEXEI. Of course, go tell him.

ELENA. Here's what we'll do, Larion Larionovich, first of all off to the bath . . . Someone's already there—Captain Myshlaevsky . . . Otherwise, you know, after the train . . .

LARIOSIK. Yes, of course, it's terrible! . . . It's terrible! . . . Why it took me eleven days to get from Zhitomir to Kiev . . .

NIKOLKA. Eleven days! . . . Ay-ay-ay! . . .

LARIOSIK. Terrible, terrible! . . . Such a nightmare!

ELENA. Now, if you please!

LARIOSIK. I'm sincerely obliged. . . . Oh, excuse me, Elena Vasilievna, I can't take a bath.

ALEXEI. Why can't you take a bath?

LARIOSIK. Excuse me, please. Some rascals stole the suitcase with my underwear in it from the hospital train. They left the suitcase with the books and manuscripts, but the underwear was all lost.

ELENA. Well, that's a misfortune we can correct.

NIKOLKA. I'll give him some!

LARIOSIK (*intimately, to* Nikolka). But I think I have one shirt here. I wrapped the collected works of Chekhov in it. Now, would you be so kind as to give me some shorts?

NIKOLKA. With pleasure. They'll be too big for you, but we'll pin them up with safety pins.

LARIOSIK. I'm sincerely obliged to you.

ELENA. Larion Larionovich, we'll put you in the library. Nikolka, show him the way!

NIKOLKA. Follow me, please.

Lariosik and Nikolka *exit.*

ALEXEI. Now there's a character! The first thing I'd do is give him a haircut. Well, Lenochka, light a candle for me, I'm going to my room; I still have a lot of work to do, and I keep getting interrupted here. (*He exits.*)

The doorbell rings.

ELENA. Who's there?

TALBERG'S VOICE. It's me, me. Open up, please.

ELENA. Thank God! Where've you been? I was so worried.

TALBERG (*entering*). Don't kiss me, I've just come in from outside, you might catch cold.

ELENA. Where've you been?

TALBERG. I was held up at the German headquarters. Important business.

ELENA. Well, come on, come on, hurry and get warmed up. We'll have tea right now.

TALBERG. Wait, I don't want any tea, Lena. And whose coat is that, may I ask?

ELENA. Myshlaevsky's. He just came in from the lines, completely frozen.

TALBERG. Still, you could have put things away.

ELENA. I'll do it right away. (*She hangs the coat behind the door.*) You know, there's more news. My cousin from Zhitomir just arrived unexpectedly, the famous Lariosik. Alexei put him up in our library.

TALBERG. I knew it! Señor Myshlaevsky by himself isn't enough! Now some cousins from Zhitomir turn up too. This isn't a house, it's a hotel. I can't understand Alexei at all.

ELENA. Volodya, you're just tired and in a bad mood. Why don't you like Myshlaevsky? He's a very good man.

TALBERG. Remarkably good! He practically lives in taverns.

ELENA. Volodya!

TALBERG. However, I have no time for Myshlaevsky now. Lena, close the door. Lena, a terrible thing has happened.

ELENA. What?

TALBERG. The Germans are leaving the Hetman to the whim of fate.

ELENA. Volodya, what are you saying?! Where did you hear that?

TALBERG. Just now, at the German headquarters, in strictest secrecy. No one knows, not even the Hetman himself.

ELENA. What will happen now?

TALBERG. What will happen now . . . H'mm . . . It's nine-thirty. So . . . What will happen now? . . . Lena!

ELENA. What did you say?

TALBERG. I said "Lena"!

ELENA. Well, what about "Lena"?

TALBERG. Lena, I have to flee immediately.

ELENA. Flee? Where?

TALBERG. To Germany, Berlin. H'mm . . . My dear, you can imagine what will happen to me if the Russian army doesn't defeat Petlyura, and he takes Kiev?

ELENA. We could hide you.

TALBERG. My dearest, how could you hide me! I'm not a needle. There's not a man in town who doesn't know me. Hide the assistant to the Minister of War! Unlike Señor Myshlaevsky, I cannot sit coatless in someone else's apartment. They'd find me in a minute.

ELENA. Wait! I don't understand. . . . This means we must both run away?

TALBERG. No, that's just the point. The whole terrible picture is clear now. The town is surrounded on all sides, and the only way of getting out is on the German headquarters train. They don't take women. They gave me one place. Thanks to my connections.

ELENA. In other words, you want to leave alone?

TALBERG. My dear, it's not that "I want" to, but there's no other way that I can! Don't you see—this is a catastrophe! The train leaves in half an hour. You make the decision—as quickly as possible.

ELENA. In half an hour? As quickly as possible? Then I've decided—go.

TALBERG. You're a clever girl. I've always said that. What else was I going to say? Yes, that you're a clever girl! However, I've said that already.

ELENA. How long are we going to be apart?

TALBERG. A month or two, I think. I'll just sit out this whole mess in Berlin, and when the Hetman returns . . .

ELENA. What if he doesn't return at all?

TALBERG. Impossible. Even if the Germans withdraw from the Ukraine, the Entente will occupy it and restore the Hetman. Europe needs the Hetman's Ukraine as a buffer against the Moscow Bolsheviks. You see, I've taken everything into consideration.

ELENA. Yes, I see, except for one thing: how will it look that the Hetman is still here, that troops are being drawn up—and suddenly you run away and everyone sees you do it. Won't that be a little awkward?

TALBERG. My dear, that's naive of you. I'm telling you this in secret, I say: "I'm running away," because I know you will never tell anyone. Colonels of the General Headquarters don't run away. They travel on orders. In my pocket I have orders from the Hetman's ministry to go to Berlin. Not bad, eh?

ELENA. Not bad at all. But what's going to happen to everyone else?

TALBERG. Allow me to thank you for comparing me to "everyone." I'm not "everyone."

ELENA. But you'll warn my brothers.

TALBERG. Of course, of course. To some extent, I'm actually glad that I'm going alone for such a long time. No matter what happens, you hold onto our rooms.

ELENA. Vladimir Robertovich, these are my brothers! Do you really think that they'd squeeze us out? You don't have the right . . .

TALBERG. Oh no, no, no . . . Of course not. . . . But you know the proverb: *Qui va à la chasse, perd sa place.* Now one more favor, the last. Hm . . . Of course, when I'm gone . . . hm . . . that Shervinsky will be coming here . . .

ELENA. He comes here whether you are here or not.

TALBERG. Unfortunately. You see, my dear, I don't like him.

ELENA. May I ask why?

TALBERG. His interest in you is becoming too persistent, and I would like it.... Hm ...

ELENA. What would you like?

TALBERG. I can't tell you what. You are an intelligent woman of excellent upbringing. You understand quite well how you must conduct yourself so as not to cast a shadow on the Talberg name.

ELENA. Very well. I won't cast a shadow on the Talberg name.

TALBERG. Why such a dry answer? After all, I'm not implying that you could be unfaithful to me. I know very well that could not happen.

ELENA. Why do you presume that it could not happen, Vladimir Robertovich?

TALBERG. Elena, Elena, Elena! I don't recognize you. Here are the fruits of association with Myshlaevsky. A married woman—to be unfaithful! ... It's a quarter to ten! I'll be late!

ELENA. I'll pack for you right away ...

TALBERG. My dear, never mind, never mind, just the small case, there's some linen in it. Only, for God's sake, do it as fast as possible. I'll give you one minute.

ELENA. Still you must say goodbye to my brothers.

TALBERG. Of course, naturally. Only don't forget, I'm going on orders.

ELENA. Alyosha! Alyosha! (*She runs out.*)

ALEXEI (*entering*). Yes, yes ... Oh, hello Volodya.

TALBERG. Hello, Alyosha.

ALEXEI. What's all the fuss?

TALBERG. Well, you see, I must inform you of some important news. Tonight the position of the Hetman has become extremely serious.

ALEXEI. What do you mean?

TALBERG. Serious in the extreme.

ALEXEI. What's wrong?

TALBERG. It's very possible that the Germans will not provide help, and it will be necessary to repulse Petlyura with our own forces.

ALEXEI. What are you saying?

TALBERG. It may very well be.

ALEXEI. Something about this stinks. . . . Thanks for telling me.

TALBERG. Now the second thing. . . . Since I am leaving on orders right now . . .

ALEXEI. Where, if it is not a secret?

TALBERG. To Berlin.

ALEXEI. Where? To Berlin?

TALBERG. Yes. No matter how I struggled, I couldn't squirm out of it. Such an annoyance!

ALEXEI. For long, may I inquire?

TALBERG. For two months.

ALEXEI. Oh, so that's how it is!

TALBERG. And so, allow me to wish you all the best. Take care of Elena. (*He holds out his hand.*)

Alexei *hides his hand behind his back.*

What does that mean?

ALEXEI. That means that I do not like your orders.

TALBERG. Colonel Turbin!

ALEXEI. I am listening, Colonel Talberg.

TALBERG. You'll answer to me for that, Mr. Brother of my wife!

ALEXEI. And when would you like that to be, Mr. Talberg?

TALBERG. When . . . It's five to ten. . . . When I return.

ALEXEI. Well, God knows what'll happen when you return.

TALBERG. You . . . you . . . I been wanting to have a talk with you for a long time.

ALEXEI. Don't you dare upset your wife, Mr. Talberg!

ELENA (*entering*). What were you talking about?

ALEXEI. Nothing, nothing, Lenochka!

TALBERG. Nothing, nothing, dear! Well, goodbye Alyosha!

ALEXEI. Goodbye Volodya!

ELENA. Nikolka! Nikolka!

NIKOLKA (*entering*). Here I am. Oh, he came?

ELENA. Volodya is going away on orders. Say goodbye to him.

TALBERG. Goodbye, Nikolka.

NIKOLKA. Bon voyage, colonel, sir.

TALBERG. Elena, here's some money for you. I'll send some from

Berlin right away. My respects to you all. (*He heads hurriedly toward the entrance hall.*) Don't see me off my dear, you'll catch cold. (*He exits.* Elena *goes after him.*)

ALEXEI (*in an unpleasant voice*). Elena, you'll catch cold.

A pause.

NIKOLKA. Alyosha, how can he go away like that? Where is he going?

ALEXEI. Berlin.

NIKOLKA. Berlin . . . At a time like this . . . (*Looking out the window.*) He's bargaining with the cab-driver. (*Philosophically.*) Alyosha, you know, I've noticed that he looks like a rat.

ALEXEI (*mechanically*). Quite right, Nikolka. And our house is like a ship. Well, go see to our guests. Go on, go on.

Nikolka *exits.*

The whole division will be bivouacking with the angels. "Extremely serious." "Serious in the extreme." The rat! (*He exits.*)

ELENA (*returns from the entrance hall, looks out the window*). He's gone . . .

SCENE TWO

The table is set for supper.

ELENA (*at the piano, plays the same chord over and over*). He left. How he left . . .

SHERVINSKY (*suddenly appears on the threshold*). Who left?

ELENA. My God! How you scared me, Shervinsky! How did you get in without ringing?

SHERVINSKY. Why your door's open—wide open. Hello, Elena Vasilievna. (*He takes a huge bouquet out of some paper.*)

ELENA. How many times have I asked you not to do this, Leonid Yurievich. It's unpleasant for me when you spend money on me.

SHERVINSKY. As Karl Marx said, money exists to be spent. May I take off my cloak?

ELENA. And what if I said no?

SHERVINSKY. I would sit at your feet all night wearing my cloak.

ELENA. Oh, Shervinsky, that's an infantry compliment.

SHERVINSKY. I'm sorry, it's a guard officer's compliment. (*He takes off the cloak in the entrance hall, revealing a magnificent Cossack outfit.*) I'm so happy to see you! It's been so long since I've seen you!

ELENA. If my memory does not deceive me, you were here yesterday.

SHERVINSKY. Ah, Elena Vasilievna, what is "yesterday" in times like these! So, who left?

ELENA. Vladimir Robertovich.

SHERVINSKY. But he was supposed to return today!

ELENA. Yes, he returned . . . and left again.

SHERVINSKY. For where?

ELENA. Such wonderful roses!

SHERVINSKY. For where?

ELENA. Berlin.

SHERVINSKY. Berlin? And for long, may I ask?

ELENA. Two months or so.

SHERVINSKY. Two months! What are you saying! It's sad, sad, sad . . . I'm so upset, I'm so upset!! . . .

ELENA. Shervinsky, that's the fifth time you've kissed my hand.

SHERVINSKY. I am, one might say, crushed . . . My God, this is it! Hurrah! Hurrah!

NIKOLKA'S VOICE. Shervinsky! The Demon![2]

ELENA. Why are you so wildly happy?

SHERVINSKY. I am happy . . . Ah, Elena Vasilievna, you won't understand! . . .

ELENA. You aren't very subtle, Shervinsky.

SHERVINSKY. I, not subtle? If you please, why not? . . . No, I'm subtle. It's just that I'm, you know, upset. . . . So, he's gone away, but you stayed here.

ELENA. As you see. How is your voice?

SHERVINSKY (*at the piano*).

2. An allusion to the romantic hero of Anton Rubinstein's opera *The Demon*, based on Lermontov's narrative poem "The Demon" (1829–41).

Ma...ma...mia...mi...
He's far away, he's ...
he's far away, he won't find out ...
He's ...

I'm in incomparable voice. I left home in a cab, and it seemed my voice had left too, and when I got here, it turned out that I was in fine voice.

ELENA. Did you bring the music?

SHERVINSKY. Of course, of course ... You are an absolute goddess!

ELENA. The only good thing about you is your voice, and your obvious vocation is to be an opera singer.

SHERVINSKY. I do have a little of the basic raw material for that. You know, Elena Vasilievna, once I was singing the epithalamion in *Zhmerinka*—there's a high "F" there as you know, but I took "A" and held it for nine bars.

ELENA. How many bars?

SHERVINSKY. I held it for seven bars. It's useless for you not to believe me. I swear it! Countess Hendrikova was there ... She fell in love with me after that "A."

ELENA. And what happened then?

SHERVINSKY. She poisoned herself. Potassium cyanide.

ELENA. Oh, Shervinsky! It's really a disease with you, honestly. Gentlemen, Shervinsky! Supper is on the table!

Alexei, Studzinsky, *and* Myshlaevsky *enter.*

ALEXEI. Hello, Leonid Yurievich. Welcome.

SHERVINSKY. Viktor! He's alive! Well, thank God! Why are you wearing a turban?

MYSHLAEVSKY (*wearing a turban made from a towel*). Hello, adjutant.

SHERVINSKY (*to* Studzinsky). My respects, captain.

Lariosik *and* Nikolka *enter.*

MYSHLAEVSKY. Allow me to introduce you. Captain Studzinsky, the senior officer of our division, and this is Monsieur Surzhansky. He and I just had a bath together.

NIKOLKA. Our cousin from Zhitomir.

STUDZINSKY. Glad to meet you.

LARIOSIK. Sincerely happy to make your acquaintance.

SHERVINSKY. Lieutenant Shervinsky, Uhlan Regiment of Her Imperial Majesty's Light Guard, and personal Adjutant of the Hetman.

LARIOSIK. Larion Surzhansky. Sincerely happy to make your acquaintance.

MYSHLAEVSKY. No need for you to feel overwhelmed. It's the *former* Light, *former* Guard, *former* regiment . . .

ELENA. Gentlemen, come to the table.

ALEXEI. Yes, yes, please, it's already twelve; we have to get up early tomorrow.

SHERVINSKY. Oh, such splendor! What's the occasion for the feast, may I ask?

NIKOLKA. The last supper of our division. We move out tomorrow, Lieutenant . . .

SHERVINSKY. Aha . . .

STUDZINSKY. Where do we sit, colonel?

SHERVINSKY. Yes, where?

ALEXEI. Wherever you like, wherever you like. Please, be seated! Lenochka, you be the hostess.

They sit down.

SHERVINSKY. So, therefore, he's left, and you've stayed?

ELENA. Shervinsky, be quiet.

MYSHLAEVSKY. Lenochka, will you have some vodka?

ELENA. No, no, no! . . .

MYSHLAEVSKY. Well, some white wine then.

STUDZINSKY. May I pour you some, colonel?

ALEXEI. *Merci.* Please pour yourself some.

MYSHLAEVSKY. Your glass.

LARIOSIK. I . . . basically, I don't drink vodka.

MYSHLAEVSKY. Well of course—I don't either. But one glass. How can you eat herring without vodka? I simply can't understand it.

LARIOSIK. I am sincerely obliged to you.

MYSHLAEVSKY. I haven't had any vodka for a long, long time.

SHERVINSKY. Gentlemen! Elena Vasilievna's health! Hurrah!

STUDZINSKY.
LARIOSIK. } Hurrah!
MYSHLAEVSKY.

ELENA. Shh! What is wrong with you gentlemen! You'll wake up the whole street. As it is, they keep saying we have drunken parties every day.

MYSHLAEVSKY. Oh, it's good! Vodka freshens you up. Don't you think so?

LARIOSIK. Yes, quite true.

MYSHLAEVSKY. I beg you—another glass apiece. Colonel . . .

ALEXEI. Take it easy, Viktor, we move out tomorrow.

NIKOLKA. And we *will!*

ELENA. What's going on at the Hetman's, tell us.

STUDZINSKY. Yes, yes, what's happening?

SHERVINSKY. Everything is in fine shape. What a supper there was at the palace yesterday! . . . For two hundred people. Grouse . . . The Hetman in the national costume.

ELENA. But, they say the Germans are leaving us to the whim of fate?

SHERVINSKY. Don't believe any of the rumors, Elena Vasilievna.

LARIOSIK. I thank you, most respected Viktor Viktorovich. You know . . . basically, I do not drink vodka.

MYSHLAEVSKY (*drinking up*). Shame on you, Larion!

SHERVINSKY.
NIKOLKA. } Shame!

LARIOSIK. I thank you humbly.

ALEXEI. Nikolka, don't drink too much vodka.

NIKOLKA. No sir, colonel. I'll have some white wine.

LARIOSIK. How do you down it so adroitly, Viktor Viktorovich?

MYSHLAEVSKY. It is achieved through practice.

ALEXEI. Thanks, captain. And some salad?

STUDZINSKY. Thank you very much.

MYSHLAEVSKY. Golden Lena! Have some white wine. My joy! Red-headed Lena, I know why you're so upset. Forget it. Everything's for the best.

SHERVINSKY. Everything's for the best.

MYSHLAEVSKY. No, no—to the bottom, Lenochka, to the bottom!

NIKOLKA (*takes his guitar, sings*).

> Who should drink a cup,
> Who should be healthy . . .
> drink a cup . . .[3]

ALL (*sing*).

> Joy to Elena Vasilievna!
> —Lenochka, drink up!
> —Drink up . . . drink up!

> Elena *drinks.*

> —Bravo!

> *They applaud.*

MYSHLAEVSKY. You look wonderful today. I swear it. And that robe is just right for you, on my word of honor. Gentlemen, look what a robe she has, absolutely green!

ELENA. Vitenka, this is a dress, and it's gray, not green.

MYSHLAEVSKY. Well, so much the worse. It makes no difference. Gentlemen, just look—wouldn't you say she's a beautiful woman?

STUDZINSKY. Elena Vasilievna is very beautiful. To your health!

MYSHLAEVSKY. Lovely Elena, allow me, I'll hug and kiss you.

SHERVINSKY. Now, now—Viktor, Viktor!

MYSHLAEVSKY. Leonid, get away. Get away from another man's wife!

SHERVINSKY. Allow . . .

MYSHLAEVSKY. It's all right for me, I'm a childhood friend.

SHERVINSKY. You're a pig, not a childhood friend . . .

NIKOLKA (*getting up*). Gentlemen, the division commander's health!

> Studzinsky, Shervinsky, *and* Myshlaevsky *stand up.*

LARIOSIK. Hurrah! . . . Excuse me, gentlemen, I'm not a military man.

---

3. A traditional toasting song.

MYSHLAEVSKY. Never mind, never mind. Larion. That's the way to do it!

LARIOSIK. Most respected Elena Vasilievna! I cannot express, how wonderful it is for me to be at your home.

ELENA. That's very nice of you.

LARIOSIK. Most respected Alexei Vasilievich . . . I cannot express how wonderful it is to be at your home! . . .

ALEXEI. That's very nice of you.

LARIOSIK. Gentlemen, the cream-colored curtains . . . behind them you can rest your soul . . . you forget about all the horrors of the Civil War. And our wounded souls so thirst for peace . . .

MYSHLAEVSKY. Allow me to ask, do you write poetry?

LARIOSIK. Me? Yes . . . I do write.

MYSHLAEVSKY. I thought so. Excuse me for interrupting you. Continue.

LARIOSIK. Please . . . The cream-colored curtains . . . They separate us from the whole world . . . Incidentally, I am not a military man . . . Oh! Pour me another glass.

MYSHLAEVSKY. Bravo, Larion! Oh, the sly devil—and he said he didn't drink. You're a nice fellow, Larion, but you make a speech about as well as a deeply respected boot.

LARIOSIK. No, don't say that, Viktor Viktorovich, I've made more than one speech . . . at a meeting of my late father's colleagues . . . in Zhitomir . . . Well, the tax inspectors were there . . . They gave it to me too . . . Oh, how they cursed me!

MYSHLAEVSKY. Tax inspectors are well-known jackals.

SHERVINSKY. Drink Lena, drink, my dear!

ELENA. You want to get me drunk? Ooh, what a repulsive person!

NIKOLKA (*at the piano, sings*).

      Tell me, oh soothsayer, favorite of the gods,

      What is my fate in my life ahead?

      And to the joy of my enemies nearby

      Will I soon be covered 'neath the dirt of the grave?[4]

4. These lines are from a song based on Pushkin's poem "The Song of Oleg the Wise."

LARIOSIK (*sings*).

> So louder, oh music, sound the victory![5]

ALL (*sing*).

> Our foe is on the run, and we're victorious,
> So for the ...

LARIOSIK. The tsar!

ALEXEI. What's wrong with you, what is *wrong* with you![6]

ALL (*hum the line without words*).

. . . .

> We'll shout a loud "Hurrah! Hurrah! Hurrah!"

NIKOLKA (*sings*).

> And coming toward him from the forest dark ...

They all sing.

LARIOSIK. Ooh! How gay things are here, Elena Vasilievna, dear one! Lights! ... Hurrah!

SHERVINSKY. Gentlemen! The health of his majesty, the Hetman of all the Ukraine. Hurrah!

A pause.

STUDZINSKY. Sorry. I'm going to fight tomorrow, but I will not drink that toast, and I don't advise the other officers to.

SHERVINSKY. Captain!

LARIOSIK. An absolutely unanticipated event.

MYSHLAEVSKY (*drunk*). Because of him, that devil, I got my feet frozen off. (*He drinks.*)

STUDZINSKY. Colonel, do you approve of the toast?

ALEXEI. No, I do not.

SHERVINSKY. Colonel, allow me, I'll propose one!

STUDZINSKY. No, just allow *me*, I'll propose one!

---

5. This is the refrain (*not* in Pushkin's poem in any form) from the song based on Pushkin's "The Song of Oleg the Wise." No author is cited in A. I. Chernov, *Narodnye russkie pesni i romansy* (New York, 1953), II, 349.

6. They hum the tsarist national anthem, which could have been fatal at that time.

LARIOSIK. No, just allow *me*, I'll propose one. To the health of Elena Vasilievna, and also to her most respected husband who has departed for Berlin!

MYSHLAEVSKY. Ho-ho! Good guess, Larion! It would be hard to come up with a better one!

NIKOLKA (*sings*).
     Tell me the whole truth, don't be afraid . . .[7]

LARIOSIK. Forgive me, Elena Vasilievna, I am not a military man.

ELENA. Never mind, never mind, Larion. You are a sincere man, a good one. Come here.

LARIOSIK. Elena Vasilievna! Oh, my God, red wine! . . . I spilled . . .

NIKOLKA. We'll pour salt on it . . . salt . . . never mind.

STUDZINSKY. As for your Hetman! . . .

ALEXEI. One moment, gentlemen! . . . What's really going on? Did we pledge ourselves to him as a joke or what? If your Hetman had started the formation of the officers' corps instead of playing this damned comedy with Ukrainianization, there wouldn't be a whiff of Petlyura anywhere in the Ukraine. But that's not the main thing—we would be able to smash the Bolsheviks in Moscow like flies. And at the best moment! They say they're gobbling cats there. He would have saved Russia, the scoundrel!

SHERVINSKY. The Germans would not allow the formation of an army—they're afraid of that.

ALEXEI. That's not true, sir. What was needed was to explain to the Germans that we are no danger to them. Of course! We lost the war. Now we have something more terrifying than the war, than the Germans, than generally anything on earth—we have the Bolsheviks. What was needed was to tell the Germans: "What do you need? You need grain, sugar? There, take it, stuff yourselves, fill your gullets,—but just help us see that our peasants don't get sick with the Moscow disease!" But now it's too late, now our officers have turned into café sitters. A café army! Just try to get one. Like hell he'll go fight for you. He's got cash in his pocket, the bastard. He sits in a café on Kreshchatik Street, and all that headquarters guards officer bunch with him. Well, isn't

7. A continuation of Pushkin's "The Song of Oleg the Wise."

that just fine, sir! They give Colonel Turbin a division: go on, fly, hurry up, form up, move out, Petlyura's coming! . . . Excellent, sir! And then I took a good look at them yesterday and, I give you my word of honor, my heart sank for the first time.

MYSHLAEVSKY. Alyosha, my dear commander! You have an artilleryman's heart! I drink your health!

ALEXEI. It *sank* because there are a hundred and twenty students for every hundred cadets, and they carry a rifle as if it were a shovel. And then yesterday on the square . . . Snow was falling, fog in the distance . . . You know, I seemed to see a coffin . . .

ELENA. Alyosha, why are you saying such gloomy things? Don't you dare!

NIKOLKA. Please don't get upset, colonel, sir, we will not surrender.

ALEXEI. And now, gentlemen, I am sitting here among you, and all the time I have a single, nagging doubt. Oh! If we could have foreseen all this earlier! Do you know what this Petlyura of yours is? He's a myth, he's black fog. He doesn't exist at all. Take a look out the window, look, what's there. The snowstorm is there, some shadows . . . There are two forces in Russia, gentlemen— the Bolsheviks and us. We will meet yet. I see more threatening times. I see . . . Well, all right! We will not hold Petlyura back. But of course he won't come for long. And then after him the Bolsheviks will come. Because of that I am going! Against all odds, but I'll go! Because when we meet them, things will really get hot. Either we will bury them, or, more likely, they us. I drink to our meeting, gentlemen!

LARIOSIK (*at the piano, sings*).

> The thirst for meetings
> Promises, speechings
> Everything on the earth
> Isn't worth a fa-la-la[8]

NIKOLKA. Great, Larion! (*He sings.*)

> The thirst for meetings
> Promises, speechings

All sing chaotically, Lariosik *suddenly begins to sob.*

8. Perhaps Lariosik's own improvisatoin.

ELENA. Lariosik, what's wrong?

NIKOLKA. Larion!

MYSHLAEVSKY. What is it Larion, who has offended you?

LARIOSIK (*drunk*). I got scared.

MYSHLAEVSKY. Of whom? The Bolsheviks? Well, we'll show them soon enough! (*He takes out his Mauser.*)

ELENA. Viktor, what are you doing?

MYSHLAEVSKY. I'm going to shoot the commissars. Which of you are commissars?

SHERVINSKY. The Mauser's loaded!!

STUDZINSKY. Captain, sit down this instant!

ELENA. Gentlemen, take it away from him!

They take away the Mauser. Lariosik *exits.*

ALEXEI. What's wrong with you, have you gone out of your mind? Sit down this instant! I'm to blame for this, gentlemen.

MYSHLAEVSKY. I must have fallen into the company of Bolsheviks. Very pleasant. Hello, comrades! Let's drink to the health of the commissars. They're really very nice!

ELENA. Viktor, don't drink anything more!

MYSHLAEVSKY. Shut up, you commissar's wife!

SHERVINSKY. God, he's really drunk.

ALEXEI. Gentlemen, I'm to blame. Pay no attention to what I said. It's just that my nerves are on edge.

STUDZINSKY. Oh, no, colonel. Please believe that we understand everything you said and share your opinion. We will defend the Russian Empire forever!

NIKOLKA. Long live Russia!

SHERVINSKY. Allow me to say something. You have misunderstood me. The Hetman will do just as you think should be done. When we manage to get rid of Petlyura and the allies help us smash the Bolsheviks, that's when the Hetman will place the Ukraine at the feet of His Imperial Majesty, the Emperor Nikolai Alexandrovich ...

MYSHLAEVSKY. What Alexandrovich? And he says I'm drunk.

NIKOLKA. The emperor has been killed ...

SHERVINSKY. Gentlemen! The news of His Imperial Majesty's death . . .

MYSHLAEVSKY. Is somewhat exaggerated.

STUDZINSKY. Viktor, you are an officer!

ELENA. Gentlemen, let him finish!

SHERVINSKY. Was fabricated by the Bolsheviks. Do you know what happened in Emperor Wilhelm's palace when the Hetman's entourage was presented? Emperor Wilhelm said: "And about everything else this man will speak to you . . ."—the curtains drew aside, and our sovereign walked out .

Lariosik *enters.*

He said: "Gentlemen, officers, go to the Ukraine and form your units. When the time comes I will personally lead you to the heart of Russia, to Moscow!" And he burst into tears.

STUDZINSKY. He has been killed!

ELENA. Shervinsky, is that true?

SHERVINSKY. Elena Vasilievna!

ALEXEI. Lieutenant, that's a fairy tale! I've already heard that story.

NIKOLKA. All the same. Even if the emperor is dead, long live the emperor! Hurrah! . . . The national hymn! Shervinsky! The hymn! (*He sings.*)

God save the tsar! . . .[9]

SHERVINSKY. STUDZINSKY. MYSHLAEVSKY. } God save the tsar!

LARIOSIK (*sings*). Strong, powerful . . .

NIKOLKA. STUDZINSKY. SHERVINSKY. } Rule on . . .

ELENA. ALEXEI. } Gentlemen, what's wrong with you! This is unnecessary!

MYSHLAEVSKY (*cries*). Alyosha, can they be the people! Why they're bandits. A professional union of regicides. Peter the Third . . .

9. The tsarist national anthem again.

Well, what did he do to them? What? They howl: "We don't want war!" Fine . . . It was he who stopped the war. And then what? His own nobleman socks the Tsar in the puss with a bottle! . . . A prince gives it to Pavel Petrovich on the ear with a cigar box. . . . And that . . . I forget his name . . . the one with the sideburns, the nice guy . . . O.K., he thinks, I'll do something nice for the peasants, I'll free them, the striped devils. So they gave it to him with a bomb for that?[10] They should be flogged, the good-for-nothings. Alyosha! Ooh, I don't feel so good, fellows . . .

ELENA. He's sick!

NIKOLKA. The captain's sick!

ALEXEI. In the bathroom.

> Studzinsky, Nikolka, *and* Alexei *pick up* Myshlaevsky *and carry him out.*

ELENA. I'll go see what's happening to him.

SHERVINSKY (*blocking the door*). There's no need, Elena!

ELENA. Gentlemen, gentlemen, you have to . . . Chaos . . . They've filled the room with smoke . . . Lariosik, Lariosik!

SHERVINSKY. What are you doing, you'll wake him up!

ELENA. Because of you I drank too much myself. Lord, my legs won't work.

SHERVINSKY. Here, come here . . . will you allow me . . . beside you?

ELENA. Sit down . . . Shervinsky, what's going to happen to us? How will all this end? Hm? I had a bad dream. In general everything around here has gotten worse and worse lately.

SHERVINSKY. Elena Vasilievna! Everything will be all right, and I don't believe in dreams.

ELENA. No, no, my dream is prophetic. It's as if we're all going by boat to America and we're sitting in the hold. And then a gale. The wind howls. It's cold, oh so cold. Waves. And we're in the hold. The water rises right to our feet . . . We climb up on some sort of plank bed. And suddenly rats. Such enormous, repulsive ones. So terrifying that I woke up.

10. The reference is to Tsar Alexander II during whose reign many reforms (including emancipation of the serfs) were carried out, and who was assassinated in 1881.

SHERVINSKY. And do you know what, Elena Vasilievna? He won't come back.

ELENA. Who?

SHERVINSKY. Your husband.

ELENA. Leonid Yurievich, that's brazen. What business of yours is it whether he comes back or not?

SHERVINSKY. It's very much my business. I love you.

ELENA. I've heard. And you're still making things up.

SHERVINSKY. I swear it, I love you.

ELENA. Well, love me and keep it to yourself.

SHERVINSKY. I don't want to, I'm tired of that.

ELENA. Wait, wait! Why did you remember my husband when I mentioned the rats?

SHERVINSKY. Because he looks like a rat.

ELENA. What a pig you are, really, Leonid! First of all, he doesn't look like one at all.

SHERVINSKY. Like two drops of water. The pince nez, the sharp nose . . .

ELENA. Very, very handsome of you! To say nasty things about a man who is absent—and to his wife besides!

SHERVINSKY. What kind of wife are you to him?

ELENA. What do you mean?

SHERVINSKY. Look at yourself in the mirror. You are beautiful, intelligent, intellectually developed, as they say. In general a woman with a capital "W." You are a fine accompanist on the piano. And compared to you he's a coat rack, a careerist, a headquarters nothing.

ELENA. Behind his back! Wonderful! (*She shuts his mouth.*)

SHERVINSKY. I'll say it to his face too. I've wanted to for a long time. I'll say it and challenge him to a duel. You're unhappy with him.

ELENA. And with *whom* will I be happy?

SHERVINSKY. With me.

ELENA. You're not suitable.

SHERVINSKY. Oho, ho! . . . Why am I not suitable?

ELENA. What's good about you?

SHERVINSKY. Just take a good look.

ELENA. Trifles, adjutants' toys, and you're as cute as a cherub. And the voice. And nothing else.

SHERVINKSY. I knew it! What a curse! Everyone says the same thing! Shervinsky—the adjutant, Shervinsky—the singer . . . But Shervinsky has a soul, *that* no one notices. And Shervinsky lives like a homeless dog, and Shervinsky has no one on whose bosom to rest his head.

ELENA (*pushes his head away*). You miserable Lovelace![11] I know about your escapades. You tell the same thing to everyone. And you did to that lanky one of yours. Faugh, painted lips . . .

SHERVINSKY. She's not lanky. She's a mezzo-soprano. Elena Vasilievna, I didn't tell her anything of the sort and I never will. That's very wrong on your part, Lena, so wrong on your part, Lena.

ELENA. I'm not Lena to you!

SHERVINSKY. Well, it's wrong on your part, Elena Vasilievna. In general you have no feeling for me.

ELENA. Unfortunately, I like you very much.

SHERVINSKY. Aha! You like me. And you don't love your husband.

ELENA. No, I do.

SHERVINSKY. Lena, don't lie. Women who love their husbands don't have eyes like that. I have seen feminine eyes. One can see everything in them.

ELENA. But yes, you are experienced, of course.

SHERVINSKY. Look at the way he left?!

ELENA. And you would have done the same thing.

SHERVINSKY. Me? Never! It's disgraceful. Admit that you don't love him.

ELENA. Well, all right: I don't love him or respect him. I don't respect him. Satisfied? But nothing follows from that. Take your hands away.

SHERVINSKY. But why did you kiss me then?

ELENA. You're lying! I have never kissed you! A liar with epaulets!

SHERVINSKY. I'm lying? . . . But at the piano? I was singing "Almighty God" . . . and we were alone. And I'll even tell you when—

---

11. The hero of Samuel Richardson's *Clarissa, or the History of a Young Lady.* For Russians he is the equivalent of Casanova.

the eighth of November. We were alone, and you kissed me on the lips.

ELENA. I kissed you for your voice. Understand? For your voice. It was a motherly kiss. Because you have a remarkable voice. And nothing more.

SHERVINSKY. Nothing?

ELENA. This is torture. I swear it is! Dirty dishes. These drunks. My husband's gone away somewhere. Light all around . . .

SHERVINSKY. We'll get rid of the light. (*He puts out the overhead light.*) Is it all right like that? Listen, Lena, I love you very much. I won't let you go in any case. You're going to be my wife.

ELENA. You persist like a snake . . . like a snake.

SHERVINSKY. What kind of snake am I?

ELENA. You use every occasion and you tempt. You won't get anything. Nothing. No matter what he is like, I'm not going to wreck my life because of you. You might turn out to be even worse.

SHERVINSKY. Lena, how lovely you are!

ELENA. Go away! I'm drunk. You got me drunk on purpose. You are a well known no-good. Our whole life is crashing down. Everything is falling apart, being destroyed.

SHERVINSKY. Elena, don't be afraid, I won't abandon you at a time like this. I'll be beside you, Lena.

ELENA. Let me go. I'm afraid of casting a shadow on the Talberg name.

SHERVINSKY. Lena, leave him altogether and marry me . . . Lena!

They kiss.

Will you get divorced?

ELENA. Oh, let it all go to the devil!

They kiss.

LARIOSIK (*suddenly*). Don't kiss—or I'll throw up.

ELENA. Let go! My God! (*She runs out.*)

LARIOSIK. Ooh! . . .

SHERVINSKY. Young man, you saw nothing!

LARIOSIK (*hazily*). No, I *did* see.

SHERVINSKY. What did you see?

LARIOSIK. If you have a king, play the king, but don't touch the
queens! ...Don't touch! ...Ay! ...

SHERVINSKY. I wasn't playing cards with you.

LARIOSIK. Yes you were.

SHERVINSKY. Lord, how drunk!

LARIOSIK. We'll just see what Mama says to you when I die. I said
I was not a military man, I shouldn't have so much vodka. (*He
falls on* Shervinsky's *chest.*)

SHERVINSKY. Plastered!

The clock strikes three, plays the minuet.

CURTAIN

ACT II

SCENE ONE

THE HETMAN'S OFFICE *in the palace. A huge desk, telephones on it. A separate field telephone. On the wall a huge map in a frame. Night. The office is brightly lit. The door opens, and the lackey lets* SHERVINSKY *in.*

SHERVINSKY. Hello, Fyodor.

LACKEY. Good evening, lieutenant, sir.

SHERVINSKY. What! No one's here? And which of the adjutants is on duty at the telephones?

LACKEY. His Highness Prince Novozhiltsev.

SHERVINSKY. But where is he?

LACKEY. I don't know. He left half an hour ago.

SHERVINSKY. How can that be? And the telephones sat here for half an hour without a duty officer?

LACKEY. But no one called. I was at the doors the whole time.

SHERVINSKY. It's not important that no one called! And if someone *had* called? At a time like this? The devil knows what's going on!

LACKEY. I would have taken the message. He arranged that I should write them down until you came.

SHERVINSKY. You? Write down military messages?! . . . What is wrong with him—softening of the brains? Ah, I see, I see! He got sick?

LACKEY. Not at all. He left the palace altogether.

SHERVINSKY. That is . . . what do you mean, out of the palace altogether? You're joking, dear Fyodor. He departed from the palace without finishing his duty hours? Does that mean he departed for an insane asylum?

LACKEY. I don't know. Only he gathered up his toothbrush, towel and soap from the adjutants' quarters. I gave him a newspaper too.

SHERVINSKY. What newspaper?

LACKEY. I'm making the report, lieutenant: he wrapped up the soap in yesterday's issue.

SHERVINSKY. Well I'll ... and there's his saber.

LACKEY. And he left in his civilian clothes.

SHERVINSKY. Either I've gone out of my mind or you have. Did he at least leave me a note? Did he tell you to pass anything on to me?

LACKEY. He ordered me to give his respects.

SHERVINSKY. You may go, Fyodor.

LACKEY. Yes, sir. Permission to report, lieutenant?

SHERVINSKY. Well?

LACKEY. He received unpleasant news.

SHERVINSKY. From where? From home?

LACKEY. Not at all. On the field telephone. And he immediately rushed away. His face changed very much at the news.

SHERVINSKY. Fyodor, I hope that the facial changes of His Highness's adjutants does not concern you. You say too much.

LACKEY. I beg your pardon, lieutenant. (*He exits.*)

SHERVINSKY (*speaks into the telephone on the* Hetman's *table*). Twelve-twenty-three ... *Merci* ... Is this Prince Novozhiltsev's apartment? ... Ask Sergei Nikolaevich ... What? At the palace? He's not at the palace. I'm speaking from the palace myself ... Wait, Seryozha, why that's your voice! ... Sergei ... Please ...

The phone rings off.

What boorishness! I heard quite clearly that it was he himself. (*A pause.*) Shervinsky, Shervinsky ... (*He rings up on the field telephone, the telephone squawks.*) Headquarters of the Svyatoshin unit ... Ask the HQ commander ... What—he's not there! His assistant ... Headquarters of the Svyatoshin unit? ... What the hell! ... (*He sits down at the table, rings.*)

The Lackey *enters.*

(*He writes a note.*) Fyodor, give this note to the courier immediately. He should go to my apartment on Lvov Street right away; there he will be given a bundle when he presents this note. Bring it here immediately. Here are two rubles for the cab. Here's a note to the commander for his pass.

LACKEY. Yes, sir. (*He exits.*)

SHERVINSKY (*touches his sideburns, pensively*). I swear, what a hell of a mess!

The telephone on the table rings.

I'm listening . . . Yes . . . His Highness's personal adjutant Lieutenant Shervinsky . . . Your health, Your Excellency . . . What, sir? (*A pause.*) Bolbotun?! . . . What, with the entire headquarters staff? . . . Yes, sir! . . . Yes, sir, I'll inform him . . . Yes, sir, Your Excellency . . . His Highness must be there at twelve midnight. (*He hangs up the receiver.*)

The phone rings off. A pause.

I'm dead! (*He whistles.*)

Off-stage a hollow command: "Attention! At ease!"—then the many voices of the guards shouting: "Good evening, Your Highness!"

LACKEY (*opens both halves of the door*). His Highness!

Enter the Hetman. *He is wearing a very rich Cossack jacket, raspberry red trousers and Caucasian type boots without heels or spurs. Glittering general's shoulder straps. Short-clipped graying mustache, a smoothly shaved head, about forty-five.*

HETMAN. Hello, lieutenant.

SHERVINSKY. Good evening, Your Highness.

HETMAN. Have they arrived?

SHERVINSKY. May I ask who?

HETMAN. What do you mean, "who"? I set a conference for eleven forty-five here. The commander of the Russian army, the chief of the garrison, and the representatives of the German staff were to be here. Where are they?

SHERVINSKY. I don't know. No one has arrived.

HETMAN. They're always late. Give me an account of the last hour. Quickly!

SHERVINSKY. I must inform Your Highness—I just went on duty. Cornet Prince Novozhiltsev who was on duty before me . . .

HETMAN. I have long wanted to make it clear to you and the other adjutants that you should speak Ukrainian. This is disgraceful, really! Not one of my officers speaks the language of the country, and this makes the most negative impression on the Ukrainian units. I request this urgently.

SHERVINSKY. *Slukayu,* Your Highness. Duty adjutant, cornet . . . prince . . . (*Aside.*) How the hell do you say "prince" in Ukrainian! . . . Dammit! (*Aloud.*) Novozhiltsev, temporarily fulfilling the duties. I think . . . *ya dúmayu . . . ya dumáyu . . . dumováyu . . .*[12]

HETMAN. Speak Russian!

SHERVINSKY. Yes, Your Highness. Cornet Prince Novozhiltsev, who was on duty before me, apparently got suddenly ill and left for home before my arrival . . .

HETMAN. What are you saying? Left his duty-post? What's wrong with you? Are you in your right mind? You mean that he left his duty post? I.e. he abandoned his post? What's really going on here? (*He calls up on the telephone.*) Commandant's? . . . Give me a detail immediately . . . You should be able to tell from my voice who's speaking. A detail to the apartment of my adjutant, Cornet Novozhiltsev, arrest him and take him to the commandant's. Immediately.

SHERVINSKY (*aside*). That's what he deserves! That'll teach him to disguise his voice on the telephone. The boor!

HETMAN. (*on the telephone*). This instant! (*To* Shervinsky.) Well, did he leave a note?

SHERVINSKY. Yes, sir. But there's nothing on the tape.

HETMAN. What was he thinking about? Has he gone crazy? Nuts? Why I'll shoot him right now, right here on the palace parapet.

---

12. The Hetman wants his men to speak Ukrainian, not Russian; but most stumble, just as Shervinsky does here.

I'll show you all. Get connected to the commandant's headquarters immediately! Get him up here right now! The same for the garrison chief and all the regimental commanders. Move it!

SHERVINSKY. May I report, Your Highness, news of extreme importance.

HETMAN. What other news is there?

SHERVINSKY. Five minutes ago I was called from the commandant's headquarters and informed that the commandant of Your Highness's volunteer army had suddenly fallen ill and left for Germany with his whole headquarters on a German train.

A pause.

HETMAN. Are you in your right mind? You have sick eyes . . . Have you thought about what you are reporting? What has happened? A catastrophe, or what? Have they fled? Why don't you say something? Well? . . .

SHERVINSKY. Precisely, Your Highness, a catastrophe. At ten this evening the Petlyura units ripped through the city front and Bolbotun's cavalry rode through the opening . . .

HETMAN. Bolbotun's? . . . Where? . . .

SHERVINSKY. On the other side of the Slobodka, ten versts beyond.

HETMAN. Wait . . . wait . . . so . . . what the? . . . Here's what . . . In any case, you're a fine, alert officer. I noticed that a long time ago. Here's what we'll do. Get in touch with the headquarters of the German commander immediately, and ask his representatives to come here to see me. Quickly, my dear fellow, quickly!

SHERVINSKY. Yes, sir. (*On the telephone.*) The third. *Seien Sie bitte so liebenswürdig, Herrn Major von Dust an den Apparat zu bitten.*

A knock on the door.

Ja . . . Ja . . .

HETMAN. Yes, come in.

LACKEY. The representatives of the German commander, General Von Shratt and Major Von Dust ask to be received.

HETMAN. Ask them in immediately. (*To* Shervinsky.) Forget that.

The Lackey *admits* Von Shratt *and* Von Dust. *Both in gray uniforms.* Shratt *is gray-haired, long-faced.* Dust *has a purple face. Both wearing monocles.*

SHRATT. *Wir haben die Ehre, Euer Durchlaucht zu begrüssen.* Unfortunately, ze German command can not this do.

HETMAN. What? Inform me why, General.

SHRATT. *Physisch unmöglich.* It is physically impossible. *Erstens,* first of all, according to our information, Petlyura has zwei hundert tousand men, excellently armed. And besides the German command is the division gathering taking to Germany.

SHERVINSKY (*aside*). The bastards!

SHRATT. Thus, at our disposal enough forces there are not. *Zweitens,* second, the whole Ukraine is on the side Petlyura's.

HETMAN. Lieutenant, underline that sentence in the protocol.

SHERVINSKY. Yes, sir.

SHRATT. I against haf noting. Underline. Thus, it is impossible Petlyura to stop.

HETMAN. This means the German command is suddenly leaving me, the army and government to the whim of fate?

SHRATT. *Nyet,* we are ordered to take measures Your Highness to save.

HETMAN. What measures does the command propose?

SHRATT. Instant evacuation of Your Highness. The train car right now, and to Deutschland.

HETMAN. Forgive me, I understand none of this. How can that be? . . . Sorry. Perhaps the German command has evacuated Prince Belorukov?

SHRATT. Precisely so.

HETMAN. Without my permission? (*Upset.*) I will not agree. I am lodging a protest with the German government against such acts. I still have the possibility of gathering an army within the city and defending Kiev with my own means. But the responsibility for the destruction of the capital lies on the German command. And I think that the governments of England and France . . .

SHRATT. The government of England! The government of France!!

. . . The German government feels itself strong enough not to permit the destruction of the capital.

HETMAN. Is that a threat, general?

SHRATT. A warning, Your Highness. There are no armed forces at Your Highness's disposal. The situation is catastrophic . . .

DUST (*quietly,* to Shratt). *Mein General, wir haben gar keine Zeit. Wir müssen* . . .

SHRATT. *Ja-ja* . . . Your Highness, allow me a final word: we have just intercepted news that Petlyura's cavalry is eight versts from Kiev. And it will tomorrow morning enter . . .

HETMAN. I am the last to find out!

SHRATT. Your Highness, do you know what will happen to you in the event you are captured? Your Highness has been sentenced. It is an extremely sad sentence.

HETMAN. What kind of a sentence?

SHRATT. I beg your pardon, Your Highness. (*A pause.*) To be hanged. (*A pause.*) Your Highness, I would like an answer in moments. At my disposal only ten short minutes I have, after that I absolve myself of responsibility for Your Highness's life.

A long pause.

HETMAN. I will go!

SHRATT. Ah, you'll go? (*To* Dust.) Be so kind, do it secretly and with no noise.

DUST. Oh, no noise at all! (*He shoots at the ceiling twice with his revolver.*)

Shervinsky *is upset.*

HETMAN (*taking hold of his revolver*). What does this mean?

SHRATT. Oh, be at ease, Your Highness. (*He disappears behind the curtain of the right-hand door.*)

Off-stage rumbling, shouts: "Guard, to arms!" Clatter of feet.

DUST (*opening the middle doors*). *Ruhig!* Quiet there! General

Von Shratt caught his revolver with his trousers, and it accidentally fired, hitting his forehead.

Voices off-stage: "The Hetman! Where is the Hetman!"

The Hetman is quite all right. Your Highness, kindly step out here ... Guard ...

HETMAN (*in the middle doors*). Everything's quiet, stop the alarm.

DUST (*at the door*). Please let the doctor through with his instruments.

The alarm quiets down. A German Army Doctor, carrying a case and medical bag enters. Dust locks the middle door with key.

SHRATT (*coming out from behind the curtain*). Your Highness, I'll ask you to disguise yourself in a German uniform, as if you are I— and I am wounded. We will carry you out of town secretly so that no one will know, so that it will not cause indignation among the guards.

HETMAN. Do as you wish.

The field telephone rings.

Lieutenant, the telephone!

SHERVINSKY. His Highness's office ... What? How's that? ... (*To the* Hetman.) Your Highness, two Serdyuk regiments have gone over to Petlyura's side ... The enemy cavalry has appeared in an exposed section. What should I tell them, Your Highness?

HETMAN. What? Tell them to slow down the cavalry, well, for at least half an hour! I must leave. I'll give them armored cars!

SHERVINSKY (*on the telephone*). You hear? ... Hold them back for at least half an hour! His Highness will give you armored cars!

DUST (*taking a German uniform out of the box*). Your Highness! Where do you wish to do it?

HETMAN. In the bedroom.

Hetman and Dust exit to the right.

SHERVINSKY (*at the front of the stage*). Flee, or what? Will Elena go or not? (*Decisively, to* Shratt.) Your Excellency, I ask you most respectfully to take me with the Hetman, I am his personal adjutant. In addition, with me ... my ... fiancée ...

SHRATT. Unfortunately, lieutenant, not only can I not take your fiancée—but I can't take you. If you want to go, go to the station where our staff train is. But I forewarn you—there are no places—there is already a personal adjutant there.

SHERVINSKY. Who?

SHRATT. What's his ... Prince Novozhiltsev.

SHERVINSKY. Novozhiltsev! When did he manage that?

SHRATT. When there is a catastrophe, everyone becomes very nimble. He was at our staff headquarters just now.

SHERVINSKY. And there, in Berlin, will he serve the Hetman?

SHRATT. Oh, *nyet!* The Hetman will be alone. No entourage. We will just to the border take those who want to save their necks from your *muzhiks,* and there it's everyone for himself.

SHERVINSKY. Oh, thank you very much, I know how to save my neck here too ...

SHRATT. Right, lieutenant. One should never leave one's homeland. *Heimat ist Heimat!*

The Hetman *and* Dust *enter. The* Hetman *is disguised as a German general. He's upset, smokes.*

HETMAN. Lieutenant, burn all of the papers here.

DUST. *Herr Doktor, seien Sie liebenswürdig.* Your Highness, be seated.

They sit the Hetman *down. The* Doctor *bandages his head all over.*

DOCTOR. *Fertig.*

SHRATT (*to* Dust). The car!

DUST. *Sogleich.*

SHRATT. Your Highness, lie down.

HETMAN. But the people must be informed ... A manifesto? ...

SHRATT. A manifesto? ... If you please ...

HETMAN (*hollowly*). Lieutenant, write ... God hasn't given me the strength ... and I ...

DUST. Manifesto? . . . There is no time for manifestoes . . . Do it by telegram from the train . . .

HETMAN. Forget it!

DUST. Your Highness, lie down.

They put the Hetman *on a stretcher.* Shratt *hides. They open the middle door, the* Lackey *appears.* Dust, *the Doctor and the* Lackey *carry the* Hetman *out the left door.* Shervinsky *helps them as far as the door, returns.* Shratt *enters.*

SHRATT. All *ist in ordnung.* (*He looks at his wristwatch.*) One A.M. (*Puts on a cap and cape.*) Goodbye, Lieutenant. I don't advise you to sit around here. You can leave with no difficulty. Take off your shoulder straps. (*He listens.*) You hear?

SHERVINSKY. Running fire.

SHRATT. Precisely. A pun! "Running!" Do you have a pass for the side door?

SHERVINSKY. Yes, sir.

SHRATT. *Auf Wiedersehen.* Hurry. (*He exits.*)

SHERVINSKY (*crushed*). Real German work. (*He suddenly comes to life.*) Well, sir, there's no time. None . . . none . . . none . . . (*At the table.*) Oh, his cigarette case! Gold! The Hetman forgot it. Leave it here? Impossible, the lackeys'll snatch it. Oho! Must weigh a pound. A historical treasure. (*Hides the cigarette case in his pocket.*) Well, now . . . (*At the table.*) We aren't going to burn any papers—with the exception of the list of adjutants. (*He burns the papers.*) Am I a swine or not a swine? No, I am not a swine. (*On the telephone.*) Fourteen-fifty three . . . Yes . . . Division? . . . Get the commander to the telephone! On the double! . . . Wake him up. (*A pause.*) Colonel Turbin? . . . Shervinsky speaking. Listen carefully, Alexei Vasilievich: the Hetman has flown the coop. . . . *Flown the coop!* . . . Yes I'm serious . . . No, there's time until dawn . . . Tell Elena Vasilievna not to go out of the house tomorrow for any reason . . . I'll come to hide in the morning. Goodbye. (*The dial tone.*) And my conscience is clean and at ease . . . Fyodor!

The Lackey *enters.*

Did the courier bring the bundle?

LACKEY. Yes, sir.

SHERVINSKY. Give it to me quickly!

The Lackey *exits, then returns with the bundle.*

LACKEY (*disturbed*). May I ask what happened to His Highness?

SHERVINSKY. What kind of question is that. The Hetman is asleep. And you just keep quiet in general. You're a good man, Fyodor. There's something in your face . . . something . . . attractive . . . proletarian . . .

LACKEY. Yes, sir.

SHERVINSKY. Fyodor, bring me my towel, razor, and soap from the adjutants' room.

LACKEY. Yes, sir. Do you want a newspaper?

SHERVINSKY. Quite right. And a newspaper.

The Lackey *exits through the left door. Meanwhile,* Shervinsky *puts on a civilian overcoat and hat, takes off his spurs. He wraps his saber and* Novozhiltsev's *in the bundle. The* Lackey *appears.*

Does this hat suit me?

LACKEY. Of course, sir. Will you take the razor in your pocket?

SHERVINSKY. The razor in my pocket . . . Well, now . . . Dear Fyodor, allow me to leave you fifty Ukrainian rubles as a memento.

LACKEY. Thank you very much, sir.

SHERVINSKY. Allow me to shake your honorable working hand. Don't be surprised—I'm a democrat by nature. Fyodor! I have never been in the palace—I never served as adjutant.

LACKEY. I understand.

SHERVINSKY. I don't know you. In general—I'm an opera singer.

LACKEY. Did he really run away?

SHERVINSKY. Slipped right out.

LACKEY. Oh, the rogue!

SHERVINSKY. An indescribable bandit!

LACKEY. So it looks like we've all been left to the whim of fate?

SHERVINSKY. You can see for yourself. It's not half so bad for you—but what about me?

The telephone rings.

Yes . . . Ah! Captain! . . . Yes! Toss everything and get the hell out . . . It means I know what I'm talking about . . . Shervinsky . . . Good luck. Goodbye! . . . Dear Fyodor, no matter how pleasant it is for me to chat with you, you can see yourself that I have no time . . . Fyodor, while I am in power—I bequeath this office to you. What are you looking at? Strange fellow! You just imagine what sort of blanket you could get out of this curtain. (*He disappears.*)

A pause. The telephone rings.

LACKEY. Yes . . . How can I help you? . . . You know what? Toss everything and get the hell out . . . Fyodor's speaking . . . Fyodor! . . .

SCENE TWO

AN EMPTY, *gloomy room. A sign: "Headquarters of the First Cavalry Division." A blue and gold flag. A kerosene lamp at the entrance. Evening. The clatter of horses' hooves outside the windows from time to time. A concertina softly plays familiar tunes.*

TELEPHONE OPERATOR (*on the telephone*). It's me, Franko, plug in the line again . . . plug it in I say! . . . Do you hear me? . . . This is the headquarters of the cavalry division.

The telephone sings signals. Noise off-stage. Hurricane *and* Kirpaty *lead in a* Sechevnik[13] Deserter. *His face is bloody.*

BOLBOTUN. What's this?
HURRICANE. We caught a deserter, colonel, sir.

13. A man from the *Sech*, the home of the Cossacks.

BOLBOTUN. Of what regiment?

Silence.

Of what regiment, I said?

Silence.

TELEPHONE OPERATOR. It's me again! I'm calling from the headquarters, Franko, plug in the line! This is the headquarters of the cavalry division! ... Do you hear! ... God dammit!

BOLBOTUN. What are you doing, you mother-fucker! Eh? What are you doing? ... At a time when every honorable Cossack went to the defense of the Ukrainian republic against the White Guards and those yid Communists, at a time when every farmer has stood up in the ranks of the Ukrainian army, you're hiding in the bushes? Do you know what the Hetman's officers and those commissars do with our farmers? They bury them alive! Understand? So I'll bury *you* alive in a grave myself! Myself, Sotnik[14] Galanba!

A voice off-stage: "The Sotnik is ordered to the Colonel!"
A flurry.

Where did you take him?

KIRPATY. Beyond the stacks, the son of a bitch, he run off, he was hiding!

BOLBOTUN. Oh you rotten swine!

Galanba *enters, cold, black, with a black peaked cap.*

Pan Sotnik, interrogate the deserter ... Franko, the disposition! Quit fooling around with the telephone!

TELEPHONE OPERATOR. Immediately, colonel, sir, immediately! What am I supposed to do with it? "Quit fooling around ..."

GALANBA (*with a cold face*). What regiment?

Silence.

What regiment?

DESERTER (*crying*). I'm not a deserter. Have pity, *pan* Sotnik! I was crawling to the field hospital. My feet are completely frozen.

14. An untranslatable Cossack rank.

TELEPHONE OPERATOR (*on the telephone*). Where's the disposition? I'm asking nicely. The commander of the cavalry division is asking for the disposition ... Do you hear? ... What are you going to do with this telephone?!

GALANBA. Your feet are frozen? And why didn't you take a pass from the headquarters of your regiment? Eh? What regiment? (*He starts to swing.*)

Horses crossing a log bridge can be heard.

DESERTER. The Second Sechevoi.

GALANBA. We know you *Sechevik* guys. All deceivers. Traitors. Bolsheviks. Get off your boots, get them off. And if your feet aren't frozen, and you're lying, then I'll shoot you right here. Men! The lamp!

TELEPHONE OPERATOR (*on the telephone*). Send us an orderly for the agreement ... To the slobodka! ... Right! ... Right! ... Yes! ... Gritsko! Let the orderly take the disposition for our headquarters. All right? ... Pan Colonel, the disposition will be here immediately ...

BOLBOTUN. Good.

GALANBA (*taking out his Mauser*). And here's the condition for you: if your feet are healthy—I'll have you in the next world. Get back so I don't hit anyone.

The Deserter *sits down on the floor, takes his boots off. Silence.*

BOLBOTUN. That's right. So that he'll be an example to others.

They shine the lamp on the Deserter.

KIRPATY (*with a sigh*). Frozen ... He told the truth.

GALANBA. You should have gotten a signed order. An order, you swine! And not run away from your regiment ...

DESERTER. There's no one to get an order from. There's no doctor in our regiment. There's no one. (*He cries.*)

GALANBA. Take him under arrest! And he goes to the hospital under arrest! After the doctor bandages his foot, return him here to the headquarters and give him fifteen lashes, so he'll know what happens when you run away from your regiment without documents. HURRICANE (*leading him out*). Go on, go on!

A concertina off-stage. A voice sings mournfully: "Ay, my little apple, where are you rolling, you'll land with the Gaydamaks and never return . . ."[15] *Anxious voices outside the window: "Stop them! Stop them! Past the bridge . . . They ran on the ice."*

GALANBA (*out the window*). Men, what's going on there? What is it?

A voice: "Some kind of Jews, pan Sotnik, they ran out of the Slobodka past the bridge on the ice."

Men! Reconnaissance! To your horses! To your horses! Mount up! Mount up! Kirpaty! Well, get going after them! But take them alive! Alive!

BOLBOTUN. Franko, hold the line.

TELEPHONE OPERATOR. I'll hold it, colonel, sir, I'll hold it!

Hoofbeats off-stage. Hurricane *appears, leading* a Man carrying a basket.

MAN with basket. Hey, fellows, I didn't do anything. What's wrong? I'm a craftsman . . .

GALANBA. What did they arrest you for?

MAN with basket. Please, comrade officer . . .

GALANBA. What? Comrade? Who's a comrade to you here?

MAN with basket. Sorry, Mister Officer.

GALANBA. I'm no "Mister" to you. The "Misters" are all with the Hetman in the city now. And we're going to rip the guts out of your "Misters." Boy, hit him one, you're closer. Punch this Mister in the mouth. Now, do you see what kind of Misters there are here? You see?

MAN with basket. I see.

GALANBA. Get a light on him, men! Now it seems to me that he's a Communist.

15. From "Little Apple," a Russian folk song.

MAN with basket. Whatd'ya mean! What do you mean, please! I'm a bootmaker, if you'll be so kind as to see.

BOLBOTUN. Why do you speak the Muscovite tongue so very well?

MAN with basket. We're from Kaluga, sir. From the Kaluga district. And our lives are no longer happy since we came here to you in the Ukraine. I'm a bootmaker.

GALANBA. Your papers!

MAN with basket. Passport? Immediately. My passport is clean, one may say.

GALANBA. What's the basket for? Where were you going?

MAN with basket. There are boots in the basket, Your ... Your High ... boots ... b ... We work for the store. We live in the Slobodka ourselves and we take the boots to town.

GALANBA. Why at night?

MAN with basket. It's just the right timing so as to be in town in the morning.

BOLBOTUN. Boots ... Oh ho ho ... that's good!

Hurricane *opens the basket.*

MAN with basket. I'm sorry, Honored Citizen, they are not mine, they're from my boss's store.

BOLBOTUN. From his boss's! That's even better. The boss's stuff is good stuff. Men, take a pair of the "boss's stuff" each.

They pass out the boots.

MAN with basket. Citizen Military Minister! Without these boots I'll be dead. I'll be all ready to lie right down in the grave! There are two thousand rubles worth here ... it's my boss's ...

BOLBOTUN. We'll give you a receipt.

MAN with basket. Please, what good is a receipt to me? (*He rushes at* Bolbotun, *who hits him on the ear. He rushes at* Galanba.) Mister Cavalryman! Two thousand rubles worth. The main thing is, that if I were a bourgeois, or say, a Bolshevik ...

Galanba *hits him on the ear.*

(*He sits down on the ground, crushed.*) What's going on? But all right, take it! I suppose this is to supply the army? ... Only, let me add a pair into the bargain then. (*He starts to take off his boots.*)

TELEPHONE OPERATOR. Look, colonel, sir, what is he doing?

BOLBOTUN. What are you doing, making fun of us, you slime? Get away from the basket. Are you going to be getting underfoot any longer? Any longer? Well, my patience has ended. Get back, men. (*He takes his revolver out.*)

MAN with basket. What're you doing! What're you doing! What're you doing!

BOLBOTUN. Get out of here!

The Man with the basket *rushes to the door.*

EVERYONE. Thank you very much, colonel, sir!

TELEPHONE OPERATOR (*on the telephone*). Yes! . . . Yes! . . . Fine! . . . Fine! . . . Colonel, sir! Colonel, sir! Couriers have come to headquarters from two of the Hetman's *serdyuk*[16] regiments. The commander is conducting negotiations with them about coming over to our side.

BOLBOTUN. Fine! When those regiments are with us, Kiev is ours.

TELEPHONE OPERATOR (*on the telephone*). Gritsko! And we have new boots! . . . Right . . . Right . . . Yes, yes . . . Fine! Fine, colonel, sir, please come to the telephone.

BOLBOTUN (*on the telephone*). Colonel Bolbotun, commander of the First Cavalry Division . . . I'm listening . . . Right . . . Right . . . I am leaving immediately. (*To Galanba.*) *Pan* Sotnik, order all four regiments to their horses right away! We've taken the approaches to the city. *Slava!*[17] *Slava!*

HURRICANE.
KIRPATY. } *Slava!* the attack!

A flurry of activity.

GALANBA (*out the window*). Mount up! Mount up! To your horses!

A roar outside the window: "Hurrah!" Galanba *runs out.*

16. *Serdyuks* were one kind of Cossack.
17. "Glory!" ("Hurrah!")

BOLBOTUN. Dismantle the telephone! Bring my horse!

The Telephone Operator *dismantles the telephone. A flurry of activity.*

HURRICANE. The commander's horse!

VOICES. First company, forward at a trot! Next company, forward at a trot! . . .

Clatter of hooves, whistling outside the window. Everybody runs off stage. Then the concertina resounds, flying past the window . . .

CURTAIN

ACT III

SCENE ONE

THE VESTIBULE *of the Alexander Gymnasium. Rifles in piles. Boxes, machine guns. A gigantic staircase. A portrait of Alexander I at the top. Through the windows dawn can be seen. Rumbling off-stage: the division is passing through the corridors of the gymnasium to the sound of music.*

NIKOLKA (*off-stage he starts singing an absurd tune from a soldiers' song*).
> The night breathed with the ecstasy of love,[18]
> Filled with vague thoughts and thrills,

CADETS (*sing deafeningly*).
> I waited for you with a reckless greed for happiness,
> I waited for you and was thrilled at the window.

NIKOLKA (*sings*).
> Our little corner I decorated with flowers ...

STUDZINSKY (*at the bottom of the stairs*). Division, halt!

Off-stage the division halts with a thunderous stamp.

As you were! Captain!

MYSHLAEVSKY. First battery! Stand to! Forward march!

The division marches off-stage.

STUDZINSKY. Left! Left!

MYSHLAEVSKY. Hup! Hup! Hup! First battery, halt!

FIRST OFFICER. Second battery, halt!

18. "The Letter," a song by V. Mazurievich.

The division halts.

Myshlaevsky. The battery may smoke,—at rest!

A hum of voices off-stage.

First Officer (*to* Myshlaevsky). Captain, five of my platoon are missing. Apparently, they've run off. Rotten little students!

Second Officer. In general it's all a swinish mess. You can't figure out anything.

First Officer. Why isn't the commander here? We were supposed to move out at six, and it's already quarter to seven.

Myshlaevsky. Quiet, lieutenant, they called him to the palace by telephone. He'll be here soon. (*To the* Cadets.) What the matter, frozen?

First Cadet. Yes, sir, Captain, sir. It's cold.

Myshlaevsky. Why are you standing in place? Blue as a corpse. Stamp your feet, in open order. After the command "at rest" you're not a monument. Everybody's his own stove. Livelier! Hey, second platoon, break up the desks in the classrooms, get the stoves going! On the double!

Cadets (*shout*). Boys, into the classrooms! Break up the desks, get the stoves going!

Noise, flurry of activity.

Maxim (*appears from his little room, in horror*). Your Excellency, what are you doing? Put the desks in the stoves?! What kind of abuse is that. The director ordered me . . .

First Officer. This is his fourteenth appearance.

Myshlaevsky. And what are we supposed to put in the stoves, old man?

Maxim. Firewood, sir, firewood.

Myshlaevsky. And where is your firewood?

Maxim. We don't have any firewood.

Myshlaevsky. Well then get the bloody hell out of here, you old fool! Hey, second platoon, what the hell? . . .

Maxim. Oh my Lord, saints above us! What is happening! Tatars, absolute Tatars! There were many soldiers . . . (*He exits. Shouts off-stage.*) Sirs, soldiers, what are you doing?!

CADETS (*break up the desks, saw them, put them in the stoves. They sing.*)

> Through the sky a storm is sweeping,
> Whipping snowy whirlwinds round;
> It resembles childish weeping,
> Or a wild beast's wailing sound.[19]

MAXIM. Oh, who heats stoves like this?

CADETS (*sing*).

> Hey you, my Sasha Kanasha!
> (*Sadly.*) Have mercy on us Lord, for the last time . . .

A sudden explosion nearby. A pause. A flurry.

FIRST OFFICER. A shell.

MYSHLAEVSKY. The explosion was somewhere close.

FIRST CADET. Maybe it was aimed at us, captain.

MYSHLAEVSKY. Nonsense! Petlyura just spit, that's all.

The song dies out.

FIRST OFFICER. Captain, I think we will be forced to see Petlyura today. I wonder what he looks like?

SECOND OFFICER (*gloomy*). You'll find out, don't be in a rush.

MYSHLAEVSKY. It has little to do with us. If we're ordered—we'll see him. (*To the* Cadets.) Cadets, what do you . . . Why have you gone sour? More gaily!

CADETS (*sing*).

> And when by the white stairs
> They lead us to a blue realm . . .[20]

SECOND CADET (*runs up to* Studzinsky). The division commander!

19. The words are from Pushkin's lyric poem "A Winter Evening." Several composers used the poem for songs, including M. L. Yakovlev in Pushkin's lifetime and Dargomyzhsky in 1840.

20. A paraphrase from the last stanza of A. Vertinsky's "Your fingers smell of incense."

STUDZINSKY. In ranks! Division, attention! Straighten it out in the middle! Officers! Officers!

MYSHLAEVSKY. First battery, attention!

Alexei *enters.*

ALEXEI (*to* Studzinsky). The list! How many are missing?

STUDZINSKY (*softly*). Twenty-two men.

ALEXEI (*tears up the list*). Is our support on Demievka? Recall them!

STUDZINSKY (*to the* Second Cadet). Recall the support men!

SECOND CADET. Yes, sir. (*He runs out.*)

ALEXEI. I want you officers and the division to listen carefully to what I'm going to say—that is an order. To listen and remember. And having remembered, to carry it out.

Silence.

During the night, in our position, in the position of the entire Russian army, and I would say, in the governmental position of the Ukraine, sharp and sudden changes have taken place . . . Therefore, I am informing you that I am disbanding our division.

Dead silence.

The battle with Petlyura is over. I order you all, including the officers, to immediately take off your shoulder straps, all badges of rank, and to immediately flee and hide in your houses.

A pause.

I'm finished. Carry out the order!

STUDZINSKY. Colonel! Alexei Vasilievich!

FIRST OFFICER. Colonel! Alexei Vasilievich!

SECOND OFFICER. What does this mean?

ALEXEI. Silence! No discussions! Carry out the order! On the double!

THIRD OFFICER. What does this mean, colonel? Arrest him!

Noise.

CADETS.

Arrest him! . . .

We don't understand anything!...
What, arrest him?!...
Have you gone crazy?!...
Petlyura's broken through!...
So that's it! I knew it!...
Quiet!...

FIRST OFFICER. What does this mean, colonel?
THIRD OFFICER. Hey, first platoon, after me!

Distraught Cadets *run in with rifles.*

NIKOLKA. Gentlemen, what are you doing?
SECOND OFFICER. Arrest him! He's betrayed us to Petlyura!
THIRD OFFICER. Colonel, you're under arrest!
MYSHLAEVSKY (*holding back the* Third Officer). Hold it, hold it, lieutenant!
THIRD OFFICER. Hands off, captain, let me by! Cadets, take him!
MYSHLAEVSKY. Cadets, get back!
STUDZINSKY. Alexei Vasilievich, look what's happening.
NIKOLKA. Get back!
STUDZINSKY. Get back, I say! Don't listen to the junior officers!
FIRST OFFICER. Gentlemen, what is this?
SECOND OFFICER. Gentlemen!

An uproar. Revolvers in the hands of the Officers.

THIRD OFFICER. Don't listen to the senior officers!
FIRST CADET. A revolt in the division!
FIRST OFFICER. What are you doing?
STUDZINSKY. Shut up! Attention!
THIRD OFFICER. Take him!
ALEXEI. Shut up! I will say something else!
CADETS.

No talking!
We don't want to listen!
We don't want to listen!

NIKOLKA. Let him talk!
THIRD OFFICER. Quiet, cadets, calm down! Let him say his piece!
We won't let him out of here!

MYSHLAEVSKY. Get your cadets back this second.

FIRST OFFICER. Attention! In place!

CADETS. Attention! Attention! Attention!

ALEXEI. Yes . . . Oh, I'd really be clever if I went into battle with a complement of men such as the Lord God has sent me in the person of you people. But, gentlemen, that which is forgivable in a young volunteer, is unforgivable (*to the* Third Officer) in you, lieutenant! I thought that each of you would understand that a calamity had occurred, and that your commander's tongue doesn't move to report disgraceful things. But you're not subtle. Whom do you wish to defend? Answer me.

Silence.

Answer when the commander asks a question! Whom?

THIRD OFFICER. We promised to defend the Hetman.

ALEXEI. The Hetman? Fine! Today at three o'clock in the morning, abandoning the army to the whim of fate, the Hetman fled, disguised as a German officer, in a German train, to Germany. So, that at the time when the lieutenant is getting ready to defend the Hetman, he's already been gone for a long time. He'll make it to Berlin in fine shape.

CADETS.

To Berlin?!

What's he talking about?!

We don't want to listen?!

FIRST CADET. Gentlemen, why are they listening to him?

STUDZINSKY. Shut up!

A roar. Dawn in the windows.

ALEXEI. But that's a small part of it. Simultaneously with this swine, another swine fled in the same direction—His Eminence, Prince Belorukov, commander of the entire army. So, my friends, not only is there no one to defend, there's not even anyone to command us, because the Prince's staff took off with him.

A roar.

CADETS.

It can't be!
That cannot be so!
It's a lie!

ALEXEI. Who said "lie"? Who said "lie"? I was just at headquarters. I checked all the information. I answer for every word I've said! ... And so, gentlemen! Here we are—two hundred men. And there—Petlyura. But what am I saying—not *there*, but *here*! My friends, his cavalry is in the suburbs of the city! He has an army of two hundred thousand, and we have—in place us, two or three home guard cavalry groups, and three batteries. Understand? One of you here got a revolver out at me. He frightened me terribly. A little kid!

THIRD OFFICER. Colonel, sir.

ALEXEI. Shut up! So here's how it is. If you would all carry out the decision to defend . . . what? whom? . . . —in a word, go into battle—I wouldn't lead you, because I won't take part in a farce, all the more so that you'll all pay for this farce with your blood—and absolutely senselessly!

NIKOLKA. Those headquarters bastards!

Roars and howls.

CADETS.

What are we to do now?
Lie down in the grave!
Shame! . . .
Go to hell! . . . What is this, an open discussion?
Stand at attention!
They've driven us into a trap.

THIRD CADET (*runs in crying*). First they shouted, "Forward, forward!" And now, "Back!" I'll find the Hetman—and kill him!

FIRST OFFICER. Get that crybaby the hell out! Listen, cadets: if what the colonel says is true, rally round me! We'll get to the troop trains —and on to the Don, to Denikin![21]

21. Denikin was a White general.

CADETS.

> To the Don! To Denikin!
> Sure, sure . . . what kind of crap is that!
> It's impossible to get to the Don! . . .

STUDZINSKY. Alexei Vasilievich, that's true, we have to abandon everything and lead the division to the Don.

ALEXEI. Captain Studzinsky! Don't you dare! I'm commanding the division! I will give the orders—and you will carry them out! To the Don? Listen, you! There on the Don you'll find the same thing, if you manage to get there. You'll find the same generals and the same kind of headquarters staff crowd.

NIKOLKA. The same kind of headquarters bastards!

ALEXEI. Absolutely right. They'll make you fight with your own people. And when the people split your heads, those bastards will run abroad . . . I know it's the same way in Rostov as it is in Kiev. There there are divisions without ammunition, there the cadets have no boots, and the officers sit in cafés. Listen to me, my friends! I am a wartime officer—I was entrusted with the job of pushing you into the fight. If it only were for something! But it's for nothing! I proclaim publicly that I will not lead you and will not permit you to go! I am telling you—it's the end of the White movement in the Ukraine. It's the end of it in Rostov-on-the-Don, everywhere! The people are not with us. They are against us. That means it's over! The coffin! The lid's closed! And I, officer Alexei Turbin—I who have been through the war with the Germans, as Captains Studzinsky and Myshlaevsky can attest, I am taking all responsibility on my own conscience. I take it all, I am warning you, and because I care about you I am sending you home. I have finished.

A roar of voices. A sudden explosion.

Tear off your shoulder straps, abandon your rifles, and get home immediately!

The Cadets *tear off their shoulder straps, abandon their rifles.*

MYSHLAEVSKY (*shouts*). Quiet! Colonel, will you permit me to set fire to the gymnasium building?

ALEXEI. I will not.

A cannon shot. The glass rattles.

MYSHLAEVSKY. A machine gun!

STUDZINSKY. Cadets, to your homes!

MYSHLAEVSKY. Cadets, sound dismissal, to your homes!

A horn off-stage. The Cadets *and* Officers *disperse running.* Nikolka *smashes the light control box with his rifle and runs out. The lights go out. At the stove* Alexei *tears up papers, sets fire to them. A long pause.* Maxim *walks in.*

ALEXEI. Who are you?

MAXIM. I'm the watchman here.

ALEXEI. Get the devil out, they'll kill you here.

MAXIM. Where would I go, Your Excellency? I've got no reason to leave official property. They broke up the desks in two classrooms, they've done so much damage I don't know how to tell it. And the lights . . . There've been many armies here, but none like this—excuse me . . .

ALEXEI. Get away from me, old man.

MAXIM. You can slash with a sword, but I won't leave. I was told by Mr. Director . . .

ALEXEI. Well, what did Mr. Director tell you?

MAXIM. Maxim, you alone will stay . . . Maxim, see that . . . And what have you done . . .

ALEXEI. Old fellow, do you understand Russian? They will kill you. Go somewhere to a cellar, hide there, so that there's no sign of you.

MAXIM. Who's going to answer for things? Maxim answers for everything. All kinds have been here—there've been ones for the tsar and ones against the tsar, hard-bitten soldiers, but break up the desks . . .

ALEXEI. Where are the class-rolls? (*He smashes open a cupboard with his foot.*)

MAXIM. Your High Excellency, why there's a *key* for it. It's the gymnasium's cupboard and you use your foot. (*He walks away, crosses himself.*)

A cannon shot.

MAXIM. Queen of Heaven . . . Holy Mother . . . Lord Christ . . .

ALEXEI. That's it! Go ahead! Blast away! A concert! Music! Well, you'll hit me one of these days, *pan* Hetman! Stinking snake!

Myshlaevsky *appears above. A faint ray of light pierces through the window.*

MAXIM. Your excellency, at least you tell him. What is this? He smashed the cupboard with his foot!

MYSHLAEVSKY. Don't get underfoot, old man. Get out.

MAXIM. Tatars. Absolute Tatars . . . (*He disappears.*)

MYSHLAEVSKY. (*from the distance*). Alyosha! I set fire to the storeroom! Petlyura'll have a fig instead of overcoats!

ALEXEI. For God's sake, don't hang around. Run home.

MYSHLAEVSKY. This won't take long. I'll put two more bombs in the hay—and then I'll get out. What are you sitting here for?

ALEXEI. I can't go until the support troops arrive.

MYSHLAEVSKY. Alyosha, is that necessary? Eh?

ALEXEI. What are you saying, captain?

MYSHLAEVSKY. Then I'll stay with you.

ALEXEI. What do I need you for, Viktor? I order you: go to Elena immediately! Guard her! I'll be right on your heels. What's wrong, have you gone crazy, or what? Are you going to obey or not?

MYSHLAEVSKY. All right, Alyosha. I'll run to Lenka!

ALEXEI. Look and see if Nikolka's gone. Take him by the collar, for God's sake.

MYSHLAEVSKY. All right! Alyosha, be careful, don't take any chances!

ALEXEI. Don't teach the teacher!

Myshlaevsky *disappears.*

Serious, "Serious in the extreme" . . . And when the white srairs lead us to a blue realm . . . If only the support troops haven't run into trouble . . .

NIKOLKA (*appears above, crawling*). Alyosha!

ALEXEI. What are you doing, playing jokes on me or what?! Get home this instant, take off your shoulder straps! Out!

NIKOLKA. I will not go without you, colonel.

ALEXEI. What? (*Takes out his revolver.*)

NIKOLKA. Shoot, shoot your own brother!

ALEXEI. You blockhead!

NIKOLKA. Curse, curse your own brother. I know why you're sitting there! I know you, commander, you're waiting for death to save you from disgrace, that's what! Well, I'm going to guard you then. Lenka would kill me.

ALEXEI. Hey, somebody! Take Cadet Turbin away! Captain Myshlaevsky.

NIKOLKA. They've all gone already.

ALEXEI. Well wait then, you scoundrel, I'll talk to you when we get home!

Noise and clatter of feet. The Cadets *who have been at the outpost run in.*

CADETS (*running past*). Petlyura's cavalry's right behind us!

ALEXEI. Cadets! Obey this order! Take the cellar tunnel to Podol! I'll cover you. Tear off your shoulder straps on the way!

Off-stage a brisk whistling growing nearer, a concertina resounds hollowly: "And it hums, and howls . . ."[22]

Run, run! I'll cover you! (*Rushes to the upstairs window.*) Run, I implore you. Have pity on Lenka.

A close explosion of a shell. The glass breaks. Alexei *falls.*

NIKOLKA. Colonel! Alyosha, Alyosha, what have you done!

ALEXEI. Sub-officer Turbin, throw heroism to the devil! (*He falls silent.*)

NIKOLKA. Colonel . . . it can't be! Alyosha, get up!

Clatter of feet and noise. The Gaidamaks *run in.*

HURRICANE. Here! Look! Look! Hold him, men! Hold him!

22. A Ukrainian folk song.

Kirpaty *shoots at* Nikolka.

GALANBA (*running in*). Alive! Take him alive, men!

Nikolka *crawls away upstairs, bares his teeth.*

KIRPATY. Ooh, what a wolf cub! Ah, the son of a bitch!

HURRICANE. You won't get away! You won't get away!

The Gaidamaks *appear.*

NIKOLKA. Hangmen, I won't surrender! I won't surrender, you bandits! (*Hurls himself over the railing and disappears.*)

KIRPATY. Oh, an acrobat! (*He shoots.*) He's gone.

GALANBA. What did you let him get away for, men! Eh, you good for nothings! . . .

Concertina: "it hums and it howls . . ." Off-stage a shout: "Glory, glory!" Bugles off-stage. Bolbotun. *Behind him* Gaidamaks *with banners. The colors float up the stairs. A deafening march.*

SCENE TWO

THE TURBIN'S APARTMENT. *Dawn. No electricity. A candle is burning on the dining-room table.*

LARIOSIK. Dear Elena Vasilievna! Do what you wish with me! If you want, I'll get my things and go to look for them?

ELENA. Oh, no, no. What's wrong with you, Lariosik! They'd kill you on the street. We'll wait. My God, it's already dawn. What a terrible dawn! What's going on there? I would like to know just one thing—where are they?

LARIOSIK. My God, how terrible civil war is!

ELENA. Do you know what? I'm a woman, they won't touch me. I'll go see what's going on in the street.

LARIOSIK. Elena Vasilievna, I won't let you! Why I . . . I simply won't let you! . . . What would Alexi Vasilievich say to me?! He ordered that you shouldn't be allowed to go in the street no matter what, and I gave him my word.

ELENA. I'm close . . .

LARIOSIK. Elena Vasilievna!

ELENA. Just to find out what's happening . . .

LARIOSIK. I'll go myself . . .

ELENA. Let it go . . . We'll wait . . .

LARIOSIK. Your husband did very well to leave. That was a very wise act. Now he'll get through this terrible mess in Berlin and return.

ELENA. My husband? My husband? . . . Never mention his name in this house again. Do you hear?

LARIOSIK. Very well, Elena Vasilievna . . . I always manage to say the wrong thing . . . Maybe you'd like some tea? I could set up the samovar . . .

ELENA. No, that's not necessary . . .

A knock.

LARIOSIK. Wait, wait, don't open it—we have to ask who's there. Who's there?

SHERVINSKY. It's me! Me . . . Shervinsky . . .

ELENA. Thank God! (*She opens it.*) What does this mean? A catastrophe?

SHERVINSKY. Petlyura has taken the city.

LARIOSIK. Taken it? God, how horrible!

ELENA. Where are they? In battle?

SHERVINSKY. Don't be disturbed, Elena Vasilievna. I warned Alexei Vasilievich several hours ago. Everything is absolutely all right.

ELENA. What do you mean all right? And the Hetman? The troops?

SHERVINSKY. The Hetman fled last night.

ELENA. He fled? Abandoned the army?

SHERVINSKY. Precisely. Prince Belorukov too. (*He takes off his overcoat.*)

ELENA. The wretches!

SHERVINSKY. Indescribable swindlers!

LARIOSIK. And why isn't the electricity on?

SHERVINSKY. They shot up the station.

LARIOSIK. Ay-ay-ay . . .

SHERVINSKY. Elena Vasilievna, may I hide here? They'll be looking for officers now.

ELENA. Well of course.

SHERVINSKY. Elena Vasilievna, if you only knew how happy I am that you are alive and well.

A knock at the door.

Larion, ask who's there . . .

LARIOSIK. Who's there?

MYSHLAEVSKY'S VOICE. Your own, your own . . .

Lariosik *opens the door.* Myshlaevsky *and* Studzinsky *enter.*

ELENA. Thank the Lord! But where are Alyosha and Nikolai?

MYSHLAEVSKY. Easy, easy, Lena. They'll be right here. Don't be afraid about anything, the streets are still free. The outpost men will accompany them both. Ah, this one's here already? Well, you must know everything . . .

ELENA. Thanks, everything. Well, Germans! Germans!

STUDZINSKY. Never mind . . . never mind, sometime we'll recall everything . . . Never mind!

MYSHLAEVSKY. Hello, Larion!

LARIOSIK. Oh, Vitenka, what terrible events!

MYSHLAEVSKY. Yes, first class events.

ELENA. What a sight you are! Go get warmed up, I'll set up the samovar for you right away.

SHERVINSKY (*from the fireplace*). Can I help you, Lena?

ELENA. That's not necessary. I'll do it myself. (*She runs out.*)

MYSHLAEVSKY. Were you in good health, pan adjutant? *Chomu zh tse* . . . Why are you without your aiguillettes? . . . "Officers, go to the Ukraine and form your units" . . . And he burst into tears. In a pig's eye!

SHERVINSKY. What does the farcical tone mean?

MYSHLAEVSKY. It ended as a farce, *that's* why the farcical tone. You promised us his majesty the emperor and drank the health of his eminence. Apropos—where is that eminence now, at the present time?

SHERVINSKY. What's it to you?

MYSHLAEVSKY. This is what it is to me: if this same "eminence" turned up in my hands right now, I'd take him by the feet and smash his head against the pavement until I felt complete satisfaction. And your headquarters staff bunch ought to be drowned in a toilet.

SHERVINSKY. Mr. Myshlaevsky, I'll ask you not to forget yourself!

MYSHLAEVSKY. Bastards!

SHERVINSKY. Wha-a-t?

LARIOSIK. Why quarrel?

STUDZINSKY. As the senior officer, I'll ask you to cease this conversation immediately! It's totally absurd and will lead to nothing! Really, why are you bothering the man? Lieutenant, calm down.

SHERVINSKY. Captain Myshlaevsky's behavior lately has been insufferable . . . And the main thing is his boorishness! Am I to blame for the catastrophe or what? On the contrary, I warned you all. If it hadn't been for me, there's a question whether he'd be sitting here alive right now or not!

STUDZINSKY. Quite right, lieutenant. And we are very obliged to you.

ELENA (*enters*). What is it? What's the matter?

STUDZINSKY. Elena Vasilievna, don't worry, everything will be in perfect order. I give you my word. Go back to your room.

Elena exits.

Viktor, apologize, you have no right.

MYSHLAEVSKY. Well, all right, forget it, Leonid! I got carried away. Really, it's such an offense!

SHERVINSKY. Rather strange . . .

STUDZINSKY. Forget it, there's absolutely no time for that. (*He sits down by the fire.*)

A pause.

MYSHLAEVSKY. Really, where are Alyosha and Nikolka?

STUDZINSKY. I'm worried myself . . . I'll wait five minutes, and then I'll go to meet them . . .

A pause.

MYSHLAEVSKY. What happened then, does this mean he took off while you were there?

SHERVINSKY. While I was there: I was there until the very last minute.

MYSHLAEVSKY. A remarkable spectacle! I would have paid dearly to be present at that! Why didn't you kill him like a dog?

SHERVINSKY. You should go kill him yourself!

MYSHLAEVSKY. I would, rest assured of that. Well, did he say anything to you in parting?

SHERVINSKY. Of course he did! He embraced me, thanked me for faithful service . . .

MYSHLAEVSKY. And broke into tears . . .

SHERVINSKY. Yes, he broke into tears . . .

LARIOSIK. Broke into tears? Really? . . .

MYSHLAEVSKY. Perhaps he gave you some farewell gift? A gold cigarette case with a monogram, for example?

SHERVINSKY. Yes, he gave me his cigarette case.

MYSHLAEVSKY. Oh, the devil! . . . Excuse me, Leonid. I'm afraid you'll get angry again. Basically you're not a bad person, but you do have peculiarities . . .

SHERVINSKY. What do you mean by that?

MYSHLAEVSKY. Well, how can I phrase it? . . . You ought to be a writer . . . You have a rich imagination . . . He burst into tears . . . Well, suppose I said, "Show us the cigarette case!"

Shervinsky *shows the cigarette case without a word.*

He won! Really, with a monogram!

SHERVINSKY. What should you say, Captain Myshlaevsky?

MYSHLAEVSKY. This instant. In your presence, gentlemen, I beg his pardon.

LARIOSIK. Never in my life have I seen such a beautiful thing! It must weigh a full pound.

SHERVINSKY. Seven-eighths.

A knock at the window.

Gentlemen!

They stand up.

MYSHLAEVSKY. I don't like games . . . Why not at the door?

SHERVINSKY. Gentlemen . . . revolvers . . . better throw them out. (*He hides the cigarette case behind the fireplace.*)

Studzinsky *and* Myshlaevsky *go up to the window and cautiously moving the curtain aside they look out.*

STUDZINSKY. Oh, I can't forgive myself!

MYSHLAEVSKY. What the devil!

LARIOSIK. Oh, my God! (*He rushes off to inform* Elena.) Elena . . .

MYSHLAEVSKY. Where are you going, you devil? . . . Have you gone crazy! . . . As if one could! . . . (*He shuts his mouth.*)

All run out. A pause. They carry in Nikolka.

We have to get Lenka away somewhere . . . My God! And where's Alyosha? . . . Killing me would be too little! . . . Put him down, put him down . . . right on the floor . . .

STUDZINSKY. Better on the divan. Look for the wound, the wound, look for it!

SHERVINSKY. His head's hit! . . .

STUDZINSKY. Blood in his boot . . . Take off his boots . . .

SHERVINSKY. Let's move him . . . over there . . . Really, he can't stay on the floor . . .

STUDZINSKY. Lariosik! Get a pillow and blanket on the double! Put it on the divan.

They move Nikolka *to the divan.*

Cut the boots off! . . . Cut them! . . . Alexei Vasilievich has bandages in the study.

Shervinsky *runs out.*

Get some alcohol! My Lord, how did he ever get here? What is this? . . . Where's Alexei Vasilievich?

Shervinsky *runs in with iodine and bandages.* Studzinsky *bandages* Nikolka's *head.*

LARIOSIK. Is he dying?

NIKOLKA (*coming around*). O-oh! ...

MYSHLAEVSKY. It could drive you mad! ... Tell us just one thing, where's Alyosha?

STUDZINSKY. Where is Alexei Vasilievich?

NIKOLKA. Gentlemen ...

MYSHLAEVSKY. What?

Elena *comes walking straight in.*

Lenochka, don't worry. He fell and hit his head. It's nothing dangerous.

ELENA. He's been wounded! What are you saying?!

NIKOLKA. No, Lenochka, no ...

ELENA. And where's Alexei? Where is Alexei? (*Insistently.*) You were with him. Say one word, where's Alexei?

MYSHLAEVSKY. What are we to do now?

STUDZINSKY (*to* Myshlaevsky). This cannot be! It cannot! ...

ELENA. Why aren't you saying anything?

NIKOLKA. Lenochka ... In a minute ...

ELENA. Don't lie! Just don't lie!

Myshlaevsky *makes a sign to* Nikolka—"*Keep quiet.*"

STUDZINSKY. Elena Vasilievna ...

SHERVINSKY. Elena, what are ...

ELENA. I understand everything! They've killed Alexei!

MYSHLAEVSKY. What's the matter with you, Lena, what's the matter! Where did you get that idea?

ELENA. Look at his face. Look. But I didn't need his face! I knew it, I felt it—when he left I knew how it would end!

STUDZINSKY (*to* Nikolka). Tell us, what happened to him?!

ELENA. Larion! They've killed Alyosha ...

SHERVINSKY. Get some water ...

ELENA. Larion! They've killed Alyosha! Yesterday you were sitting with him at the table—remember? And he's been killed.

LARIOSIK. Elena Vasilievna, dear ...

SHERVINSKY. Lena. Lena ...

ELENA. And you?! Senior officers! You all came home, but they killed the commander? . . .

MYSHLAEVSKY. Lena, have some feeling for us, what are you saying?! We all carried out his order, all of us!

STUDZINSKY. No, she's absolutely right! I'm guilty on all counts! I shouldn't have left him! I'm the senior officer and I will correct my mistake! (*He takes his revolver.*)

MYSHLAEVSKY. What are you doing? . . . No, stop! No, stop!

STUDZINSKY. Take your hands off!

MYSHLAEVSKY. What, and I'll remain alone? You're guilty of absolutely nothing! Nothing! I saw him last, and I warned him and carried out all his orders. Lena!

STUDZINSKY. Captain Myshlaevsky, release me this instant!

MYSHLAEVSKY. Give up the revolver! Shervinsky!

SHERVINSKY. You have no right! What do you want to do, make things even worse? You have no right. (*He holds* Studzinsky.)

MYSHLAEVSKY. Lena, order him! It's all because of what you said. Take the revolver away from him!

ELENA. I said it from grief. My mind was not clear. Give up the revolver.

STUDZINSKY (*hysterically*). No one dares reproach me! No one! No one! I carried out all of Colonel Turbin's orders!

ELENA. No one! . . . No one! . . . I was crazy.

MYSHLAEVSKY. Nikolka, tell us . . . Lena, be brave. We'll find him . . . We'll find him . . . Tell us straight out . . .

NIKOLKA. They have killed the commander . . .

Elena *faints.*

CURTAIN

ACT IV

Two months later. *The Eve of the Epiphany (Twelfth Night) 1919. The apartment is lit up.* Elena *and* Lariosik *are decorating the Christmas tree.*

Lariosik (*on a stepladder*). I think that this star . . . (*He listens mysteriously.*)

Elena. What are you doing?

Lariosik. No, I just imagined it . . . Elena Vasilievna, I assure you this is the end, they will take the city.

Elena. Don't be in a hurry, Lariosik, nothing is known yet.

Lariosik. I think that this star would be very well placed right here.

Elena. Climb down, Lariosik, otherwise I'm afraid you'll break your neck.

Lariosik. Well, what are you saying Elena Vasilievna! It's a Christmas tree with a capital "C," as Vitenka says. I'd like to see the person who could say the tree's not beautiful! Oh, Elena Vasilievna, if you only knew! . . . The tree reminds me of the irretrievable days of my childhood in Zhitomir . . . Fires . . . A little green Christmas tree . . . (*A pause.*) However, I'm happier here, much happier, than in my childhood. I would never leave here . . . I would spend my entire life under the Christmas tree at your feet and I wouldn't go anywhere . . .

Elena. You would get bored. You're such a poet, Larion.

Lariosik. No, what sort of poet am I? What the he . . . Oh, excuse me, Elena Vasilievna!

Elena. Recite, recite something new. Well, recite. I like your poetry very much. You are very talented.

LARIOSIK. Do you sincerely think so?

ELENA. Quite sincerely.

LARIOSIK. Well, all right . . . I'll recite . . . I'll recite . . . It is dedicated . . . Well, in a word, it is dedicated . . . No, I'm not going to recite poetry to you.

ELENA. Why not?

LARIOSIK. No, what for? . . .

ELENA. And to whom is it dedicated?

LARIOSIK. To a certain woman.

ELENA. A secret?

LARIOSIK. A secret. To you.

ELENA. Thank you, dear.

LARIOSIK. What good are thanks to me! . . . You can't make an overcoat out of thanks . . . Ay, forgive me, Elena Vasilievna, I've caught that from Myshlaevsky. You know, expressions like that just pop out . . .

ELENA. I see. In my opinion you're in love with Myshlaevsky.

LARIOSIK. No, I'm in love with you.

ELENA. You shouldn't fall in love with me, Larion, you shouldn't.

LARIOSIK. You know what? Marry me.

ELENA. You're an appealing person. But that's impossible.

LARIOSIK. He won't come back! . . . And how can you be alone? Alone, without support, without care. Well, true, I'm pretty crum . . . weak support, but then I'd love you very much. My whole life. You are my ideal. He won't come. Especially now that the Bolsheviks are attacking. He won't come back!

ELENA. He won't come back. But that's not the point. Even if he did come back, my life with him is still over.

LARIOSIK. They cut him off . . . I couldn't look at you when he left. My heart would have bled. Why it was awful to look at you, I swear . . .

ELENA. Did I really look so bad?

LARIOSIK. Awful! A nightmare! Thin, so thin . . . Your face—yellow, yellow as could be . . .

ELENA. You, Lariosik, are an inimitable person. Come here, and I'll kiss you on your forehead.

LARIOSIK. On the forehead? Well, if it's to be the forehead—then the forehead!

Elena *kisses his forehead.*

Of course, how could anyone love me!

ELENA. Very easily. Only I'm already having a romance.

LARIOSIK. What? A romance? Who? You? You have a romance? It can't be!

ELENA. You mean I'm not good enough?

LARIOSIK. You—are holy! You . . . But who is he? Do I know him?

ELENA. Very well.

LARIOSIK. I know him very well? . . . Wait . . . Who? Wait, wait, wait! . . . A young man . . . you haven't seen anything . . . Go with the king, but don't touch the queen . . . And I thought that was a dream. Damn him, the lucky guy!

ELENA. Lariosik! That's not nice!

LARIOSIK. I'm leaving . . . I'm leaving . . .

ELENA. Where, where?

LARIOSIK. I'll go to the Armenian for some vodka and drink myself senseless . . .

ELENA. Then I'll allow you that . . . Larion, I will be your friend.

LARIOSIK. I've read, I've read in novels . . . what "I'll be a friend" means—the lid's closed, of course! The end! (*He puts on his overcoat.*)

ELENA. Lariosik, come back right away! The guests will soon be here!

> *Opening the door,* Lariosik *bumps into the arriving* Shervinsky *in the entrance hall. The latter is wearing a grubby hat, tattered overcoat, and dark blue glasses.*

SHERVINSKY. Hello, Elena Vasilievna! Hello, Larion!

LARIOSIK. Uh . . . hello . . . hello . . . (*He disappears.*)

ELENA. My God! What a sight you are!

SHERVINSKY. Well thank you, Elena Vasilievna. I've already tested it. I'm riding along in a cab today, and some sort of proletarians or other are already flitting, flitting along the sidewalks. And one of them says in such a caressing voice: "Eh, a Ukrainian boss-man! Wait till tomorrow," he says, "Tomorrow we'll take you out of that cab!" I have an experienced eye. As soon as I took a look at him I understood that I had to go home and change clothes. Congratulations. Petlyura's had it!

ELENA. What are you saying?

SHERVINSKY. The Reds will be here tonight. Ergo, Soviet power et cetera.

ELENA. What are you so happy about? One could think you were a Bolshevik yourself!

SHERVINSKY. I'm a sympathizer! And I rented the crummy coat from a yard man. It is a nonpartisan crummy coat.

ELENA. Please take off that monstrosity this instant!

SHERVINSKY. Yes, ma'am! (*He takes off the coat, hat, galoshes, and glasses, and he is left in a magnificent suit with a frock coat.*) There, congratulate me, I'm straight from my debut. I sang and was accepted.

ELENA. Congratulations.

SHERVINSKY. Lena, isn't there anyone home? How's Nikolka?

ELENA. Sleeping . . .

SHERVINSKY. Lena, Lena . . .

ELENA. Let . . . Wait a minute, why did you shave your sideburns?

SHERVINSKY. It's easier to put make-up on.

ELENA. It's easier for you to make up as a Bolshevik this way. Oh, you sly, cowardly creature! Don't be afraid, no one will touch you.

SHERVINSKY. Well, let them try to touch a man whose voice spans two whole octaves and two notes above besides! Lenochka! May I explain something?

ELENA. Go ahead.

SHERVINSKY. Lena! It's all over with now . . . Nikolka is getting well . . . They're driving Petlyura out . . . I've made my debut . . . Now a new life is beginning. We cannot torture ourselves any longer. He will not come back. He's been cut off, Lena! I'm not a bad fellow, I swear it! . . . I'm not bad. Look at yourself. You're alone. You'll wither . . .

ELENA. Will you reform?

SHERVINSKY. But what do I have to reform, Lenochka?

ELENA. Leonid, I will become your wife if you change. And above all if you stop lying!

SHERVINSKY. Am I really such a liar, Lenochka?

ELENA. You aren't a liar, but God knows what you are—hollow as a nut . . . What kind of thing is all this?! He saw his majesty, the emperor, behind the curtain. And he burst into tears . . . And nothing of the sort really happened. That lanky mezzo-soprano— it turns out she's simply a waitress in Semadena's cafe . . .

SHERVINSKY. Lenochka, she had been working there for a very short time, while she had no *engagement*.

ELENA. It appears she had an *engagement*!

SHERVINSKY. Lenochka, I swear by the memory of my late mother— and my father too—there was nothing between us. I'm an orphan.

ELENA. It makes no difference to me. Your dirty secrets are of no interest to me. The other thing is what's important—that you stop boasting and lying. Once you told the truth—when you were telling about the cigarette case—and no one believed you, you had to present evidence. Tfu! . . . Shame . . . Shame . . .

SHERVINSKY. It was precisely in regard to the cigarette case that I made up everything. The Hetman did not present it to me, he didn't embrace me, and he didn't burst into tears. He simply forgot it on the table, and I took it.

ELENA. You swiped it from the table?

SHERVINSKY. I hid it. It's of historical value.

ELENA. My God, that was all we needed! Give it to me! (*She takes away the cigarette case and hides it.*)

SHERVINSKY. Lenochka, the cigarettes in it are mine.

ELENA. Thank your lucky stars that you were smart enough to tell me about it. And if I had found out?

SHERVINSKY. How could you find out?

ELENA. Savage!

SHERVINSKY. Absolutely not. Lenochka, I have changed incredibly much. I don't recognize myself, on my word of honor! Whether catastrophe has had its effect on me—or Alexei's death . . . I'm a different man now. And materially you have nothing to worry about, Lenochka, why I . . . oho-ho . . . Today at the debut I finished singing and the director says to me, "Leonid Yurievich," he says, "you show great promise. You should go to Moscow," he says, "to the Bolshoi Theater . . ." He came up to me, embraced me, and . . .

ELENA. And what?

SHERVINSKY. And nothing . . . He went down the hall . . .

ELENA. You are incorrigible!

SHERVINSKY. Lena!

ELENA. But what are we going to do with Talberg?

SHERVINSKY. Divorce. Divorce. Do you know his address? A telegram to him and a letter saying it's all over! Over!

ELENA. Well, all right! I'm bored and lonely. Melancholy. All right! I agree!

SHERVINSKY. "You have conquered, Galilean!"[23] Lena! (*He sings.*) "And you'll be the queen of the wor-r-rld" . . . That "G" is pure! (*He points to* Talberg's *portrait.*) I demand that it be thrown out! I can't stand to look at it!

ELENA. Oho, such a tone!

SHERVINSKY (*fondly*). Lenochka, I cannot stand to look at it. (*He knocks the portrait out of the frame and throws it into the fireplace.*) Rat! And my conscience is clear and at rest!

ELENA. The jabot suits you very much . . . You're handsome, what can I say! . . .

SHERVINSKY. We won't go under . . .

ELENA. Oh, I don't fear for you! . . . You won't go under!

SHERVINSKY. Lena, let's go into your room . . . I'll sing, you'll accompany . . . Why we haven't seen each other for two months. Always with people and more people.

ELENA. But they'll be here soon.

SHERVINSKY. And we'll come back in then.

> *They exit, close the door. The piano is heard. In an excellent voice,* Shervinsky *sings the epithalamion from "Nerone."*

NIKOLKA (*enters, wearing a black cap, on crutches. He is pale and*

23. This line and the following one are from Boito's opera *Nerone*, first produced in 1924. The story involves a conflict between Nero and the Christians, ending with the burning of the city and the death of the Christians.

weak. He is wearing a student's jacket). Ah! . . . They're practicing! (*He sees the frame of the portrait.*) Ah! . . . They've knocked him out of it. I understand . . . I guessed long ago. (*He lies down on the divan.*)

LARIOSIK (*appears in the entrance hall*). Nikolasha! You're up? Alone? Wait a second, I'll bring you a pillow. (*He brings a pillow to* Nikolka).

NIKOLKA. Don't get upset, Larion, I don't need it. Thanks. Apparently, Larion, I am going to remain a cripple like this.

LARIOSIK. What are you saying, Nikolasha, you should be ashamed!

NIKOLKA. Listen, Larion, why aren't they here yet?

LARIOSIK. They aren't here yet, but they soon will be. You know, I was just walking along the street—wagons and more wagons, and in them *those* guys with their tails between their legs. Apparently the Bolsheviks really gave them a licking.

NIKOLKA. That's what they deserve!

LARIOSIK. But nevertheless I got some vodka. For the first time in my life I was lucky. I'm that kind of person. I'll go out when the weather is magnificent. The sky is clear, the stars are shining, no cannons are firing . . . Everything in nature is satisfactory. But as soon as I show myself on the street—it just has to start snowing. And really, I went out and wet snow hit me right in the face. But I got a bottle! . . . That'll show Myshlaevsky what I'm capable of. I fell down twice, clunked the back of my head, but I held the bottle in my hands.

SHERVINSKY'S VOICE. "You bless our love . . ."

NIKOLKA. Look, do you see? . . . A shattering piece of news! Elena is getting divorced. She's going to marry Shervinsky.

LARIOSIK (*drops the bottle*). Already?

NIKOLKA. Oh, Lariosik, oh, oh! . . . Look what you've done, Larion, what's wrong with you? . . . Ah-ah . . . I understand! You are head over heels too?

LARIOSIK. Nikol, when speaking of Elena Vasilievna, such expressions as "head over heels too" are out of place. Understand? She is pure gold!

NIKOLKA. She is red-haired, Larion, red. A real misfortune! She's red-haired, that's why everyone likes her. As soon as someone sees that, they start dragging in bouquets. So that we always have bouquets in our apartment, standing around like little brooms. And Talberg used to get furious. Well, pick up the glass, otherwise Myshlaevsky will be here in a second and he'll kill you.

LARIOSIK. Don't tell him. (*Picks up the glass.*)

A bell. Lariosik lets in Myshlaevsky and Studzinsky. Both are in civilian clothes.

MYSHLAEVSKY. The reds have smashed Petlyura! Petlyura's troops are leaving the city!

STUDZINSKY. Yes, yes! The reds are already in the Slobodka. They'll be here in half an hour.

MYSHLAEVSKY. And so, tomorrow we'll have a Soviet Republic here . . . Hey, it smells like vodka! Who drank vodka ahead of time? Confess! What is going on in this home which has been saved by God!! . . . Do you wash the floors with vodka?! . . . I know whose work this is! Why do you break everything?! Why do you break everything! Those are golden hands—in the full sense of the word! Whatever they touch—pow, splinters! Well, if you have such an itch, go ahead, smash the tea service!

Off-stage the piano plays the whole time.

LARIOSIK. What right do you have to criticize me! I don't like it!

MYSHLAEVSKY. Why is it everyone shouts at me? Soon they'll start beating me! However, I'm in a good mood today, for some reason. Peace, Larion, I'm not mad at you.

NIKOLKA. But why isn't there any shooting?

MYSHLAEVSKY. They're coming quietly, politely. And without any opposition!

LARIOSIK. And the main thing, most surprising of all, is that everyone is happy—even the inveterate bourgeoisie. That's how much Petlyura had bothered everyone!

NIKOLKA. I wonder what the Bolsheviks look like?

MYSHLAEVSKY. You'll see, you'll see.

LARIOSIK. Captain, your opinion?

STUDZINSKY. I don't know, I don't understand anything now. The best thing for us to do would be to get up and follow Petlyura.

How we, White Guards, can get along with the Bolsheviks I can't imagine!

MYSHLAEVSKY. Follow Petlyura where?

STUDZINSKY. Hook up with some wagon and go away to Galicia.

MYSHLAEVSKY. And then where.

STUDZINSKY. And from there to the Don, to Denikin, and fight the Bolsheviks.

MYSHLAEVSKY. You mean go under the command of the generals again? That's a very clever plan. It's too bad Alyoshka is lying in the ground, he could tell you many interesting things about the generals. But it's too bad, the commander is at rest.

STUDZINSKY. Don't torture me, don't remind me.

MYSHLAEVSKY. No, if you please, he's not here, so I'll talk a bit. In the army again? Fight again? . . . And he burst into tears? . . . Thanks, thanks anyway, I already had my laugh. Especially when I saw Alyosha in the anatomy theater.

Nikolka *begins to cry.*

LARIOSIK. Nikolasha, Nikolasha, don't do that, stop!

MYSHLAEVSKY. Enough! I've been fighting since 1914. For what? For the fatherland? But what kind of fatherland is it when all they've left me is disgrace?! And I should go to those "eminences" again?! No thanks. See? (*He makes a fig sign.*) A fig to them.

STUDZINSKY. Please explain yourself in words.

MYSHLAEVSKY. I'll explain myself right now, rest assured of that. Am I really an idiot? No, I, Viktor Myshlaevsky, declare that I am not going to have anything to do with those generals any more. I'm finished!

LARIOSIK. Viktor Myshlaevsky has become a Bolshevik.

MYSHLAEVSKY. Yes, if you like, I'm for the Bolsheviks!

STUDZINSKY. Viktor, what are you saying?

MYSHLAEVSKY. I'm for the Bolsheviks, only against the Communists.

STUDZINSKY. That's ridiculous. One should know what one's talking about.

LARIOSIK. Allow me to tell you they are one and the same thing: Bolshevism and Communism.

MYSHLAEVSKY (*mocking him*). "Bolshevism and Communism." Well, I'm for the Communists then . . .

STUDZINSKY. Listen, Captain, you used the word "fatherland." What kind of fatherland is it when there are Bolsheviks. Russia is finished. You remember, the commander said it and the commander was right: there they are—the Bolsheviks! . . .

MYSHLAEVSKY. The Bolsheviks? . . . Fine! Very happy!

STUDZINSKY. But they'll mobilize you.

MYSHLAEVSKY. And I'll go and I'll serve. Yes!

STUDZINSKY. Why?

MYSHLAEVSKY. I'll tell you why! Because! Because Petlyura has how many, did you say? Two hundred thousand! Those two hundred thousand have their heels greased and they blow away at the mere word "Bolsheviks"! Did you see it? Great! Because behind the Bolsheviks there are peasants as thick as locusts . . . And what can I oppose them with? Riding pants with piping. They can't stand to see the piping . . . They get the machine guns out in a second. Wouldn't this be fine . . . In front the Red Guards like a wall, behind the speculators and all kinds of trash with the Hetman,—and in between—me? Thank you very much! No, I'm sick and tired of playing the dung in the ice hole. Let them mobilize me! At least I'll know that I'm serving in the Russian army. The people are not with us. The people are against us. Alyosha was right!

STUDZINSKY. What the hell kind of Russian army can there be when they've put an end to Russia?! And they'll shoot us anyway!

MYSHLAEVSKY. And they'll be right to do so! They'll deliver us to the Cheka, curse us, write us off. They'll feel more at ease and we will too . . .

STUDZINSKY. I am going to fight them!

MYSHLAEVSKY. Be my guest, put on your coat! Go on! Blow! . . . Fire away at the Bolsheviks, shout at them, "I won't let you." They've already thrown Nikolka down the stairs once! Did you see his head? But they'll tear yours off completely. And rightly so—don't butt in. This is not our cause now!

LARIOSIK. I am opposed to the horrors of the civil war. In essence, why spill blood?

MYSHLAEVSKY. Were you in the war?

LARIOSIK. I have a white slip, a medical deferment, Vitenka. Weak lungs. And besides that I'm my mama's only son.

MYSHLAEVSKY. Correct, Comrade White-Slip.

STUDZINSKY. We had a Russia—a great power! . . .

MYSHLAEVSKY. And it will be! . . . It will!

STUDZINSKY. Yes, it will, it will—you wait!

MYSHLAEVSKY. It will not be the former one, it'll be a new one. A new one! And you tell me this. When they slam you to pieces on the Don—and I predict that they will slam you to pieces—and when your Denikin tears off abroad—and I predict that for you too—then where?

STUDZINSKY. Abroad too.

MYSHLAEVSKY. You're about as necessary there as a third wheel on a cannon! No matter where you go, they'll spit in your mug from Singapore to Paris. I won't go, I'll be here, in Russia. And let whatever happens to her happen! . . . Well, I'm finished, enough, I close the meeting.

STUDZINSKY. I see that I'm alone.

SHERVINSKY (*runs in*). Wait, wait, don't close the meeting. I have a special announcement. Elena Vasilievna Talberg is getting divorced from her husband, former colonel of the general staff Talberg, and is marrying . . . (*He bows, indicates himself with his hand.*)

Elena *enters.*

LARIOSIK. Oh! . . .

MYSHLAEVSKY. Quit it, Larion, what business have bulls like us in a china shop? Lovely Lena, allow me, I will embrace and kiss you.

STUDZINSKY. Congratulations, Elena Vasilievna.

MYSHLAEVSKY (*goes after* Lariosik *who has run into the entrance hall*). Larion, congratulate them—this is awkward of you! Then you come back here again.

LARIOSIK (*to* Elena). I congratulate you and wish you happiness. (*To* Shervinsky.) Congratulations . . . Congratulations.

MYSHLAEVSKY. But you're quite a fellow, yes indeed! Why, what a woman! She speaks English, plays the piano, and in addition she knows how to set up the samovar. Lena, I'd marry you myself, with pleasure.

ELENA. But I wouldn't marry you, Vitenka.

MYSHLAEVSKY. Well, there's no need. I love you anyway. And basically I'm a military man and a bachelor. I like for the house to be comfy like a barracks, without women or children . . . Larion, pour! We have to congratulate them.

SHERVINSKY. Wait, gentlemen! Don't drink that wine! I'll bring something myself right away. Do you know what kind of wine this is? Oho, ho, ho! . . . (*He glances at* Elena, *withers.*) Well, it's just a mediocre wine. Ordinary Abrau-Durseau.

MYSHLAEVSKY. Lena, this is your doing! Marry, Shervinsky . . . you're completely cured! Well, I congratulate you and wish you . . .

The door in the entrance hall opens, Talberg *enters, wearing a civilian coat, carrying a suitcase.*

STUDZINSKY. Gentlemen! Vladimir Robertovich . . . Vladimir Robertovich . . .

TALBERG. My respects.

A dead pause.

MYSHLAEVSKY. It's a trick!

TALBERG. Hello, Lena! You seem surprised?

A pause.

Rather odd! It would seem I should be more surprised—finding such a merry group at such a sad time in my own house. Hello, Lena. What does this mean?

SHERVINSKY. Here's what . . .

ELENA. Wait . . . Gentlemen, will you all go out for a moment and leave me alone with Vladimir Robertovich.

SHERVINSKY. Lena, I don't want to!

MYSHLAEVSKY. Hold it, hold it . . . We'll fix everything up. Keep calm . . . Should we get out, Lenochka?

ELENA. Yes.

MYSHLAEVSKY. I know you're an intelligent woman. In case of anything, call me. Personally. Well, gentlemen, let's have a smoke, we'll go into Larion's room. Larion, pick up the pillow and we'll go.

All exit, Larion—for some reason—on tiptoes.

ELENA. Be seated.

TALBERG. What does this mean. I'd like an explanation.

A pause.

What sort of game is this? Where's Alexei?

ELENA. Alexei was killed.

TALBERG. Impossible! . . . When?

ELENA. Two months ago—within two days after your departure.

TALBERG. Oh, my God, that's terrible! But I did warn him. You remember?

ELENA. Yes, I remember. And Nikolka is crippled.

TALBERG. Of course, this is all terrible . . . But of course I'm not to blame for this whole story . . . And agree that this is no reason for the occurrence of such a, I would say, stupid display.

A pause.

ELENA. Tell me, how did you return? The Bolsheviks will be here today . . .

TALBERG. I am quite up to date on things. The Hetman thing turned out to be a stupid operetta. The Germans deceived us. But in Berlin I managed to get official orders to the Don, to General Krasnov. You must abandon Kiev immediately . . . there's no time left . . . I'll follow you.

ELENA. But you see, I'm getting divorced from you and I'm marrying Shervinsky.

TALBERG (*after a long pause*). All right! Very well! Making use of my absence to get involved in a vulgar love affair . . .

ELENA. Viktor!

Myshlaevsky *enters.*

MYSHLAEVSKY. Lena, are you giving me complete power to make matters clear?

ELENA. Yes. (*She exits.*)

MYSHLAEVSKY. I understand. (*He walks up to* Talberg.) Well? Out! (*He hits him.*)

Talberg *is at a loss. He goes to the entrance hall, exits.*

MYSHLAEVSKY. Lena! Personally!

Elena *enters.*

He's gone. He's agreeing to the divorce. We had a pleasant chat.
ELENA. Thank you, Viktor! (*Kisses him and runs out.*)
MYSHLAEVSKY. Larion!
LARIOSIK (*enters*). Has he left already?
MYSHLAEVSKY. He left!
LARIOSIK. You are a genius, Vitenka!
MYSHLAEVSKY. "I am a genius—Igor Severyanin."[24] Put out the lights, light up the Christmas tree, and play a march.

Lariosik *turns out the lights in the room, illuminates the tree with electric lights, runs into the next room. A march.*

Gentlemen, come in!

Shervinsky, Studzinsky, Nikolka *and* Elena *enter.*

STUDZINSKY. Very pretty! And how cozy it got all at once!
MYSHLAEVSKY. Larion's work. Well, now let us congratulate you properly. Larion, enough!

Lariosik *enters with a guitar, hands it to* Nikolka.

Congratulations, lovely Lena, once and for all. Forget about everything. And in general—your health! (*He drinks.*)
NIKOLKA (*strums the strings of the guitar, sings*).
Tell me, sorcerer, favorite of the gods,
What will my life be?[25]
Will I be covered with earth in my grave,
To the joy of my enemies?

24. The title of a famous poem by Igor-Severyanin (he hyphenated his name), a well-known decadent poet who became a leader of the "Ego-Futurist" movement in the years just before the Revolution.
25. See note 5.

Then louder, music, play a victory,
We have conquered and the foe is running, running, running!
MYSHLAEVSKY (sings).
So, for the Soviet of People's Commissars ...

All except Studzinsky *take up the tune.*

We thunder a loud "Hurrah! Hurrah! Hurrah!"
STUDZINSKY. Well, what the hell is this! You should be ashamed!
NIKOLKA (sings on).
From the dark forest
The inspired sorcerer goes to meet him ...
LARIOSIK. Wonderful! Fires ... The Christmas tree ...
MYSHLAEVSKY. Larion! Give us a speech!
NIKOLKA. Right, a speech!
LARIOSIK. Gentlemen, really, I don't know how! And besides, I'm very bashful.
MYSHLAEVSKY. Larion, make a speech!
LARIOSIK. Well, if the group wants it, I'll do it. Only I beg you to excuse it—after all I didn't prepare. Gentlemen, Elena! We have met at the hardest and most terrible of times, and we have all gone through very, *very* much . . . including me. I have gone through one of life's dramas . . . And my frail ship has long been blown about on the waves of the civil war . . .
MYSHLAEVSKY. That's really good about the ship . . .
LARIOSIK. Yes, ship . . . Until it approached this harbor with the cream-colored curtains, people whom I like so much . . . Incidentally, among them too I found a drama . . . Well, it's not worth talking about sad things. Times changed. Then Petlyura perished . . . Everyone is alive . . . yes . . . and we are all together again . . . And even more than that—there's Elena Vasilievna, she too has gone through very very much and deserves happiness, because she is a remarkable woman. And I want to tell her in the words of the writer: "We will rest, we will rest . . ."[26]

Distant cannon shots.

26. A quotation from Chekhov's *Uncle Vanya*—a speech near the end of the play.

MYSHLAEVSKY. So! ... We've rested! ... Five ... six ... nine! ...

ELENA. Not battle again?

SHERVINSKY. No. That's a salute!

MYSHLAEVSKY. Quite right: A sixteen gun battery is saluting.

Off-stage, in the distance, growing closer all the time, a band is playing the "International."

Hear that, gentlemen? The Reds are coming!

They all go to the window.

NIKOLKA. Gentlemen, this evening is a great prologue to a new historical play.

STUDZINSKY. For some a prologue, but for others—an epilogue.

THE END

ZOYA'S APARTMENT

A Play in Four Acts

INTRODUCTION

Zoya's Apartment WAS FIRST PRESENTED at the Vakhtangov Theater by A. D. Popov on October 28, 1926—only three weeks after the turbulent première of *The Days of the Turbins*.[1] Even at the rehearsals the director and actors had serious doubts about the comedy's ideological acceptability, and Popov said they tried to make it more palatable by playing it farcically rather than lyrically, trying to make the characters seem as coarse and vulgar as possible. This prevented neither the violent attacks of the critics, some of whom considered it pornographic, nor the considerable popular success which the play enjoyed. It played three of the six nights that the Vakhatangov Theater was open at first, and it was even performed by theaters in other cities, including Kiev and Sverdlovsk. However, the play was temporarily banned after the première, and it underwent forced revision several times. *Zoya's Apartment* was shown more than one hundred times in Moscow before it was totally banned, apparently at the beginning of 1929 along with *The Days of the Turbins* and *The Crimson Island*.

The Vieux Colombier Theater in Paris decided to put on the play in 1935, using a translation made by Marie Reinhardt. However, numerous interpolations were made by the theater, all critical of the Soviet Union. Bulgakov objected and had his brother Nikolai (who lived in Paris) intervene; on June 4 Nikolai sent a telegram and a letter informing Bulgakov that the alterations had been removed. It was apparently for, or at least in connection with this production that Bulgakov completely rewrote *Zoya's Apartment*. According to his widow the play had originally been written in some five days, so Bulgakov felt that even apart from the new production it should be revised. The rewriting was extensive, affecting more than forty percent of the text. None of the alterations change the basic plot.

97

While a few of the changes were clearly dictated by political considerations,[2] the majority make the play better artistically—excess verbiage was trimmed, language was polished, crude farcical elements were removed, and all of the dialogue relating to the nature of the enterprise in Zoya's apartment was made much subtler. If one compares such scenes as the one in which Zoya persuades Alla to join her enterprise, the superiority of the 1935 version of the play is obvious.

Zoya's Apartment was Bulgakov's first major comedy in a line which was to continue through *The Crimson Island* (1927), *Adam and Eve* (1931), *Bliss* (1934), *Ivan Vasilievich* (1935)—and back to *Zoya's Apartment* in 1935. Although all of these plays are satires and share many of the same character types and situations, there is a major difference between *Zoya's Apartment* and the others. The other plays involve utopias of one sort or another. *Zoya,* which has no flight to another world and no discussion of utopian ideas, deals exclusively with Moscow life. In theme and spirit, the play is closest to Bulgakov's feuilletons about Moscow during the period of the New Economic Policy—"Moonshine Lake," "Forty Times Forty," "Four Portraits," "A Treatise on Housing," and others. This particular theme like so many others finds its final expression in *The Master and Margarita.*

Zoya, like most comedies, is both social and topical. In this respect the play is dated—but the version of 1935 has far fewer topical allusions than the 1926 version. Since few plays of the twenties have been published it may seem (on the basis of those plays usually performed) that *Zoya* is unusual in terms of subject matter or genre. Actually, the play was far from innovative in these areas; many other playwrights witnessed and used the exotic "flowers of NEP."[3] In memoirs we can read about the cafés which turned into bordellos at night, where thieves, prostitutes, and writers mingled. Pornographic books and postcards were sold in front of churches, gambling casinos were widespread, and the crime rate was very high: in the area in Moscow known as the "catacombs," now the site of the Gorky Street Post Office, there was an unfinished building in which ten murders a week supposedly took place. In "The Bar" restaurant, cabaret entertainers were available, as were cocaine and heroin. The restaurant's flourishing business ended when a tax-collector found out that its profits were much greater than reported. Ehrenburg wrote that the moral climate of Moscow at this time was like that of California during the gold fever combined with that of an exaggerated situation in a Dostoevskian novel. This atmosphere, these grotesque people and events seemed to call for a special theatrical genre—the satiric melodrama.

The term "satiric melodrama" was first widely used in March of 1926, after Boris Romashov's *The End of Krivorylsk* was produced, but it came to be applied to a group of earlier NEP satires as well. Among them were: *The Sweet Soufflé* (1924), followed by Nikolai Erdman's *The Warrant* (1925), Alexei Fayko's *Evgraf, Seeker of Adventures* (1926), and Romashov's *The End of Krivorylsk*. All of these plays were produced before *Zoya*, and it is interesting that both Erdman and Fayko were personal friends of Bulgakov.

In all of these plays one finds Khlestakovian scoundrels, Nepmen, as they were called, trying to amass fortunes to go abroad before times change. In *The Sweet Soufflé* the adventurer Rak persuades a director of a Soviet bank to aid him in illegal enterprises, and his character and background are very similar to the character and background of Ametistov in *Zoya;* similar to Goose *(Gus')* is the banker Koromyslov, who uses his new bank car to transport his mistress. The ending of the play is like the ending of *Zoya:* the GPU men (secret police)—the Soviet equivalent of the Greek fates— arrest Rak.[4] In Fayko's *Evgraf* a scene in a restaurant resembles the party scene in *Zoya:* there is a fashion show, music, and drunks. The hero Evgraf stabs Abram Matveich, an acquaintance who is a thief and who keeps trying to tempt Evgraf into working for him. Evgraf, like Cherubim stabbing Goose, uses a Finnish knife.

These plays, like *Zoya,* blend elements of melodrama, farce, and vaudeville. Yet they were fairly well received by the critics, while *Zoya* and Erdman's *The Warrant* were treated harshly by them. Some critics called *Zoya* pornographic, but it was not much more so than the plays of Erdman or Fayko.[5] The attacks on the play were in part a continuation of the attacks on *Days;* Bulgakov's literary enemies would have greeted any new play with denigration. But *Zoya* and *The Warrant* were different from the other plays in one important respect—they contained no positive heroes, and regeneration of their scoundrels was not implied. *The Warrant* was somewhat less open to attack because its basic plot is that of *The Inspector General*, but *Zoya* showed a world peopled with nothing but scoundrels, with not a Komsomol member in sight. There is no one to explain that Zoya and her friends are not typical of the Soviet Union during NEP, nor is there anyone to blame everything on the tsarist legacy of petty bourgeoise's desire for luxury. And the plain-clothesmen who finally apprehend Zoya (but not Cherubim or Ametistov) are anything but heroic.

Another way in which Bulgakov departs from Soviet conventions is in the characterization of these "former people." The critics accused Bulgakov of making these rascals attractive—a criticism which would also be made of his portrayal of Charnota in *Flight*. Militant critics naturally wanted characters to be either totally positive or totally negative—puppets wearing white or black. Bulgakov could not or would not subordinate his characters to the demands of typical didactic satire; his characters seemed to refuse to stay cardboard figures to be laughed at and not with. Rather they came alive as individuals—individuals who were not unredeemably evil. The result was that the critics accused him of "good-naturedly" poking fun at the vices of his characters, of describing their world in "soft tones."

Despite these differences of approach to characterization and attitude, Bulgakov's play very definitely belongs with the other plays discussed—it breaks no new ground in terms of satiric targets or genre. The difference between *Zoya* and all of the other plays is that Bulgakov is a better playwright. The themes, characters, and even turns of phrase may be conventional for the time, but Bulgakov handles them better than the other writers, and understands the unique requirements of the stage. The single most important factor is economy of means, of which most of the other writers seem to have had little knowledge. Bulgakov has far fewer main characters. In Romashov's *The Sweet Soufflé,* for example, there are thirty-four *named* characters and many extras. Erdman, who would seem to be superior to Fayko and Romashov, is the only one besides Bulgakov who does not introduce a confusing number of characters. Another characteristic of these plays is the incredible number of scene changes, combined with great prolixity. The plots are generally dizzyingly complex and hard to follow; and the authors are little inclined to plan suspense by careful clues and revelations—things just suddenly happen. In all of these ways, Bulgakov's play is unusual. There is little superfluous detail, and the plot is designed to interest, not instruct. As he showed in *Flight,* Bulgakov could handle panoramic views and geographic scene changes as well as anyone, but he obviously felt that NEP-time Moscow did not deserve that sort of treatment.

Unlike Bulgakov's other satires, *Zoya's Apartment* lacks a central character—either negative or positive. Despite the number of interesting and well-drawn comic figures, the focus of the play is not on any one of them. The most likely candidate for this role would be Ametistov—but he is peripheral to the main dramatic situations. Goose, who could have been made the real subject of the satire, never emerges as a main character. He is a Babbitt without Babbitt's naive and touching dreams or his somehow attractive weaknesses. Goose is a target and nothing more. The portrait is neither savage enough to insure revulsion nor humanized enough for the viewer to get involved or see himself in Goose. As for Zoya herself, we know that she is a terribly practical and realistic person who is ready to deal with whomever and whatever she must in order to get along. She does not escape to the world of drugs as Obolyaninov does, nor does she take refuge in fantasies as Ametistov does. In spite of her larcenous way of life and certain demonic traits (she tempts people to evil, and two characters call her a devil), she is fairly good-hearted —especially toward the burdensome Obolyaninov. But generally we do not know too much about her—she usually talks only about plans of action or she gives orders. Her speeches are short and she never seems to take a large part in the action, even though she is the mastermind behind the original scheme. She can no more be considered the central character than Ametistov or Goose. This is unusual since in most satires a single figure who is either the embodiment of a vice (Tartuffe) or the instigator of events which reveal the vices of a society (Khlestakov) dominates the play. If, despite the quality of the characterization, character is not the key to *Zoya's Apartment,* what is?

The answer would seem to be atmosphere and scene. *Zoya's Apartment* is a vision, a picture of the underside of NEP. Written in five days, it must have been perceived whole. The world of *Zoya's Apartment* is a closed, complete world. We have no sense of life going on outside the apartment. There is no weather in this world, no passing of time. This is a world of no exits in which everyone is involved in feverish activity which leads nowhere. The opening stage directions refer to the blend of music playing as a "hellish concert," and this first scene is ended by apocalyptic, sudden darkness as Manyushka goes to the Chinese laundry—a more primitive hell than that of the apartment. The final party scene, with the "Dead Body" present, presages Satan's Ball in *The Master and Margarita*. However, Zoya and Woland have very different sorts of guests. The guests who attend the Ball of the Full Moon are guilty of major crimes; those who attend Zoya's party are guilty of crimes that are petty by comparison. Like the Devil's Ball, Zoya's party is cinematic in its presentation. It is not what people say that lingers afterward—it is the blue smoke, a Chinaman sitting in a niche, and the torches burning as the guests wander through *Zoya's Apartment*. If Bulgakov has imprinted these images upon our memories, his play is a success.

NOTES

1. It also played at the Baku Workers Theater, one of the best provincial theaters. It premièred on October 31, 1926, directed by Arseny Ridal.

2. For example, references to Ametistov arguing with "old Kalinin," selling pictures of the leaders *(portrety voždej)* on the train, connection to the People's Commissariat of Education, etc., were deleted. Certain risqué touches are also removed. On the other hand, the secret police are presented in an even less favorable light in the 1935 version.

3. The New Economic Policy, known as NEP, was introduced by Lenin in March of 1921, as a result of agricultural disasters and a labor paralysis. NEP was considered a betrayal by many Communists, because it allowed a partial restoration of free trade, gave the peasants the right

to sell surplus goods independently, and allowed private enterprises to be set up, leased from the government. This last is the important fact for *Zoya's Apartment*. The term "Nepman" was used for the business-men who appeared to fill the need for an entrepreneurial and managerial class to get the economy working. Since those with such experience were usually non-party and of bourgeois background, they were regarded with mistrust—especially since many of them were arrested for having not paid taxes, or for misappropriation of funds. The Nepmen realized from the beginning that this period of freedom was only temporary, and many of them hurried to make their money and emigrate. In *Zoya* Goose is a trust director. Trusts coordinated the interests of different industries and were heavily subsidized by the government; trust directors were given a free hand to build up the chosen industries to their former levels. Much of the money Goose was throwing around theoretically belonged to the government. During NEP it was claimed that literally thousands of shady businesses were operating in Moscow.

4. Another play of this type which ends with the arrest by agents is Alexander Popovsky's *Comrade Tsatkin and Co.* (1926). Erdman's *The Warrant* is slightly more original: at the end the police refuse to arrest the evil-doers, and the play ends as the main character says to his mother: "Mama if they won't even arrest us, how will we live?".

5. In Bulgakov's next satire, *The Crimson Island,* he alludes to *Zoya:* the head of the theater objects to what he imagines are "pornographic" elements in a new play, and says he won't allow any *Zoya's Apartment* in his theater.

Discussions of pornography and free love were quite topical when *Zoya's Apartment* premièred. Sergei Malashkin's story "The Moon from the Right Side, or Unusual Love" had been published in September 1926; and it created a storm of interest and criticism. (The heroine has twenty-two "husbands," including six in one night; various orgies are described, including one "Athenian night" during which a drunken audience smoking opium is lectured on free love.)

Cast of Characters

Zoya Denisovna Peltz, a widow, 35 years old.

Pavel Fyodorovich Obolyaninov, 35 years old.

Alexander Tarasovich Ametistov, a manager, 38 years old.

Manyushka, Zoya's maid, 22 years old.

Anisim Zotikovich Portupeya, representative of the House Committee, 42 years old.

Gan-dza-lin, or Gasoline, a Chinese, 40 years old.

Cherubim, a Chinese, 28 years old.

Alla Vadimovna, 25 years old.

Boris Semyonovich Goose, Director of Repairs for the Commercial Trust of Refractory Metals.

Lizanka, 28 years old.

Madame Ivanova, 30 years old.

Marya Nikiforovna.

Robber, an attorney.

The Dead Body, Ivan Vasilievich.

First Lady.

Second Lady.

Third Lady.

A Seamstress.

A Cutter.

First Stranger.

Second Stranger.

Third Stranger.

Fourth Stranger.

ACT I

THE ANTEROOM, *living room, and bedroom of Zoya's apartment are visible. A May sunset is blazing in the windows. Outside the windows, the courtyard of the huge building is playing like some horrible musical snuffbox. A phonograph sings: "On this earth is the whole human race! ..."*[1] *Someone shouts: "We buy primuses!" Someone else shouts: "Knives and scissors sharpened! ..." A third: "Samovars soldered! ..." The phonograph: "He honors one holy idol! ..." From time to time a trolley rumbles by. Occasional automobile horns. A hellish concert. Then it quiets down somewhat, and an accordion plays a gay polka.*

ZOYA (*changing clothes in front of a mirrored wardrobe, she is singing the polka*). Let's go, let's go, my sweet angel ... Here's the paper! ... I got it ... Here's the paper!
MANYUSHKA (*appearing suddenly*). Zoya Denisovna! Portupeya's come sneaking around.
ZOYA (*in a whisper*). Get him out, get him out! Tell him I'm not home!
MANYUSHKA. But he's come in the back way, the rat!
ZOYA. Kick him out! Kick him out! Tell him I've gone out. (*She hides in the mirrored wardrobe.*)
PORTUPEYA (*appearing suddenly*). Zoya Denisovna, are you home?
MANYUSHKA. She ain't home, I tell you, she ain't. And what are you doing, Comrade Portupeya, coming right into a lady's bedroom?
PORTUPEYA. Under Soviet power, bedrooms aren't allowed.[2] Maybe

1. From an aria in *Faust.*
2. A reference to the chronic housing shortage in the Soviet Union. People were assigned not apartments or even rooms, but specific amounts of "living space."

you'd like a separate bedroom arranged for you? When will she be here?

MANYUSHKA. And just how would I be knowing? She doesn't make reports to me.

PORTUPEYA. I suppose she's run off to her lover-boy?

MANYUSHKA. Comrade Portupeya, how uncultured of you—who are you saying that about?

PORTUPEYA. Don't play the fool, Manya! We know all about your goings on. At the House Committee everything's out in the open, like in the palm of your hand. The House Committee is an unslumbering eye. We sleep with one eye shut, but we keep the other open. That's our job.

MANYUSHKA. You ought to get out of here, Anisim Zotikovich. Why'd you sneak in the bedroom?

PORTUPEYA. Don't you see I'm carrying a briefcase? Who do you think you're talking to? This means I can go in anywhere. I'm an official person, I have immunity. (*He tries to hug* Manyushka.)

MANYUSHKA. Well I'll tell your wife, and she'll tear your whole official person to shreds!

PORTUPEYA. Just a minute, you fidget!

ZOYA (*in the wardrobe*). Portupeya, you are a pig!

MANYUSHKA. Oh! (*She runs out.*)

ZOYA (*coming out of the wardrobe*). A fine House Committee chairman you are! Just fine!

PORTUPEYA. I thought you really weren't here. Why was she lying? And what a sly one you are, Zoya Denisovna . . .

ZOYA. You're an indelicate sort of fruit, Portupeya! In the first place, you say nasty things. What is "lover-boy" supposed to mean? Does that refer to Pavel Fyodorovich?

PORTUPEYA. I am a simple man. I didn't go to the university.

ZOYA. Too bad. In the second place, I'm not dressed, and you are hanging around my bedroom. And in the third place, I'm not at home.

PORTUPEYA. What do you mean, not at home? That's pretty strange!

ZOYA. In brief, what do you want from me? More doubling up? New people moving in?

PORTUPEYA. As usual. You are alone, but you have six rooms.

ZOYA. What do you mean alone—what about Manyushka?

PORTUPEYA. Manyushka is a servant—she has sixteen square yards of living space in the kitchen.

ZOYA. Manyushka!

MANYUSHKA (*appearing*). What is it, Zoya Denisovna?

ZOYA. Who are you?

MANYUSHKA. Your niece, Zoya Denisovna.

PORTUPEYA. What do you call Zoya Denisovna?

MANYUSHKA. *Ma tante.*

PORTUPEYA. Oh, what a wench!

ZOYA. You may go, Manyushka.

Manyushka *flits out.*

PORTUPEYA. This is imposible, Zoya Denisovna. What kind of cock-and-bull story is it you keep giving me? Manyushka! . . . Your niece? She's your niece like I'm your aunt!

ZOYA. Portupeya, you are a boor!

PORTUPEYA. The front room is empty too!

ZOYA. Excuse me, he is traveling on business.

PORTUPEYA. What are you saying, Zoya Denisovna! He's not in Moscow at all. Let's put it objectively: he left you some money from the State Porcelain Trust and vanished from Moscow. A mythical being. And because of you the General Meeting of the House Committee gave me such a reception that I barely got out of there alive.

ZOYA. What does that gang want?

PORTUPEYA. Who are you saying that about?

ZOYA. About your General Meeting.

PORTUPEYA. Zoya Denisovna, do you know that if there were any-one else in my place . . .

ZOYA. That's the point—*you* are in your place, not anyone else.

PORTUPEYA. A resolution was made to double you up, and half of them were hollering for you to be evicted altogether!

ZOYA. Evicted? (*She gives him the finger.*)

PORTUPEYA. How am I to take that?

ZOYA. Take it as a finger!

PORTUPEYA. All right. But may I drop dead if I don't move a worker in here tomorrow! We'll see how you give him the finger! Excuse me. (*He starts to go.*)

ZOYA. Portupeya, tell me one thing. How is it that in your co-operative's building Monsieur Goose-Bagazhny occupies eight rooms on the first floor all by himself?

PORTUPEYA. I beg your pardon, Goose took that apartment on contract. He's going to pay for all of our heating.

ZOYA. Forgive me for an impertinent question: how much did he give you personally to get that apartment away from Firsov?

PORTUPEYA. A little more careful, Zoya Denisovna, I am a person with responsibilities!

ZOYA. In the inner pocket of your vest there are some banknotes. Series VM, the first number is 425900. Check it.

PORTUPEYA (*unbuttons his vest, gets out the money, and he is dumb-founded*).

ZOYA. Allez-oop!

PORTUPEYA. Zoya Denisovna, you are in cahoots with the devil, I noticed that a long time ago.

A pause.

ZOYA. Therefore, Manyushka and the mythical being remain.

PORTUPEYA. Have a heart, Zoya Denisovna, believe me—Manyushka is impossible! The entire building knows she is a servant.

ZOYA. Well, all right, I believe you. I'll let one person in here to double up.

PORTUPEYA. And the rest—what about those other rooms?

ZOYA. Here!

PORTUPEYA (*reads*). This certifies that Citizeness Peltz is permitted to open a demonstration sewing shop and a school ... Oho, ho! ... for the sewing of work-clothes for the wives of workers and civil servants ... Supplementary dwelling place ... Oh my God! Was it Goose that fixed up this document for you?

ZOYA. Oh, what difference does it make? Well then, esteemed comrade, a copy of this item to your bandits and, of course, I no longer exist.

PORTUPEYA. Well of course, the situation is simpler with a document like this!

ZOYA. By the way, they gave me a fifty-ruble note today at Miur's, but it's counterfeit. Take a look, you're the specialist on banknotes.

PORTUPEYA. Oh, what a tongue! (*He looks at it.*) It's genuine!

ZOYA. And I say it's counterfeit. Take the nasty thing and throw it away.

PORTUPEYA. All right, I'll throw it away.

ZOYA. Well now, my dear, march! I have to get dressed.

PORTUPEYA (*starts to go*). Only you decide today who you're going to let double up in here. I'll drop by a little later.

ZOYA. All right.

Somewhere a piano starts playing and a voice sings: "Don't sing to me, my beauty, songs of melancholy Georgia ..."[3]

PORTUPEYA (*stopping at the door, hollowly and sadly*). How does that work—Goose gives out the banknotes, but he writes down the serial numbers?

ZOYA. And what did you think?

Portupeya *exits through the living room and anteroom, and at the same time* Obolyaninov *appears. He looks terrible.*

OBOLYANINOV. Zoyka, may I? (*He throws down his hat and cane.*)

ZOYA. Pavlik! Of course you may. What is it Pavlik? Again?

OBOLYANINOV. I can't help myself ... Send the Chinaman ... To the Chinaman, I beg you ...

ZOYA. Very well, very well ... (*She shouts.*) Manyushka!

Manyushka *appears.*

ZOYA. Pavel Fyodorovich is not well, off to the Chinaman immediately!

Darkness. Zoya's apartment disappears. A vile cellar room rises up, illuminated by a small kerosene lamp. Underwear and shirts on ropes. Gandzalin *stands over a burning spirit-lamp. In front of him is* Cherubim.

3. A song by Rachmaninoff, the words taken from a lyric poem by Pushkin: "Don't sing to me, my beauty,/ Songs of melancholy Georgia;/ They remind me/ Of another life and a distant clime."

GANDZALIN. You Chinese swindrel, you bandit! You store the dishes, you store a cocaine, whel it go? How can I berieve you, who can?

CHERUBIM. No silee, shutee up! You bandit youlself!

GANDZALIN. Get out of laundley-loom light now, you clook!

CHERUBIM. What? What? You kickee out pool Chinese? What? They stole my silk jacket flom me on Svetnoi Boulevald, a bandit take away cocaine, almost killee me—look. (*He points to a scratch.*) I wolked fol you, and now you kickee me out. Who going to feed pool Chinese in Moscow? Bad comlade! It too little to kill you.

GANDZALIN. If you gonna kill, Communist porice will dlop in on you. Just lemembel that!

A pause.

CHERUBIM. What? You kickee out helpel? I gonna hang you on gates!

A pause.

GANDZALIN. Ale you gonna steal, gonna lob?

CHERUBIM. No! No!

GANDZALIN. Sweal it—by God!

CHERUBIM. By God!

GANDZALIN. Sweal it: by God, Jesu!

CHERUBIM. By God, by God, by the Lold!

GANDZALIN. Put on youl lobe, you'll keep to wolk!

CHERUBIM. Me hungly, no ate two days, givee me some blead!

GANDZALIN. Thele's white blead in bag.

A knock.

Who? Who? Who?

MANYUSHKA (*outside*). Open up, Gasoline, it's a friend!

GANDZALIN. A-ah! Manyuska! (*He opens the door.*)

MANYUSHKA (*enters*). Why've you got the door closed on me? A fine laundry, you don't answer knocks!

GANDZALIN. Ah, Manyuska, herro, herro!

MANYUSHKA. Well, Gasoline, let's go to our friends. Obolyaninov is sick again.

GANDZALIN. I can no come light now, I will give you medicine.

MANYUSHKA. No, you just come yourself, dish it out in their presence —otherwise they'll say you're cutting it too thin here at your place.

CHERUBIM. What? Molphine?

> Gandzalin *says something in Chinese.* Cherubim *answers him in Chinese.*

GANDZALIN. Manyushka, he go, he do what necessaly.

MANYUSHKA. Does he know how?

GANDZALIN. Yes, no wolly. (*He gets a little box out of the corner, gives it to* Cherubim, *speaks Chinese.*)

CHERUBIM. You no have to teachee me. Le's go, gill!

GANDZALIN (*to* Cherubim). You behave bettel now, you bling back five lubles. You undelstand?

MANYUSHKA. Why are you bawling him out? He's as quiet as a cherubim!

GANDZALIN. Oy, the charoobum, a bandit!

MANYUSHKA. Well, goodbye, Gasoline!

GANDZALIN. Goodbye, Manyuska! And when you going to mally me?

MANYUSHKA. Eeukh! When did I promise?

GANDZALIN. Ah, Manyuska. Who said?

MANYUSHKA. Kiss a lady's hand, but don't lunge at her lips! Let's go!

> Manyushka *exits with* Cherubim.

GANDZALIN. Nice gill, Manyuska! Manyuska—tasty gill. (*He starts to sing sadly in Chinese.*)

> *The kerosene lamp and spirit-lamp go out. Darkness. The laundry disappears. Zoya's bedroom, living room, and ante-room appear.* Obolyaninov, Cherubim, *and* Zoya *are in the bedroom.* Obolyaninov *buttons his cuffs, straightens his sleeves, livens up.*

OBOLYANINOV. How much do I owe you, my friend. Hey, China-man!

CHERUBIM. Seven lubles.

ZOYA. Why seven and not five? Crooks!

OBOLYANINOV. Never mind, Zoya, never mind. He is a deserving Chinaman. (*He pats his pockets.*)

ZOYA. Wait, Pavlik, I'll pay! (*She gives money to* Cherubim.)

CHERUBIM. Thankee . . .

OBOLYANINOV. Look how he smiles, Zoya! A perfect cherub! A talented Chinaman! . . .

CHERUBIM. Talent vely little . . . (*Intimately.*) You want, I bling you it evely day? You no tellee Gandzalin . . . We got evelything—molphine, alcohol . . . You want, can dlaw you pletty things? (*He opens his shirt, shows the tattoo on his chest—a dragon which is alternately terrifying and distorted.*)

OBOLYANINOV. Astounding! Zoyka, look!

ZOYA. What a horror! Did you do that yourself?

CHERUBIM. Myself did. In Shanghai.

OBOLYANINOV. Listen, my cherub, can you come here every day? I am not well, I have to be treated with morphine. You'll prepare the injection, agreed?

CHERUBIM. Agleed!

ZOYA. Careful, Pavlik, he might be some kind of tramp.

OBOLYANINOV. What are you saying, no! . . . Why it's written on his face that he is a virtuous man from China. Listen, Chinaman, you're not a Party member are you?

CHERUBIM. We wash clothes.

ZOYA. Clothes? You come back in an hour, I'll make a deal with you—you can iron for my sewing shop.

CHERUBIM. All light . . .

ZOYA. Manyushka, see the Chinaman out!

MANYUSHKA (*appearing*). If you please! (*She goes out into the ante-room with* Cherubim.)

> Obolyaninov *opens the bedroom curtain and reveals evening in Moscow outside. The first lights. The noise gets more hollow. A voice begins: "They remind me . . ."*[4] *and then dies out.*

4. See note 3.

CHERUBIM (*in the anteroom*). Goodbye, Manyushka, I coming in an houl. Manyuska, I comee evely day, I tookee job with Obolyanu.

MANYUSHKA. What job?

CHERUBIM. I gonna bling medicine. Kissee me, Manyuska!

MANYUSHKA. Forget it—if you please . . . (*She opens the door.*)

CHERUBIM (*mysteriously*). I when I am lich, you gonna kiss me? Lich, pletty . . .

MANYUSHKA. Go on, go on, for Lord's sake . . .

Cherubim *exits.*

MANYUSHKA. How strange can you get!

OBOLYANINOV (*at the bedroom window*). "They remind me . . ."

ZOYA. Pavlik, I got the paper. (*A pause.*) Count, why is it you refuse to answer a lady?

OBOLYANINOV. Forgive me, I was thinking. And please, don't call me "Count."

ZOYA. Why not?

OBOLYANINOV. Today some character in hunting boots comes and says, "You're the former Count? . . ."

ZOYA. Well?

OBOLYANINOV. He threw his cigarette butt on the floor . . . I leave to come here, and as I'm riding along past the zoo on the trolley I see a sign: "The former chicken is on display." I ask the guard, "If it's a former chicken, what is it now?" He answers, "Now she's a rooster."[5] I don't understand anything . . .

ZOYA. Oh, Pavlik, Pavlik . . . (*A pause.*) Well, Pavlik, make up your mind. Do you agree (*in a whisper*) to the enterprise?

OBOLYANINOV. It makes no difference to me now . . . I agree . . . I can't bear to see any more former chickens! I've got to get out of here at any price!

ZOYA. Oh, yes! You are wasting away here! I will take you to Paris! By Christmas we will have a million francs, I guarantee it.

5. After the Revolution it became very important to establish what one had been "formerly." For example, a former aristocrat (like Obolyaninov) might not be eligible for certain jobs or rations. This is also an allusion to sex operations such as the ones described in Bulgakov's *Heart of a Dog.*

OBOLYANINOV. But how will we manage to get out?

ZOYA. Goose will help.

OBOLYANINOV. The former goose! . . . I imagine him as omnipotent! I'm thirsty, Zoya. Do you have any beer?

ZOYA. Manyushka!

Manyushka *appears.*

Buy some beer!

MANYUSHKA. I'll bring it right away.

She flits into the dining room, from there to the anteroom where she tosses a scarf over her head, and goes out—forgetting to close the door behind her.

OBOLYANINOV. But now I'm afraid all of a sudden . . . aren't you frightened that they'll catch you?

ZOYA. We will do it intelligently, they won't catch us. Let's go into the mythical person's room, Pavlik, I don't want to chat here in the open.

Zoya exits with Obolyaninov *through the living room and closes the door behind her.* Zoya's *and* Obolyaninov's *voices are heard hollowly behind the door. Somewhere outside a stupid and thin voice begins to sing: "It was evening, the stars did shine,/ The frost outside was crackling,/ I was walking along the street . . ."*[6]

AMETISTOV (*enters the anteroom*). "The little baby! (*Sadly.*) He's turned blue and he's shaking all over!" (*He puts a beat-up suitcase on the floor, looks around.* Ametistov *is wearing torn trousers, a soiled field-jacket, a cap, and some sort of medal on his chest.*) Phooey, dammit to hell! Flapping three miles from the Kursk Station with a suitcase is quite a trick too, I'll tell you that! Now I ought to have a drink of beer! Oh, my miserable Fate, you've dragged me up to the fifth floor again! Will you give me anything here? (*He looks through the door into the kitchen.*) Hey, comrades, who's here? Is Zoya Denisovna home? Hm . . . (*He looks into the living room, hears the voices of Zoya and*

6. From a popular song.

Obolyaninov, *sneaks up a little closer, eavesdrops*.) Oh-ho-ho! I got here at just the right time.

MANYUSHKA (*enters the anteroom carrying beer bottles*). Lord! Didn't I shut the door?

Ametistov *returns to the anteroom*.

MANYUSHKA. What's this? Who do you want?

AMETISTOV. *Pardon! Pardon!* Don't get upset, comrade! Beer! Precisely at the right time. I've been dreaming of beer all the way from Kursk Station!

MANYUSHKA. Just who do you want?

AMETISTOV. Zoya Denisovna. And with whom have I the pleasure to be speaking?

MANYUSHKA. I am Zoya Denisovna's niece.

AMETISTOV. Very pleased to meet you! Very! I didn't have the slightest idea that Zoyechka had such a pretty little neice! I am Zoya Denisovna's cousin. (*He kisses* Manyushka's *hand*.)

MANYUSHKA (*dumbfounded*). Zoya Denisovna! Zoya Denisovna!

Ametistov *runs after* Manyushka *into the living room, carrying his suitcase.* Zoya *and* Obolyaninov *enter the living room to answer* Manyushka's *shout.*

AMETISTOV. My dear little cousin. *Je vous salue!*

Zoya *is petrified.*

Introduce me to this citizen, my little cousin . . .

ZOYA. It's you, my . . . You . . . Pavel Fyodorovich, this is Ametistov, my cousin.

AMETISTOV. *Pardon, pardon* . . . (*to* Obolyaninov.) Putnikovsky, a non-Party member, a former nobleman.

OBOLYANINOV (*struck*). Very happy to . . .

AMETISTOV. Cousin, permit me to ask you for a few words *à part!*

ZOYA. Excuse me, Pavlik, I have to exchange a few words with Alexander Tarasovich . . .

AMETISTOV. *Pardon, pardon*, Vasily Ivanovich . . . such an insignificant amount of time has passed, and you have even forgotten my name, cousin! It's a bitter pill, ay-ay-yay!

OBOLYANINOV. Please, please ... (*He disappears.*)

ZOYA. Manyushka, go pour some beer for Pavel Fyodorovich.

Manyushka *exits. A pause.*

ZOYA. They shot you in Baku?

AMETISTOV. *Pardon, pardon,* what kind of logic is that? If they shot me in Baku, how can I arrive in Moscow like this? They were shooting me by mistake, quite innocently ...

ZOYA. My head is spinning.

AMETISTOV. From joy?

ZOYA. I don't understand a thing ...

AMETISTOV. Well, naturally, I flew in under the wings of the May amnesty ...[7] By the way, where did you get that niece?

ZOYA. What niece? That's my maid, Manyushka.

AMETISTOV. So-o, I see, for the purposes of retaining your living space. (*Stentorianly.*) Manyushka!

Manyushka, *confused, appears.*

AMETISTOV. My dear! Bring me some beer, I'm dying! Some niece you are, the deuce take you! (*Dumbfounded,* Manyushka *exits.*) And I kissed her hand! Such disgrace!

ZOYA. Where do you plan to stay? Keep it in mind that there is a crisis in living space in Moscow.

AMETISTOV. I know. With you, naturally.

ZOYA. And what if I tell you that I can't take you?

AMETISTOV. Oh, so that's how it is? You're being rotten! Well, so what, be rotten, be rotten! You are kicking out your cousin who has trudged here on foot from the Kursk Station? An orphan? Go ahead, kick him out! So what, I'll go ... (*He picks up his suitcase.*) And I won't even drink the beer . . . Only you will be sorry for this, my dear cousin ...

ZOYA. Oh, so you want to frighten me? No, sir, that won't work!

AMETISTOV. Why frighten you? I am a decent man, a gentleman (*in a whisper*) and if I were not myself, if I were to go to the GPU

---

7. On May Day each year the government granted amnesty to many political prisoners.

and report on the kind of workshop it is that you are organizing in your apartment . . . I heard everything, dear Zoya Denisovna! (*He starts to leave.*)

ZOYA. Wait! How did you get in without ringing?

AMETISTOV. To hell with this subterfu . . . and I haven't even kissed you, my little cousin.

ZOYA (*pushes him away*). This must be Fate!

Manyushka *enters, brings in a bottle of beer and a glass.*

ZOYA. Manyushka, was it you that didn't lock the door? Oh, Manyushka! . . . Well, never mind! Go, apologize to Pavel Fyodorovich for me . . .

Manyushka *exits.*

AMETISTOV (*drinks beer*). Oo-o, that's good! Moscow has first-class beer! You managed to keep the apartment, I see—good girl, Zoya!

ZOYA. Fate! . . . Obviously, I am going to have to bear my cross some more!

AMETISTOV. Do you want me to take offense and leave?

ZOYA. No! What do you want first?

AMETISTOV. First—a pair of pants.

ZOYA. Do you mean you have no trousers? What's in the suitcase?

AMETISTOV. Six decks of cards and "Are Miracles Possible?" I owe thanks to those miracles. If it weren't for them, I'd have kicked off from hunger! It's no joking matter to go from Baku to Moscow in a freight and passenger train! . . . You see, in the Baku Culture Center I grabbed 100 brochures entitled "Are Miracles Possible?" as a memento, and I sold them for a ruble apiece on the train. . . . They are possible, little Zoya, and here I am! . . . Marvelous beer! Comrades, buy a brochure! . . .

ZOYA. Are the cards marked?

AMETISTOV. What do you think I am, madame?

ZOYA. Cut it, Ametistov! Where have you been roaming for the last seven years?

AMETISTOV. The Whites were coming . . . So the Reds gave me money to be evacuated to Moscow, and so I got myself evacuated to the Whites in Rostov and started working for them . . . Then

I got money from the Whites to be evacuated—and I went to the Reds and became the head of an agitation group for them. The Reds gave me money for evacuation, and I went to the Whites in the Crimea—there I simply served as the manager of a restaurant in Sevastopol. . . . I ran into one group of players, and they took me for 15,000 at *chemin* in one evening . . .

ZOYA. You! that means they must have been real specialists!

AMETISTOV. Ignorant scoundrels, I tell you, ignorant! . . . Well, and then you know what happened, after the Whites came the Reds. And I set off plunging around the Soviet system. In Stavropol I was in the fire department, in Voronezh I managed a food supply department . . . finally, I decided that I had no future career there, and then I decided to move through Party channels. I'll get through all this bureaucratism, I thought, through all those probation periods. And then a friend of mine, Chemodanov, Karl Petrovich, died in my apartment, a pure soul he was—and a Party member . . .

ZOYA. In Voronezh?

AMETISTOV. No, this was in Odessa now. I thought, what loss is it to the Party? One man dies, and another immediately takes his place in the ranks. I wept over the deceased, took his Party Card, and I was off to Baku. A quiet place, I thought, I can set up a *chemin-de-fer* game. So I make my appearance like that, as Chemodanov. And next my door opens, and it's a friend of Chemodanov—pow! A real *tableau!* He has nine, I've busted . . . I head for the windows, but the windows are on the second floor . . .

ZOYA. Well done!

AMETISTOV. No, I had bad luck, what are you saying! At the trial I made such a concluding speech—would you believe it, not only the spectators who were from the intelligentsia—the professors—were weeping, but even the guards and prosecutors were! Well, they were going to shoot me . . . Well, what was there for me to do? . . . I had to come to Moscow. Oh, Zoyka, you have grown callous here in your apartment. You have torn yourself off . . . torn yourself off from the masses!

ZOYA. All right! You heard everything?

AMETISTOV. I was lucky, Zoechka!

Zoya. I will let you stay.

Ametistov. Zoechka!

Zoya. Shut up! I will give you a job as manager of our enterprise—but watch out, Ametistov, if you pull some kind of fast one, I'll risk everything to put an end to you! Be careful, Ametistov, you've told me too much about yourself!

Ametistov. So, I have entrusted the mournful tale of a mendicant to a serpent? *Mon Dieu!*

Zoya. Shut up, you numbskull! Where is the necklace you were supposed to pawn for me just before you left?

Ametistov. Necklace? Wait, wait . . . The one with the little diamonds?

Zoya. Bastard! You bastard! . . .

Ametistov. *Merci, madame!* Just see how Zoechka receives her relatives!

Zoya. Do you have any documents?

Ametistov. I have a whole pocket full of documents—the whole question is which of these documents is, so to speak, the freshest . . . (*He takes out some papers.*) Karl Chemodanov—no possibility of that! Siguradze, Anton . . . no, that's no good.

Zoya. This is awful, I swear. You are Putnikovsky!

Ametistov. No, Zoechka, I got mixed up. Putnikovsky is in Moscow now—so that is eliminated. Maybe my own name would be best. I think that in eight years it must have been forgotten in Moscow. There, register me as Ametistov! Hold on, I had a Hernia Certification exempting me from military service too . . . (*He gets out a paper.*)

Zoya (*takes a magnificent pair of pants out of the wardrobe*). Put on these trousers.

Ametistov. God bless your good little heart. Turn away, sweetie-pie!

Zoya. I really needed you! Try to return the trousers, they are Pavel Fyodorovich's.

Ametistov. Your morganatic spouse?

Zoya. You be polite to him, he's my husband!

Ametistov. What is his last name?

Zoya. Obolyaninov.

Ametistov. The Count? Well! . . . Congratulations, cousin! Though he probably hasn't got a thing left. A counter-revolutionary, judging by his physiognomy . . . (*He comes out from behind the screen, admires the trousers he has put on.*) Nice humane trousers! In trousers like these you immediately feel like you're up on a podium . . .

ZOYA. You get your names disentangled . . . You're putting me in an absurd position. Pavlik.

Obolyaninov *enters.*

ZOYA. Forgive me, Pavlik, we were talking business.

AMETISTOV. We got carried away by reminiscences of our childhood . . . Zoechka and I grew up together, you know. I was weeping, really . . . look at the pants . . . *pardon, pardon,* I was robbed on the road . . . my second suitcase was filched in Taganrog—a really grotesque situation! I hope you have nothing against this? Among members of the nobility, it is nothing . . .

OBOLYANINOV. Of course, of course, by all means . . .

ZOYA. Pavlik, Alexander Tarasovich here is going to work as manager for us. You don't have anything against that, do you?

OBOLYANINOV. Please, by all means . . . if you recommend Vasily Ivanovich . . .

AMETISTOV. *Pardon, pardon,* Alexander Tarasovich . . . Are you surprised? That is my stage name—on stage Vasily Ivanovich Putnikovsky, but in life—Alexander Tarasovich Ametistov. It's a well-known name—many of its representatives were shot by the Bolsheviks . . . that story would make a whole novel! You will weep when I tell you about it . . .

OBOLYANINOV. That'll be very nice. Where do you come from?

AMETISTOV. Me? Where did I come from, you ask? At this very moment I came from Saratov. This story is a whole novel too, you will weep when . . .

OBOLYANINOV. Are you non-Party, may I inquire?

AMETISTOV. *Quelle question?* What are you saying?

OBOLYANINOV. But you had . . . on your chest . . . some kind of medal . . . however, I guess I just imagined that.

AMETISTOV. Oh, no, no—that was for the road. You know, it helps a lot on the train—to get your seat reservation without waiting in line, all kinds of things . . .

MANYUSHKA (*appearing*). Portupeya is here.

ZOYA. Call him in. (*To* Ametistov). He is Chairman of the House Committee, bear that in mind.

PORTUPEYA. Good evening, Zoya Denisovna; hello, Citizen Obol-yaninov. Well, how about it, have you made up your mind, Zoya Denisovna?

ZOYA. Yes. Here are some documents. Register Alexander Tarasovich Ametistov, he has just arrived. He is going to be manager of the workshop.

PORTUPEYA. Aha, so you intend to work here?

AMETISTOV. Of course, of course . . . A small glass of beer, esteemed comrade?

PORTUPEYA. *Merci.* Don't mind if I do. It's hot, you know, and I'm always on my feet running around here . . .

AMETISTOV. Yes, bad weather, as they say. You have a huge building here, dear comrade . . . such a huge one! . . .

PORTUPEYA. And don't remind me—it is a real torment! And do you happen to have a Hernia Certificate exempting you from military service?

AMETISTOV. Yes, sir. (*Gives him the paper.*) Are you a Party member, comrade?

PORTUPEYA. I am a sympathizer.

AMETISTOV. Ah, very good! (*He puts on his medallion.*) I am a former Party member myself. (*Softly, to* Obolyaninov.) *Devant les gens* . . . cunning . . .

PORTUPEYA. Why did you leave the Party?

AMETISTOV. Petty fractional conflicts . . . There is much I do not agree with . . . I looked around and saw, no, things aren't working out! Then I told them straight to their faces . . .

PORTUPEYA. Straight to their faces?

AMETISTOV. Why not, what do I have to lose besides my chains? At one time I played a very important role . . . No, I said, this is not it! We have deviated—that's the first thing. We have lost the purity of our line—that's the second. We have abandoned our precepts! Oh, so that's the way it is, they said? Well, we'll fix you then . . . Hot-tempered people they are! Your health!

OBOLYANINOV. He's a genius, I swear it.

ZOYA (*softly*). A scoundrel! Well, enough politics! So, Comrade Portupeya, I begin business tomorrow.

AMETISTOV. So, we are beginning. To the success of the workshop and to the health of its head, Zoya Denisovna, Comrade Peltz! Hurrah! (*He drinks some beer.*) And now to the health of our esteemed House Committee Chairman and sympathizer . . . (*Softly.*) . . . what's his name?

ZOYA (*softly*). Anisim Zotikovich Portupeya.

AMETISTOV. Just what I was going to say: Anisim Zotikovich Portupeya! Hurrah!

> *Outside a piano begins to play, little boys start singing: "May you live a long, long time . . ."*

AMETISTOV. Absolutely right! May you live a long, long time—a long, long time!

CURTAIN

ACT II

THE LIVING ROOM *of Zoya's apartment has been turned into a work-shop. Mannequins with doll-like faces, billows of material. A* SEAM-STRESS *has a sewing machine crackling away; there is a* CUTTER *with a tape measure hanging over her shoulder.* THREE LADIES.

FIRST LADY. Oh, not like that, deary! . . . You have to take out the whole corner, take it out, or it will create the impression that I am missing two ribs. For God's sake, take it out, out! . . .
CUTTER. All right.
SECOND LADY (*cracks to the* Third). And just imagine it—madame, she says, you need your hair trimmed first. I run right over to *Jean* on Kuznetsky, of course, I get my hair trimmed, I run back to her shop, and she puts the straw hat on me—and imagine it—my head immediately starts looking like a big pot!
THIRD LADY. He-he-he!
SECOND LADY. Oh, it's funny to *you,* dear.
FIRST LADY. It's bulging in the rear, my dear, bulging.
CUTTER. What's wrong, madame?
SECOND LADY. And what effrontery! She tells me, "It's because you have broad cheekbones."

The doorbell rings.

AMETISTOV (*running in*). *Pardon, pardon,* I'm not looking . . .
SECOND LADY. Monsieur Ametistov, what do you think, do I have broad cheekbones?
AMETISTOV. You? *Qu'est-ce que vous dîtes, madame?* You have no cheekbones at all. (*He disappears.*)
FIRST LADY. Who is he?
CUTTER. The main manager of the school.
FIRST LADY. It's a chic place.

AMETISTOV (*returning*). *Pardon, pardon,* I'm not looking . . . Your manteau is enchanting!

SECOND LADY. What's enchanting about it? Do I really have a rear-end like that?

AMETISTOV. An absolutely correct rear-end, *madame.*

The doorbell.

(*Aside.*) Oh, may you drop dead! *Pardon, pardon!* (*He flies out.*)

FIRST LADY (*taking off her manteau*). Well, by Friday?

CUTTER. Impossible, *madame,* Varvara Nikolaevna will not be finished.

FIRST LADY. Oh, this is awful! What about Saturday?

CUTTER. By Wednesday, *madame.*

FIRST LADY. Goodbye. (*She exits.*)

The Seamstress *gives a bundle to the* Second Lady.

SECOND LADY. Thank you.

AMETISTOV (*flying in*). *Au revoir, madame.*

The doorbell.

AMETISTOV (*aside*). Well, what the hell? *Pardon, pardon!* . . . (*He flies out.*)

The Second Lady *exits.*

SEAMSTRESS (*wraps up a bundle in paper, gives it to the* Third Lady). Here is your package.

THIRD LADY. *Merci.* (*She exits.*)

CUTTER (*sits down in exhaustion*). Oo-oo! . . .

AMETISTOV. Well, dear comrades, close the shop! Enough!

The Seamstress *and* Cutter *get ready to go.*

AMETISTOV. Take a rest, comrades, do as the work code says . . . Go out to Sparrow Hills, it's a golden autumn, the foliage . . .

SEAMSTRESS. Who cares about foliage, Alexander Tarasovich! . . . If only I can make it to bed!

AMETISTOV. Oh, how well I understand you! I myself dream of only one thing—if only I could lie down! I'll have some nighttime reading in the history of materialistic philosophy and fall asleep! You don't have to clean up, comrades! Comrade Manyushka will do it all.

The Seamstress *and* Cutter *exit.*

They torment me, the cursed females. Nothing but rears and ribbons! (*He gets out a bottle of cognac and a glass, drinks up.*) Dammit to hell!

Zoya *enters.*

AMETISTOV. Well, Zoechka, dear directress, what about it—are you going to get Alla Vadimovna in the very near future?
ZOYA. It won't work!
AMETISTOV. *Pardon, pardon* . . . you listen to me. How much does she owe you?
ZOYA. Three thousand.
AMETISTOV. There's your trump!
ZOYA. She'll pay.
AMETISTOV. She won't pay, I tell you, she has eyes that suggest a bad credit rating. You can always tell from his eyes whether a person has money or not. I judge by myself—when I'm flat, I'm pensive, thoughts overwhelm me, I feel drawn toward Socialism. I tell you that girl is pensive, she needs money desperately, and she has no money. Just think about it—what a specimen, a real ornament for the apartment! Listen to Ametistov! Ametistov is a big man!

The doorbell.

Now who?
MANYUSHKA. Alla Vadimovna wants to know if she can see you.
AMETISTOV. There! Put the pressure on her, pressure!
ZOYA. All right, don't get in an uproar. (*To* Manyushka.) Ask her in.
ALLA (*enters*). Hello, Zoya Denisovna!
ZOYA. I'm very glad to see you, Alla Vadimovna.
AMETISTOV. Let me kiss your hand, my adored Alla Vadimovna! Alla Vadimovna, if you see the new dresses we got from Paris

today! You will throw your dress out the window! I give you the word of a former cuirassier!

ALLA. You were a cuirassier?

AMETISTOV. *Mais oui.* I must fly, I will leave you alone. (*He disappears after winking to* Zoya.)

ALLA. You have an excellent manager, Zoya Denisovna. Tell me, is he really a former cuirassier?

ZOYA. Unfortunately, I cannot really say . . . Sit down, Alla Vadimovna.

ALLA. Zoya Denisovna, I have come to see you about an important matter.

ZOYA. Yes?

ALLA. Oh, how unpleasant . . . I was supposed to pay you today . . . I'm so ashamed, Zoya Denisovna, but I . . . my finances have been very bad lately . . . I am constrained to ask you to wait . . . (*A pause.*) You are killing me with your silence, Zoya Denisovna!

ZOYA. What can I say, Alla Vadimovna? (*A pause.*)

ALLA. Goodbye, Zoya Denisovna, you are right, of course . . . Well, I will employ all efforts to get the money and pay off the debt . . . Goodbye, Zoya Denisovna.

ZOYA. Best wishes, Alla Vadimovna.

Alla *goes to the door.*

ZOYA. So things are really that bad?

ALLA. Zoya Denisovna, I am in debt to you, but that does not give you the right to speak to me in a tone like that! . . .

ZOYA. Oh, no, Allochka, you can't get away with that! It is precisely a matter of tone! Lots of people owe people money! If you had simply come to me and said, "My affairs are rotten," we would have thought up a way out together . . . but you came in to me like a statue . . . As if to say, "I'm a society lady, but you're a dressmaker. . . ." Well, if that's the way it is, why ask a dressmaker questions?

ALLA. Zoya Denisovna, it just seemed that way to you, I swear it! I am so crushed by my debt that I didn't know how to look you in the face.

ZOYA. Enough about the debt! So, you have no money? Answer simply and like a friend. How much do you need?

ALLA. A lot. So much that it's cold in the pit of my stomach!

ZOYA. For what purpose?

A pause.

ALLA. I want to go abroad.

ZOYA. I see. So not a damned thing is working out here.

ALLA. Not a damned thing!

ZOYA. Well, what about *him* . . . I don't want to know who he is, I don't need his name . . . Well, in a word, doesn't he have any money to set you up a little better here?

ALLA. Since my husband died, I have had no one, Zoya Denisovna.

ZOYA. Oy! . . .

ALLA. It's the truth.

ZOYA. You didn't succeed in getting away then—three months ago?

ALLA. I didn't succeed.

ZOYA. I will try to fix it for you.

ALLA. If you do that, I will be indebted to you for life!

ZOYA. Don't worry, comrade! . . . And, if you want, I will give you an opportunity to earn the money—you will pay off your debts.

ALLA. Zoechka, there is no opportunity for me to earn money in Moscow. That is, in any decent kind of work, as I understand it.

ZOYA. Why so? There is decent work in this shop. Be a mannequin for me—that is my offer.

ALLA. But, Zoechka, one gets paid pennies for that!

ZOYA. Pennies! Well, that is a flexible concept . . . I offer you a salary of 1000 rubles a month, I cancel your debt, and besides that I will help you emigrate. We work only in the evenings—every other day. Well?

A pause.

ALLA. Every other day? . . . Evenings? . . . (*She understands.*) That's a joke!

ZOYA. There are only four months before Christmas. In four months you are free, your debts paid, and no one, do you hear, no one will ever learn that Alla worked as a mannequin. In the spring you will see the great boulevards.

Somewhere outside a voice sings hollowly to a piano: "We will leave the place where we suffered so . . ."[8]

(*In a whisper.*) Is your beloved in Paris . . .

ALLA. Yes . . .

ZOYA. In the spring you are arm in arm with him, and he will never know.

ALLA. So *that's* the kind of workshop this is! So that's it! Work only in the evenings . . . Do you know who you are, Zoyka? You are the devil! You won't tell anyone, ever?

ZOYA. I swear it.

A pause.

Well, will you dive into the water all at once? *Allez!* . . .

ALLA. Agreed. I'll come three days from now.

ZOYA. Óop! (*She flings open the wardrobe, a blinding light flares up —Paris gowns glitter in it.*) Pick one, any of them—it's my gift!

Darkness. Zoya and Alla disappear in it. Then a burning lamp rises up. Evening has fallen. By the lamp sit Ametistov and Zoya.

AMETISTOV. There, you see what it means when Alexander Ametistov says something? I told you so!

ZOYA. You are not stupid, Alexander Ametistov.

AMETISTOV. Zoechka, just remember that half of your wealth has been created by my hands! You won't abandon your cousin? You'll take me with you? Won't you? Ah, Nice, Nice, when will I see you. The azure sea—and me on the shore in white pants!

ZOYA. I have one favor to ask you: don't speak French! At least don't speak it in front of Alla. She stares at you.

AMETISTOV. What is that supposed to mean? Perhaps I speak poorly.

ZOYA. You don't speak it poorly—you speak it nightmarishly!

8. From a popular song.

AMETISTOV. Zoya, that's insolence, *parole d'honneur:* I've been playing *chemin de fer* since I was ten, and now you say I speak French poorly!

ZOYA. And another thing. Why do you lie all the time? Just what kind of cuirassier, what the hell kind of cuirassier were you? And who needs it.

AMETISTOV. There is no greater pleasure for you than to say rotten things to people! If it were in my power, I'd ship you to Siberia just for your character.

ZOYA. Cut the babbling! Forget it, Goose is coming in a minute. I'm going to change clothes. (*She exits.*)

AMETISTOV. Goose? Why didn't you say so before? (*He gets panicky.*) Goose! Goose! And where is that Skylark Nest, the Heavenly Empire?! Niece Manyushka!

MANYUSHKA (*appearing*). Here I am!

AMETISTOV. I wonder what you are doing hanging around in there? What am I going to do, move everything by myself?

MANYUSHKA. I was washing the dishes.

AMETISTOV. You'll have time for the dishes. Help me!

He begins to move things around in the apartment and turn on lights. Obolyaninov *enters. He is wearing a frock coat.*

OBOLYANINOV. Good evening.

AMETISTOV. Maestro, my respects!

OBOLYANINOV. Excuse me, I've been meaning to ask you for a long time—call me by my first name and patronymic.

AMETISTOV. Why get offended? Such an eccentric! Among men of our circle . . . And what's so bad about the word "maestro"?

OBOLYANINOV. It is simply an unusual word which sets my teeth on edge—like the word "comrade."

AMETISTOV. *Pardon, pardon!* There is a big difference. Apropos of difference—you don't happen to have a cigarette?

OBOLYANINOV. Here you are.

AMETISTOV. *Merci beaucoup.* (*Looking around the apartment.*) *Voilà.* Why it's paradise! Count, you just cheer up! Why are you sitting like a kneading-trough?

OBOLYANINOV. What is a kneading-trough?

AMETISTOV. O.K., you aren't one to cheer up with! What do you think of the apartment?

OBOLYANINOV. Very cozy. It vaguely reminds me of my old apartment.

AMETISTOV. Was it a good one?

OBOLYANINOV. Very nice, only they took it away from me!

AMETISTOV. Really!

OBOLYANINOV. Some sort of guys with red beards came and tossed me out . . .

AMETISTOV. Who could imagine it! . . . Tell me! Such a sad story.

ZOYA (*enters*). Pavlik! Hello, my dear! Come into my room.

> *She exits with* Obolyaninov. *A code ring of the doorbell: three longs, two shorts.*

AMETISTOV. There he is! Damn him!

> Manyushka *runs out. After a while* Cherubim *enters.*

AMETISTOV. Where did you disappear to?

CHERUBIM. I had to ilon some shilts.

AMETISTOV. Well, to hell with you and your shirts. Did you bring the cocaine?

CHERUBIM. Yes.

AMETISTOV. Give it here! Listen you, Sham-poo-tea, look me in the eyes.

CHERUBIM. I am lookee you in eyes.

AMETISTOV. On your word of honor—did you cut it with aspirin?

CHERUBIM. No, no!

AMETISTOV. Ooh, I know you, you bandit! But if you cut it any, God will punish you!

CHERUBIM. Be little-little punishment.

AMETISTOV. Not little-little—he'll nail you to your spot! He'll clonk you on the head—and cross out one Chinaman! Don't cut the cocaine with aspirin! . . . No, it's good cocaine.

> Cherubim *puts on a Chinese coat and hat.*

AMETISTOV. And another thing! What the hell are you shaving your hair for? The price would be completely different if you had a braid!

A code doorbell rings. Marya Nikiforovna *enters.*

MARYA NIKIFOROVNA. Hello, Alexander Tarasovich! Hello, little Cherubim!

AMETISTOV. Go get dressed, Marya Nikiforovna, or it'll be too late. We are going to demonstrate new ensembles.

MARYA NIKIFOROVNA. They were sent? Oh, how nice! (*She runs out.*)

Cherubim *lights a Chinese lantern in a niche, it begins to emit smoke.*

AMETISTOV. Not too much.

CHERUBIM. I not too much ... (*He exits.*)

A code doorbell. Lizanka *enters.*

LIZANKA. Greetings to the manager of this nunnery!

AMETISTOV. *Bon soir* ...

Lizanka *goes out. A code doorbell. Hearing it,* Ametistov *runs to the mirror, spruces up.* Madame Ivanova *enters. A very beautiful, haughty woman.*

AMETISTOV. Hello, Madame Ivanova!

IVANOVA. Give me a cigarette.

AMETISTOV. Manyushka! A cigarette!

Manyushka *runs in, gives cigarettes to* Ivanova. *A pause.*

AMETISTOV. Is it cold outside?

IVANOVA. No.

AMETISTOV. We have a surprise: the ensembles have arrived from Paris.

IVANOVA. That's good.

AMETISTOV. They're wonderful!

IVANOVA. So.

AMETISTOV. Did you come on the trolley?

IVANOVA. Yes.

AMETISTOV. I suppose there were lots of people on the trolley?
IVANOVA. Yes.

A pause.

AMETISTOV. Your match ... went out ...
IVANOVA. Thank you. (*She exits.*)
AMETISTOV. (*to* Manyushka). Now there's a woman, by God! A man could live his entire life with her and not get bored! Not like you— always rumbling and grumbling ...

An imperious ring of the doorbell.

It's him! I recognize the ring of a Commercial Director! Excellent. He's ringing! Open up. Then hurry and change. Cherubim will help you.
CHERUBIM (*running through*). Goose coming!
MANYUSHKA. Lord! It's Goose! (*She runs out.*)
AMETISTOV. Zoya. Goose! Get to work, I am disappearing! (*He disappears.*)
ZOYA (*in an evening dress*). How happy I am, dear Boris Semyonovich!
GOOSE. Hello, Zoya Denisovna, hello!
ZOYA. Sit here, it's cozier here . . . Ay-ay-yay, what a bad man you are! A neighbor, a close acquaintance, you could have dropped in at least once . . .
GOOSE. Believe me, I could with pleasure, but . . .
ZOYA. I'm joking. I know you are up to your ears in work.
GOOSE. Don't remind me—it gives me insomnia.
ZOYA. Poor man, you have overworked yourself, you need some amusement.
GOOSE. There is no question of my amusing myself. (*He looks around the room.*) And you have a very nice place.
ZOYA. The workshop owes its existence to you.
GOOSE. Well, it's a trifle. About the workshop. I have come to see you partly on business. Only this is just between you and me. I need a Paris gown. You know, the latest thing, for about three hundred rubles.
ZOYA. I understand. A gift?

GOOSE. Between you and me.

ZOYA. Oh, you devil, in love! Well, confess it, you are in love?

GOOSE. Just between you and me.

ZOYA. Don't worry, I won't tell my husband. Oh, men, men! Well, all right. My manager will show you some ensembles now, and you pick out everything you like. And later we will have supper. Today you are mine, and I will not let you go!

GOOSE. *Merci.* You have a manager? Let's see what kind of manager you have.

ZOYA. You'll see him in a minute. (*She disappears.*)

AMETISTOV (*appears suddenly, wearing a frock coat*). *Quand on parle du soleil, on voit sa rayon*—which in translation means: "when one speaks of the sun, one sees its rays."

GOOSE. Are you telling me about the rays?

AMETISTOV. You, most deeply esteemed Boris Semyonovich! Allow me to introduce myself—Ametistov!

GOOSE. Goose.

AMETISTOV. You desire to have an ensemble? It's a good thing you've thought of, most deeply esteemed Boris Semyonovich. I can assure you that you won't find a selection like this anywhere else in Moscow. Cherubim!

Cherubim *appears.*

GOOSE. If you please, he's a Chinaman!

AMETISTOV. Yes sir, a Chinaman, with your blessing! Pay no attention to him, most respected Boris Semyonovich! He's a most ordinary son of the Celestial Empire, and he differs only in one quality—exemplary honesty.

GOOSE. But why a Chinaman!

AMETISTOV. He is my old and devoted servant, precious Boris Semyonovich. I brought him out of Shanghai where I had wandered for many years collecting materials.

GOOSE. That's remarkable. Materials for what?

AMETISTOV. For a large ethnographic work—I'll get around to telling you about my wanderings some other time, most deeply esteemed Boris Semyonovich. You will simply weep. Cherubim, give us something refreshing.

CHERUBIM. Light away. (*He disappears and immediately reappears carrying some champagne.*)

AMETISTOV. If you please.

GOOSE. Champagne? You have set up a remarkable business, Mr. Manager.

AMETISTOV. *Je pense!* Having worked at Paquin's in Paris, one may acquire tastes . . .

GOOSE. You worked in Paris?

AMETISTOV. For five years, dear Boris Semyonovich! Cherubim, you may go.

GOOSE. You know, if I believed in a life after death, I would say he really is a cherub.

AMETISTOV. And looking at him, one begins to believe almost involuntarily. Your health, highly respected Boris Semyonovich! And also the health of your Refractory Metals Trust! Hurrah! Hurrah! Hurrah! No, no! To the bottom! Don't insult your firm!

GOOSE. You have set up the business well.

AMETISTOV. *Milles mercis!* So, is she a blonde? A brunette?

GOOSE. Who?

AMETISTOV. *Pardon, pardon* . . . that esteemed creature for whom the ensemble is destined.

GOOSE. Just between you and me, she's a lovely brunette.

AMETISTOV. You have taste. I'll have another glass—and I'll ask you to get up. Your beautiful coat simply begs for a lovely brunette. You have tremendous taste, Boris Semyonovich! Cherubim!

Cherubim *appears.*

AMETISTOV. Ask the maestro in, and also Mademoiselle Liza.

CHERUBIM. Light away! (*He disappears.*)

Obolyaninov *comes in.* Obolyaninov *sits down at the piano.*

AMETISTOV. Get settled a little more comfortably, dear Boris Semyonovich, have some almonds. (*He claps his hands.*) Atelier!

Obolyaninov *begins to play. The curtain is flung open, and on a brightly lit stage* Lizanka *appears wearing a lux-*

urious and rather low-cut gown. Goose *looks at all of this in surprise.*

LIZANKA (*in a whisper.*) Should I beat it!

AMETISTOV. Beat it, Lizanka!

The curtain closes.

What do you think of this, priceless Boris Semyonovich?

GOOSE. Um—yes ...

AMETISTOV. Another glass?

GOOSE. You are a truly charming manager!

AMETISTOV. Why what are you saying, Boris Semyonovich, I acquired some manners in my time, I spent some time at the Imperial Court ...

GOOSE. You were at the court? ...

AMETISTOV. Oh, Boris Semyonovich! When I tell you certain secrets, you will burst into tears! ... Atelier!

The curtain is flung open, and on the stage Marya Nikiforovna *appears in a very low dress.* Obolyaninov *plays the piano.* Marya Nikiforovna *walks along the stage in time to the music.*

AMETISTOV. More animation! (*Softly.*)

MARYA NIKIFOROVNA (*softly*). Ignoramus!

AMETISTOV. *Vous êtes très aimable.*

The curtain closes.

Atelier!

Obolyaninov *plays "The moon is shining"*[9] *and on-stage* Manyushka *dances wearing an extremely low-cut Russian dress.*

CHERUBIM (*suddenly looks out, says in a whisper*). Manyuska, when you dance, lookee at me, no lookee at guests ...

MANYUSHKA (*in a whisper*). Go away, you jealous devil!

9. A Russian folk song ("Svetit mesjac, svetit jasnyj").

OBOLYANINOV (*suddenly*). I am playing, the maid is dancing on a stage, what is going on?

AMETISTOV. Shh . . . (*In a whisper.*) Manyushka, get the hell off the stage, set up dinner for two!

The curtain closes.

GOOSE (*suddenly*). Atelier!

AMETISTOV. Quite right, Boris Semyonovich. Atelier!

The curtain is flung open. Obolyaninov *plays a languorous waltz. On the stage is* Madame Ivanova *in a dress which is as low-cut as anything possible on the stage.* Ametistov *jumps up on the stage, dances with* Madame Ivanova, *whispers to her.*

AMETISTOV. Basically, I am very unhappy, Madame Ivanova . . . my dream is to go away to Nice with a woman I love . . .

MADAME IVANOVA (*in a whisper*). Babbler!

The dance ends.

AMETISTOV. Mademoiselle, please model the gown for monsieur. (*He disappears.*)

Madame Ivanova *comes off the stage like a figure from inside a picture frame and turns around in front of* Goose.

GOOSE (*confused*). I am very grateful to you . . . to the depths of my soul . . .

MADAME IVANOVA. Don't you dare look at me like that! You are insolent!

GOOSE (*confused*). Who said I was looking at you?

MADAME IVANOVA. No, you are insolent—there's something African in you. I like men like you. (*She abruptly disappears behind the curtain.*)

GOOSE (*furiously*). Atelier!

AMETISTOV. (*appears suddenly, the lights flare up*). Pardon, entr'-acte!

CURTAIN

ACT III

A GRAYISH DAY. AMETISTOV *is sitting in the living room beside the telephone looking sad.*

AMETISTOV (*after hiccoughing*). God damn it to hell! I can't get rid of it!

A pause. Obolyaninov *enters looking bored.*

AMETISTOV (*hiccoughing*). *Pardon!*

The telephone rings.

Cherubim, the telephone!

CHERUBIM (*on the telephone*). Yes silee . . . fol . . . fol . . . Goose— callee you. (*He exits.*)

AMETISTOV (*on the telephone*). Comrade Goose? How are you, Boris Semyonovich? Is your health good? Why, of course . . . we're waiting, we're waiting . . . just a little while . . . (*He hiccoughs abruptly.*) Pardon, someone must be thinking of me . . . What? A secret, a secret, a surprise awaits you, Boris Semyonovich . . . Goodbye, sir. (*He hiccoughs.*)

OBOLYANINOV. That fellow Goose is an amazingly vulgar man, don't you think so?

AMETISTOV. No, I don't. A man who earns five thousand rubles a months cannot be vulgar. (*He hiccoughs.*) Who's that thinking of me I'd like to know? What the hell does he have to do that for? Yes, sir, I respect Goose . . . Who trudges around Moscow on foot?—You do.

OBOLYANINOV. Excuse me, Monsieur Ametistov, I do not trudge, I walk.

AMETISTOV. Oh, don't take offense! What a person, by God! Well, all right, you walk, but he rides in an automobile. You sit in one room, *pardon, pardon,* perhaps the expression "you sit" is in-

139

decorous in high society—thus you *repose,* let us say. But Goose has seven rooms. You pound on your piano . . . *pardon,* you *play* for a month to get one hundred rubles, but Goose gets five thousand. You play, but Goose dances!

OBOLYANINOV. That's because this government has created conditions for life in which it is impossible for a decent person to live.

AMETISTOV. *Pardon, pardon!* A decent person can live under any conditions. I am a decent person, however I exist. I came to Moscow without any pants, brother, and now . . .

OBOLYANINOV. Excuse me, what kind of brother am I to you?

AMETISTOV. Why don't you stop being such an untouchable! What kind of trifles are these between members of the gentry?

OBOLYANINOV. Are you really a member of the gentry?

AMETISTOV. I like that question! Can't you see for yourself? (*He hiccoughs.*) Dammit . . .

OBOLYANINOV. But you see, I've never run across your name.

AMETISTOV. There are lots of names you've never run across! It's a well-known name from the Penza Province. Oh, signor! If you only knew what I bore, what I suffered from the Bolsheviks . . . They pillaged my estate, they burned my house down . . .

OBOLYANINOV. In what province was your estate?

AMETISTOV. Mine? Are you asking that about mine?

OBOLYANINOV. Well yes, the one they burned . . .

AMETISTOV. Oh, *that?* I don't want to think about it, because it's too painful for me . . . White columns, as I now recall . . . seven columns, one more beautiful than the next . . . Oh, but why talk about it! And pure-bred cattle! And a brick factory!

OBOLYANINOV. My aunt, Varvara Nikolaevna, had a fine stable.

AMETISTOV. What does it matter what your Aunt Varvara had? I personally had one, and what a great one it was! Why are you so depressed? Cheer up, old man!

OBOLYANINOV. I am feeling melancholy.

AMETISTOV. Imagine, I am too. Why? I don't know! Some sort of premonition . . . Cards are a cure for melancholy . . .

OBOLYANINOV. I don't like cards, I like horses. I had one horse, Pharaoh . . .

A voice begins to sing hollowly: "They remind me ..."[10]

AMETISTOV. And I like to play faro ...

OBOLYANINOV. ... a red coat, yellow sleeves, a black cross-belt ... Pharaoh ...

AMETISTOV. ... oh, your opponent starts betting, and you're bathed in sweat, sir! But then, when you trump his card in the middle of things, wham! It lies there as if cut down by a scythe! ... Who's got me all upset?! Oh! I'd like to get out of Moscow as fast as possible!

OBOLYANINOV. Yes! Yes! As fast as possible! I can't live here! ...

AMETISTOV. Don't get all unnerved, old fellow! Three more months —and we'll leave for Nice. Have you ever been in Nice, count?

OBOLYANINOV. Many times.

AMETISTOV. I was there too of course, only it was in early childhood. Oh, oh, oh! My late mother took me there . . . two governesses traveled with us, and my nanny. I had curly hair, you know . . . I wonder if there are any card sharps in Monte Carlo?

OBOLYANINOV. I don't know. Oh, I don't know anything ...

AMETISTOV. I've had it! Now there's exotic flora! Count, my colleague! Shall we take off for the "Bavaria" as soon as Zoechka comes?

OBOLYANINOV. You simply dumbfound me with what you say! There's dirt and nastiness in the beer-halls ...

AMETISTOV. You must not have seen the lobsters that they brought to the "Bavaria" yesterday. Every lobster was as big as a . . . Well, so as not to exaggerate, as big as a guitar! Cherubim!

Cherubim *appears.*

Listen, my dear major domo of the yellow race, if Zoya Denisovna comes, tell her that the Count and I have gone to the Tredyakov Gallery for a little while. Let's go, pops! Ho! Lobsters! (*He goes out with* Obolyaninov.)

CHERUBIM. Manyuska! They left!

MANYUSHKA (*runs out, kisses* Cherubim). What it is I like about

10. See note 3.

you, I can't imagine! You're yellow as an orange, but I like you!
Are you Chinese Lutherans?

CHERUBIM. Luthelans? We little-little washee clothes . . . Listen,
Manyuska, to impoltan business. We soon going, Manyuska! I
takee you Shanghai.

MANYUSHKA. I am not going to Shanghai.

CHERUBIM. You going.

MANYUSHKA. Who are you ordering around? What am I, your wife
or something?

CHERUBIM. I mallee you, Manyuska, in Shanghai.

MANYUSHKA. You have to ask me whether I will go or not. Did I
sign a contract with you or something?

CHERUBIM. Maybe you wantee mally Gandzalin?

MANYUSHKA. And even if it were Gandzalin, I'm a free woman, why
are you puffing up your Chinese cheeks, I'm not afraid of you!

CHERUBIM. Gandzalin?

MANYUSHKA. Never mind! Never mind!

CHERUBIM (*becomes terrifying*). Gandzalin!

MANYUSHKA. What's wrong with you?

CHERUBIM (*grabs* Manyushka *by the throat, takes out a knife*). I
going to cut youl thloat now. (*He chokes* Manyushka.) Tellee, you
kissee Gandzalin?

MANYUSHKA. Oy! Let go of my throat, little angel . . . Remember
your slave Maria, oh Lord . . .

CHERUBIM. You kissee him? You kissee?

MANYUSHKA. Little Cherubim, crystal one . . . I didn't kiss him . . .
don't cut the throat of an orphan . . . have pity on my young
life . . .

CHERUBIM (*puts the knife away*). You going to mally Gandzalin?

MANYUSHKA. No, no, no! . . .

CHERUBIM. You going to mally me?

MANYUSHKA. No . . . I *will*, I *will*. What is he doing, comrades?

CHERUBIM. I ploposed to you.

MANYUSHKA. What a proposal! What a fiancé with a knife . . .
You're a robber, you're a criminal, Cherubim!

CHERUBIM. No . . . I not climinal! I was sad . . . evelyone pulsecute
me . . . want to putee pool Chinaman in plison fol cocaine . . .

Gandzalin tyllanize ovel me muchee . . . I wash clothes all night long . . . he takee money, givee me folty kopeks . . . I suffeled cold . . . Chinaman can not live in cold Moscow . . . Chinaman useful live in Shanghai. . . . Listen, Manyuska, you get leady now, we soon going to go, I thought up way to getee many ten-luble notes . . .

MANYUSHKA. Oy, Cherubim, what did you think up? I'm afraid for you . . .

The doorbell.

Get into the kitchen!

Cherubim *disappears. She opens the door.*

Oy, my God, my Lord!

GANDZALIN. Herro, Manyuska!

MANYUSHKA. Oy! Go away, Gasoline . . .

GANDZALIN. No! I why go? I no go. You alone, Manyuska? I come to makee you ploposal.

MANYUSHKA. Go away, Gasoline!

GANDZALIN. No, why? What have you been saying to me, huh? You been saying you love. You fool Gandzalin?

MANYUSHKA. Why are you lying like that? I didn't tell you anything. Now I'll just call Zoya Denisovna . . .

GANDZALIN. You lie. She no home. Manyuska, you lie velly much! I love you!

MANYUSHKA. Have you got a knife? Tell me the truth, if you've got a knife . . .

GANDZALIN. I havc knife. To make a ploposal.

CHERUBIM (*appearing suddenly*). Who ploposal?

GANDZALIN. A-a-ah! So hele helpel! Oh, you! . . .

CHERUBIM. You get out of apaltment! Get out! . . . This is my apaltment, Zoya's, mine!

MANYUSHKA. Oy, what's going to happen!

GANDZALIN. Youl's? You bandit! You snatch apaltment. You wele rike dog? And you . . . I going to make ploposal to Manyuska!

CHERUBIM. I alleady make. She my wife. She rove me.

GANDZALIN. Stop! She my wife, she rove me!

MANYUSHKA. He's lying, little Cherubim, he's lying!

CHERUBIM. Get out my apaltment!

GANDZALIN. You get out! I will tell porice evelything, what kind Chinese chalactel you ale!

CHERUBIM. To the porice? . . . (*He hisses.*)

GANDZALIN (*hisses*).

MANYUSHKA. Little rabbits, dear boys! Just don't cut each other, you devils!

CHERUBIM. Ah-ah-ah! . . . (*Suddenly pulls out his knife, rushes at* Gandzalin.)

MANYUSHKA. Help! Help! Help!

GANDZALIN (*throws himself into the mirrored wardrobe, slams the door behind him.*)

The doorbell.

MANYUSHKA. Help! Throw that knife down, you damned devil!

The doorbell.

CHERUBIM. I stab him latel. (*He locks the wardrobe with a key, hides the key in his pocket and disappears.*)

Manyushka *opens the door and into the anteroom walk two strange men in civilian clothes, both carrying briefcases.*

FIRST STRANGER. Hello, comrades! Were you calling for help?

MANYUSHKA. Why no, what kind of help? I was singing . . .

SECOND STRANGER. A-ah!

MANYUSHKA. And what do you want, comrades?

FIRST STRANGER. Comrade, we are the commission. We have come to inspect your workshop.

MANYUSHKA. But the directress is not here right now . . . There is no work today . . .

FIRST STRANGER. And who might you be?

MANYUSHKA. I am a student model.

SECOND STRANGER. Well, then you show us around. Otherwise, we will have to make two trips.

MANYUSHKA. Well, please then . . .

FIRST STRANGER. What's in here?

MANYUSHKA. This is the measuring room.

FIRST STRANGER. It's a good room, and what's this? Are things measured on them? (*He points to the mannequins.*)

MANYUSHKA. Of course, on the mannequins ...

FIRST STRANGER. Then what are the models for?

MANYUSHKA. That's for when the dresses are measured while walking—so then they put them on a student ...

FIRST STRANGER. Aha.

SECOND STRANGER (*pulls the curtain aside.* Cherubim *turns out to be standing behind the curtain with an iron in his hand*). Hm, a Chinaman!

MANYUSHKA. He comes to us from the laundry. He irons skirts ...

FIRST STRANGER. Aha.

Cherubim *spits on the iron and exits with it.*

FIRST STRANGER. Well, let's go further. (*He walks on, behind him goes* Manyushka.)

SECOND STRANGER (*having been left alone, he quickly takes out some keys, opens one wardrobe, examines it, closes it, opens a second, jumps away from it. In the wardrobe, hunched up, sits* Gandzalin *with a knife in his hand*). A second one! S-sh! . . . You sit in here?

GANDZALIN. I sitting.

SECOND STRANGER (*in a whisper*). And what do you do here?

GANDZALIN (*tearfully*). I hide a little . . . Chelubim bandit . . . just now want stab me . . . save me . . .

SECOND STRANGER. Quiet you! I'll save you, I'll save you. But who are you?

GANDZALIN. I am Gandzalin, honolable Chinese. I made ploposal to maid, and he almost stab me! He bling opium hele to this apaltment.

SECOND STRANGER. Aha, so, so . . . Get yourself out of the wardrobe, go to the police department and wait for me there. Only don't get any ideas about running away, I'll find you at the bottom of the sea.

GANDZALIN. I no lun away, only you take Chelubim—he bandit! (*He hops out of the wardrobe, exits into the anteroom, disappears.*)

Second Stranger *exits where* Manyushka *and the* First
Stranger *went. After a little while all three return.*

FIRST STRANGER. Well! Everything is *fine*—it's light and airy. It's
an excellently set up workshop.
SECOND STRANGER. What can one say?
FIRST STRANGER (*to* Manyushka). Well, here's what we'll do, comrade—tell the directress that the commission was here and found
the workshop in exemplary order. We will send you a paper.
SECOND STRANGER. My respects to her.

They both exit into the anteroom. Manyushka *closes the
door behind them.*

CHERUBIM (*flies out like a storm, carrying his knife*). A-ah, they
leave? Tell the porice? I showee you! (*He rushes to the ward-
robe.*)
MANYUSHKA. You devil! Help! Help! Help!
CHERUBIM (*opens the wardrobe and turns to stone*). The bastald!
He had key!

CURTAIN

ACT IV

NIGHT. *Zoya's living room is illuminated by lamps with shades. The Chinese lantern is burning in its niche.* CHERUBIM *is sitting in the niche wearing his exotic clothing—he looks like a Buddha. Outside the doors one can hear the strumming of two guitars, and one can hear several voices singing: "Hey once, now twice . . ." The mannequins stand there smiling, one cannot determine if they are alive or dead. There are many flowers in vases.*

AMETISTOV (*looking out the doors*). Cherubim! Some champagne!
CHERUBIM. Light away! (*He exits. After a little while he returns and again sits down in the niche.*)

> *The sounds of the guitars are replaced by a piano on which a fox-trot is being played. In through the doors comes* The Dead Body. *It looks around mournfully, walks over to* Cherubim.

DEAD BODY. Madame, may I ask you . . .
CHERUBIM. I not any madam.
DEAD BODY. What the hell. (*It walks up to one of the mannequins.*) One *tour*, madame, don't you wish to? As you wish . . . Smile, please . . . only watch out that you don't have to cry afterwards . . . (*Then it goes up to the second mannequin.*) Madame . . . (*It puts its arms around the waist of the mannequin, begins to dance with it.*) Never in my life have I held in my arms such a waist . . . (*Looks more closely into the eyes of the mannequin, pushes it away, cries bitterly.*)
AMETISTOV (*hops out through the doors*). Ivan Vasilievich! *Pardon, pardon* . . . why are you so upset? What is it you lack in life?
DEAD BODY. Scoundrel! You!

AMETISTOV. Ivan Vasilievich, I will pour some bicarbonate of soda for you.

DEAD BODY. A new insult! Everybody else gets champagne, but I get bicarbonate of soda!

AMETISTOV. Ivan Vasilievich, my dear fellow . . .

> *During this scene the door at the back of* Zoya's *half-lit bedroom opens, and* Portupeya *appears noiselessly in the bedroom, hides behind the portière, and observes what is happening. From the doors appears* Robber.

ROBBER. Ivan Vasilievich, what's wrong with you? ,

DEAD BODY. They're giving me bicarbonate of soda!

MARYA NIKIFOROVNA (*appears in the living room*). Ivan Vasilievich, dear!

DEAD BODY. Everybody get away from me! . . .

> Zoya *appears in the living room.*

ROBBER. Zoya Denisovna, accept my deepest apologies, from Ivan Vasilievich too.

ZOYA. It's nothing, things like this happen.

AMETISTOV. Get busy—take him to dance.

> Marya Nikiforovna *draws the crying* Dead Body *toward the doors.* Ametistov *follows them.*

ROBBER. Zoya Denisovna, your *soirée* is enchanting! Oh, by the way, so as not to forget when I'm saying goodbye . . . how much do I owe you?

ZOYA. We pool our money for these *soirées* . . . Two hundred rubles.

ROBBER. I see . . . I will pay for Ivan Vasilievich too. That means two hundred plus two hundred . . .

ZOYA. Four hundred . . .

ROBBER. Right . . . (*He hands her the money.*) *Merci.* Zoya Denisovna, one dance.

ZOYA. Oh no, I don't dance.

ROBBER. Oh, Zoya Denisovna, why not? (*He exits.*)

Cherubim *suddenly moves, looks toward the side where the anteroom is.* Manyushka *has looked out of there and made some sort of sign.* Zoya *nods her head. At this time* Alla Vadimovna *appears noiselessly from the doors. She is wearing an overcoat and a veil.*

ZOYA (*in a whisper*). Hello, Allochka! (*To* Manyushka.) Take Alla Vadimovna into her room, put her gown on her.

Manyushka *exits with* Alla *through the bedroom.* Cherubim *disappears noiselessly.* Portupeya *moves the portière aside and appears.*

ZOYA (*trembles, steps back*). What does this mean, Portupeya? How did you get in here?

PORTUPEYA (*in a whisper*). Through the back door. I have the keys to all the apartments. Well there, Zoya Denisovna, what a workshop! Well, now I understand everything!

ZOYA (*gives some money to* Portupeya). Disappear, be quiet! When they've all left, come back again!

PORTUPEYA. Zoya Denisovna, be more careful! . . .

ZOYA. Go on . . .

Portupeya *exits through the bedroom,* Zoya *behind him. A soft fox-trot can be heard on the other side of the doors. Through the doors comes* Goose. *He is looking gloomy.*

GOOSE. Goose, you're drunk! . . . You're so drunk, Mr. Commercial Director of Refractory Metals, that you can't get your tongue straightened out! . . . You're the only one who knows why you're drunk, but you won't tell anyone, because you're proud! . . . Women are whirling around you and cheering up the Director, but you are not cheerful . . . Your soul is gloomy . . . (*To a mannequin.*) . . . oh, mannequin! . . .

Zoya *appears noiselessly in the bedroom.*

To you alone, silent mannequin, I will entrust my secret: I . . .

ZOYA. Am in love!

GOOSE. A-ah, Zoyka! You overheard me? Well, so what . . . Zoya! A snake has entrapped my heart . . . Oh, Zoya, I'm almost sure that she's no good . . . but she has conquered me!

ZOYA. Is it worth tormenting yourself, dear Goose! You will find another!

GOOSE. Oh, no, never! But it makes no difference, Zoya, show me someone else so that I can forget about her for a while anyway— and squeeze her out of my heart . . . Zoya, she doesn't love me!

ZOYA. Oh, my Goose, my old friend, wait a few minutes and you will see a woman who will make you forget everything in the world! And she will be yours, because what woman can resist you, Goose?

GOOSE. Thank you, Zoyka, for the kind words!

> Obolyaninov *and* Ametistov *come out of the doors, both wearing frock coats.*

GOOSE. I want to reward you, how much do I owe you?

ZOYA. Goose, I don't want to take anything from you.

GOOSE. You don't want to take it, but I want to give it. Take five hundred rubles!

ZOYA. *Merci.*

GOOSE (*to* Ametistov). A-ah! Mr. Manager! You have set up a paradise in which an exhausted soul has rested! Take this!

AMETISTOV. *Danke sehr.*

GOOSE (*to* Obolyaninov). Count! You play the piano beautifully! Please! (*He hands him some money.*)

OBOLYANINOV. *Merci.* When times change I will send you my seconds.

GOOSE. I'll give them some too!

AMETISTOV. Bravo! Boris Semyonovich! Boris Semyonovich, your attention please! A change of decorations! Now a new gown is to be modelled. Light! (*He turns out the light.*)

> *For a few moments the entire apartment is in darkness, then the lights pour a dim light on everything. In the living room sit* Goose, Zoya, Robber, Dead Body, Marya Nikiforovna, Lizanka *and* Madame Ivanova. Obolyaninov

is at the piano. Ametistov *rises up by the curtain which covers over the niche.*

AMETISTOV. Attention! The lilac gown! Shown in Paris! The price— six thousand francs! *Atelier!*

Obolyaninov *begins a waltz.* Alla *steps out on the stage to the music.*

EVERYONE. Bravo!!

GOOSE. What is this?

ALLA. Oh, it's you? How did you get here?

GOOSE. How do you like that question? She asks how I got here when I ought to be asking her how she got here.

ALLA. I have begun work as a model.

GOOSE. As a model! The woman I love! The woman whom I intend to marry, after abandoning my wife and two babies, has begun working as a model? And do you know, unhappy woman, where you have begun?

ALLA. In a dress shop.

GOOSE. Well, of course, it's spelled "dress shop," and pronounced "bordello!"

ROBBER. Wh-a-at! What is that?

GOOSE. Dear comrades, have you ever seen a dress shop where the outfits are shown at night, to music?

DEAD BODY. True! . . . What's the reason for the music? Be so kind.

AMETISTOV. *Pardon, pardon . . .*

ZOYA. Aha, now I see! (*She imitates* Alla.) "I haven't had anyone, Zoya Denisovna, since my husband died . . ." Oh, you clown, you clown! Why I asked you, I warned you! Thanks for the scandal, Allochka!

GOOSE. Zoya Denisovna, you are displaying my fiancée as a model.

ALLA. I am not your fiancée!

GOOSE. Between us, she is my mistress!

DEAD BODY. Thank God, they've cheered up! . . .

OBOLYANINOV. I'll ask you not to offend the woman!

GOOSE. Leave me alone, piano player!

ZOYA. Gentlemen, this is a small misunderstanding, it will be cleared

up immediately. Gentlemen, I'll ask you into the next room . . .
Please be so kind, Ametistov!

AMETISTOV. *Pardon, pardon,* please, gentlemen, please! A general
and grandiose fox-trot. And then a small intimate explanation . . .
Such events are not rare in high society . . . Ivan Vasilievich!
Lizanka, get busy!

The women lead the men through the doors. Ametistov *and*
Obolyaninov *exit with them.* Zoya *remains in the niche and
listens to the conversation.*

GOOSE. You? In an atelier?!

ALLA. And just how did *you* get into this dress shop?

GOOSE. Me? I'm a man! I wear trousers! And not dresses that have
necklines down to the waist! I came here because you drank all
of my blood! And why did you?

ALLA. I came for money.

GOOSE. Why do you need money?

ALLA. I want to go abroad.

GOOSE. I won't give you any for that. Again this damned abroad!

ALLA. And I wanted to get it here.

GOOSE. You had everything in Moscow—even birds' milk! I pro-
posed to you seven times! Abroad! . . . What do you think—that
everyone is waiting for you abroad? That in Paris the president
is upset that Alla Vadimovna has not come!

ALLA. Yes, he's upset, only not the president—but my fiancé!

GOOSE. Who? Fiancé? Fiancé? Well, do you know, if you have a
fiancé, you . . . you . . . are trash!

ALLA. Don't you dare insult me! I hid it, true. But I didn't at all
suppose that you would fall in love with me! I wanted to get
money from you to go abroad and take off! . . .

GOOSE. Take it, but stay!

ALLA. No, not for anything!

GOOSE. A-ah, now! . . . When you're wearing my rings, that's something to stay for! . . . You just look at your fingers!

ALLA (*tears off the rings, throws them on the floor*). Take that!
And that!

GOOSE. To hell with the rings! Answer me, are you going with me or not?

ALLA. No, I'm not!

GOOSE. I'll count to three. One! Two! . . . I'll count to ten!

ALLA. Stop it, Boris Semyonovich, don't bother counting. I will not go. I do not love you.

GOOSE. Loose woman!

ALLA. How dare you . . .

ZOYA (*in the niche*). Ooh, the damn fool!

AMETISTOV (*appearing suddenly*). Pardon, pardon, Boris Semyonovich!

GOOOSE. Get out!

AMETISTOV. *Pardon, pardon,* Boris Semyonovich! . . . Alla Vadimovna, please, you must rest! . . . She will calm down . . .

ALLA (*going*). Zoya Denisovna, I am very sorry that I was the cause of a scandal . . . I will return the gown to you . . .

ZOYA. I will make a gift of it to you—for stupidity, you little idiot!

GOOSE. Stop! Where are you going? Abroad?

ALLA. I'll escape even if I die trying.

Ametistov *throws an overcoat around* Alla, *and she disappears.*

GOOSE. I will not let you do that.

ZOYA. Calm him down, calm him.

AMETISTOV. All right, all right, I will. Go to your guests . . .

Zoya *exits, closes the door behind her.*

GOOSE (*into space*). You'll end up selling things in the Smolensk Market, you'll land in a hospital! And then I'll see how you look in your lilac gown . . . (*He drops to the rug in grief.*)

AMETISTOV. Boris Semyonovich, the rug is dirty! . . . It'll all work out! Is she the only one in the world? To hell with her! She isn't even pretty, *entre nous soit,* quite *ordinaire.*

GOOSE. Go away, I am grieving . . .

AMETISTOV. Now that's excellent! You grieve a bit . . . Here's a little liqueur and some cigarettes for you . . . (*He disappears.*)

Off-stage a fox-trot.

GOOSE (*grieving*). Goose is grieving . . . Why are you grieving, poor man? Because you suffered an irreparable tragedy . . . Oh, how unhappy I am! I had achieved everything that a man can achieve, and now poisonous love has cut me down, and I'm lying on the rug. And where? In a whore house! . . . Alla! Come back! (*Loudly.*) Alla! Come back!

AMETISTOV (*appearing*). Not so loud, Boris Semyonovich, or the proletariat downstairs will hear . . . (*He disappears, closing the door.*)

> Cherubim *appears noiselessly, walks over to* Goose.

GOOSE. Go away, I'm grieving . . .

CHERUBIM. Why fol you glieving?

GOOSE. Not a single human face can I see—only you are sympatico . . . Cherubim, little Chinaman . . . Sadness is ripping me apart, and that's why I'm on the rug . . .

CHERUBIM. Sadness . . . I too sad . . .

GOOSE. Oh, Chinaman! What have you to be sad about? The whole future is in front of you . . .

CHERUBIM. Did madam tlick you? All madams muchee no good . . . So what? You gettee new madam . . . Many madams in Moscow . . .

GOOSE. I can't get another madam.

CHERUBIM. You no havee money?

GOOSE. Oh, dear Chinaman! How could it ever happen that I wouldn't have money? But the one thing my brain cannot think up is how to turn money into love! Look! (*He tosses fat wads of ten-ruble notes out of his pockets.*) I got five thousand this morning! And this evening—a blow which has laid me low! And here I lie on the open road, and may every passerby spit on the conquered Goose as I spit on these ten-ruble notes!

CHERUBIM. You spitee on money? Funny! You havee money, but no madam! . . . I havee madam, but whele money? You lettee me feel money? . . .

GOOSE. Feel it . . .

CHERUBIM. Ah, ten-luble notes, ten-luble notes, dealies . . . (*He suddenly strikes* Goose *under the shoulder-blade with his Finnish knife.* Goose *falls silent without a cry.*) Ten-luble notes . . . and walm Shanghai! (*He puts the money in his pockets, tears the watch and chain from* Goose's *body and the rings from his fingers, wipes his knife off on* Goose's *jacket, picks* Goose *up, puts him in an armchair, turns up the light, and says in a whisper.*) Manyuska!

MANYUSHKA (*looking out*). What do you want?

CHERUBIM. Shh . . . Now we flee to Shanghai . . . to lailload station . . .

MANYUSHKA. What have you done, you devil?

CHERUBIM. I stab Goose . . .

MANYUSHKA. Ah . . . You demon! . . . Demon! . . .

CHERUBIM. You flee, ol I gonna stab you! Pletty soon gonna be bloody mess! . . .

MANYUSHKA. My Lord! My Lord! (*She disappears with* Cherubim.)

AMETISTOV (*entering quietly*). Boris Semyonovich, I just came in for a second to check. . . . Well, how do you feel? Hey, how you've gotten over the excitement! Your hand is all cold . . . (*He looks more closely.*) What's this? Son of a bitch! The bandit! A bloody mess! This, ladies and gentlemen, was not in the program! What should I do now? Hm? He's come to a bad end! *Kaput!* Cherubim! Yes . . . of course, he robbed him and took off . . . Ah! I am an idiot! There's Nice for you! There's "abroad" for you! (*A pause—absently.*) "It was in the evening, and the stars were shining . . ."[11] What am I sitting here for? Get moving! (*He throws off his frock coat and tie, runs into* Zoya's *bedroom, opens the desk, takes some papers and money out, puts them in his pocket, removes his ancient suitcase from under the bed, and takes out of it his service-jacket; he puts this and a cap on.*) My faithful comrade, my suitcase, again we are alone together. But where should we head now? Explain to me, comrade, where we should head? Oh, my star, my inconsolable star! . . . Oh, my Fate! Farewell, Zoya, forgive me! I could do no other! Farewell, Zoya's apartment! (*He disappears with the suitcase.*)

A pause. The door into the bedroom opens quietly, and the

11. A refrain from a soldier's song: "Nightingale, nightingale."

First *and* Second Strangers *enter, and behind them are two other* Strangers.

ZOYA (*appearing in the living room*). Boris Semyonovich, are you alone? Where is Ametistov? (*She looks more closely.*) Oh, my God, my God! We are done for! Oh, my God! (*Softly, through the door.*) Pavel Fyodorovich!

Obolyaninov *enters.*

ZOYA. Pavlik, disaster has struck! Look! (*She points to* Goose.)
OBOLYANINOV (*having looked at him*). What's wrong?
ZOYA. Pavlik, it's disaster! The Chinaman did it! He and Ametistov! Pavlik, we have to run! Run, right now!
OBOLYANINOV. What do you mean, run?
ZOYA. Pavlik, wake up, can't you see that there's been a murder in the apartment! And what am I . . . Oh, the money in the bedroom! Run . . .
FIRST STRANGER (*coming out*). Take it easy, citizeness, we have warrants.
OBOLYANINOV. Zoya, what is going on in this apartment?
ZOYA. Oh, I understand! It's the end, Pavlik! Be a man. Remember, we aren't guilty!
SECOND STRANGER. Who is dancing in there?
ZOYA. Those are my guests. Just remember, we are not part of the murder. The Chinaman and Ametistov did that.
FIRST STRANGER. Take it easy, citizeness. (*He goes to the door and opens it.*) Your documents, citizens!

Darkness. Light appears again. The First Stranger *is sitting at a little table, the* Second Stranger *is examining the room, the* Third Stranger *is standing by the door smoking. From the door leading into the bedroom* PORTUPEYA *appears quietly, enters the living room, is surprised.*

FIRST STRANGER. What do you want, citizen?
PORTUPEYA. This is rather strange. I could ask the same thing: what do you want here in this apartment? I am the representative of the House Committee.

FIRST STRANGER. A-a-ah, how very pleasant.
PORTUPEYA. I want Zoya Denisovna.
SECOND STRANGER. Immediately. (*He exits, then returns with* Zoya *and* Obolyaninov. *They are both pale and taciturn.* Zoya *is supporting* Obolyaninov *by the arm.* Portupeya *is dumbfounded.*)
SECOND STRANGER. Well, what did you want to tell Zoya Denisovna?
PORTUPEYA (*sensing things are bad*). And who might you be?
FIRST STRANGER. Did you know Goose?
PORTUPEYA. Of course, he lives in our building.
SECOND STRANGER. Lived.
PORTUPEYA (*shuddering*). Comrades, I noticed a long time ago that this was a suspicious apartment . . . I was going to inform tomorrow . . .
ZOYA. The bastard! I paid him money! He has my banknotes in his pockets right now!

Portupeya *tries to swallow a banknote.*

SECOND STRANGER (*taking the banknote away*). Are you defective, or what? Do you munch banknotes?
FIRST STRANGER. They cut up Goose right under your nose, and you're busy using banknotes as hors-d'oeuvres!
PORTUPEYA (*falls to his knees*). Comrades! I am not very conscious!
. . . (*With pathos.*) Comrades, taking into consideration my ignorance and unenlightenment as my heritage from the tsarist regime, consider a suspended sentence! . . . What am I saying . . . I don't know myself . . .
FIRST STRANGER. All right, get up. (*To* Zoya.) *Put on your coat, madam, it is time to go.*

Portupeya *sobs bitterly.*

FIRST STRANGER. Don't sob, you'll go together.
ZOYA (*pointing to* Obolyaninov). Just remember that my husband is sick. Don't you insult him . . .
FIRST STRANGER. He will be put in a hospital . . .
ZOYA. Farewell, farewell, my apartment! . . .
OBOLYANINOV. My mind is clouded . . . Tuxedo . . . blood . . . (*To the*

Second Stranger.) Excuse me, please, I wanted to ask you—why are you wearing tuxedos?

SECOND STRANGER. We intended to come to your place as guests.

OBOLYANINOV. Excuse me, please, but one must never wear yellow shoes with a tuxedo.

SECOND STRANGER (*to the* First Stranger). Didn't I tell you so?!

THE END

FLIGHT

Eight Dreams

A Play in Four Acts

Immortality—is a calm, bright shore;
Our journey—a striving toward it.
Let him rest, who has ended his flight!
              ZHUKOVSKY [1]

---

1. The epigraph is from Vasily Zhukovsky's poem "A Singer in the Camp of Russian Soldiers" (1812).

INTRODUCTION

Flight WAS THE FIRST of Bulgakov's plays to be banned before it was premièred. Bulgakov worked on the play from 1926 to 1928, and after much public discussion the play was given permission to be staged only at MXAT. This was on the 11th of October 1928. By the 24th of October it was banned.

Despite a speech by Gorky, a defense by Nemirovich-Danchenko, and the approval of Lunacharsky and Stanislavsky, the Central Repertory Committee saw *Flight* as a glorification of White generals. The chief complaints apparently had to do with the figure of Charnota, who was too attractive for the censors' liking. The censors, never famous for subtlety of understanding, apparently did not sense the irony in the comic scenes. At any rate, the play was banned. However, the theater did not give up hope of staging it. In January of 1929 the director N. N. Litovtseva was again working on *Flight,* and Nemirovich-Danchenko was preparing to oversee the rehearsals. By January 30, however, whatever pressure had been applied had failed, and Leonidov wrote Stanislavsky: "Bulgakov's *Flight* has been banned totally. If the author will agree to change the play basically, then they will discuss it again as a newly-written play." But Bulgakov refused. He did not choose to completely rewrite the play. In 1933 the theater again discussed doing *Flight*—this was a year after *The Days of the Turbins* had been granted permission to play again. Presumably the theater felt that it might be safe to try again with *Flight.* The play was then rehearsed a few times by Stanislavsky. But by March 1934 Stanislavsky was convinced that *Flight* would not be granted permission.

It was the critics who were responsible for the first ban of *The Days of the Turbins,* but it was Stalin who was behind the banning of *Flight*. On February 2, 1929, he wrote a letter to the playwright Bill-Belotserkovsky in which he aired his views:

> *Flight* is a manifestation of an attempt to elicit pity, if not liking, for certain levels of anti-Soviet émigré society—therefore an attempt to justify or half-justify the White Guard movement. *Flight,* as it stands, is an anti-Soviet phenomenon.

It is difficult to understand Stalin's objections to *Flight,* which seems the most politically orthodox of all Bulgakov's plays.

Formally, *Flight* was one of the most unorthodox of Bulgakov's plays, and it is perhaps because of its blend of tragedy, melodrama, farce, and comedy that the critics were suspicious of it. The nightmarish "dreams" of *Flight* were light-years away from the conventional realistic scenes of *The Days of the Turbins.* Of the two plays *Flight* is the more Bulgakovian in form. Bulgakov was not allowed free rein in the writing of *The Days of the Turbins*—a striking dream sequence was cut, the panoramic view of Kiev was edited out, the number of scenes reduced. But in *Flight* the curtain did not come down between acts—the actors of one scene were extinguished in darkness and those in the next were illuminated. As a "mystical" writer, Bulgakov favored fade-out/fade-in techniques which fit well with his view of the world as a place where events happen suddenly and irrevocably. The darkness at the end of the "dreams" (as the scenes are called) in *Flight* is not just a theatrical device—it is a comment. For example, at the end of the First Dream, the stage directions read: "Mist eats up the monastery. The first dream ends." And at the end of the play: "Constantinople begins to be extinguished and is extinguished forever." In general *Flight* is a very "literary" play—it has an evocative series of epigraphs (unique in Bulgakov's plays), and the long poetic stage directions are meant for a reader.

There are other differences between *The Days of the Turbins* and *Flight.* In *The Days of the Turbins* we are shown the cozy apartment of the Turbins which serves as a refuge for them as the world outside is crumbling. The characters in *Days,* for the most part, adjust to the new order of things. The Turbin world is basically a well-ordered and static one—even Alexei's death does not destroy this impression. In *Flight,* however, disorder is everywhere, the apocalypse has come. The characters run, looking for refuge and never finding it. Each hiding place turns out to be a trap of one sort or another—the monastery, Khludov's camp, Constantinople.

The plays are remarkably dissimilar thematically as well as formally—even though both show the Civil War from the point of view of the Whites. *Flight* does not, as some critics claim, describe what later happens to the characters in *Days.* The only character in the earlier play who would belong in *Flight* is Studzinsky, who is planning to join the White forces elsewhere and continue the fight against the Bolsheviks. Some of the characters in *Flight* may have traits reminiscent of figures from *The Days of the Turbins,* but they are not the same, nor are they meant to be. *Flight* is not a sequel—it shows another side of the White movement. The *Whites* in the first play (except for Studzinsky) have become disillusioned and they come to accept the inevitability of a Bolshevik victory. In *Flight* we see the fate of Whites who kept fighting. The play shows the reasons for the White failure, and what the punishment for this failure is.

In historical or political terms, *Flight* is unsatisfying. The reasons for the White defeat (the people are not with them) are simple-minded; the return to the fatherland of Khludov, Serafima, and Golubkov rings suspiciously like a socialist-realist ending, even though the character of Khludov is based on the real General Slashchov. The White émigrés are shown as either swine if they manage to be happy away from the fatherland (Korzukhin), or frivolous (Charnota). Most of the émigrés, of course, are depicted as utterly miserable—poverty-stricken both physically and spiritually. This is an understandable "punishment" for a character like Khludov who has committed terrible acts of cruelty, but why should Charnota, who has simply been born on the White side, end as a vagabond? The author of *The Days of the Turbins* would not have punished White officers merely for happening to be on the wrong side, but the author of *Flight* seems to view the matter more simply.

Read as a denigration of the Whites who emigrated, the play seems to be political propaganda—intelligent propaganda to be sure. To read the play simply as a political statement, however, is to ignore its central theme: the ways in which one group of people react to the violent disintegration of their world. Serafima and Go-lubkov can represent any innocent bystanders swept into the cen-trifuge of history; Khludov could be any military leader who has committed crimes against humanity in the name of military expediency.

CAST OF CHARACTERS

SERAFIMA VLADIMIROVNA KORZUKHINA, a young St. Petersburg lady.

SERGEI PAVLOVICH GOLUBKOV, the son of an idealist professor from St. Petersburg.

AFRIKAN, Archbishop of Simferopol and Karasubazar, Spiritual Head of a distinguished army; he is also the chemist MAKHROV.

PAISY, a monk.

THE DECREPIT FATHER SUPERIOR.

BAEV, commander of a regiment in Budyonny's[2] cavalry.

A BUDYONNY SOLDIER.

GRIGORY LUKIANOVICH CHARNOTA, a Zaporozhe Cossack by descent, a cavalry man, a major-general in the White army.

BARABANCHIKOVA, a lady, existing only in the imagination of GENERAL CHARNOTA.

LYUSKA, the camp wife of GENERAL CHARNOTA.

KRAPILIN, CHARNOTA's orderly, who perishes because of his own eloquence.

DE BRISAR, commander of a Hussar regiment in the White army.

ROMAN VALERIANOVICH KHLUDOV.

GOLOVAN, Cossack captain, KHLUDOV's adjutant.

COMMANDANT of the railway station.

STATIONMASTER.

NIKOLAEVNA, wife of the STATIONMASTER.

OLKA, daughter of the STATIONMASTER, four years old.

---

2. Budyonny was a famous Cossack commander in the Civil War.

PARAMON ILICH KORZUKHIN, husband of SERAFIMA.

TIKHI, head of counter-intelligence.

SKUNSKY
GURIN } counter-intelligence agents.

THE COMMANDER-IN-CHIEF OF THE WHITE ARMY.

A LITTLE FACE IN THE TICKET BOOTH.

ARTUR ARTUROVICH, the cockroach king.

A FIGURE wearing a bowler hat and quartermaster corps shoulder straps.

A TURKISH WOMAN, a loving mother.

A BEAUTIFUL PROSTITUTE.

A GREEK DON JUAN.

ANTOINE GRISHCHENKO, KORZUKHIN's lackey.

MONKS, WHITE STAFF OFFICERS, CONVOY COSSACKS OF THE WHITE COMMANDER-IN-CHIEF, COUNTER-INTELLIGENCE AGENTS, COSSACKS in burkas, ENGLISH, FRENCH, and ITALIAN SAILORS, TURKISH and ITALIAN POLICEMEN, GREEK and TURKISH URCHINS, ARMENIANS and GREEKS in windows, the CROWD in Constantinople.

The First Dream takes place in Northern Tavria in October of 1920.

The Second, Third, and Fourth—the beginning of November 1920, in the Crimea.

The Fifth and Sixth—Constantinople in the summer of 1921.

The Seventh—Paris in the fall of 1921.

The Eighth—the fall of 1921 in Constantinople.

ACT I

DREAM ONE

...I dreamed of a monastery ...[3]

ONE CAN HEAR *a chorus of monks singing hollowly in the catacomb:* "Holy Father Nikolai, pray to God for us ..."

Darkness, and then the inside of a monastery church appears, dimly lit by tiny candles in front of the ikons. An unsteady flame reveals a little booth in which candles are sold, a broad bench beside it, a window covered with a shutter, the chocolate-colored face of a saint, the faded wings of seraphims, golden halos. Outside the window it is a dismal October evening with sleet and snow. On the bench lies BARABANCHIKOVA *covered from the head down with a horse blanket.*

The chemist MAKHROV, *wearing a sheepskin jacket, has stationed himself at the window and keeps trying to make out something outside.*

In the Father Superior's high arm chair sits SERAFIMA, *wearing a black fur coat. Judging by her face, she is not well.*

At SERAFIMA's *feet on a small bench, beside a suitcase, sits* GOLUBKOV, *a young man who looks like a St. Petersburger, wearing a black overcoat and gloves.*

GOLUBKOV (*listening to the singing*). Do you hear, Serafima Vladimirovna? I knew they had a catacomb below . . . Really, how strange this all is! You know, at times it begins to seem to me that I am having a dream, honestly! It's been a month now that

---

3. Most of the epigraphs appear to have been made up by Bulgakov. Exceptions are noted as they occur.

I have been fleeing with you Serafima Vladimirovna, through villages and cities, and the further we go, the more incomprehensible everything around us becomes . . . you see, now you and I have landed in a church! And do you know, when all this mess happened today, I began to miss St. Petersburg, by God I did! Suddenly I remembered so distinctly the green lamp in the study . . .

SERAFIMA. These moods are dangerous, Sergei Pavlovich. Avoid getting melancholy during such wanderings. Wouldn't it have been better for you to stay there?

GOLUBKOV. Oh no, no, it's irrevocable, and let whatever happens happen! And afterward, well you already know what brightens up my difficult road . . . Since we met accidentally in the heated freight car under that lantern, you remember . . . not really very much time has passed, but still it seems to me that I have known you for a long, long time! Thinking about you eased this flight through the autumn darkness, and I will be proud and happy when I get you to the Crimea and deliver you to your husband. And though I'll miss you, I'll take joy in your joy.

Serafima *silently puts her hand on* Golubkov's *shoulder.*

(*Stroking her hand.*) Don't you have a fever?

SERAFIMA. No, it's a trifle.

GOLUBKOV. What do you mean trifle? A fever, by God, a fever!

SERAFIMA. Nonsense, Sergei Pavlovich, it'll pass . . .

A muffled cannon shot. Barabanchikova *stirs and moans.*

Listen madame, it is impossible for you to continue without help. One of us will make his way into the village, there's surely a midwife there.

GOLUBKOV. I'll run there.

Barabanchikova *silently grabs him by the hem of his overcoat.*

SERAFIMA. Why don't you want him to, dear one.

BARABANCHIKOVA (*capriciously*). There's no need.

Serafima *and* Golubkov *are nonplussed.*

MAKHROV (*softly, to* Golubkov). A mysterious personage, extremely mysterious!

GOLUBKOV (*in a whisper*). You think that...

MAKHROV. I don't think anything, but just so . . . it's hard times, sir, you meet just about everyone on your path through life! Some strange lady lies in a church...

The singing underground ceases.

PAISY (*appears noiselessly, black, frightened*). Documents, get your little documents ready, honorable sirs! (*He blows out all of the candles except one.*)

Serafima, Golubkov, *and* Makhrov *get out their documents. Barabanchikova sticks out her hand and lays her passport on the horse blanket.*

BAEV (*enters wearing a short fur jacket, spattered with mud, excited. Following* Baev *is a* Budyonny Soldier *with a lantern*). And may they go straight to hell, these monks! Oh, what a nest! You, holy papa, where's the spiral staircase to the bell tower?

PAISY. Here, here, here . . .

BAEV (*to the* Soldier). Take a look.

The Soldier *disappears through the iron door with his lantern.*

(*To* Paisy.) Was there a light in the bell tower?

PAISY. What do you mean, what do you mean! What light!

BAEV. A light was flashing! Well, if I discover anything in the bell tower, I'll put every last one of you up against the wall and with your grey-haired Satan too! You were waving lanterns to the Whites!

PAISY. My Lord! What're you saying?!

BAEV. And who are these people? You already said that there was not a single soul in the monastery who didn't belong here!

PAISY. They're refugees, ref . . .

SERAFIMA. Comrade, the barrage caught us all in the settlement, and

we ran for the monastery. (*She indicates* Barabanchikova.)
There is a woman and her birth pains are beginning . . .

BAEV (*goes to* Barabanchikova, *takes her passport, reads*). Barabanchikova, married . . .

PAISY (*darkening from terror, whispers*). Lord, Lord, just let this pass! (*He is ready to run away.*) Holy, glorious, great martyr Dmitry . . .

BAEV. Where's your husband?

Barabanchikova *moans*.

Fine time and place she's found to have a baby! (*To* Makhrov.) Document!

MAKHROV. Here's my identification! I'm a chemist from Mariupol.

BAEV. There are a lot of you chemists here on the front line.

MAKHROV. I was going to buy provisions, cucumbers . . .

BAEV. Cucumbers!

SOLDIER (*appears suddenly*). Comrade Baev! I discovered nothing in the bell tower, but here's what . . . (*He whispers in* Baev's *ear.*)

BAEV. What! Where from?

SOLDIER. What I'm saying is correct. The main thing is, it's dark, comrade commander.

BAEV. Well O.K., O.K., let's get going. (*To* Golubkov *who is holding out his document.*) There's no time, no time, later. (*To* Paisy.) So the monks aren't getting mixed up in the Civil War?

PAISY. No, no, no.

BAEV. You just pray? And it would be interesting to know who you pray for. For the black baron or for Soviet power? Well, all right, we'll see each other soon, we'll straighten this out tomorrow! (*He exits with the* Soldier.)

> *A muffled command is heard outside the windows, and everything grows quiet, as if nothing had happened.* Paisy *crosses himself avidly and frequently, lights candles, and disappears.*

MAKHROV. They've taken off . . . Not in vain is it said: "And he causeth them to receive a mark in their right hands, or in their foreheads. . . ."[4] The stars were five-pointed, did you notice?

GOLUBKOV (*in a whisper, to* Serafima). I am completely confused, this area is in the hands of the Whites, so where did these Reds come from? A surprise attack? . . . Why did all this happen?

BARABANCHIKOVA. It happened because General Krapchikov is an ass-sitter and not a general! (*To* Serafima.) *Pardon, Madame.*

GOLUBKOV (*mechanically*). Well?

BARABANCHIKOVA. Well what—well? They sent him a dispatch that the Red cavalry was in the rear, and he, damn his soul, put off the decoding until morning and sat down to play whist.

GOLUBKOV. Well?

BARABANCHIKOVA. He declared a little slam in hearts.

MAKHROV (*softly*). Oho, ho, what an interesting personage!

GOLUBKOV. Excuse me, you are apparently in on things; I had information that the headquarters of General Charnota was supposed to be here in Kurchulan.

BARABANCHIKOVA. My what detailed information you have! Well, his headquarters was here, how could it not be? Only the whole thing left.

GOLUBKOV. And where did it move to?

BARABANCHIKOVA. It's quite definite—into the marsh.

MAKHROV. And how do you know all this, madam?

BARABANCHIKOVA. Why, you're very curious, archbishop.

MAKHROV. Come now, why are you calling me "archbishop"?

BARABANCHIKOVA. Well all right, all right, this is a boring conversation. Leave me alone.

> Paisy *runs in, again extinguishes all the candles except one, looks out the window.*

GOLUBKOV. What now?

PAISY. Oh, sir, we ourselves don't know who else God has sent or whether we will be alive through the night! (*He disappears in such a way that it seems as if he has fallen through the earth.*)

> *The clatter of many horses' hooves is heard, the reflections of a flame dance in the window.*

4. Revelations, 13:16.

SERAFIMA. A fire?

GOLUBKOV. No, those are torches. I don't understand anything Serafima Vladimirovna! White troops, I swear it, Whites! It's happened! Serafima Vladimirovna, we're again in the hands of the
Whites, thank God! Officers wearing shoulder straps!

BARABANCHIKOVA (*sits up, wrapping herself in the horse blanket*).
You, you damned intellectual, shut up immediately. "Shoulder
straps," "shoulder straps." This isn't St. Petersburg, it's the Crimea,
a perfidious land! If they pin shoulder straps on you, that doesn't
mean that you've become a White! And if it's a detachment in
disguise? Then what?

Suddenly a bell tolls softly.

Well, they've started to ring! They've been caught red-handed,
the monk-idiots! (*To* Golubkov.) What kind of trousers are they
wearing?

GOLUBKOV. Red! . . . But there some more have ridden in, they have
on blue ones with red sides . . .

BARABANCHIKOVA. "Ridden in with sides"! . . . The devil take you!
With stripes?

The distant command of De Brisar *is heard: "First squad-
ron, dismount!"*

What's that? It can't be! His voice! (*To* Golubkov.) Well, shout
now, shout boldly now, you have my permission! (*Throws off
the horse blanket and rags and jumps up in the person of General
Charnota. He is wearing a long Circassian coat with crushed silver
shoulder-straps. A revolver, which had been in his hand, he puts in
his pocket; he runs to the window, throws it open, shouts.*) Hello,
Hussars! Hello, Don Cossacks. Colonel Brisar, report to me!

The door opens and Lyuska *runs in first, wearing a nurse's
cap, a leather jacket and high boots with spurs. After her
come* De Brisar, *his face covered with a beard, and the
orderly* Krapilin, *carrying a torch.*

LYUSKA. Grisha! Gri-Gri! (*Throws herself on* Charnota's *neck.*) I don't believe my eyes! Alive? You saved yourself?! (*She shouts out the window.*) Hussars, listen! You've gotten General Charnota away from the Reds!

Noise and shouts outside.

LYUSKA. Why we were getting ready to have a funeral service for you!

CHARNOTA. I saw death as close as your cap. When I went to Krapchikov's headquarters and he sat me down to play whist, the bitch of a tomcat . . . a little slam . . . and wham! Machine guns! There you are—Budyonny, as if dropped from the sky! They wiped out headquarters! I returned the fire, then through the window, across some gardens into the settlement to Barabanchikov's, the teacher. Give me your documents I tell him! And in his panic he gets and slips me the wrong documents! I crawl over here to the monastery, I look, the documents are female, a woman's— Madam Barabanchikova—and the certification says she's pregnant! Reds all around, well, I say, put me in the church just as I am! I lie down, I have labor pains, I hear spurs coming, clink, clink! . . .

LYUSKA. Who was it?

CHARNOTA. A Budyonny commander.

LYUSKA. Oh!

CHARNOTA. I think, where are you clinking to, Budyonny man? Death's lying for you under this horse blanket! So, lift it, lift it— right now! They'll bury you with music! And he took the passport, but didn't lift the horse blanket.

Lyuska whistles.

(Charnota *runs out, shouts through the doors.*) Greetings, Cossacks! Good going, men!

Shouts are heard. Lyuska *runs out after* Charnota.

DE BRISAR. Well, *I'll* lift the horse blanket! I'll be a devil with black spots if I don't have the pleasure of hanging someone in this monastery! Obviously the Reds forgot these guys in their hurry! (*To*

Makhrov.) Well, I don't even have to ask you for a document. It's obvious from your hair what kind of bird you are! Krapilin, light here.

PAISY (*flies in*). What are you doing? What are you doing? That's His Eminence! That's His Eminence Afrikan!

DE BRISAR. What are you babbling about, you black-tailed Satan?

Makhrov *throws off his cap and sheepskin jacket.*

(*He looks into* Makhrov's *face.*) What's this? Your Eminence, is it really you? How did you get here?

AFRIKAN. I came to Kurchulan to bless the Don army corps, but the Reds caught me during an attack. Thank God, the monks provided me with documents.

DE BRISAR. The devil knows what's going on! (*To* Serafima.) Woman, your document!

SERAFIMA. I am the wife of the Assistant Minister of Commerce. I got stuck in St. Petersburg, but my husband is already in the Crimea. I am fleeing to him. Here are my false documents, and here is my real passport. My name is Korzukhina.

DE BRISAR. *Mille excuses, madame!* And you, caterpillar in civvies, I suppose you're the Chief Procurator?

GOLUBKOV. I'm not a caterpillar, thank you, and certainly not the Chief Procurator! I am the son of the renowned idealist professor and myself an assistant professor. I am fleeing from St. Petersburg to you, to the Whites, because it is impossible to work in St. Petersburg.

DE BRISAR. Very nice! It's Noah's Ark!

An iron hatch raises up from the floor, a decrepit Father Superior *comes up out of it, and behind him—a choir of* Monks *carrying candles.*

FATHER SUPERIOR (*to* Afrikan). Your Eminence! (*To the* Monks.) Brothers! We have been fortunate enough to save and preserve our leader from the hands of the impious Socialists!

The Monks *drape the agitated* Afrikan *in his mantle, hand him his crozier.*

Your Eminence! Take up this crozier again, and strengthen your flock with it.

AFRIKAN. O God of hosts, look down from heaven and behold, and visit this vine; the vineyard which Thy right hand hath planted!

THE MONKS (*abruptly begin singing*). Εἰς πολλὰ ἔτη δέσποτα! . . .[5]

Charnota *looms in the doorway,* Lyuska *with him.*

CHARNOTA. What's wrong with you, Holy Fathers, are you out of your minds or what? You've picked the wrong time for this ceremony! Really, a choir! . . . (*With a gesture he motions for them to leave.*)

AFRIKAN. Brothers! Leave now!

The Father Superior *and* Monks *exit into the earth.*

CHARNOTA (*to Afrikan*). Your Eminence, why have you arranged a church service here? We've got to beat it! The whole corps is right at our heels, they'll catch us. Budyonny will choke us off at the sea! The entire army is leaving. We're going to the Crimea! To get under the wing of Roman Khludov!

AFRIKAN. All-merciful Lord, what is this? (*He grabs up his sheepskin jacket.*) Do you have a two-wheeled cart with you? (*He disappears.*)

CHARNOTA. Bring me a map! Krapilin, a light! (*He looks at the map.*) Everything's closed! A coffin!

LYUSKA. Oh Krapchikov, Krapchikov, you fool!

CHARNOTA. Wait! I've found a crack! (*To De Brisar.*) You will take your regiment, you will go to Almanaika. Draw them after you a little, then to Babi Gai and swim across even if it's up to your gullet! After you, I'll move forward with the Don men to the farms of the Molokans, and then, even though later than you, I'll go out on Arbat Point, and we'll join forces there. Move out within five minutes!

DE BRISAR. Yes sir, Your Excellency!

CHARNOTA. Tfu! . . . Let me have a drop to drink, Colonel.

GOLUBKOV. Serafima Vladimirovna, do you hear? The Whites are

5. A Greek prayer meaning, "For all ages, a ruler." This follows the quotation from Psalm 80, 14–15.

leaving. We must run with them, otherwise we'll fall into the hands of the Reds again. Serafima Vladimirovna, why don't you answer, what's wrong?

LYUSKA. Give me some too.

De Brisar *hands the flask to* Lyuska.

GOLUBKOV (*to* Charnota). General, sir, I implore you, take us with you! Serafima Vladimirovna has gotten sick . . . We are fleeing to the Crimea . . . Is there a field hospital with you?

CHARNOTA. You studied at the university?

GOLUBKOV. Of course, yes . . .

CHARNOTA. You produce the impression of a totally uneducated person. Well, suppose a bullet lands in your head on Babi Gai, a field hospital will help you a lot, eh? You might also ask if we have an X-ray machine. Oh, the intelligentsia! . . . Give me some more cognac!

LYUSKA. We have to take them. She's a beautiful woman, the Reds will get her . . .

GOLUBKOV. Serafima Vladimirovna, get up! We must go!

SERAFIMA (*hoarsely*). Do you know, Sergei Pavlovich, it seems to me I really am sick . . . You go alone, and I'll lie down here in the monastery, something's making me very hot . . .

GOLUBKOV. My God! Serafima Vladimirovna, that's unthinkable! Get up, Serafima Vladimirovna!

SERAFIMA. I want a drink of water . . . and to go to St. Petersburg . . .

GOLUBKOV. What is this?

LYUSKA (*victoriously*). It's typhus, that's what it is.

DE BRISAR. Madame, you must run, it'll be bad for you with the Reds. But I'm not an expert at talking. Krapilin, you're eloquent, persuade the lady!

KRAPILIN. Precisely so, you must go!

DE BRISAR (*glancing at his wrist watch*). It's time! (*He runs out.*)

His command is heard: "Mount!"—then hooves clattering.

LYUSKA. Krapilin! Pick her up, take her forcibly!

KRAPILIN. Yes ma'am! (*Together with* Golubkov *he picks her up and they lead her out under the arms.*)

LYUSKA. Into the cart with her!

They exit.

CHARNOTA (*alone, he finishes the Cognac, looks at his watch*). It's time.

FATHER SUPERIOR (*grows up out of the trap door*). White general! Where are you going? You mean you really will not defend the monastery which gave you shelter and safety?!

CHARNOTA. Why are you upsetting me, papa? Tie up the tongues of the bells, sit down in your catacomb! Goodbye! (*He disappears.*)

His shout is heard: "Mount up! Mount up!"—then a frightening clatter of hooves, and everything becomes silent. Paisy *appears from the trap door.*

PAISY. Father Superior! Oh, Father Superior! What are we to do? The Reds will gallop up any moment! And we rang for the Whites! What are we to do—accept the martyr's crown?

FATHER SUPERIOR. And where is His Eminence?

PAISY. He galloped off, he galloped off in the cart!

FATHER SUPERIOR. Pastor, unworthy pastor! . . . Who abandoned his flock! (*He shouts hoarsely into the catacomb.*) Brothers! Pray!

From the earth is heard hollowly: "Holy Father Nikolai, pray to God for us. . . ." Darkness envelops the monastery. The first dream ends.

DREAM TWO

. . . My dreams become more and more painful . . .

FROM THE DARKNESS *emerges the waiting room hall of an unknown and large railroad station somewhere in the northern part of the Crimea. In the rear section of the hall there are windows of ex-*

traordinary dimensions, and beyond them one can feel the black night with blue electric moons.

A brutal frost, incomprehensible in the beginning of November in the Crimea, has occurred. Sivash, Chongar, Perekop, and this station are icebound. The windows have frosted over, and from time to time fiery, snakelike reflections from passing trains flow across the icy mirrors. Portable iron black stoves and kerosene lamps on the tables are burning.

In the very back, over the exit to the main platform, is a sign in old orthography: "Dispatcher's Office."

A glass partition, inside it a green official-type lamp and two green lights of conductors' lamps, resembling the eyes of monsters. Beside this—against a dark, peeling background, a white youth on a horse is striking a scaly dragon with a lance. This youth is St. George, and a faceted, varicolored ikon-lamp is burning in front of it.

The waiting room is occupied by WHITE STAFF OFFICERS. Most of them are wearing hoods and earflaps. There are countless field telephones, staff maps with flags, typewriters in the back. Varicolored signals flash on the telephones now and then; the telephones sing in tender voices.

The front line of the staff has been at this station for three days, and for three days they have not slept, but they work like machines. And only an experienced and observant eye could see the uneasy film over the eyes of all these people. And one other thing can be discerned in their eyes—fear and hope when they turn to where the first-class buffet once was.

There, separated from everyone by a high buffet cabinet, behind a desk, hunched up on a high stool, sits ROMAN VALERIONOVICH KHLUDOV. The man's face is as white as bone, his hair is black, combed in the eternal, indestructible officer's style. KHLUDOV is snub-nosed, like Pavel I, clean-shaven like an actor, seems younger than any of those around, but his eyes are old. He is wearing a soldier's greatcoat, he's belted by a strap around this coat, as somewhat in peasant woman style, somewhat as landowners belted their bathrobes. Cloth shoulder straps, and a general's black zigzag is sewn carelessly on them. He wears a dirty officer's cap with colorless insignia, mittens on his hands. KHLUDOV is wearing no weapons.

He is sick with something, this man, sick from head to foot.
He frowns, twitches, likes to change intonations. He asks himself
questions, likes to answer them himself. When he wants to depict
*a smile, he bares his teeth. He inspires terror. He is sick—*ROMAN
VALERIANOVICH.

Beside KHLUDOV, *in front of a table on which there are several*
telephones, sits and writes the industrious Cossack captain who is in
love with KHLUDOV, GOLOVAN.

KHLUDOV (*dictates to* Golovan). . . . Comma. But Frunze[6] did not
wish to play the part of the designated enemy on maneuvers.
Period. This is not chess and not the never-to-be-forgotten Tsar-
skoe Selo. Period. Signature—Khludov. Period.
GOLOVAN (*hands what he has written to someone*). Encode it and
send it to the commander-in-chief.
FIRST STAFF OFFICER (*after being lit up by a signal light on the*
telephone, moans into the telephone). Yes, yes sir . . . yes sir . . .
Budyonny? . . . Budyonny? . . .
SECOND STAFF OFFICER (*moans into a telephone*). Taganash . . .
Taganash . . .
THIRD STAFF OFFICER (*moans into a telephone*). No, to Karp Ra-
vine . . .
GOLOVAN (*lit up by a signal light, gives* Khludov *the receiver*). Your
Excellency . . .
KHLUDOV (*into the receiver*). Yes. Yes. Yes. No. Yes. (*Returns the*
receiver to Golovan.) Send the commandant to me.
GOLOVAN. The commandant!

A running series of voices echoes: "The commandant, the
commandant!" The commandant, *a pale, squinty-eyed,*
confused officer wearing a red peaked cap runs between
the tables, stands before Khludov.

KHLUDOV. I've been expecting the armored train "Officer" for Taganash for an hour. What is going on? What is going on? What is
going on!

6. M. V. Frunze, a Bolshevik general, People's Commissar of the Army and
Navy.

COMMANDANT (*in a dead voice*). Your Excellency, the stationmaster proved to me that the "Officer" could not get through.

KHLUDOV. Give me the stationmaster.

COMMANDANT (*runs off, talking to someone in a sobbing voice as he does so*). What am I going to do?

KHLUDOV. Tragedies are beginning for us. The armored train has been wrecked by paralysis. The armored train is walking with a cane, and it cannot get through. (*He rings.*)

A sign flares up on the wall: "Counter-intelligence Section."
At the ring Tikhi *comes out of the wall, stops by* Khludov, *quiet and attentive.*

KHLUDOV (*turns to him*). No one loves us, no one. And that's the reason for the tragedies just like in the theater.

Tikhi *is quiet.*

(*Furiously.*) Are these charcoal fumes from the stove, or what?!

GOLOVAN. There aren't any at all, no fumes.

The commandant *appears before* Khludov—*and behind him is the* stationmaster.

KHLUDOV (*to the* stationmaster). You have proved that the armored train cannot get through?

STATIONMASTER (*talks and moves, but he has been a dead man for days.*) Yes, sir, Your Excellency. There is no physical power-potential. They were switching by hand, and blocked it up completely, a traffic jam.

KHLUDOV. The second one is giving off fumes?

GOLOVAN. Immediately! (*To someone off to the side.*) Pour water in that stove!

STATIONMASTER. Fumes, fumes!

KHLUDOV (*to the* stationmaster). For some reason it seems to me that you have a favorable attitude toward the Bolsheviks. Don't be afraid, speak to me honestly. Every man has his convictions, and he should not conceal them. Sly one!

STATIONMASTER (*talks nonsense*). Your Most Esteemed Excellency, why such suspicion? I have little children . . . While still the sovereign Emperor Nikolai Alexandrovich . . . Olga and Pavlik, babies . . . I haven't slept for thirty hours—God is my witness— and I am known personally by the chairman of the State Duma Mikhail Vladimirovich Radzyanko . . . I have children . . .

KHLUDOV. An honest man, eh? No? One needs love, and without love one can do nothing in war! (*Reproachfully to* Tikhi.) They don't love me. (*Dryly.*) Get a field engineer. Force it, switch it! You've got fifteen minutes for the "Officer" to get beyond the exit semaphore! If in that time this order has not been carried out, arrest the commandant! And hang the stationmaster on the semaphore, with a lighted sign under him: "Sabotage."

At this moment a slow, tender waltz is heard in the distance. At one time they danced to this waltz at high-school balls.

STATIONMASTER (*languidly*). Your Most Esteemed Excellency, my children haven't even gone to school yet . . .

Tikhi *takes the* stationmaster *by the arm and leads him away. The* commandant *goes after them.*

KHLUDOV. A waltz?

GOLOVAN. Charnota is approaching, Your Excellency.

STATIONMASTER (*comes to life on the other side of the glass partition, shouts into telephone*). Khristofor Fyodorovich! I implore you by God and Christ: run all of the trains completely off the fourth and fifth lines and on to Taganash. There'll be army engineers! Force it however you want! I implore you, in the name of the Lord!

NIKOLAEVNA (*has appeared beside the* stationmaster). What's going on, Vasya, what is it?

STATIONMASTER. Oh, woe, Nikolaevna! Woe on our family! Olka, pull Olka here, no matter what she's wearing, pull!

NIKOLAEVNA. Olka? Olka? (*She disappears.*)

The waltz breaks off. The door from the platform opens

and Charnota *enters wearing a felt cloak and Cossack hat, and he approaches* Khludov. Lyuska, *who has run in with* Charnota, *remains in the back by the doors.*

CHARNOTA. My composite cavalry division has arrived from the Chongarsky defile, Your Excellency.

Khludov *is silent, looks at* Charnota.

Your Excellency! (*Points somewhere into the distance.*) What is it you are doing? (*Abruptly takes off his Cossack hat.*) Roma! You're of the general staff! What are you doing? Roma, stop it!

KHLUDOV. Shut up!

Charnota *puts his Cossack hat on.*

Leave your transport here, go to Karp Ravine, stand there.

CHARNOTA. Yes, sir. (*He walks away.*)

LYUSKA. Where?

CHARNOTA (*dully*). To Karp Ravine.

LYUSKA. I'm with you. I'll give up these wounded men and typhoid Serafima!

CHARNOTA (*dimly*). You may perish.

LYUSKA. Well, then thank God! (*She exits with* Charnota.)

A clanging, pounding, and then the agonized wail of the armored train is heard. Nikolaevna *tears across the partition, dragging* Olka *who is bundled up in a scarf.*

NIKOLAEVNA. Here she is, Olka, here she is!

STATIONMASTER (*into the telephone*). Khristofor Fyodorovich, you got it through?! Thank you, thanks! (*Grabs* Olka *in his hands, runs to* Khludov. Tikhi *and the* commandant *run behind him.*)

KHLUDOV (*to the* stationmaster). Well, what, my dear fellow, did it get through? Did it get through?

STATIONMASTER. It got through, Your Most Esteemed Excellency, it got through!

KHLUDOV. Why is the child here?

STATIONMASTER. Olechka, a child . . . a capable girl. I've been serving for twenty years and I haven't slept for two days.

KHLUDOV. Yes, a girl . . . Hoopla. Does she play hoopla? Yes? (*Gets a caramel out of his pocket.*) Girl, here! The doctors forbid me to smoke, my nerves are shot. But the caramels don't help, I still smoke and smoke.

STATIONMASTER. Take it, Olyushenka, take it . . . The general is a kind man. Say "merci," Olyushenka . . . (*Picks up* Olka *in his arms, takes her away behind the partition, and* Nikolaevna *disappears with* Olka.)

> *Again the waltz is heard and becomes more distant. Through a door, not the one through which* Charnota *entered, but from another one,* Paramon Ilych Korzukhin *enters. He is an extraordinarily European-looking man wearing glasses, a very expensive fur coat, and carrying a briefcase. He approaches* Golovan, *gives him a card.* Golovan *hands the card to* Khludov.

KHLUDOV. I'm listening.

KORZUKHIN (*to* Khludov). May I introduce myself. Assistant Minister of Commerce, Korzukhin. The Council of Ministers has empowered me to direct three requests to you, Your Excellency. I have just come from Sevastopol. First: I have been commissioned to find out about the fate of five workers arrested in Simferopol and brought here to headquarters by your orders.

KHLUDOV. So. Oh yes, of course, you came from the other platform. Captain! Present the arrested men to the assistant minister.

GOLOVAN. Please follow me.

> *Receiving general and intense attention, he leads* Korzukhin *to the main door at the back, opens it a little, and points somewhere up high.* Korzukhin *shudders. He returns to* Khludov *with* Golovan.

KHLUDOV. Is your first question answered? I'll listen to the second.

KORZUKHIN (*agitated*). The second touches directly on my ministry. Cargoes of especially important sort have gotten stuck here at this station. I request the permission and assistance of Your Excellency in moving them quickly to Sevastopol.

KHLUDOV (*softly*). And what cargo specifically?

KORZUKHIN. Furs for export, destined for abroad.

KHLUDOV (*smiling*). Ah, export furs! And what cars is this cargo in?

KORZUKHIN (*gives him a paper*). Please.

KHLUDOV. Captain Golovan! Run the cars designated here into a blind alley, pour on the kerosene, and burn them!

> *Taking the paper,* Golovan *disappears.*

(*Softly.*) More briefly, the third question?

KORZUKHIN (*stiffening*). The situation at the front? . . .

KHLUDOV (*having yawned*). Well, what can the situation at the front be? Chaos! There's artillery fire, they've shoved a stove with charcoal fumes under the nose of the commander of the front, the Commander-in-Chief has sent me some Kuban men as a gift, but they're barefoot. There's no restaurant, no girls! Green melancholy! So we sit here on stools like parrots. (*Changing his intonation, he hisses.*) The situation? Go to Sevastopol, Mr. Korzukhin, and tell those rear-guard louses to pack their bags! The Reds will be here tomorrow! And you also tell them that their foreign sluts aren't going to see any sable cuffs! Fur goods!

KORZUKHIN. This is unheard of! (*Looks around as if being hunted.*) I will have the honor of reporting this to the Commander-in-Chief.

KHLUDOV (*politely*). Please do.

KORZUKHIN (*moving backward, goes out the side door; on his way he asks*). Which train is going to Sevastopol next?

> *No replies to him. A train can be heard approaching.*

STATIONMASTER (*dead with terror, presents himself to* Khludov). A special train from Kerman Kelmachi!

KHLUDOV. Attention! Officers!

> *The entire staff rises. In the doors through which Kor-*
> *zukhin exited two escort Cossacks wearing crimson hoods*
> *appear, followed by the White Commander-in-Chief, wear-*
> *ing a Cossack cap crushed onto the back of his head, an*
> *extremely long greatcoat, and a Caucasian saber, and fol-*

lowing behind him comes the Archbishop Afrikan, blessing the staff.

COMMANDER. Hello, gentlemen!

STAFF. We wish you health, Your Excellency!

KHLUDOV. I request permission to present my report to Your Excellency confidentially.

COMMANDER. Yes. Everyone leave the room. (*To* Afrikan.) Your Eminence, I will have a confidential talk with the commander of this front.

AFRIKAN. Good luck! Good luck!

Everyone goes out and Khludov *is left alone with the* Commander-in-Chief.

KHLUDOV. The enemy took Yushun three hours ago. The Bolsheviks are in the Crimea.

COMMANDER. The end?!

KHLUDOV. The end.

Silence.

COMMANDER (*through the door*). Your Eminence!

Upset, Afrikan *appears.*

Your Eminence! We have been abandoned by the West European powers, deceived by the perfidious Poles, and in this terrible hour we can hope only for the mercy of God!

AFRIKAN (*understanding that a calamity has happened.*) Ay, yai, yai!

COMMANDER. Pray, Holy Father!

AFRIKAN (*before St. George the Victor*). Almighty God! Why? Why dost Thou send his new ordeal upon Thy children, the glorious army of Christ? The power of the Cross is with us, it puts down the foe with arms which are blessed . . .

The face of the stationmaster *appears behind the glass partition; he is in agony from terror.*

KHLUDOV. Your Eminence, forgive me for interrupting you, but you are disturbing the Lord God to no end. Clearly He abandoned us long ago. What is all this anyway? Nothing like this ever happened before, but now the waters of the Sivash parted, and the Bolsheviks walked across as if on ballroom parquet. St. George the Victor is laughing!

AFRIKAN. What are you saying, valorous general?

COMMANDER. I am categorically against such a tone. You are obviously ill, general, and I regret that you did not go abroad for treatment last summer as I advised.

KHLUDOV. Oh, so that's how it is? And who, Your Excellency, would have kept your soldiers on Perekop Rampart? And who would have sent Charnota from Chongar to Karp Ravine with music tonight? Who would have done the hanging? Who would have done the hanging, Your Excellency?

COMMANDER (*growing dark*). What is the meaning of this?

AFRIKAN. Lord, look down on them, enlighten and strengthen them! "Every kingdom divided against itself is brought to desolation!"[7]

COMMANDER. However, this is not the time . . .

KHLUDOV. No, not the time. You must return to Sevastopol immediately.

COMMANDER. Yes. (*Takes out an envelope, hands it to* Khludov.) Please open it immediately.

KHLUDOV. Oh, it was already prepared? You foresaw? That's good. "Lord, now lettest Thou Thy servant depart . . ."[8] Yes, Sir. (*He shouts.*) A train for the Commander! Escort! Staff!

STATIONMASTER (*rushes to the telephone on the other side of the partition*). For Kerman Kelmachi! Get me the signal! Get me the signal!

The Escort Cossacks *and all of the* Staff Officers *appear.*

COMMANDER. The commander of this front . . .

The Staff *salutes.*

will inform you of my order! May the Lord send us all the strength and wisdom to live through the evil times in Russia! I

7. Matthew, 12:25.
8. Luke, 2:29.

warn each and every one of you honestly that there is no more territory for us after the Crimea.

Suddenly the door is flung open and De Brisar *appears, his head wrapped in gauze, and salutes the* Commander-in-Chief.

DE BRISAR. I wish you health, Your Imperial Highness! (*To the* Staff, *mysteriously.*) "Countess, if you want, for a simple rendezvous I will gladly name ..."⁹

COMMANDER. What's this?

GOLOVAN. Count de Brisar, commander of the Hussar regiment. He has been wounded in the head.

KHLUDOV (*as if in a dream*). Chongar ... Chongar ...

COMMANDER. Put him on my train with me, to Sevastopol! (*He goes out quickly, accompanied by the* Cossack *escorts.*)

AFRIKAN. Lord! Lord! (*He blesses the* Staff, *goes out quickly.*)

DE BRISAR (*being drawn away by the* Staff Officers). Sorry! . . . "Countess, for a single rendezvous ..."

THE STAFF OFFICERS. To Sevastopol, count, to Sevastopol ...

DE BRISAR. Sorry! . . . Sorry! . . . (*He disappears.*)

KHLUDOV (*opens the envelope. He reads, bares his teeth. To* Golovan). Send a courier to General Barbovich at Karp Ravine. Order him to break away from the enemy, ride at a fast trot to Yalta and embark!

A rustling of whispers is heard through the Staff: *"Amen, amen ..." Then a tombal silence.*

Another courier to General Kutepov—to break off, go to Sevastopol and load on board ships. To Fostikov—for him to go to Theodosia with the Kuban Cossacks. To Kalinin—to go to Kerch with the Don Cossacks. Charnota—to Sevastopol! Everyone onto the ships! The staff to pack up and go to Sevastopol at once! The Crimea is being surrendered.

GOLOVAN (*going out hastily*). Couriers! Couriers!

Groups of Staff Officers *begin to melt away. The maps are*

---

9. A line from Tchaikovsky's opera *The Queen of Spades,* based on Pushkin's short story of the same title. The hero, who ends insane, says this.

being rolled up, telephones begin to disappear. A train shrieking and departing is heard. Confusion, no longer any order. At this point the door which Charnota *went out through is flung open and* Serafima *appears, wearing a felt cloak. Behind her*—Golubkov *and* Krapilin *attempting to hold her back.*

GOLUBKOV. Serafima Vladimirovna, come to your senses, you can't go in here! (*To the surprised* Staff Officers.) The woman has typhus! . . .

KRAPILIN. Just so, typhus.

SERAFIMA (*resonantly*). Which one here is Roman Khludov?

Silence follows this absurd question.

KHLUDOV. Never mind, let her through to me. *I* am Khludov.

GOLUBKOV. Don't listen to her, she is ill!

SERAFIMA. We're fleeing from St. Petersburg, we keep fleeing and fleeing . . . Where to? To get under the wing of Roman Khludov! Always Khludov, Khludov, Khludov . . . I even dream of Khludov! (*She smiles.*) And now I've managed to see him face to face: he sits on a stool, while the bags hang around. Bags and more bags! . . . You brute! Jackal!

GOLUBKOV (*desperately*). She has typhus! She is delirious! . . . We've come from the attack echelon!

Khludov rings; Tikhi *and* Gurin *emerge from the wall.*

SERAFIMA. Well, so what! They're coming and they'll put an end to all of you!

A rustling in the group of Staff Officers: "*Oh-ho, a Communist!*"

GOLUBKOV. What's wrong with you! What is wrong with you! She is the wife of Assistant Minister Korzukhin! She doesn't know what she's saying!

KHLUDOV. That's good, because when people know what they're saying here, you can't get a word of truth out of them.

GOLUBKOV. She is Korzukhin's wife!

KHLUDOV. Stop, stop, stop! Korzukhin's wife? He's the fur goods one! So that good-for-nothing has a Communist wife besides? Ooh! What a blessed coincidence! Well, I'll settle with him now! If only he hasn't had a chance to leave, bring him here to me!

Tikhi *makes a sign to* Gurin, *and he disappears.*

Tikhi (*softly, to* Serafima). What is your first name and patronymic?

Golubkov. Serafima Vladimirovna . . . Serafima . . .

Gurin *leads in* Korzukhin. *He is deathly pale, senses calamity.*

You are Paramon Ilych Korzukhin?

Korzukhin. Yes, I am he.

Golubkov. Thank God, you've ridden out to meet us! At last!

Tikhi (*amiably, to* Korzukhin). Your wife, Serafima Vladimirovna, has come to you from St. Petersburg.

Korzukhin (*looks in* Tikhi's *and* Khludov's *eyes, sensing some kind of trap*). I don't know any Serafima Vladimirovna, this is the first time in my life I've ever seen this woman. I'm not expecting anyone from St. Petersburg. This is a trick.

Serafima (*having glanced at* Korzukhin, *dully*). Ah, he renounces me! Ooh, you snake!

Korzukhin. This is blackmail!

Golubkov (*desperately*). Paramon Ilych, what are you doing? This cannot be!

Khludov. An honest man, eh? Well, it's your luck, Mr. Korzukhin! Fur goods! Get out!

Korsukhin *disappears.*

Golubkov. I implore you to interrogate us! I'll prove that she's his wife!

Khludov (*to* Tikhi). Take them both, interrogate them!

Tikhi (*to* Gurin). Take them away to Sevastopol.

Gurin *takes* Serafima *by the arm.*

Golubkov. But you are an intelligent man! . . . I'll prove it! . . .

Serafima. And there was only one man we found along the way . . . Oh, Krapilin, eloquent man, why won't you step in for us? . . .

They lead Serafima *and* Golubkov *away.*

KRAPILIN (*standing before* Khludov). Yes, sir. As it is written in books: jackal! What did you cut the throats of those soldiers at Perekop for, you vicious animal? But then you came across one human being, a woman. She felt sorry for the men you hanged, that's all. But no one'll get by you, no one'll get by! Right away you catch a person and—wham, into a bag. Do you feed on carrion?

TIKHI. Should I get him out of here, Your Excellency?

KHLUDOV. No. There are occasionally good ideas about the war flitting through his speech. Talk on, soldier, talk on.

TIKHI (*beckons to someone with his finger, and two* counter-intelligence agents *come out of the door of the counter-intelligence section. In a whisper*). A board.

A third agent *appears with a piece of plywood.*

KHLUDOV. What's your name, soldier?

KRAPILIN (*rising to fatal heights*). What is a name? My name is an unknown one—Krapilin, an orderly! But you'll perish, jackal, you'll perish in a ditch, you mad dog! Just keep waiting here on your stool! (*Smiling.*) But no, you'll flee, you'll flee to Constantinople! You're brave only about hanging women and locksmiths!

KHLUDOV. You are mistaken, soldier, I've gone to the Chongar Road with music, and I was wounded twice there.

KRAPILIN. Every district in Russia spits on your music! (*Suddenly, he comes to himself, shudders, falls to his knees, speaks plaintively.*) Your Excellency, have mercy on Krapilin! I was delirious!

KHLUDOV. No! You're a bad soldier! You began well, but ended nastily. You're crawling around at my feet? Hang him! I can't stand to look at him!

The counter-intelligence agents *immediately throw a black bag over* Krapilin's *head and drag him away.*

GOLOVAN (*appearing*). Your orders have been carried out, Your Excellency. The couriers have been dispatched.

KHLUDOV. Everybody on the train, gentlemen. Captain, get my escort and car ready!

They all disappear.

(*Alone, he takes the telephone receiver, talks into it.*) The Commander of the Front speaking. Order the armored train "Officer" to go as far down the line as it can, and have it fire and keep firing! Fire at Taganash, fire! Have it stamp them into the earth in parting! Then have the tracks blown up behind it and head off for Sevastopol. (*He puts the receiver down, sits alone, hunched up on the stool.*)

The distant howl of the armored train flies past.

What am I sick with? Am I sick?

A salvo rings out from the armored train. It is so heavy that the sound is almost inaudible, but the electricity immediately goes off in the waiting room of the station, and the icy windows crash down. Now the platform is revealed. Bluish electrical moons are visible. Under the first of these, on an iron post, hangs a long black bag, under it a piece of plywood with a charcoal inscription: "Orderly Krapilin—a Bolshevik." There is another bag under the next pole, beyond that nothing can be seen.

KHLUDOV (*alone in the semidarkness, he looks at the hanged* Krapilin). I am sick, I am sick. Only I don't know with what.

Olka appears in the semidarkness, let loose in the panic. She is crawling along the floor in felt boots.

STATIONMASTER (*searching through the semidarkness and muttering sleepily*). Fool, that fool Nikolaevna . . . Olka, where is Olka? Olechka. Olya, where did you go, little fool, where did you go? (*Grabs up* Olka *in his arms.*) Come to my arms, to your father's arms . . . And don't look over there . . . (*He's happy that he is not noticed, vanishes in the darkness, and the second dream ends.*)

END OF THE FIRST ACT

ACT II

DREAM THREE

...A needle gleams in a dream...

SOME SORT of gloomy lighting. Autumn twilight. An office in counter-intelligence in Sevastopol. One window, a desk, a couch. A multitude of newspapers on a little table in a corner. A cabinet. Door-curtains. TIKHI is sitting at the table in civilian clothes. The door opens, and Gurin admits Golubkov.

GURIN. In here ... (He disappears.)
TIKHI. Sit down, please.
GOLUBKOV (wearing an overcoat, a hat in his hands). Thank you. (He sits down.)
TIKHI. You are, it would seem, a member of the intelligentsia?

Golubkov coughs timidly.

And I am sure you realize how important it is to us, and therefore to the high command, to know the truth. The Reds are spreading nasty rumors about counter-intelligence. In point of fact, this organization performs the most difficult and absolutely clean work relating to the security of the state from the Bolsheviks. Do you agree with this?
GOLUBKOV. I, you see ...
TIKHI. Are you afraid of me?
GOLUBKOV. Yes.
TIKHI. But why? Did we do you any harm while bringing you here to Sevastopol?
GOLUBKOV. Oh no, no, I couldn't say that.

TIKHI. Please have a smoke. (*Offers him cigarettes.*)

GOLUBKOV. I don't smoke, thank you. I implore you, tell me how she is?

TIKHI. Who interests you?

GOLUBKOV. Her . . . Serafima Vladimirovna, the one arrested along with me. I swear this is simply an absurd incident! She had an attack, she is seriously ill!

TIKHI. You are upset, calm down. I'll tell you about her a little later.

Silence.

Well, enough of this playing assistant professor! This comedy bores me! You swine! In whose presence are you sitting down! Stand at attention! Hands at your sides!

GOLUBKOV (*rising*). My God!

TIKHI. Listen now, what's your real name?

GOLUBKOV. I'm dumbfounded . . . my real name is Golubkov!

TIKHI (*takes out his revolver, aims at* Golubkov. *He covers his face with his hands*). Do you understand that you are in my hands? No one is going to come to your aid! Understand?

GOLUBKOV. I understand.

TIKHI. So, we'll make a bargain: you are going to tell the whole truth. Look here. If you start to lie, I'll switch on this needle (*he switches on the needle, which, getting hot from the electricity, begins to gleam*) and I'll touch you with it. (*He cools the needle.*)

GOLUBKOV. I swear that I really . . .

TIKHI. Shut up! Just answer my questions! (*He puts away his revolver, takes a pen, speaks in a bored voice.*) Sit down, please. Your first name, patronymic, and surname?

GOLUBKOV. Sergei Pavlovich Golubkov.

TIKHI (*writes, bored*). Where is your permanent residence?

GOLUBKOV. St. Petersburg.

TIKHI. Why did you come from Soviet Russia to the control of the Whites?

GOLUBKOV. I set out for the Crimea some time ago, because in St. Petersburg there are living conditions under which I cannot work. And I met Serafima Vladimirovna in a train; she was also fleeing here, and I came with her to the Whites.

TIKHI. Why did she come to the Whites calling herself Serafima Korzukhina?

GOLUBKOV. I am firmly . . . I know that she really is Serafima Korzukhina!

TIKHI. In your presence at the station Korzukhin said that that was a lie.

GOLUBKOV. I swear he was lying!

TIKHI. Why should he lie?

GOLUBKOV. He was afraid, he felt that some danger was threatening him.

Tikhi *puts down his pen, moves his hand toward the needle.*

What are you doing? I'm telling the truth!

TIKHI. Your nerves are shot, Mr. Golubkov. I am writing down your testimony, as you see, and I am not doing anything else. Has she been a member of the Communist Party for a long time?

GOLUBKOV. That is impossible!

TIKHI. So. (*Pushes a piece of paper over to* Golubkov, *gives him a pen.*) Write down everything that you just testified to, I will dictate to you so that it will be easier for you. I warn you that if you stop, I will touch you with the needle. If you do not stop, you have nothing to fear, nothing threatens you. (*He switches on the needle, which casts its lights on the paper, dictates.*) "I, the undersigned . . .

Golubkov *begins to write the dictation.*

. . . Golubkov, Sergei Pavlovich, under interrogation by the Counter-intelligence Section of the Front Commander's Staff on October 31, 1920 testified colon Serafima Vladimirovna Korzukhin . . ."—don't stop—". . . a member of the Communist Party comma from the city of St. Petersburg to the region occupied by the Armed Forces of South Russia for Communist propaganda and the establishment of ties with the underground in the city of Sevastopol period. Assistant Professor . . . signature." (*He takes the paper from Golubkov, cools the needle.*) I thank you for this honest testimony, Mr. Golubkov. I am completely convinced of your innocence. Excuse me if I was a little harsh with you at times. You are free. (*He rings.*)

GURIN (*enters*). Yes, sir!

TIKHI. Take this prisoner out to the street and release him, he is free.

GURIN (*to* Golubkov). Go on.

Golubkov *goes out with* Gurin, *forgetting his hat.*

TIKHI. Lieutenant Skunsky!

Skunsky *enters. Very gloomy.*

TIKHI (*lighting the lamp on the desk*). Evaluate this document! How much will Korzukhin give to buy himself off?

SKUNSKY. Here, at the gangway? Ten thousand dollars. Less in Constantinople. I advise you to get a confession from Korzukhina.

TIKHI. Yes. Find some pretext to postpone Korzukhin's embarkation for half an hour.

SKUNSKY. My share?

Tikhi *holds up two fingers.*

I'll send agents right away. Get it from her as fast as possible. The cavalry is on the way to embark right now. (*Exits.*)

Tikhi *rings.* Gurin *enters.*

TIKHI. The prisoner Korzukhina. Is she conscious?

GURIN. She seems to be a little better right now.

TIKHI. Bring her.

Gurin *exits, then in a few moments leads in* Serafima. *She has a fever.* Gurin *exits.*

You are ill? I will not detain you long, sit on the couch, there, over there.

Serafima *sits down on the couch.*

Admit that you came for propaganda, and I will release you.

SERAFIMA. What? . . . Eh? . . . What propaganda? My God, why did I come here?

A waltz is heard, it draws nearer, and there is a pounding of hooves outside the window.

Why are they playing a waltz here?

TIKHI. Charnota's cavalry is going down to the wharf, don't be distracted. Your cohort Golubkov testified that you came here for propaganda.

SERAFIMA (*lies down on the couch, breathes out heavily*). All of you leave the room, don't keep me from sleeping . . .

TIKHI. No. Pull yourself together, read this. (*He shows what* Golubkov *wrote to* Serafima.)

SERAFIMA (*squints, reads*). St. Petersburg . . . the lamp . . . he's gone out of his mind . . . (*She suddenly grabs the document, crumples it up, runs to the window, smashes the glass with her elbow, screams.*) Help me! Help me! A crime's being committed here! Charnota! Here, help me!

TIKHI. Gurin!

Gurin *runs in, grabs* Serafima.

Take away the document! Oh, damn it to hell!

The waltz instantly breaks off. A face under a Cossack hat flashes in the window. A voice: "What's going on in there?" Voices, knocking on doors, and noise are heard. The door opens, Charnota *appears in a felt Cossack cloak, two others behind him are also wearing them.* Skunsky *runs in.* Gurin *releases* Serafima.

SERAFIMA. Charnota! It's you! Charnota! Intercede! Look what they're doing to me. Look what they've forced him to write!

Charnota *takes the document.*

TIKHI. Please leave the counter-intelligence office immediately!

CHARNOTA. No! What do you mean leave? What are you doing to the woman?

TIKHI. Lieutenant Skunsky, call the guard!

CHARNOTA. I'll show you the guard! (*Drags out his revolver.*) What are you doing to the woman?

TIKHI. Lieutenant Skunsky, extinguish the light!

The light is extinguished.

(In the darkness.) "You'll pay dearly for this, General Charnota!"

Darkness. The dream ends.

DREAM FOUR

*... And a mixed multitude
went up also with them* ...[10]

TWILIGHT. *An office in a palace in Sevastopol. The office is in strange shape; one portière-curtain on a window is half-torn; there is a whitish square spot on the wall where a large military map had been. On the floor is a wooden box, apparently containing papers. There is a fire in the fireplace.* DE BRISAR *is sitting motionlessly near the fireplace, his head bandaged. The* COMMANDER-IN-CHIEF *enters.*

COMMANDER. Well, how's your head?

DE BRISAR. It doesn't hurt, Your Excellency. The doctor gave me pyramidon.

COMMANDER. So. Pyramidon? *(Absently.)* What is your opinion, do I look like Alexander the Great?

DE BRISAR *(without surprise).* Your Excellency, unfortunately I have not seen any portraits of His Majesty for a long time.

COMMANDER. Of whom are you speaking?

DE BRISAR. Of Alexander the Great, Your Excellency.

COMMANDER. His Majesty? ... Hm ... You know, Colonel, you need a rest. I have been very glad to shelter you here in the palace, you did your duty for the fatherland honorably. But now you get going, it's time.

DE BRISAR. Where do you order me to go, Your Excellency?

10. Exodus, 12:38.

COMMANDER. Onto the ship. I will take care of you abroad.

DE BRISAR. Yes, sir. When we are victorious over the Reds, I will be happy to be first to salute Your Majesty in the Kremlin!

COMMANDER. Colonel, we must not put these questions so sharply. Your views are too extreme. And so, I thank you, go now.

DE BRISAR. Yes, sir, Your Excellency. (*He goes to the exit, stops, sings mysteriously.*) "Countess, for a single rendezvous . . ." (*He disappears.*)

COMMANDER (*right after him, he says through the door*). Admit the remaining visitors to me automatically, one every three minutes. I'll receive as many as possible. Send a Cossack to escort Colonel De Brisar to my ship! Write the doctor on the ship that pyramidon is not the medicine he needs. He is obviously abnormal! (*He returns to the fireplace, falls to thinking.*) Alexander of Macedonia . . . *There* are the good-for-nothings!

Korzukhin *enters*.

What do you want?

KORZUKHIN. Assistant Minister Korzukhin.

COMMANDER. Ah! Just at the right time! I wanted to call you in spite of all this confusion. Mr. Korzukhin, do I look like Alexander of Macedonia?

Korzukhin *is nonplussed*.

I'm asking you seriously, do I? (*He grabs a newspaper from the mantel, jabs it at* Korzukhin.) Aren't you the editor of this newspaper? That means you are responsible for everything that is printed in it? This is your name, isn't it? Editor—Korzukhin? (*He reads.*) "Like Alexander of Macedonia, the Commander-in-Chief walks back and forth along the platform . . ." What is this swinish rot? Were there any railroad platforms during Alexander of Macedonia's times? And do I resemble him? Further, sir! (*He reads.*) "One glance at his merry face should disperse every worm of doubt . . ." A worm is not a cloud and not a battalion, it cannot be dispersed! And I'm merry? Am I very merry? Where did you get this illiterate, mercenary rabble, Mr. Korzukhin? How dare you print this shameful rubbish two days before the catas-

trophe? I'll have you put on trial in Constantinople! Take pyramidon if you have a headache.

The telephone rings deafeningly in the next room. The
Commander *goes out, slamming the door.*

KORZUKHIN (*taking a deep breath*). That's just what you deserve,
Paramon Ilych! What the hell, I ask, dragged me to this palace?
To complain about one maniac to another? So they seized Sera-
fima Vladimirovna, well what can I do. So she'll perish, well the
Kingdom of Heaven be hers! Why should I lose my own life be-
cause of her? Alexander of Macedonia is a boor! Put me on trial?
Excuse me, Paris is not Sevastopol! To Paris! And may you all
be damned, both you and all your spawn now and forever after!
(*He heads for the doors.*)

AFRIKAN (*entering*). Amen. Something's happening, Mr. Korzukhin, eh?

KORZUKHIN. Yes, yes, yes ... (*Slips out stealthily.*)

AFRIKAN (*looking at the boxes*). Ay, yai, yai! Lord, Lord! "And
the children of Israel journeyed from Rameses to Succoth, about
six hundred thousand on foot that were men, beside children ..."
Ah, ah ... "And a mixed multitude went up also with them ..."[11]

Khludov *enters rapidly.*

You are here, Your Excellency? And Mr. Korzukhin was just
here, it's strange ...

KHLUDOV. You sent a Bible to Headquarters as a gift for me?

AFRIKAN. Of course, of course ...

KHLUDOV. I remember, sir. I read it at night in my railway car, from
boredom. "Thou didst blow with thy wind, the sea covered them:
they sank as lead in the mighty waters."[12] Of whom was that said?
Eh? "I will pursue, I will overtake, I will divide the spoil; my
lust shall be satisfied upon them; I will draw my sword, my hand
shall destroy them."[13] A good memory, eh? And he was spread-

11. Exodus, 12:37.
12. Exodus, 15:10.
13. Exodus, 15:9.

ing slander that I'm abnormal! And what are you hanging around here for?

AFRIKAN. Hanging around! Roman Valerianovich! I am waiting for the Commander-in-Chief . . .

KHLUDOV. All things come to him who waits. That's in the style of your Bible. Do you know what you're waiting for here?

AFRIKAN. What?

KHLUDOV. The Reds.

AFRIKAN. Could they be here so fast?

KHLUDOV. Anything can happen. You and I are sitting here, quoting the Holy Writ, but at this very time, just imagine, cavalry is approaching Sevastopol from the north at a trot . . . (*He leads* Afrikan *to the window*.) Look . . .

AFRIKAN. Fire in the sky as bright as the dawn! Oh, Lord!

KHLUDOV. Precisely. Onto the ship immediately, Holy Father, immediately!

Frequently crossing himself, Afrikan *exits.*

He's gone!

COMMANDER (*enters*). Ah, thank God! I've been waiting anxiously for you! Well, did they all get out?

KHLUDOV. The Greens[14] gave the cavalry a good going over along the road. But, basically, it may be considered that they've gotten out. And as for me I rode along comfortably. I hid in a corner of the railroad car; I didn't bother anyone nor they me. Basically, Your Excellency, it was as dark as a kitchen.

COMMANDER. I don't understand, what do you mean?

KHLUDOV. This was in childhood. Once I went into the kitchen at twilight—cockroaches all over the stove. I struck a match—scratch, and they ran away. I take the match and put it out. I hear them rustling—brush-brush, shush-shush . . . And it's like that now too—darkness and rustling. I look and I wonder: where are they running to? Like the cockroaches, into a bucket. Off the kitchen table—plop!

COMMANDER. General, I thank you for all that you have done for

14. Peasant guerrillas of mixed loyalties.

the Crimea with your vast strategic talent, and I won't delay you any longer. I'm moving over to the hotel myself immediately.

KHLUDOV. A little closer to the water?

COMMANDER. If you don't stop forgetting yourself, I'll have you arrested.

KHLUDOV. I foresaw that. My escort is in the vestibule. There would be a big scandal—I'm popular.

COMMANDER. No, this is not a matter of illness. It's been a whole year now that you've been hiding your hate for me under this disgusting buffoonery.

KHLUDOV. I won't hide it, I hate you.

COMMANDER. Envy? Longing for power?

KHLUDOV. Oh no, no. I hate you because you got me into all this. Where are the promised Allied divisions? Where is the Russian Empire? How could you enter battle with them when you are powerless? Do you understand how much a man can hate when he knows that nothing will come of this and who must do it nevertheless? You became the reason for my illness! (*Calming down.*) However, this is not the time in general, we are both headed for nonexistence.

COMMANDER. I advise you to remain here at the palace, that's the best way for you to become nonexistent.

KHLUDOV. That's an idea. But I still haven't thought it over properly.

COMMANDER. I'm not keeping you, general.

KHLUDOV. Driving a faithful servant away? "Him, who in ceaseless battle spilled blood like water for thee?"

COMMANDER (*banging the chair on the floor*). Clown!

KHLUDOV. Alexander of Macedonia is a hero, but why break chairs?

COMMANDER (*at the words "Alexander of Macedonia" he gets furious*). If you say one more word! ...If you ...

ESCORT (*grows up out of the earth*). Your Excellency, the Cavalry School from Simferapol has arrived. Everything is ready!

COMMANDER. It is? Let's go! (*To Khludov.*) We will meet again! (*Exits.*)

KHLUDOV (*alone, sits down by the fireplace, his back to the door*). Empty—and a good thing too. (*Suddenly he gets up anxiously, opens the door, revealing a suite of dark and abandoned rooms with chandeliers in dark muslin bags.*) Hey, who's here? There's no one. (*He sits down.*) So, do I remain? No, that won't solve my problem. (*Turns around, talks to someone.*) Will you go away or not? Why, it's nonsense! I'll get past you just as I got through the fog yesterday, like an arrow. (*He walks as if passing through something.*) Well there, I smashed you. (*Sits down, is silent.*)

The door opens quietly and Golubkov *enters. He is wearing an overcoat, without a hat.*

GOLUBKOV. For God's sake, permit me to come in for one minute!

KHLUDOV (*not turning around*). Please, please come in.

GOLUBKOV. I know that this is insane effrontery, but I was promised that I would be let in to see you specifically. But they've all dispersed somewhere, so I just came in.

KHLUDOV (*not turning around*). What do you need of me?

GOLUBKOV. I have dared to have recourse to you, Your Excellency, to inform you of the terrible crimes which are being committed in counter-intelligence. I had recourse to you in order to complain about the beastly crime the cause of which is General Khludov.

Khludov *turns around.*

(*Recognizing* Khludov, Golubkov *staggers back.*) Oh . . .

KHLUDOV. That is interesting. But you are alive, aren't you, you haven't been changed, I hope? What is your complaint?

Silence.

You make a pleasant impression. I've seen you somewhere. So be so kind as to tell me, what your complaint is. And don't be cowardly, please. You came to say something, so say it.

GOLUBKOV. All right. The day before yesterday you ordered a woman arrested at the station . . .

KHLUDOV. I remember, yes. I remember. I recall. I recognize you. Please, to whom did you intend to complain about me here?

GOLUBKOV. To the commander-in-chief.

KHLUDOV. Too late. He's not here. (*Points out the window.*)

Small lights flicker in the distance, and a dim glow can be seen.

The bucket of water. He has sunk into nonexistence forever. There's no one else to complain to about General Khludov. (*Walks up to the table, takes one of the telephone receivers, speaks into it.*) Vestibule? . . . Captain Golovan . . . Listen, captain, take the escort with you and go to counter-intelligence, there's a woman there I had picked up . . . (*To* Golubkov.) Korzukhina?

GOLUBKOV. Yes, yes, Serafima Vladimirovna!

KHLUDOV (*into the telephone*). Serafima Vladimirovna Korzukhina. If she hasn't been shot, bring her here to me in the palace immediately. (*Puts the receiver down.*) We will wait.

GOLUBKOV. If she hasn't been shot, you say? If she hasn't been shot? . . . They shot her? Oh, if you did that . . . (*He cries.*)

KHLUDOV. Behave like a man.

GOLUBKOV. Ah, you're still taunting! All right, I'll behave . . . But if she's not alive, I'll kill you!

KHLUDOV (*apathetically*). So what, maybe that's the best out. But no, unfortunately, you won't kill anyone. Keep quiet!

Golubkov sits down and falls silent.

(*Turning away from* Golubkov, *he talks to someone.*) If you have become my companion, soldier, talk to me. Your silence oppresses me, even though I imagine that your voice must be heavy and bronze. Or else leave me alone. You know that I am a man of great will power, and I will not surrender to the first apparition—people get cured of that. Just understand that you simply fell under a wheel, and it wiped you out and crushed your bones. And it's senseless to go tagging about after me. Do you hear, my relentless, eloquent orderly?

GOLUBKOV. With whom are you talking?

KHLUDOV. Eh? With whom? We'll soon find out. (*He cuts the air with his hand.*) With no one, with myself. Yes. So who is she to you? Your mistress?

GOLUBKOV. No, no! I met her by chance, but I love her! Ah, I'm a miserable madman! Why, why did I get her up and persuade her to ride off into these devilish paws when we were in the monastery? . . . Ah, I'm a miserable man!

KHLUDOV. Yes indeed, why did you slip into my path? What brought you here? And now when the machine has broken down, you have appeared to demand of me that which I cannot give. She's not here and won't be. They've shot her.

GOLUBKOV. Villain! Villain! Senseless villain!

KHLUDOV. And now I'm getting it from two sides: a living, talking, absurd one, and from the other a silent orderly. What's wrong with me? My soul has split, and I hear words vaguely, as if through water into which I am sinking like lead. Both of them, damn them, are hanging on my legs and pulling me in to the darkness, and the darkness is calling me.

GOLUBKOV. Ah, now I understand! You're insane! Now I understand everything! The ice on Chongar, and the black bags, and the frost! Fate! Why did you oppress me? How is it I didn't save my Serafima? There he is, there he is, her blind murderer! And what can be taken from him if he's lost his mind!

KHLUDOV. There, you eccentric! (*He throws his revolver to* Golubkov.) Do me a favor, shoot. (*Into space.*) All right, leave me alone. Maybe this fellow will manage to shoot me.

GOLUBKOV. No, I can't shoot you, for me you are pitiful, terrible, disgusting!

KHLUDOV. Now what kind of comedy is this, really?

Footsteps are heard in the distance.

Stop, stop, they're coming! Maybe it's he? Now we'll find out everything.

Golovan enters.

Has she been shot?

GOLOVAN. Not at all.

GOLUBKOV. She's alive? Alive? Where is she, where?

KHLUDOV. Quiet. (*To* Golovan). In that case why didn't you bring her here?

Golovan gives a sidelong glance at Golubkov.

You can speak in his presence.

GOLOVAN. Yes, sir. Today at four o'clock Major General Charnota broke into the counter-intelligence office; threatening to use armed force, he got the prisoner Korzukhina and took her away.

GOLUBKOV. Where to? Where?

KHLUDOV. Quiet. (*To Golovan*.) Where?

GOLOVAN. Aboard the steamship *Knight*. The *Knight* left the harbor at five o'clock, and after five it put out to open sea.

KHLUDOV. That's all. Thanks. And so, there, she's alive. Your woman Serafima is alive.

GOLUBKOV. Yes, yes, alive, alive ...

KHLUDOV. Captain, take the escort, the banners, and go on board the *Saint*, I'll come immediately.

GOLOVAN. Permit me to report that ...

KHLUDOV. I'm in my right mind, I'll come, don't be afraid, I'll come.

GOLOVAN. Yes, sir. (*Disappears*.)

KHLUDOV. Well, she's probably sailing there, to Constantinople.

GOLUBKOV (*blindly*). Yes, yes, yes, to Constantinople ... Nevertheless, I will not leave you. There are the lights, they are the lights in port, look. Take me to Constantinople.

KHLUDOV. Oh, damn, damn, damn!

GOLUBKOV. Khludov, let's go, quickly!

KHLUDOV. Be quiet. (*He mutters*.) Well, there now, I've satisfied one; now I'm at liberty to talk to you a little. (*Into space*.) What do you want? For me to remain? No, he doesn't answer. He grows dim, walks away, is covered with darkness, and stands there in the distance.

GOLUBKOV (*sadly*). Khludov, you're sick! Khludov, it's delirium! Forget him! We must hurry! The *Saint* will leave and we're late!

KHLUDOV. Damn ... damn ... some Serafima ... to Constantinople ... Well, let's go, let's go! (*Exits quickly*.)

Golubkov *exits behind him. Darkness. The dream ends.*

END OF ACT TWO

ACT III

Dream Five

..."Janissary is off his stride! ..."

A STRANGE SYMPHONY. *Turkish tunes are being sung, intermingled with a Russian barrel-organ playing "The Parting,"*[15] *the moaning calls of street hawkers, the rumble of trolley cars. And suddenly Constantinople begins to glow in the precrepuscular sun. A dominating minaret and the roofs of houses are seen. Standing there is an unusual looking structure something like a carousel over which is painted a large sign in French, English, and Russian: "STOP! THE SENSATION OF CONSTANTINOPLE! COCKROACH RACES!!!"*[16] *"GAMBLING A LA RUSSE WITH POLICE PERMISSION." "SENSATION A CONSTANTINOPLE! COURSES DES CAFARDS."* Тараканьи Бега *The structure is decorated with the flags of various nations. A ticket booth with signs: "Single bets" and "Parlays." There is a sign over the booth in French and Russian: "Beginning at 5 o'clock." "Commencement a cinq heures du soir." Alongside there is an open-air restaurant beneath scrofulous laurel trees in tubs. A sign: "A Russian delicacy —Caspian roach fish. Fifty piastres per serving." Higher up, cut out of plywood, there is a painted cockroach in a frock coat, serving*

15. A Russian folk song: "No one will part us/ Not the sun, not the moon/ Parting, oh parting/ An alien shore."

16. There actually were cockroach races in Constantinople, along with Russian prostitutes and fights among sailors. A similar description of the races appears at the end of Alexei Tolstoy's *The Adventures of Nevzorov, or Ibikus* (1924), a satirical novel which ends with the evacuation of Odessa and a description of émigré life in Constantinople.

a foaming glass of beer. A laconic sign: "Beer." Higher than this structure, and behind it, the narrow alley lives its life in the broiling heat: Turkish women in yashmaks pass by, as do Turks in red fezes, foreign sailors in white; from time to time they lead past small burros carrying baskets. A small shop selling coconuts. RUSSIANS *in bedraggled military uniforms flit by. The small bells of lemonade vendors are heard. Somewhere a little boy is desperately howling: "Presse du soir!" At the exit downward from the alley to the structure stands* CHARNOTA *in a black Circassian coat without shoulder straps, intoxicated, in spite of the heat, and gloomy; he is selling rubber devils, figures with wagging tongues, and some sort of jumping dolls on a tray which he is carrying on his stomach.*

CHARNOTA. Doesn't smash, doesn't break, just turns somersaults! Buy a Red commissar for the amusement of your angelic little children! Madame! Madame! *Achetez pour vos enfants!*

A TURKISH WOMAN (a loving mother). *Boonoon fia ty nadyr? Combien?*

CHARNOTA. *Cinquante* piastres, *madame, cinquante!*

A TURKISH WOMAN (a loving mother). *Oh, eeok! Boo pakali dyr!* (*She passes by.*)

CHARNOTA. *Madame! Quarante!* Oh, why don't you drop dead! You never had any children anyway! *Gehen Sie! . . . Gehen Sie! . . .* Get to the harem! My God, what's the use of this bastardly city?

> *Constantinople moans above* Charnota. *Somewhere tenors break loose—sellers of lemons, crying sweetly: "Amboolyasi! Amboolyasi!" Basses sing in the symphony: "Kaimaki! Kaimaki!" The heat streams down. A* Small Face *rises up in the ticket booth.* Charnota *goes up to the booth.*

Maria Konstantinovna, hey, Maria Konstantinovna!

THE SMALL FACE. What do you want, Grigory Lukianovich?

CHARNOTA. You see, it's a small business matter . . . Can't you bet on Janissary for me today, on credit?

THE SMALL FACE. My goodness, Grigory, Lukianovich, I cannot.

CHARNOTA. What's the matter? Am I a swindler or a Constantinople Freemason, or a man you don't know? I should think you could trust a general who has his own commercial business right beside the races?

THE SMALL FACE. That's the way it is . . . Tell Artur Arturovich yourself.

CHARNOTA. Artur Arturovich!

ARTUR ARTUROVICH (*appears on the carousel like Punch from behind a screen, he has great difficulty buttoning his dress-shirt collar*). What's the matter? Who needs me? Ah! . . . How can I help you?

CHARNOTA. You see, I wanted to ask you . . .

ARTUR ARTUROVICH. No! (*He disappears.*)

CHARNOTA. What kind of boorishness is this? Where have you disappeared to before I told you?

ARTUR ARTUROVICH (*appears*). Well, I know what you're going to say.

CHARNOTA. That's interesting—what?

ARTUR ARTUROVICH. What I will say to you is much more interesting.

CHARNOTA. That's interesting—what?

ARTUR ARTUROVICH. *No one* gets any credit! (*He disappears.*)

CHARNOTA. What an animal!

> *Two* French Sailors *appear in the restaurant and shout:* "Un bock! Un bock!" The waiter serves beer.

THE SMALL FACE. There's a bedbug crawling on you, Grigory Lukianovich, take it off.

CHARNOTA. Well to hell with him, I won't even consider taking him off, it's absolutely useless. Let him crawl, he's not bothering me. Ah, what a city! . . . What cities haven't I seen—but nothing like this . . . Yes, I've seen many cities, enchanting cities, cities of world-wide importance.

THE SMALL FACE. What cities have you seen, Grigory Lukianovich?

CHARNOTA. Lord! Kharkov! And Rostov! And Kiev! Eh, city of Kiev, it's beautiful, Maria Konstantinovna! The monastery all aflame in the hills, and the Dnieper, oh the Dnieper! Indescribable air, indescribable light! Grass, the smell of hay, slopes, vales, the ravines by the Dnieper! And I remember what a glorious battle there was outside Kiev, a fine battle! It was warm, the sun, warm but not hot, Maria Konstantinovna. And, of course, there were lice . . . The louse—now there's an insect!

THE SMALL FACE. Phooey, what nastiness you are mouthing, Grigory Lukianovich!

CHARNOTA. Why nastiness? After all, one must make a study of insects. The louse is a military beast, a fighting one, but the bedbug is a parasite. The louse marches in squadrons, in cavalry order, it flows like lava, and then, naturally, there will be the hugest battles! (*He is sad.*) Artur!

ARTUR ARTUROVICH (*looks out, wearing a frock coat*). What are you yelling about?

CHARNOTA. Artur, I look at you and I am enraptured! Why there you are in your frock coat. You're not a man, you're a marvel of nature—tsar of the cockroaches. Well, you are lucky! But then your people are lucky in general!

ARTUR ARTUROVICH. If you begin anti-Semitism here again, I'll terminate my conversation with you.

CHARNOTA. Why, what's wrong with you? It's you who say you're a Hungarian.

ARTUR ARTUROVICH. Nevertheless . . .

CHARNOTA. So that's what I'm saying now—you Hungarians are lucky! Look here, Artur Arturovich: I want to liquidate my enterprise. (*He points to the tray.*)

ARTUR ARTUROVICH. Fifty.

CHARNOTA. Fifty what?

ARTUR ARTUROVICH. Piastres.

CHARNOTA. What's wrong with you, you're sneering at me? I sell them for fifty apiece!

ARTUR ARTUROVICH. Well, continue doing so!

CHARNOTA. So you've already made up your mind to go on sucking blood?

ARTUR ARTUROVICH. I'm not forcing you.

CHARNOTA. You're a lucky man, Artur Arturovich, you didn't fall into my hands in the Northern Crimea!

ARTUR ARTUROVICH. Well, this is not the Northern Crimea, thank God!

CHARNOTA. Take the cartridge belts too. Silver ones.

ARTUR ARTUROVICH. The cartridge belts along with the tray—two lire, fifty.

CHARNOTA. Here, take them! (*He gives the tray and cartridge belts to* Artur.)

ARTUR ARTUROVICH. Please. (*He gives money to* Charnota.)

Three men wearing hats with peacock feathers, sleeveless vests, and carrying concertinas walk by on the carousel.

(*He disappears, then again looks out, shouting.*) Five o'clock! We are beginning! Please, gentlemen!

The Russian tricolor flag is raised over the carousel. In the carousel the concertinas begin to play a rollicking march. Charnota *heads for the ticket booth first.*

CHARNOTA. Put two lire fifty on Janissary, Maria Konstantinovna!

The public flocks to the booth. A group of Italian Sailors *bursts in, behind them are* English Sailors *and then a pretty* Prostitute. *Swindlers of various types show up; a* Negro *flits by. The march thunders. A waiter flies into the restaurant, serves beer.* Artur, *wearing a frock coat and top hat, rises up over the carousel. The march ceases.*

ARTUR ARTUROVICH. *Messieurs, mesdames!* The races are open! A Russian Imperial Court game which has not been seen anywhere else in the world! Cockroach races! *Cours de cafard. Corso del piatello.* Cockroach races! The favorite amusement of the late empress in Tsarskoe Selo! *L'amusement préféré de la défunte imperatrice russe à Tsarskoe Selo.*

Two Policemen *appear—one Italian, one Turkish.*

The first heat! Racing are: Number One—Black Pearl! Number Two—the favorite, Janissary.

ITALIAN SAILORS (*applaud, shout*). *Evviva!*

ENGLISH SAILORS (*whistle, shout*). Away! Away!

A sweaty, upset Person *in a bowler and quarter-master corps shoulder straps bursts in.*

SWEATY PERSON. Am I late? Have they started?

A voice: "You'll make it!"

ARTUR ARTUROVICH. Third—Baba-Yaga! Fourth—Don't Cry, Baby! A dapple-grey cockroach!

Shouts: "Hurrah! Don't Cry, Baby!"
"It is a swindle!"
"It is a swindle!"

Sixth—Hooligan! Seventh—Button!

Whistling. Shouts: "A trap! A trap!"

ARTUR ARTUROVICH. I beg your pardon! No tricks! The cockroaches run on an open board with paper jockies! The cockroaches live in a sealed box under the observation of a professor of entomology from the Imperial University of Kazan, who was barely saved from the hands of the Bolsheviks! And so, to the start! (*He falls through into the carousel.*)

The crowd of gamblers surges toward the carousel. Little Boys appear on the stone fences. There is a rumbling inside the carousel, then dead silence. Then the concertinas begin to play "The Moon Shines",[17] through the music one can hear cockroach feet start running, with a rustling. A frantic voice in the carousel: "They're off and running!" A little Greek Boy who looks like a small devil dances on the fence, shouting "They're off! They're off!" A shout in the carousel: "Janissary is off his stride!" Rumbling.

CHARNOTA (*at the booth*). What do you mean off his stride? That cannot be!!!

A voice in the carousel: "Don't Cry, Baby!" Another voice: "Go on, go on, go on!"

Killing Artur wouldn't be enough!

The Small Face sticks itself out of the booth nervously. The Police look nervous, they glance into the carousel.

17. A Russian folk song.

A FIGURE (*running out of the carousel*). A swindle! Artur got Janissary drunk on beer!

> Artur *bursts out of the carousel. Both tails of his frock coat have been torn off, his top hat transformed into a wafer, he has no collar. His face is bloody. The crowd of gamblers is chasing him.*

ARTUR ARTUROVICH (*shouts desperately*). Maria Konstantinovna, call the police!

> *The* Small Face *disappears. The* Policemen *whistle.*

ITALIAN SAILORS (*shout*). *Ladro! Scroccone! Trufatore!*

THE PRETTY PROSTITUTE. Beat Artur up! Gianni! (*To* Artur.) Ingannatore!

ENGLISH SAILORS. Hip, hip, hurrah! Long live Button!

THE PRETTY PROSTITUTE. Brothers! *Fratelli!* Someone bribed Artur to have Button win! The favorite is waggling his feet, drunk as a pig! When has Janissary ever been off his stride?

ARTUR ARTUROVICH (*in despair*). When did you ever see a drunken cockroach? *Je vous demand un peu, où est-ce que vous avez vu un cafard saoul?* Police! Police! *Au secours!* ... Police! Help!

THE PRETTY PROSTITUTE. *Mensonge!* Lies! The whole public bet on Janissary! Beat him up, the scoundrel!

ITALIAN SAILOR (*grabs* Artur *by the throat, shouts*). *A marmalia!*

THE ITALIANS (*shout*). *Canalia!*

ARTUR ARTUROVICH (*soulfully*). They're killing me ...

ENGLISH BOATSWAIN (*to the* Italian). Stop! Keep back! (*He grabs the* Italian.)

THE FIGURE. Give him one on the ear!

THE PRETTY PROSTITUTE (*to the* Englishman). Ah, so you're defending him?!

> *The* Englishman *hits the* Italian, *he falls.*

THE PRETTY PROSTITUTE. *A soccorso, fratelli!* Help, brothers! Beat up the English! Italians, help!

> *The* English *fight with the* Italians. *The* Italians *draw knives. At the sight of the knives the public scatters in all*

directions with a howl. A little Greek Boy, *dancing on the wall, shouts: "They're slashing up the English!!!" A crowd of* Italian *and* Turkish Policemen *with revolvers bursts in from the alley, blowing whistles.* Charnota, *standing by the ticket booth, clutches his head. The dream suddenly disintegrates. Darkness. Silence takes over, and a new dream flows on.*

D R E A M   S I X

...Parting, oh, parting!...[18]

A COURTYARD *with cypresses appears, a two-storied house with a gallery. A reservoir by the stone wall, drops of water drip softly. A stone bench by a wicket gate. Beyond the house a crooked, deserted alley. The sun is setting beyond the balustrade of a minaret. The first crepuscular shadows. It is quiet.*

CHARNOTA (*entering the courtyard*). Damned Button! But who cares about Button. The fact is that I am done for irrevocably . . . She'll devour me, devour me. Should I flee, or what? But where, if I may ask, Grigory Lukianovich, will you flee? This is not your Crimea, there's no way to flee. Ay-yay-yay!

A door of the small gallery opens, and Lyuska *comes out. Dressed sloppily.* Lyuska *is hungry; because of this her eyes glitter and her face suggests an unearthly but passing beauty.*

LYUSKA. Ah, a good day to you, Your Excellency! Bonjour, Madame Barabanchikova!
CHARNOTA. Hello, Lyusenka!
LYUSKA. Why have you come so early? If I were you, I'd loaf around

18. See note 14.

until late evening—especially since it's very boring at home—there's no food, no money. But there is happy news written on your expressive face, and you don't have the tray. And the cartridge belts are missing. I think I'm beginning to understand what's going on. The money, please. Serafima and I haven't eaten anything since yesterday. If you please.

CHARNOTA. And where is Serafima?

LYUSKA. That's not important. She's doing the wash. Well, hand over the money.

CHARNOTA. There has been a catastrophe, Lyusenka.

LYUSKA. You don't say? Where are the cartridge belts?

CHARNOTA. Lyuska, I got the idea of selling them, and, you see, I put them in the tray and took the tray to the Grand Bazaar for a moment, and . . .

LYUSKA. It was stolen?

CHARNOTA. Yes . . .

LYUSKA. Of course, a man with a black beard, isn't that right?

CHARNOTA (*weakening*). What's a man with a black beard got to do with it?

LYUSKA. But he always steals from scoundrels at the Grand Bazaar. So on your word of honor it was stolen?

Charnota *nods his head.*

Well, in that case. Do you know what you are, Grisha?

CHARNOTA. What?

LYUSKA. A rotten bastard!

CHARNOTA. How dare you?

Serafima *comes out with a bucket, stops. The two who are quarreling do not notice her.*

LYUSKA. I dare because that tray was bought with my money!

CHARNOTA. You're my wife, and we have common money!

LYUSKA. The husband gets it from selling rubber devils, and the wife by selling something quite different.

CHARNOTA. What did you say?

LYUSKA. Why are you playing the fool? Did I go with that Frenchman last week to sing psalms? Did anyone ask me where I got five lire? And we lived on five lire for a week, you and I and Serafima! But that's still not all! The tray with the cartridge belts wasn't left at the Grand Bazaar, but at the cockroach races! All right, sir, let's sum it all up. The dashing knight General Charnota smashed up counter-intelligence, he had to flee from the army, and now he's in beggary in Constantinople and I with him!

CHARNOTA. What's wrong, can you reproach me for saving a woman from perishing? You can reproach me for Serafima?

LYUSKA. No! But her, Serafima, I can reproach, I can! (*She takes the bit between her teeth.*) Let immaculate Serafima live, let her go on sighing for her missing Golubkov, and let the brilliant general go on living off the dissolute Lyuska!

SERAFIMA. Lyuska!

LYUSKA. Eavesdropping doesn't seem to suit you, Serafima Vladimirovna!

SERAFIMA. I didn't mean to eavesdrop, I don't do that. I heard it accidentally, and it's a good thing I did. Why didn't you tell me anything about the five lire before?

LYUSKA. Come on, Serafima, come on, are you blind or what?

SERAFIMA. I swear to you, I didn't know anything. I thought that he brought the five lire. But don't worry, Lyuska, I'll work it off.

LYUSKA. Please, spare me the nobility!

SERAFIMA. Don't be angry, let's not quarrel. Let's clarify the situation.

LYUSKA. There's nothing to clarify. Tomorrow the Greeks will throw us out of the apartment, there's absolutely nothing to gnaw on, everything's been sold. (*She gets furious again.*) No, I can't calm down! He's the one who's got me burned up! (*To Charnota.*) Answer me, you lost it gambling?

CHARNOTA. I lost it.

LYUSKA. Oh you! . . .

CHARNOTA. Consider my position! I can't peddle devils! I was a warrior!

SERAFIMA. Lyuska, stop it, stop . . . Just stop it! How will two and a half lire help us?

Silence.

But really some malicious fate is persecuting us.

LYUSKA. Lyricism!

CHARNOTA (*abruptly, to* Lyuska). Were you with the Frenchman?

LYUSKA. Get to hell away from me!

SERAFIMA. Quiet, quiet, quiet! Cease quarreling, I'll bring supper right away.

LYUSKA. Stop it, Serafima, don't get mixed up in things that aren't your business. Don't be offended by my words. I'll go that road anyway. I'm not going to sit here without eating, I have my principles!

SERAFIMA. And I'm not going to sit here without eating, and I'm not going to live at someone else's expense. And to know that you are walking the street, earning money that way and just to sit here would be so low, so low! You should have told me everything! We've fallen into a pit together—so we will work together too!

LYUSKA. Charnota will sell his revolver.

CHARNOTA. Lyusenka, I'll sell my trousers, I'll sell anything—but not my revolver! I can't live without my revolver!

LYUSKA. It takes the place of your head. Well, go ahead and live off women!

CHARNOTA. Don't you provoke me!

LYUSKA. If you so much as touch me with a finger, I'll slit your throat in the middle of the night!

SERAFIMA. Stop it. Why are you always snapping at each other? There will be a supper, I tell you! You're doing this from hunger!

LYUSKA. What have you got in mind, you fool?

SERAFIMA. I'm not a fool at all—but I really *was* a fool! And does it make any difference what one sells? It's all such nonsense! (*She goes away to the little gallery, then returns wearing a hat. As she is leaving.*) Please, just wait for me without brawling.

Somewhere a concertina begins playing "Parting."

LYUSKA. Serafima! Simka!

CHARNOTA. Simka!

Silence.

LYUSKA. Ooh, repulsive city! Ooh, the bedbugs! Ooh, the Bosphorus! And you . . .

CHARNOTA. Shut up.

LYUSKA. I hate you, and myself, and all Russians. Outcasts from Hell! (*Exits to the gallery*.)

CHARNOTA (*alone*). To Paris or to Berlin, where should I head? To Madrid, perhaps? A Spanish city . . . Haven't been there. But I'll bet it's a hole. (*He squats down, digs around under a cypress tree, finds a butt*.) What greedy people the Greeks are, they smoke them right down to the tips, the sons of bitches! No, I don't agree with her, our Russians are better, definitely better. (*He lights up the butt and exits to the gallery*.)

Golubkov *enters the courtyard; he is wearing an English service-jacket and puttees and a Turkish fez. Carrying a hurdy-gurdy. He puts it on the ground and begins to play "Parting, oh parting . . . ," then a march.*

CHARNOTA (*shouts from the gallery*). Will you stop tearing my soul apart, you Turkish pig snout!

GOLUBKOV. What? Gri . . . Grigory Lukianovich?! I said I'd find you! I've done it!

CHARNOTA. Who is it? Is it you—assistant professor?

GOLUBKOV (*sits on the edge of the reservoir, agitated*). I've found you!

CHARNOTA (*runs down to him*). You've found me . . . found me . . . I took you for a Turk. Hello! (*He kisses Golubkov*.) What a sight! Hey, you've aged! We thought you'd stayed with the Bolsheviks. Where have you been the last six months?

GOLUBKOV. First I lounged around in a camp, then I caught typhus, lay about a hospital for two months, and now I'm trudging all over Constantinople, Khludov took me in. They've mustered him out of the army, you know!

CHARNOTA. I heard. I'm a civilian myself now, brother. We've seen everything here . . . But we haven't noticed anyone with a hurdy-gurdy yet.

GOLUBKOV. It's very handy for me to have the hurdy-gurdy. I walk

around from courtyard to courtyard—it's the way I search. Tell
me quickly, did she die? Tell me, don't be afraid. I've gotten used
to everything.

CHARNOTA. Ah, Serafima! Why die? She recovered—she's alive and
kicking!

GOLUBKOV. I've found her! (*He embraces* Charnota.)

CHARNOTA. Of course she's alive. But I must say we've fallen into a
difficult situation, sir! Everything's collapsed! We've reached the
last extremity, Seryozha!

GOLUBKOV. But where is she, where's Serafima?

CHARNOTA. She's here. She'll be here. She went to pick up men on
the *Pera*.

GOLUBKOV. What?!

CHARNOTA. Well why are you bugging your eyes out at me? We're
croaking from hunger. No cartridge belts, no money.

GOLUBKOV. So she went to the *Pera?* You're lying!

CHARNOTA. Why should I lie? I myself haven't had a smoke for half
a day now. Something's inclining me toward Madrid ... I dreamed
of Madrid all night ...

Voices are heard. Serafima *enters the courtyard, and behind
her is a* Greek Don Juan, *decorated with purchases and
carrying bottles in his hands.*

SERAFIMA. Oh no, no, it will be very comfortable, we'll sit and chat
for a while ... True, we do live in bivouac style ...

GREEK DON JUAN (*with a heavy accent*). Very, very nice! I fear I
will trouble you, madame.

SERAFIMA. Please, I will introduce you ...

Charnota *turns his back to her.*

Where are you going, Grigory Lukianovich, this is unpleasant!

GREEK DON JUAN. Very, very pleased!

SERAFIMA (*recognizing* Golubkov). My God!

Golubkov, *frowning heavily, gets up from the reservoir,
walks up to the* Greek *and punches him in the ear. The*

Greek Don Juan *drops the purchases, extremely crushed.*
Anxious Greeks *and* Armenians *appear in the windows.*
Lyuska *comes out on the gallery.*

GREEK DON JUAN. What's this? What's going on?

SERAFIMA. My God! . . . Shame, shame!

CHARNOTA. Mr. Greek!

GREEK DON JUAN. Ah, I've landed in a fly-trap, a dive! (*He is sad.*)

SERAFIMA. Forgive me, monsieur, forgive me, for God's sake! This
is terrible, it's a misunderstanding!

CHARNOTA (*taking his revolver, he turns toward the windows*).
Shove off this minute!

The Observers *get down and the windows close.*

GREEK DON JUAN (*mournfully*). Oh, my God! . . .

GOLUBKOV (*moving toward him*). You . . .

GREEK DON JUAN (*taking out his wallet and watch*). There's my
wallet and my watch, brave man! My life is dear—I have a family,
a store, little children . . . I won't say anything to the police . . .
live on, kind sir, praise God Almighty . . .

GOLUBKOV. Get out of here!

GREEK DON JUAN. Ah, Istanbul, what a place you've become! . . .

GOLUBKOV. Take the purchases!

The Greek Don Juan *wants to take the purchases, but he*
looks into Golubkov's *face and sets off running.*

LYUSKA. Mr. Golubkov? And we just mentioned you not an hour
ago! We thought you were there—in Russia. But your wit may
be considered brilliant!

GOLUBKOV. But you, Serafima Vladimirovna, what are you doing?!
I sailed and I fled and I was in the hospital, you see, my head has
been shaved . . . I fled only for you! But you, what are you doing
here?

SERAFIMA. Who gave you the right to reproach me?

GOLUBKOV. I love you, I chased after you in order to tell you that!

SERAFIMA. Leave me alone! I don't want to hear any more! All this

makes me sick! Why have you appeared in front of me again?
We're all beggars! I'm getting away from you all! . . . I want to
perish alone! God, what shame! What disgrace! Goodbye!

GOLUBKOV. I implore you, don't leave!

SERAFIMA. I'll never come back, not for anything! (*She leaves.*)

GOLUBKOV. Ah, so that's the way it is! (*Abruptly snatches* Charnota's
dagger and rushes after Serafima.)

CHARNOTA (*grabbing him from behind, takes the dagger away*).
What's wrong with you, have you gone out of your mind? You
want to go to jail?

GOLUBKOV. Let go! I'll find her anyway, I'll stop her anyway! All
right. (*He sits on the edge of the reservoir.*)

LYUSKA. What a performance, what a performance! The Greeks are
stunned by it. All right, that's enough. Charnota, open that package, I'm hungry.

GOLUBKOV. I won't let you touch the packages!

CHARNOTA. No, I won't open them.

LYUSKA. So this is how it is! My patience is exhausted! I've drunk
my Constantinople cup to the dregs! (*She takes her hat from the
gallery and some sort of package and she exits.*) Well, sir, Grigory
Lukianovich, I wish you the best of luck. Our life together is at
an end. Lyuska has acquaintances on the Orient Express, and
Lyuska has been a fool for sitting around here for six months!
Goodbye!

CHARNOTA. Where are you going?

LYUSKA. To Paris! Paris! Goodbye! (*She disappears in the alley.*)

> Charnota *and* Golubkov *sit on the edge of the reservoir in
> silence. A little* Turkish Boy *leading someone waves and
> says "This way, this way!" Behind the little* Boy *walks*
> Khludov *wearing civilian clothes. He has aged and grown
> grey.*

CHARNOTA. So here's Roman. He's turned up too. What are you
looking at—that I have no cartridge belts? I'm like you—a free
man.

KHLUDOV. Yes, I see already. Well, hello, Grigory Lukianovich. Yes,
see how each of us is walking in the footsteps of the other. (*Point-

ing to Golubkov). First I cured him, and now he's going around with the idea of curing me. Meanwhile he's playing the hurdy-gurdy. (*To* Golubkov.) Well, what's going on, no results here either?

GOLUBKOV. No, I found her. Only don't ask me any questions. Don't ask any questions.

KHLUDOV. I'm not asking you. That's your business. Only one thing is important to me—you found her?

GOLUBKOV. Khludov! I'll only ask you one thing, and you alone can do it. Go after her, she has left me, hold her back, save her from going to walk the streets.

KHLUDOV. Why can't you do that yourself?

GOLUBKOV. Here, on the reservoir, I made a firm resolution—I am going away to Paris. I'll find Korzukhin, he is a rich man, he ruined her, he is obliged to help her.

KHLUDOV. How will you go? Who will let you into France?

GOLUBKOV. I'll go secretly. I was playing my hurdy-gurdy in the port today, a captain sympathized with me; I'll put you in the hold, he said, I'll take you away to Marseilles in the hold.

KHLUDOV. What then? Must I watch over her for a long time?

GOLUBKOV. I'll return soon, and I swear to you that I'll never ask you for anything again.

KHLUDOV. That railroad station has cost me dearly. (*He turns around.*) No, not here.

CHARNOTA (*in a whisper*). A fine guardian!

GOLUBKOV (*in a whisper*). Don't look at him, he's fighting with it.

KHLUDOV. Where did she go just now?

CHARNOTA. That's not hard to guess. She went to beg the Greek's forgiveness, to Shishli Street, the second-hand store there. I know him.

KHLUDOV. Well, all right.

GOLUBKOV. Just keep her from walking the streets!

KHLUDOV. When she's at my place? She won't leave. It wasn't for nothing a certain orderly said: "There's no getting by you." However, I'm not going to start reminiscing . . . "O Lord God, remember me!" (*To* Golubkov.) You have no money?

GOLUBKOV. I don't need money!

KHLUDOV. Don't be foolish. Here are two lire, I don't have any more right now. (*He unbuttons the medallion from his watch.*) Take the medallion, in case of emergency sell it. (*He exits.*)

The evening shadows are thicker. The sweet voice of a muezzin begins to flow from the minaret: "La ilâh illa illâh."

GOLUBKOV. And now night is setting in . . . a terrible city! An unbearable city! A suffocating city! But why am I sitting here? It's time! I'll go away in the hold at night.

CHARNOTA. I'll go with you. We won't get any money, I don't even hope for that—but I simply have to go somewhere. I say—I thought of Madrid, but Paris is perhaps somehow more decent. Let's go. Our Greek landlords will be surprised and overjoyed!

GOLUBKOV (*walking*). It's never cool—neither during the day nor at night!

CHARNOTA (*goes away with him*). To Paris, and so to Paris.

The little Turkish Boy *runs up to the hurdy-gurdy, turns the handle. The hurdy-gurdy plays a march. The muezzin's voice flies from the minaret. Shadows. Here and there lights are already beginning to burn. There is a pale golden crescent in the sky. Then darkness. The dream ends.*

END OF ACT THREE

ACT IV

DREAM SEVEN

...Three cards, three cards, three cards! ...

AUTUMN SUNSET *in Paris. Mr.* KORZUKHIN's *study in his own mansion. The study is furnished in an extraordinarily impressive way. Among other things there is a safe. Besides a desk, there is a card table. On it the cards and two unlit candles stand ready.*

KORZUKHIN. Antoine!

Antoine, *a manservant of very dignified French appearance enters; he is wearing a green apron.*

Monsieur Marchand m'avait averti qu'il ne viendra pas aujourd'hui. Ne remuez pas le table. Je me servirai plus tard.

Silence.

Repondez-donc quelque chose! Well, it appears you haven't understood a thing.

ANTOINE. So, sir, Paramon Ilych, I didn't understand.

KORZUKHIN. How do you say "no, sir" in French?

ANTOINE. I don't know, Paramon Ilych.

KORZUKHIN. Antoine, you are a Russian lazybones. Remember, a person who lives in Paris should know that Russian is good only for swearing in unprintable words or, what is still worse, for promulgating some kind of destructive slogans. Neither the former nor the latter are acceptable in Paris. Study, Antoine, I'm sick of this. *Que faites-vous à ce moment?* What are you doing at this moment?

ANTOINE. *Je* . . . I'm cleaning knives, Paramon Ilych.
KORZUKHIN. How do you say "knives," Antoine?
ANTOINE. *Les couteaux,* Paramon Ilych.
KORZUKHIN. Correct. Study, Antoine.

A bell.

(*He unbuttons his pajamas, talks as he is going out.*) I'll receive now. Perhaps a partner will turn up. *Je suis à la maison.* (*He exits.*)

> Antoine *exits and returns with* Golubkov. *The latter is wearing black sailor pants, a shabby grey jacket, and he has a cap in his hands.*

GOLUBKOV. *Je voudrais parler à monsieur Korzukhin.*
ANTOINE. Please, your calling card, *votre carte.*
GOLUBKOV. What? You're Russian? And I took you for a Frenchman. How glad I am!
ANTOINE. Yes, sir, I am Russian. My name is Grishchenko.

> Golubkov *shakes* Antoine's *hand.*

GOLUBKOV. Here's the point—I have no cards. You just say that it's Golubkov from Constantinople.
ANTOINE. Yes, sir. (*He disappears.*)
KORZUKHIN (*coming out already dressed in a jacket, he mutters*). What Golubkov is this? . . . Golubkov . . . What can I do for you?
GOLUBKOV. You probably don't recognize me. We met a year ago, that awful night at a station in the Crimea when your wife was arrested. Now she's in Constantinople on the verge of ruination.
KORZUKHIN. On the verge of what? Forgive me, first of all. I have no wife, and second, I don't remember any station either.
GOLUBKOV. What do you mean? It was night . . . There was still a terrible cold-wave—you remember the cold-wave during the time the Crimea was taken?
KORZUKHIN. Unfortunately, I don't remember any cold-wave. You are surely mistaken.
GOLUBKOV. But you are Paramon Ilych Korzukhin, you were in the Crimea, why, I recognize you!

Korzukhin. I did in fact live in the Crimea for a short time, just when those half-insane generals were storming around there. But, you see, then I left; I have no connections with Russia and intend to have none. I have assumed French citizenship, I was not married, and I should tell you that for three months now a Russian émigré woman who has also assumed French citizenship, and the name Frejole, has been living in my house in the capacity of personal secretary. This enchanting creature has so touched my heart that—I tell you this in secret—I intend to marry her soon, so that any conversations about any supposedly existing wife are unpleasant for me.

Golubkov. Frejole ... So, you are renouncing a living human being! But she was traveling to join you! Remember, they arrested her? Remember, the cold, the windows, the blue moon of a street light.

Korzukhin. Well, yes, a blue moon, the cold ... Counter-intelligence tried to blackmail me once with the help of this legend about some Communist wife or other of mine. This conversation is unpleasant for me, Mr. Golubkov, I repeat.   ,

Golubkov. Ai-yai-yai! I'm dreaming my life! ...

Korzukhin. Beyond any doubt.

Golubkov. I understand. She is in your way, and so very well. Let her not be your wife. It's even better that way. I love her, understand that! And I will do everything to deliver her from the clutches of beggary. But I ask you to help her at least temporarily. You are a very rich man; everyone knows that all of your capital was abroad. Give me a loan of a thousand dollars. and as soon as we get on our feet, I'll return it to you as a holy debt. I'll work it off! I'll set this as the goal of my life.

Korzukhin. Excuse me, Monsieur Golubkov, I supposed that this conversation about my mythical wife would lead precisely to dollars. A thousand? I didn't hear wrong?

Golubkov. A thousand. I swear to you, I will return it!

Korzukhin. Ah, young man! Before talking about a thousand dollars I will tell you what one dollar is. (*He begins a ballad about the dollar and is carried away by inspiration.*) A dollar! That Great, Almighty Spirit! It is everywhere! Look there! There, far away, on the roof burns a golden ray, and high in the air alongside it a crouching black cat—a chimera! The dollar is there too! The chimera watches over it! (*He points mysteriously to the floor.*) A vague sensation, not a rumble or a noise, but as it were the breathing of a swelling earth; there trains fly like arrows—they carry the dollars. Now close your eyes and imagine—darkness, through it roll waves as big as mountains. Gloom and water—the ocean! It is terrifying, it will devour you. But there is a monster moving through the ocean, with a hissing of boilers, ripping apart millions of tons of water! It moves along, it groans, it carries fiery lights! It plows through the water; it strains—but there in the furnaces of hell where there are naked stokers, it bears its golden child, its divine heart—the dollar! And suddenly the world is disturbed!

The sounds of passing military music are heard somewhere far away.

And there they are already coming! They're coming! There are thousands of them, then millions! Their heads are soldered into steel helmets. They're coming! Next they will run! Next they will throw their breasts on barbed wire with a howl! Why will they have thrown themselves? Because somewhere they offended the divine dollar! But now the world is at peace, and everywhere, in every city, the victory horns are blowing! The dollar has been avenged! They are blowing in honor of the dollar! (*He quiets down.*)

The music moves further off.

And so, Mr. Golubkov, I think that even you yourself will stop insisting that I hand over a whole thousand dollars to an unknown young man?

GOLUBKOV. No, I am not going to insist. But I would like to tell you in parting, Mr. Korzukhin, that you are the most soulless, the most terrible man I have ever seen. And you will have retribution worked upon you, it will come! It could be no other way! Goodbye! (*He starts to leave.*)

A bell. Antoine *enters.*

ANTOINE. General Charnota.

Korzukhin. Hm . . . A Russian day. Well, invite him in, invite him.

> Antoine *exits.* Charnota *enters. He's wearing a Cossack jacket but without the silver belt and without the dagger— and he is wearing lemon-colored underpants. The expression on his face shows that* Charnota *has nothing to lose. He is voluble.*

Charnota. Hi there, Paramosha!

Korzukhin. Can it be we have met?

Charnota. Such a question! What's wrong with you, Paramon, are you dreaming? What about Sevastopol?

Korzukhin. Ah, yes, yes . . . Very happy. Forgive me, did we drink *Brüderschaft?*

Charnota. Damned if I know, don't recall . . . but once we did meet, we must have drunk it.

Korzukhin. Forgive me, please . . . You seem to be wearing underpants.

Charnota. And why does that surprise you? I'm not a woman, on whom this type of garment would not be appropriate.

Korzukhin. General, did . . . did you walk around Paris, through the streets, like this? ,

Charnota. No, I walked the streets wearing trousers, but I took them off in your anteroom. What a foolish question!

Korzukhin. Pardon, pardon!

Charnota (*softly, to* Golubkov). Did he give it?

Golubkov. No, I'm leaving. Let's get out of here.

Charnota. Well where are we going to go now? (*To* Korzukhin.) What's wrong with you, Paramon? Your fellow countrymen, who fought against the Bolsheviks for you stand before you, and you refuse them a trifling sum. Do you understand that Serafima is starving in Constantinople?

Golubkov. I'll ask you to be quiet. In a word, let's go, Grigory!

Charnota. Well, you know, Paramon, I am a sinful man. I would sign up with the Bolsheviks purposely, just to shoot you. I'd shoot you, and in an instant I'd quit the Party and leave them. But, hold it, why do you have those cards out? Do you play?

KORZUKHIN. I don't see anything surprising about that. I play and like it very much.

CHARNOTA. You play! What game do you play?

KORZUKHIN. Imagine it, *chemin-de-fer,* and I like it very much.

CHARNOTA. Then let's have a game.

KORZUKHIN. I would with pleasure, but, you see, I like playing for cash only.

GOLUBKOV. Will you stop humiliating yourself, or not, Grigory? Let's go!

CHARNOTA. There's nothing humiliating in this. (*In a whisper.*) What were you told. In an extreme emergency? Nothing could be more extreme: give me Khludov's medallion!

GOLUBKOV. There you are, please, it doesn't make any difference to me now. And I am leaving.

CHARNOTA. No, we'll leave together. I won't let you go with such a face. You'll drown yourself in the Seine. (*Holds out the medallion to* Korzukhin.) How much?

KORZUKHIN. Hm ... a decent item ... Well, what the ... ten dollars.

CHARNOTA. Really, Paramon! This item is worth much more, but you apparently aren't an expert in such matters. Well, so what, sold! (*Hands the medallion to* Korzukhin, *who gives him ten dollars. He sits down at the card table, rolls up the sleeves of his Cossack jacket, shuffles the deck.*) What's your slave's name?

KORZUKHIN. Hm ... Antoine.

CHARNOTA (*stentorianly*). Antoine!

Antoine *appears.*

Bring me a snack, dear fellow.

ANTOINE (*surprisedly but politely smiling*). Yes, sir ... *À l'instant!* (*He disappears.*)

CHARNOTA. For how much!

KORZUKHIN. Well, for these same ten dollars. A card, please.

CHARNOTA. Nine.

KORZUKHIN (*pays*). Banco, if you please.

CHARNOTA (*deals*). Nine.

KORZUKHIN. Banco again.

CHARNOTA. You wish a card?

KORZUKHIN. Yes. Seven.

CHARNOTA. But I have eight.

KORZUKHIN (*smiling*). Well, so be it, banco.

GOLUBKOV (*abruptly*). Charnota! What are you doing? Why he's doubling, and naturally he'll take everything back from you.

CHARNOTA. If you understand the game better than I, then you sit down for me.

GOLUBKOV. I don't know how.

CHARNOTA. Then don't stand in my light. A card?

KORZUKHIN. Yes, please. Ah, damn, bust!

CHARNOTA. I have three points.

KORZUKHIN. You don't draw when you have a three?

CHARNOTA. Sometimes, it all depends . . .

> Antoine *brings in a snack*.

(*Drinking up.*) Golubkov, a glass?

GOLUBKOV. I don't want any.

CHARNOTA. And you, Paramon, what about it?

KORZUKHIN. *Merci,* I've already eaten.

CHARNOTA. Aha! . . . Would you like a small card?

KORZUKHIN. Yes. A hundred and sixty dollars.

CHARNOTA. Bet. "Countess, for a single rendezvous . . ." Nine.

KORZUKHIN. Unprecedented! I bet three hundred and twenty!

CHARNOTA. I'll ask you to give me the cash, please.

GOLUBKOV. Quit. Charnota, I implore you! Quit now!

CHARNOTA. Be so kind as to busy yourself elsewhere. Look through an album or something. (*To* Korzukhin.) The cash, please!

KORZUKHIN. Right away. (*He opens the safe, bells immediately begin to jangle furiously, ringing is heard everywhere.*)

> *The light goes out and immediately goes on again.* Antoine *appears from the anteroom with a revolver in his hand.*

GOLUBKOV. What's that?

KORZUKHIN. That is the burglar alarm. Antoine, you may go, it was I who opened it.

> Antoine *exits.*

CHARNOTA. A very handy item. Bet! Eight!
KORZUKHIN. Six hundred and forty is bet?
CHARNOTA. No. The bank will not accept that stake.
KORZUKHIN. You play very well. How much will you accept?
CHARNOTA. Fifty.
KORZUKHIN. Bet! Nine!
CHARNOTA. I bust.
KORZUKHIN. The money.
CHARNOTA. Please.
KORZUKHIN. Five hundred and ninety!
CHARNOTA. Eh, Paramosha, you are a zealous gambler! That's where your soft spot is!
GOLUBKOV. Charnota, I implore you, let's go!
KORZUKHIN. Card! I have seven!
CHARNOTA. Seven and a half! I'm joking—eight.

With a groan Golubkov suddenly covers his ears and lies down on the couch. Korzukhin *opens the safe with a key. Again the ringing, darkness, again light. And it is already night on stage. Candles under small pink shades are burning on the card table.* Korzukhin *is already without his jacket, his hair is mussed up. The lights of Paris in the windows, music is heard somewhere. There are heaps of money in front of* Korzukhin *and in front of* Charnota. Golubkov *is lying on the couch sleeping.*

CHARNOTA (*sings softly*). "You'll receive a fatal blow . . . three cards, three cards, three cards . . ."[19] Bust.
KORZUKHIN. Give me four hundred! Bet three thousand!
CHARNOTA. You're on. In cash!

Korzukhin *rushes to the safe. Again darkness with ringing and music. Then light. In Paris—a blue dawn. Quiet. No music is heard.* Korzukhin, Charnota, *and* Golubkov *look like shadows. Champagne bottles litter the floor. Crumpling it,* Golubkov *stuffs money in his pockets.*

19. From Tchaikovsky's opera *The Queen of Spades*. See also note 9.

CHARNOTA (*to* Korzukhin). Do you have a newspaper to wrap it in?

KORZUKHIN. No. I'll tell you what, you give me the cash and I'll give you a check!

CHARNOTA. What's wrong with you, Paramon? Would any bank give twenty thousand to a man who appeared wearing underpants? No, thank you!

GOLUBKOV. Charnota, buy my medallion back, I want to return it!

KORZUKHIN. Three hundred dollars!

GOLUBKOV. There! (*Throws the money.*)

Korzukhin *answers by throwing him the medallion.*

CHARNOTA. Well, goodbye, Paramosha. We've been sitting here too long, it's time for us to go.

KORZUKHIN (*blocking the door*). No, stop! I have a fever, I don't understand any of this ... You've used my illness?! Listen—return the money, I'll give you five hundred dollars each as a pay-off!

CHARNOTA. " 'You're joking'—cried the perfidious beast!"

KORZUKHIN. Well, if that's the way you want it, I'll call the police immediately and tell them you robbed me. They'll grab you immediately! Bums!

CHARNOTA. Did you hear? (*Takes out his revolver.*) Well, Paramon, pray to your Parisian Notre Dame; your mortal hour has arrived!

KORZUKHIN. Help! Help!

At these cries Antoine *runs in wearing only underwear.*

Everyone's asleep! The whole villa is asleep! No one hears them robbing me!

The portière moves aside and Lyuska *appears. She is wearing pajamas. Seeing* Charnota *and* Golubkov *she turns to stone.*

You're sleeping, dear Lucy, while Russian bandits are robbing your patron!

LYUSKA. My God, my God! Apparently I have still not drained my bitter cup! ... It would seem I had a right to rest, but no, no ...

No wonder I dreamed of cockroaches tonight! Only one thing
interests me—how did you manage to get here?

CHARNOTA (*stunned*). Is it she?

KORZUKHIN (*to* Charnota). You know Mademoiselle Frejole?

Behind Korzukhin's *back* Lyuska *gets down on her knees,
imploringly clasps her hands together.*

CHARNOTA. How would I know her? I have no idea.

LYUSKA. So let's get acquainted, gentlemen! Lucy Frejole!

CHARNOTA. General Charnota.

LYUSKA. Well, gentlemen, what is the misunderstanding? (*To* Korzukhin.) My little rat, why were you screaming so desperately?
Who hurt you?

KORZUKHIN. He won twenty thousand dollars from me! And I
want him to return it!

GOLUBKOV. What utter baseness!

LYUSKA. No, no, my little toad, that's impossible! Well, if you lost,
what can you do? You're not a little boy!

KORZUKHIN. Where did Antoine buy the cards?

ANTOINE. You bought them yourself, Paramon Ilych.

LYUSKA. Antoine, you go to hell! Why are you hanging around me
in that get-up?

Antoine disappears.

LYUSKA. Gentlemen! The money belongs to you, and there will be
no misunderstandings. (*To* Korzukhin.) Go, my little boy, and
get to sleep, to sleep. You have bags under your eyes.

KORZUKHIN. I'll fire that fool Antoine! Don't allow any more Russians in my house! (*He sobs, exits.*)

LYUSKA. Well, sirs, I was very happy to see my fellow countrymen,
and I'm sorry that we will never have occasion to meet again. (*In
a whisper.*) You've won—get your legs moving! (*Loudly.*)
Antoine!

Antoine looks in the door.

The gentlemen are leaving us, see them out.

CHARNOTA. *Au revoir, mademoiselle.*

LYUSKA. *Adieu!*

> *Charnota* and *Golubkov exit.*

Glory to the Lord, they're gone! My God! When will I finally get some rest!

> *Footsteps are heard in the deserted street.*

(Looking around stealthily, she runs to the window, opens it, calls out softly.) Goodbye! Golubkov, take care of Serafima! Charnota! Buy yourself some pants!

> *Then darkness. The dream ends.*

THE EIGHTH AND LAST DREAM

... There were twelve robbers ...[20]

A ROOM *covered with rugs, low divans, a water-pipe (hookah). In the background—a solid glass wall with a glass door in it. Beyond the glass the last glow from a Constantinople minaret, laurel trees, and the top of* ARTUR's *carousel. The autumn sun is setting ... sunset ... sunset ...* KHLUDOV *is sitting in the room, on the floor, on a rug, his legs under him Turkish fashion, and he is talking to someone.*

KHLUDOV. You've tormented me long enough. But things are starting to clear up. Yes, clear up. But you must not forget that you're not the only one beside me. There are the living people too—and they hang on my legs and they demand things too. Eh? Fate tied them into the same knot with me, and now I can't get rid of them. I've reconciled myself to that. There is one thing I don't under-

---

20. From the second stanza of a very popular song based on a poem by Nikolai Nekrasov.

stand. You. How did you alone get separated from the long chain of moons and street lamps? How did you get away from eternal peace? After all, you weren't the only one. Oh no, there were many of you . . . (*He mutters.*) Well, remember me, remember, remember . . . But I'm not going to recall. (*He thinks, grows older, sags.*) Yes. So I did it all in vain. And then what? Simple—darkness, and we left. Then—heat, and every day the carousel turning around. But you are a trapper! What distance you penetrated to come after me, and then you caught me, caught me in a bag! Don't torture me any more; understand that I have decided, I swear it. As soon as Golubkov returns I will go immediately. Well, lighten my soul, nod yes. Nod just once, eloquent orderly Krapilin! So! You nodded! It's decided.

Serafima *enters quietly.*

SERAFIMA. Again, Roman Valerianovich?

KHLUDOV. What?

SERAFIMA. With whom were you talking? Why there's no one in the room except you!

KHLUDOV. You're hearing things. And anyway, I have a habit of muttering. I hope that it doesn't bother anyone, eh?

SERAFIMA (*sits down on the carpet beside* Khludov). I have been living on the other side of that wall for four months listening to you muttering at night. Do you think that's easy? On such nights I don't sleep myself. Now you're doing it even in the daytime? Poor, poor, man . . .

KHLUDOV. All right. I'll get you another room, but in the same block so that you'll be under my eye. I sold a ring, I have the money. It'll be light, windows onto the Bosphorus. Of course I cannot offer any special comfort. You'll see yourself—it's nonsense. A rout. We lost and were thrown out. And why did we lose—do you know? (*He points mysteriously over his shoulder.*) He and I know *everything.* It's inconvenient for me to be next to your room too, but I have to keep my word.

SERAFIMA. Roman Valerianovich, do you remember the day that Golubkov left? You came after me and forced me to return, remember?

KHLUDOV. When a person is going out of his mind, one must apply force. You are all somehow abnormal.

SERAFIMA. I felt sorry for you Roman Valerianovich, and I stayed only because of that.

KHLUDOV. I don't need a nursemaid—but you do!

SERAFIMA. Don't be annoyed, you hurt only yourself by doing that.

KHLUDOV. Yes, true, true . . . I can't hurt anyone any more. But remember that night, the headquarters . . . Khludov the brute, Khludov the jackal? Eh?

SERAFIMA. All that's past, and I've forgotten—and don't you remember either.

KHLUDOV (*mutters*). Yes, yes, yes . . . No, I have to remember. However . . . remember me, remember . . . I will not recall.

SERAFIMA. Here's what I've been thinking all night, Roman Valerianovich . . . Something must be decided. Tell me, how long can you and I sit here together like this?

KHLUDOV. As soon as Golubkov returns, our little club will break up. I'll hand you over to him, and then each will go his own way, helter-skelter. And that's the end. It's a suffocating city!

SERAFIMA. Ah, what madness it was to let him go then? I'll never forgive myself for that! Oh, how I miss him! Lyuska, it's Lyuska who's to blame . . . I was insane from her reproaches . . . And now, just like you, I cannot sleep, because he's probably got lost in his wanderings, and maybe he's even dead.

KHLUDOV. A suffocating city! And that scandal—the cockroach races! Everyone stares at me as if I were abnormal. And why, in fact, did you let him go? Does your husband there have some money?

SERAFIMA. I have no husband; I've forgotten him and curse him!

KHLUDOV. So what's to be done.

SERAFIMA. Let's look the truth in the face: Sergei Pavlovich is lost, he's lost. And I decided tonight: they've let the Cossacks return home, I'll petition too, I'll return with them, to St. Petersburg. Why did I, crazy woman that I am, leave?

KHLUDOV. That's intelligent. Very. An intelligent person, eh? You did nothing to the Bolsheviks, you can return peacefully.

SERAFIMA. There's only one thing I don't know, one thing that holds me back—what will happen to you?

KHLUDOV (*beckons to her mysteriously with a finger. She moves closer, and he speaks in her ear*). But . . . shh . . . it's nothing to you, but counter-intelligence is on my heels, they have good noses . . . (*He whispers.*) I will go to Russia too, we can go this very night. A ship leaves tonight.

SERAFIMA. You want to go secretly, under another name?

KHLUDOV. Under my own name. I'll appear and say: I'm Khludov, I've come.

SERAFIMA. Come to your senses, they'll shoot you immediately!

KHLUDOV. Momentarily. (*He smiles.*) Instantaneously. Eh? A cotton shirt, a cellar, snow . . . Ready! My time is melting away. Look, he's walked away and is standing in the distance.

SERAFIMA. Ah! So that's whom you mutter about! You want death? Madman! Stay here, perhaps you will recover?

KHLUDOV. I recovered today. I am completely well. I'm not a cockroach—I'm not going to swim in buckets. I remember the army, battles, snows, posts, and little lamps on the posts . . . Khludov will walk past under the little lamps.

A loud knock on the door. It opens at once, Golubkov *and* Charnota *enter. Both are dressed in decent suits.* Charnota *is carrying a small suitcase. Silence.*

SERAFIMA. Seryozha! . . . Seryozha!

CHARNOTA. Hello! Why don't you say something!

KHLUDOV. Well here they are. They've come. I *told* you . . .

GOLUBKOV. Sima! Well, how are you, Sima, hello!

Serafima *embraces* Golubkov *and cries.*

KHLUDOV (*frowning*). Charnota, let's go out on the balcony and have a little talk. (*Exits through the glass wall with* Charnota.)

GOLUBKOV. Well, don't cry, don't cry. What are you crying about, Serafima? It's I. I've returned.

SERAFIMA. I thought you had perished! Oh, if you only knew how I missed you! . . . Now everything is clear to me . . . But nevertheless, I waited long enough! Now, you will never go anywhere, I won't let you.

GOLUBKOV. Nowhere, of course, nowhere! It's all over! And now we'll decide everything! How did you get along here without me, Sima? Tell me at least a little!

SERAFIMA. I got exhausted, I couldn't sleep. As soon as you left I came to my senses, I couldn't forgive myself for letting you go! I would sit up all night looking at the lights, and I imagined you walking around Paris, ragged and hungry . . . And Khludov is sick, he's so terrifying!

GOLUBKOV. Don't, Sima, don't!

SERAFIMA. Did you see my husband?

GOLUBKOV. I saw him, I did. He renounced you, and he has a new wife—but who she is is absolutely uninteresting . . . And . . . it's better this way, and you are free! (*He shouts.*) Khludov, thanks!

Khludov *and* Charnota *enter.*

KHLUDOV. Well there, all is in order now, eh? (*To* Golubkov.) You love her? Eh? An honest man? I advise you to go where she says. And now, goodbye to you all! (*He takes his overcoat, hat, and a small suitcase.*)

CHARNOTA. Where to, may I ask?

KHLUDOV. There is a ship leaving tonight, and I am going on it. But keep quiet.

GOLUBKOV. Roman! Think it over! You can't do this!

SERAFIMA. I've already told him, he can't be held back.

KHLUDOV. Charnota! You know what? Come with me! Well?

CHARNOTA. Wait, wait, wait! I just realized! Where? Ah yes, *there!* Cleverly thought out! What is this, you've evolved some ingenious new plan? You're not of the General Staff for nothing! Or are you going to give answer? Eh? Well then you may as well know, Roman, that you will live exactly as long as it takes to remove you from the ship and get you to the nearest wall! And that under the closest guard so that they don't tear you apart along the road! You left a big memory of yourself, brother. And they'd take me, slave of God, along with you, they'd take and . . . There's a lot behind me too! Although, true, I have no street lamps in my wake!

SERAFIMA. Charnota, what are you saying to a sick man!

CHARNOTA. I am saying it in order to stop him.

GOLUBKOV. Roman! Stop, you cannot go!

KHLUDOV. You will be sad and homesick, Charnota.

CHARNOTA. Eh, you've said it! I've been sad and homesick for a long time, brother. Kiev torments me—I keep remembering the laurel, remembering the battles . . . I didn't run from death, but I won't make a special trip to the Bolsheviks for it either. And from pity I tell you this—don't go.

KHLUDOV. Well, goodbye! Goodbye! (*He exits.*)

CHARNOTA. Serafima, hold him back, he'll give up the idea!

SERAFIMA. I can do nothing. ,

GOLUBKOV. You cannot hold him back, I know him.   ,

CHARNOTA. Ah! The soul demands judgment! Well, so what, nothing can be done! Well, what about you?

SERAFIMA. Let's go and petition, Sergei. I've been thinking about it—let's go home tonight!

GOLUBKOV. Let's go, let's go! I can't wander around any more!

CHARNOTA. Well, so what, you may, they'll let you. Let's divide up the money.

SERAFIMA. What money? Korzukhin's, probably?

GOLUBKOV. He won twenty thousand dollars from Korzukhin.

SERAFIMA. Not for anything in the world.

GOLUBKOV. I don't need it either. I got here and that's enough. We'll make our way to Russia somehow. What you gave me is enough for us.

CHARNOTA. I offer for the last time. No? Nobility? Well, all right. So our paths have parted, fate has untied us. One to a noose, others to St. Petersburg, and I—where do I go? Who am I now? From today on I am the Wandering Jew! I am Ahasuerus, I am the Flying Dutchman! I am the Devil's Hound.

> *The clock strikes five. In the distance a flag raises over the carousel and hurdy-gurdies are heard—and with them Artur's chorus at the races: ". . . There were twelve robbers, and Kudeyar their Ataman . . ."*[21]

Bah! Do you hear that? The jig's alive and working! (*He throws open the door to the balcony.*)

21. More lines from the song based on Nekrasov's poem.

The chorus begins to flow more distinctly: "... The robbers spilled the blood of many honest Christians ..."

Hello again, Cockroach Tsar Artur! You'll ooh and ah now when your General Charnota appears before you in all his glory! (*He disappears.*)

GOLUBKOV. I can't bear to look at this city any more! I cannot bear to hear it!

SERAFIMA. What was it, this past year and a half, Seryozha? Dreams? Explain it to me! Where, why did we flee? Street lamps on the platform, black bags ... and then the heat! I want to be on Karavan Street again, I want to see snow again! I want to forget everything, as if it hadn't happened!

The chorus swells more broadly: "We will pray to the Lord God, we will hallow the ancient story! ..." From the distance a muezzin's voice begins to flow: "Ia ilâh illa illâh ..."

GOLUBKOV. None of it happened, none of it—it was all delirium! Forget it, forget! A month will pass, we'll make it, we'll return, and then the snow will fall and efface our footprints ... Let's go! Let's go!

SERAFIMA. Let's go! The end.

They both run out of Khludov's room. Constantinople begins to go dark and goes dark forever.

THE END

THE CRIMSON ISLAND

A dress rehearsal of a play by Citizen Jules Verne in GENNADI PANFILOVICH's theater, with music, the eruption of a volcano, and English sailors.

In four acts with a Prologue and an Epilogue.

Acts One, Two, and Four take place on an uninhabited island, Act Three in Europe, and the Prologue in GENNADI PANFILOVICH's theater.

INTRODUCTION

IN 1924 Bulgakov published a story called "The Crimson Island" in the Berlin newspaper *On the Eve*. It was subtitled: "A Novel by Comrade Jules Verne Translated from the French into the Aesopian by Mikhail A. Bulgakov." The story appears to be a parody of the kind of propagandistic stories written after the Revolution, allegories in which history is simplified and characters are either heroes or villains. "The Crimson Island" is full of hyperbole, gross caricature, incongruous juxtapositions, and funny non sequiturs. It is an amusing piece, but hardly significant; and one would not give it much attention if Bulgakov had never written a play called *The Crimson Island*.

The play was written in 1927[1] for the Kamerny Theater and its famous director A. Ya. Tairov.[2] It premièred December 11, 1928 and was very successful; but it was soon banned.[3] While the play was very popular with the public, the critics violently denounced it as "talentless, toothless, humble" and a "pasquinade on the Revolution." There was one favorable review, written by N. Novitsky for the *Repertory Bulletin*:

> *The Crimson Island* is an interesting and witty parody in which the shade of the Grand Inquisitor arises, crushing artistic creativity, cultivating slavish, absurd dramatical clichés, taking the individuality away from the actors and writer. In *The Crimson Island* we see a dark, ominous force which sets up idols, toadies and panegyrists. . . . If such a dark force does exist, the playwright's indignation and mordant wit are justified.[4]

The German press referred to the play as "the first call for freedom of press in the U.S.S.R."[5] And it was *The Crimson Island* which served as the final piece of evidence in the trial by press of Bulgakov.

In 1929 all of Bulgakov's plays were taken out of production. But the effects of this play lasted—several years later Meyerhold reproached Tairov for having put it on. One probable reason for the unusual unanimity of critical opinion is that Stalin himself did not like the play.

The main subject of *The Crimson Island* is censorship—a dangerous theme which Bulgakov explored in a very complicated way. The structure is that of a play within a play. Dymogatsky's play presents a problem to any critic and one can see why *The Crimson Island* was misread (deliberately or otherwise) at the time. The play within the play can be seen as a parody of the *xaltura* ("fake culture") being turned out by other authors at the time. There were clumsy allegorical novels, showing the dangers and decay of the West. Plays which crudely satirized the bourgeois world and glorified the Soviets were put on because they were "sound ideologically" and not because they had theatrical merit. That Dymogatsky's play is meant to be such a parody is the view of one of the best Soviet critics of Bulgakov, V. A. Sakhnovsky-Pankeev.

While it is true that Bulgakov loathed these ideological potboilers, and that the play could be seen as a "parody on opportunistic fake-culture,"[6] things are more complicated than Sakhnovsky-Pankeev is willing to admit. He says that Dymogatsky is a "talentless" writer, but Dymogatsky's play does not confirm this judgment.[7] His play is simple-minded in its view of the Revolution, its portrayal of foreigners, etc., but it is genuinely funny; and as it goes on the viewer actually comes to like some of the characters. In Sakhnovsky-Pankeev's view, the purpose of Bulgakov's play is to defend "true art from opportunists and fakes." If, as the critic says, Dymogatsky is without talent, then his play cannot represent the "real art." Real art must simply mean the good plays that were being presented, or perhaps Bulgakov's play as a whole. If one accepts this view of Bulgakov's intentions, one must conclude that his play is a failure, because Dymogatsky's play is not bad enough. Surely Dymogatsky's play could be shown full of unredeemed clichés which would have been funny, but only because of the parodistic elements, not because of anything original in the humor—as is the case here. Dymogatsky himself is not shown as either stupid enough or opportunistic enough to serve as the author of *xaltura*. In the epilogue, far from condemning him as the author of trash, Bulgakov makes the reader/viewer feel sorry for him. The ending which the censor forces the theater to add is pure *xaltura*, but the rest of the play is not.

It seems clear that if we treat Dymogatsky's play as only a parody of bad plays, and if we maintain that the only purpose of the play is to defend real art from "opportunists and time-servers" complications arise. As intelligent a critic as Sakhnovsky-Pankeev must have seen that censorship, not *xaltura*, is the subject of Bulgakov's play.[8] Another Soviet critic, B. Milyavsky, did. In a comparison of *The Crimson Island* and Mayakovsky's *The Bathhouse* Milyavsky maintains that the chief difference in the attitudes toward censorship shown in the two plays is that: "Mayakovsky comes out against bureaucratic 'management' of art. But in Bulgakov's play the very idea of state, Party management of theatrical life is ridiculed, scorned."[9]

Milyavsky is quite right in his analysis. But it was not this attitude toward censorship alone, that was responsible for the violent attacks on the play. The fact that Dymogatsky's play was a parody of bad plays did not make up for the fact that the play within the play was a funny allegory of the Revolution. The upstart Kiri-Kuki represents Kerensky, and while it is quite all right to put him in a vaudeville, it is a little more delicate a matter to have a Ki-Kum represent Lenin, and a Farra-Teytey play the role of a Trotsky. Reducing the Revolution to a rather lighthearted squabble over pearls was a dangerous thing to do, even in parodistic form. Ki and Farra may be noble in the play, but the fact is they exist in a farce, and this affects the viewer's evaluation of them. Because of this, it is no surprise when Savva, the censor, bans the play and says that it is *smenovexovskaja*.[10] But it rapidly becomes clear that Savva is using the term as simply an abusive epithet—he actually has no idea of what it really means. What Savva finally says he wants, in order to supposedly eradicate the *smenovexovskij* element, is a change in the ending. The English sailors must be liberated, and international revolution and solidarity must play a role. These changes, of course, would not really take care of the play's *smenovexovskij* features if they existed. There is one thing which could conceivably be used to claim Dymogatsky's play is *smenovexovskij*. When Likki, Tokhonga, and Betsy return to the island, it is not because they believe in the ideology of the red natives, but because they are homesick and wretched with Lord Glenarvan. Tokhonga does say something about how he "understands" slavery since he has felt it with his own skin, but Betsy and Likki make no such remarks. However, Likki's repentance speech when he gets to the island more than takes care of this objection. The political allegory, which occasionally gets quite tedious, is not the most important, or the most interesting thing about *The Crimson Island*.

In this play Bulgakov gives his audience the ultimate baring of the device—he shows exactly how and why a play is censored. We are educated simultaneously with the playwright who brings the play he has labored over to the theater, where it is immediately reduced to fodder for directors, actors, and censors. *The Crimson Island* is a play about the theater and the nature of theatrical illusion itself—a subject which Bulgakov was later to return to in his *Theatrical Novel*.

The nature of censorship is the main theme of the play, but it does not seem obtrusive until the Epilogue. It is there all along (first mentioned when Metelkin tells the prop men that *Ivan the Terrible* has been banned), but the reader, absorbed in the events of Dymogatsky's play itself, forgets the censor from the time Gennadi talks on the phone in the Prologue until Savva's arrival in Act III. Gradually the audience notices that it is not the censor Savva who is responsible for the majority of changes made in Dymogatsky's play, but the director Gennadi. Gennadi tries to anticipate Savva's every reaction—and cuts some things which Savva probably would not have reacted to. With kingly disdain for the text, he changes props and cuts an entire scene. But, of course, he is simply doing his job. As a professional, he has to make sure that the theater does not get into trouble politically. The problem is that he is so worried about what might possibly be negatively understood, that he himself does things more strictly than the censor—especially since he gives Savva credit for more subtlety of mind than Savva ever displays. It is not just Gennadi that is being attacked—his anxiety and hypocrisy are forced on him by the very existence of censorship which forces the theater to censor itself before the official censor ever arrives. In this way any impulses toward freedom are quickly destroyed—the very people who should be fighting, or at least resisting, censorship are themselves part of it. This extends to the artists themselves—if a Dymogatsky were to write another play, one could be sure that he himself would cross out the passages "Savva" might not like—or even worse, he would not permit himself to write them in the first place. The most terrible censorship is self-censorship.

NOTES

1. The typescript which I used has "Moscow, 1927" written after the title.

2. See K. N. Državin, *Kniga o Kamernom Teatre 1914–34* (L. 1934), p. 231. The production was by Tairov and L. Lukyanova, music by A. Malmer, set designer V. Ryndin.

3. According to the best available information *The Crimson Island* was played only four times, and was banned at the beginning of December 1928. On February 2, 1929 Stalin wrote a letter to Bill-Belotserkovsky calling the Kamerny a bourgeois theater and citing the fact that it put on *The Crimson Island* as proof of this.

4. Pavel Novickij, "*Bagrovyj ostrov* M. Bulgakova," *Repertuarnyj bjulleten' Glaviskusstva RSFSR,* No. 12 (M. 1928), pp. 9–10.

5. Noted by Bulgakov in his letter to Stalin.

6. V. A. Saxnovskij-Pankeev, "Bulgakov," *Očerki istorii russkoj sovetskoj dramaturgii,* ed. S. V. Vladimirov and G. A. Lapkina (L-M. 1966), II, 133.

7. Hereafter the play within the play (both are entitled "The Crimson Island") will be specified as Dymogatsky's play.

8. In his letter to Stalin, Bulgakov says that he has not written a pasquinade on the Revolution, but a lampoon about the Central Repertory Committee which, he says, "is killing creative thought; it is destroying Soviet dramaturgy and it will destroy it finally." And he adds: "I did not whisper these ideas, I put them in a dramatic lampoon and put the lampoon on the stage."

9. Boris Miljavskij, *Satirik i vremja* (M. 1963), p. 245.

10. The term (translated as "counter-revolutionary" in the play) re-

fers to the "Changing Landmarks" a movement among émigrés to accept the October Revolution, even if not necessarily in favor of Communism. The group had been aroused to patriotic feelings by the Soviet-Polish war, and by the announcement of NEP, which seemed to indicate a less dogmatic Communist line. The name came from the title of a collection of articles published in Prague in 1921 by Russian émigrés—*Smena Vex*.

The reason why Bulgakov introduces the term is because he was often associated with (and abused for) *smenovex* publications. *On the Eve* was founded as a *smenovex* organ. *Russia* was called a "changing landmarks" journal by Trotsky. Lunacharsky called *Days of the Turbins* a *smenovexovskaja* play.

CAST OF CHARACTERS

GENNADI PANFILOVICH, the theater director, he is also EDWARD GLENARVAN.

VASILY ARTUROVICH DYMOGATSKY, he is also JULES VERNE[1] and KIRI-KUKI, an upstart at the court.

NIKANOR METELKIN, the director's assistant, he is also the servant PASSEPARTOUT; he also sets up the samovar for GENNADI PANFILOVICH; he is also the talking parrot.

JACQUES PAGANEL, a member of a geographical society.

LIDIA IVANNA, she is also LADY GLENARVAN.

HATTERAS, the captain.

BETSY, LADY GLENARVAN's maid, also called ADELAIDA KARPOVNA.

SIZI-BUZI the Second, a white Arab,[2] sovereign ruler of the island.

LIKKI-TIKKI, a general, a white Arab.

PROMPTER

1. Works by Jules Verne provide many characters for Bulgakov's play. Lord Glenarvan, Paganel, and Tohonga are from *Les Enfants du Capitaine Grant*, Hatteras from *Les Voyages et aventures du Capitaine Hatteras*. Maori chieftains in *Les Enfants du Capitaine Grant* have names such as Kara-Tété (Bulgakov's Farra-Teytey) and Kai-Koumou (Bulgakov's Ki-kum). Bulgakov reverses Verne's characters in some cases; Verne's Glenarvan is pious and noble while Bulgakov's is a caricature colonialist.
2. The Russian is *arap*, which means first a "black servant" or "slave" (as in Pushkin's "The Blackamoor of Peter the Great"—*Arap Petra Velikogo*). We cannot very well translate Bulgakov's text as "white blackamoors" or "white slaves." Furthermore, in context the word also suggests the phrase *na arape*—"to be a freeloader, to get away with something." Therefore, we have simply translated the word as "Arab," or perhaps "ārab," as in the slang "dumb ārab."

Likui Isaich, the conductor.

Tohonga, an Arab guardsman.

Ki-Kum, first positive native.

Farra-Teytey, second positive native.

A Musician with a French horn.

Savva Lukich

Arab Guardsman (they're negative, but they repent), Red Natives of both sexes (positive figures and innumerable hordes), Sizi-Buzi's Harem, English Sailors, Musicians, Acting Students, Hairdressers, and Wardrobe Women.

Prologue

Part of the curtain *opens revealing the office and dressing room of* Gennadi Panfilovich. *A desk, posters, a mirror.*
Gennadi Panfilovich, *red-haired, shaved face, very experienced, is at the desk. He is upset.*
From somewhere one can hear pleasant, very rhythmic music and hollow, unnatural voices (the rehearsal of a ball is in progress).
Metelkin *is hanging in the air on tangled ropes and singing, "I loved, I suffered, but the scoundrel ruined me . . ." It is daytime.*

Gennadi. Metelkin.
Metelkin (*falling out of the air into the office*). It's I, Gennadi Panfilych.
Gennadi. He hasn't come?
Metelkin. No, Gennadi Panfilych.
Gennadi. And have you sent someone to his apartment?
Melelkin. The messenger ran over there three times today. The room's locked. He asks the landlady when he'll be home, and she says, "What's wrong with you, dearie, bloodhounds couldn't track him down!"
Gennadi. Writers! Oh! Damn him to hell!
Metelkin. Damn him to hell, Gennadi Panfilych.
Gennadi. Well, why are you squawking like a parrot? Make your report.
Metelkin. Yes, sir. The backdrop for *Maria Stuart* tore open, Gennadi Panfilych.
Gennadi. What's wrong with you, am I supposed to fix the backdrop for you or what? You're being a nuisance with these trifles. Sew it up.

METELKIN. It's all full of holes, Gennadi Panfilych. They let it down the other day, and you could see the stagehands through it.

The phone on the desk rings.

GENNADI. Put a patch on it. (*On the telephone.*) Yes. The theater. We don't give complimentary tickets. You're welcome, goodbye. (*He puts up the receiver.*) It's an amazing thing. If someone gets on the trolley, he doesn't ask the conductress for a complimentary ticket, but he considers it a sacred duty to go to the theater for nothing. Why that's gall! Eh?

METELKIN. Gall.

GENNADI. Go on.

METELKIN. Give me some money for the patch, Gennadi Panfilych.

GENNADI. Sure, right away. I've already wasted five hundred rubles on that ninny! You take it, and cut out . . . (*The telephone.*) Yes? . . . We give no complimentary tickets. Yes. (*He puts up the receiver.*) Such characters! You take . . . (*The telephone.*) We don't give them to anyone! (*He hangs up.*) Divine punishment! So, you take the backdrop . . . (*The telephone.*) Oh, for Christ's sake! . . . What? We don't give them to anyone! . . . Sorry . . . Evgeny Romualdovich! I didn't recognize your voice . . . How's that . . . with your wife? Enchanting! Please go right to the box office at quarter to eight. All the best. (*He hangs up the receiver.*) Metelkin, be a good fellow and tell the cashier to set aside two seats in the middle of the second row for that water devil.

METELKIN. Who's that, Gennadi Panfilych?

GENNADI. The Superintendent of the City Water Works.

METELKIN. Yes, sir.

GENNADI. So, you'll take . . . Is it a big hole?

METELKIN. Not at all, it's little. Five or six yards.

GENNADI. On your scale I suppose "big" means a mile and a half. Odd-ball! (*Pensively.*) *Ivan the Terrible*[3] won't be played any more . . . So, here's what you do. You take that and cut out a suitable piece. Understand?

METELKIN. I understand. (*He shouts.*) Volodya! Take a piece out

3. Probably A. K. Tolstoy's *The Death of Ivan the Terrible* (1866).

of the *Ivan the Terrible* backdrop and make a patch for *Maria Stuart* out of it! . . . *Ivan the Terrible* won't be played any more . . . They've banned it . . . Yes, there *is* a reason . . . What business is it of yours? . . .

The telephone.

GENNADI (*listens*). No, I won't give any. (*He hangs up receiver.*) What else?

METELKIN. Gennadi Panfilych, tell the student actors . . . why it's awful what they're doing. They're wiping their faces with their tails.

GENNADI. I don't understand a word.

METELKIN. I issued them frock coats for *Woe from Wit*,[4] and they're using the tails instead of rags to wipe off their make-up.

GENNADI. Oh, the thieves! O.K., I'll tell them. (*The telephone rings. Without removing the receiver.*) We do not give complimentary tickets to anyone. (*The telephone stops ringing.*) Get going.

METELKIN. Yes, sir. (*He exits.*)

GENNADI. It's after twelve. But, dear ladies and gentlemen, if you want to know who is the biggest upstart and thief in our theater life, I will tell you. It is Vaska Dymogatsky, the one who writes in various magazines under the pseudonym Jules Verne. But you tell *me*, comrades, how he pulled the wool over my eyes? How could I have trusted him?

METELKIN (*enters quickly*). Gennadi Panfilych! He's come!

GENNADI (*rapaciously*). Ah! Call him in here, call him, call him!

METELKIN. If you please. (*He exits.*)

DYMOGATSKY (*with a stack of notebooks in his arms*). Hello, Gennadi Panfilych!

GENNADI. Well, hello, most esteemed Comrade Dymogatsky, hello Monsieur Jules Verne!

DYMOGATSKY. Are you angry, Gennadi Panfilych?

GENNADI. What do you mean? What do you mean? Ha-ha! I, angry? He-he! I'm in utter ecstasy! I'm fairly trembling from rapture!

4. One of the most famous Russian comedies, written by Alexander S. Griboedov in 1822–25.

DYMOGATSKY. I've been sick, Gennadi Panfilych. Terribly sick . . .

GENNADI. Tell me about it, please do. Oh, oh, oh. With scarlatina?

DYMOGATSKY. The most ferocious influenza, Gennadi Panfilych.

GENNADI. So, so.

DYMOGATSKY. Here's what I've brought, Gennadi Panfilych.

GENNADI. What is the date today, Comrade Dymogatsky?

DYMOGATSKY. The eighteenth, new style.[5]

GENNADI. Absolutely correct. And you gave me your word of honor that you would bring the play, in its revised form, on the fifteenth.

DYMOGATSKY. Just three days, Gennadi Panfilych.

GENNADI. Three days! And do you know what has happened in those three days? Savva Lukich is leaving for the Crimea! Tomorrow at eleven A.M.!

DYMOGATSKY. What are you saying?

GENNADI. So, there, "what are you saying!" That means that if we don't show him a dress rehearsal today, then instead of a play we'll get a finger with rings on it! You, Mr. Jules Verne, have wrecked my season! That's what! I believed you, old idealist that I am! When you snapped up the advance of five hundred rubles, I guess you didn't have influenza, "new style"! Writers do not behave like this, my dear Mr. Jules Verne!

DYMOGATSKY. Gennadi Panfilych! What can we do now?

GENNADI. What can we do now? Apart from the five hundred rubles I tossed you, as if in a daze, I've also squandered money on the sets, I've turned the theater upside down, I've ruined the entire production schedule! Metelkin! Metelkin!

METELKIN (*running in*). Here I am, Gennadi Panfilych!

GENNADI. Listen—what are they doing in there?

METELKIN. Rehearsing a ball scene.

GENNADI. To hell with the ball. Order them to stop and absolutely no one is to leave the theater.

METELKIN. Should they take off their make-up?

GENNADI. There's no time! We need them all! As they are!

---

5. Russia used the Julian calendar until the Revolution. Dates given in "old style" are thirteen days behind "new style" in the twentieth century. Dymogatsky is trying to imply that he thought he had more time.

METELKIN. Yes, sir. (*He runs out.*) Volodka! Order the doorman not to let anyone out of the theater!

GENNADI (*after him*). We need all the student actors! The orchestra! It's just after twelve. Well, thank the Lord! (*On the telephone.*) Sixteen-seventeen-eighteen. Savva Lukich, please! The director of the theater, Gennadi Panfilovich . . . Savva Lukich? Hello, Savva Lukich. How *are* you today? I heard, I heard. Mending of the organism, as they say. You've just exhausted yourself. He-he! You need to rest. We need your organism. Well, here's what's up, Savva Lukich. The well-known writer Jules Verne has presented us with his new opus *The Crimson Island*. What do you mean, "dead"? He's sitting here in the theater with me right now. Oh! . . . he-he. It's a pseudonym. Comrade Dymogatsky. He signs himself Jules Verne. A terrific talent . . .

Dymogatsky *trembles and turns pale.*

GENNADI. So now, Savva Lukich, we must have an itsy-bitsy permission. What, sir? Or an itsy-bitsy ban? Ha-ha! You're as witty as ever! What. Till fall? Savva Lukich, don't ruin me! I implore you to watch the general rehearsal today . . . The play is ready, completely ready. But why do you want to bother with reading it in the Crimea? You need to go swimming, Savva Lukich, not read all sorts of nonsense! Take walks on the beach, Savva Lukich! You're murdering me! We'll go down the tubes! It's a play that is ideological to the marrow of its bones! Do you really imagine that I would permit anything like that in my theater? . . . We're beginning in twenty minutes. Well, even if by the third act, and I'll give you the first two to look over here. I'm extremely grateful. *Grand merci!* Yes, sir. I'll be waiting for you! (*He hangs up the receiver.*) Oof! Well, now just be firm, Comrade Author.

DYMOGATSKY. Is he really so frightening?

GENNADI. You'll see for yourself. And I told him ideological, ideological, but what if it's not ideological at all? Bear this in mind— in case of anything like that, I'm going to cross it out mercilessly. I've got to save my skin here. Otherwise this could be a perfect botch! I could lose my reputation . . . The worst thing is that there's not even any time to look it over. (*He looks through the notebooks.*)

DYMOGATSKY. I tried, Gennadi Panfilych.

GENNADI. Tried?! So, this must be Act One. An island inhabited by red natives who live under the rule of white Arabs . . . Tell me please, what kind of natives are these?

DYMOGATSKY. It's an allegory, Gennadi Panfilych. This has to be understood subtly.

GENNADI. Oh, my God, allegories! Look, Savva hates allegories mortally! I know, he says, I know these allegories! On the outside allegories but on the inside the Menshevism is so thick you could cut it with a knife! Metelkin! Metelkin!

METELKIN. (*running in.*) What can I do?

GENNADI. I'm appointing you to do the staging of the play. Here's a copy, my friend. Act One. An exotic island. You'll give us some bananas, palms . . . (*To* Dymogatsky.) What does he live in? Their tsar?

DYMOGATSKY. In a wig-wam, Gennadi Panfilych.

GENNADI. We need a wig-wam, Metelkin.

METELKIN. We don't have any wig-wams, Gennadi Panfilych.

GENNADI. Well, set up the cabin from *Uncle Tom.* Tropical vegetation, monkeys in the branches, eclairs and a samovar.

METELKIN. A prop samovar?

GENNADI. Oh, Metelkin, you've been in the theater for ten years, and you're still like a child! Savva Lukich is coming to watch the dress rehearsal.

METELKIN. So, yes, so . . .

GENNADI. Well, that means you serve tea. Tell the guy in the buffet to make two thick *buderbrots* with red caviar, or something.

METELKIN (*out the door*). Volodya! Run over to the guy at the buffet! A samovar for the dress rehearsal!

GENNADI. There you are! Nothing's been drunk, or eaten, but the expenses are beginning already! Look, Mr. Author. Whether there will be any profits from your play or not is still unknown—or for that matter whether the play itself will "be" or not. Yes, let's see . . . A volcano! Ay-yay . . . Can't you get along without a volcano?

DYMOGATSKY. Gennadi Panfilych! Please! I have an eruption in Act Two. Everything is built on the eruption.

GENNADI. Oof, writers, writers! You write without any restraint! Even though an eruption's a good thing! A classy thing! The public loves things like that. Listen Metelkin! Don't we have a lot of mountains?

METELKIN. We've got mountains of them. A whole shed full.

GENNADI. Well, then, here's what we'll do: order the prop man to pick up one of the crummier mountains and turn it into a volcano. In a word, get busy!

METELKIN (*exits, shouting*). Volodya, yell to the prop man, tell him to punch a hole in the top of Mt. Ararat and put fire in it! What? Yes, with smoke. And toss the Ark.

LIDIA (*enters in a rush*). Hello, Genya.

GENNADI. Hello, pussycat, hello. Well . . . here, let me introduce you . . . Vasily Arturovich Dymogatsky. Jules Verne. A well-known talent.

LIDIA. Oh, I've heard so much about you.

GENNADI. My wife, a *grande coquette*.

DYMOGATSKY. Very glad to meet you.

LIDIA. They say you've brought us a play?

DYMOGATSKY. Precisely so.

The music off-stage abruptly ceases.

LIDIA. Oh, that's very nice. We're in such need of contemporary plays. I hope I have a role, Gennadi? However, perhaps I'm not needed in your play.

DYMOGATSKY. Oh, what are you saying! That would be very, very nice!

GENNADI. Of course, my snookums, naturally. Here—Lady Glenarvan . . . A most enchanting role. Your type of woman exactly. Here, take it!

LIDIA (*seizing the role*). Finally! So that no one would think he is giving me roles because of our relation, my Gennadi has been completely ignoring me. I've acted only eight times this season . . .

GENNADI. The theater, my dear, is a temple—you shouldn't forget that either.

METELKIN (*bursts in*). The carpenter wants to know if the ship has sails.

GENNADI. Vasily Arturych?

DYMOGATSKY. Sails and a smokestack. Like the eighteen-sixties.

METELKIN (*flying off*). Volodya! . . .

GENNADI (*after him*). Metelkin! Everybody on stage! Everybody— immediately!

METELKIN (*off-stage*). Volodya! . . .

> *Desperate electric bells are heard. The curtain closes and conceals* Gennadi's *office. A huge empty stage appears. In the middle stands a volcano, made out of a mountain, emitting smoke.* Metelkin, *walking backwards away from it.*

It's working! Volodya! Put it in place!

> *The volcano moves modestly to the side. The troupe begins to come on stage: the conductor* Likui Isaich *in a frock coat. The prompter,* Likki, *in a frock coat.* Sizi-Buzi *in a frock coat, some thin-legged girls with painted lips . . . Noise, talking . . . Women's voices: "A new play . . . a new play . . ."*

SIZI-BUZI. What's going on? A rehearsal?

> *Women's voices: "They say it's terribly interesting."* Gennadi, Lidia, *and* Dymogatsky *appear. A banana tree descends softly from the sky and lands on* Dymogatsky.

DYMOGATSKY. Hey!

GENNADI. Easy, you devils, you've crushed the author!

> *Women's voices: "Volodya! . . . Volodya! . . ."*

METELKIN. Volodya, easy! Take it back up! It's too soon.

> *The banana tree goes up.*

GENNADI (*stands at the foot of the volcano and waves the notebooks*). Quiet please! Comrades, I have invited you to inform you of . . .

SIZI-BUZI. Most unpleasant news . . .

LIDIA. Quiet, Anempodist.

GENNADI. . . . Comrade Jules Verne-Dymogatsky has delivered himself of his burden. (*Someone giggles.*) It would be interesting to know who thinks this is funny? (*Voices: "We weren't laughing, Gennadi Panfilych!"*) I clearly heard a "he-he." If among the student actors there is some irrepressible comedian, he can go into some comedy theater. I will not hold him back. Incidentally, I will not allow you to use your tails to wipe the make-up off your faces. That is impermissible and I will be stern in exacting reparation from the guilty parties! So, Vasily Arturych, the most colossal talent of our time, has presented to our theater his latest opus, entitled *The Crimson Island* . . . (*Hum of noise and interest.*) . . . Attention, please! Circumstances force us to hurry, Savva Lukich is leaving us for an entire month, therefore I am ordering a dress rehearsal right now—with make-up and costumes.

SIZI-BUZI. Gennadi! You are quick as a deer, but no one knows the roles.

GENNADI. We'll use a prompter. And I hope that the actors entrusted to me by the governing body of this theater will turn out to be conscientious enough to apply all efforts and means to . . . in light of . . . and ignoring obvious difficulties . . . (*He has started to talk nonsense.*) Comrade Mukhin!

PROMPTER. Here I am.

GENNADI (*handing him a copy of the play*). Please give the lines distinctly.

PROMPTER. Yes, sir.

GENNADI. There will be corrections along the way.

PROMPTER. I understand, sir.

GENNADI. So, allow us to summarize the content of the play briefly for you. But, our talent himself is on hand . . . Vasily Arturych! Come here, please!

DYMOGATSKY. I . . . um . . . er . . . my play, in essence, is simply like . . .

GENNADI. More boldly, Vasily Arturych, we're listening.

DYMOGATSKY. It's an allegory, you see. In a word, on an island live oppressed red natives—under the rule of white Arabs . . . Their leader is Sizi-Buzi the Second . . .

LIDIA. You know, Ada, he has an inspired face.

BETSY. A very ordinary one.

GENNADI. Attention, please.

DYMOGATSKY. And then there's an eruption of a volcano . . . but that's in the second act. I love Jules Verne very much . . . I even chose his name as a pseudonym . . . Therefore in most cases my heroes have names from Jules Verne . . . here, for example, Lord Glenarvan . . .

GENNADI. Sorry, Vasily Arturovich! Allow me to do it, more so to speak, summarily . . . Your business, Jules Verne, is the muses, and ink. And so. Act One. Kiri-Kuki is a provocateur. They catch two natives (positive types). Wham! Into prison! Trial! Wham! Hang 'em! They escape! Europeans arrive. Wham! Negotiations. A holiday on the island. End of Act One. Curtain.

SIZI-BUZI. He's told it already!

GENNADI. Note that there's a holiday, Likui Isaich.

LIKUI ISAICH. Say no more, Gennadi Panfilych, I already understand.

GENNADI. Here, let me introduce you. Our choirmaster. He'll write us some music, rest assured of that. His father lived in the same house as Rimsky-Korsakov.

DYMOGATSKY. Very, very glad to meet you.

GENNADI. Exoticism, Likui Isaich. You know, natives, so good no one can tell they aren't real—but allegory at the same time.

LIKUI ISAICH. Say no more, Gennadi Panfilych, I already understand.

GENNADI. And so, the roles . . . (*A hum of noise and interest.*) . . . Sizi-Buzi the Second. The leader of the natives, the white Arab. A dull-witted villain on the throne. Well, if we need a dull-witted villain—Sunduchkov. It's yours, Anempodist!

SIZI-BUZI. *Merci.*

GENNADI. Likki-Tikki, army commander, later he regrets this. Alexander Pavlovich Rinsky. Please . . .

LIKKI-TIKKI. Should I take my frock coat off, Gennadi?

GENNADI. There's no time, Sasha. Over your suit. Native Ki-Kum, a positive type . . . Vondakleevsky. Please. Native Farra-Teytey. Also extremely positive—Shurkov . . . It's yours!

SIZI-BUZI. The play ends with the victory of the Arabs?

GENNADI. It ends without a victory of the red natives, and there's no other way it could possibly end!

SIZI-BUZI. Then I won't last beyond Act One. I won't even live until the victory celebration that way.

GENNADI. Anempodist Timofeevich! I urgently request you not to upset the students with Menshevik jokes. In general the theater— is a temple. The government has entrusted these young people to me. Lady Glenarvan ... hm ... Well, she's a grand coquette, ergo—Lidia Ivanna. That's obvious. Lida ... oh, you've already taken the script ...

A hum of noise in the female group.

BETSY. Well, of course it's obvious! How could it not be obvious?!

GENNADI. Pardon me, Adelaida Karpova. Do you wish to say something?

LIDIA. I'm sorry ...

BETSY. No, never mind, nothing. It's nice weather we're having.

LIDIA. There are actresses who suppose that ...

BETSY. What do they suppose? They suppose that it's hard for the wives of directors to get roles.

GENNADI. Mesdames, I protest categorically! ... (*A woman's voice: "How many female roles are there in all?"*) ... Two. (*A hum of disappointment.*) ... Betsy, Lady Glenarvan's maid. Adelaida Karpovna—that's for you!

BETSY. Gennadi Panfilych, I have been on stage for ten years now, and I'm past the time when I should have to carry trays.

GENNADI. Adelaida Karpovna! How can you say that—have some fear of God!

BETSY. No longer ago than last night at the general meeting, Gennadi Panfilych, you maintained that there is no God—because Savva Lukich was present. And as soon as he leaves the theater, God immediately appears on stage!

LIDIA. Well, what a character!

GENNADI. Adelaida Karpovna! I protest against that tone!

SIZI-BUZI. I told Gennadi, don't ever marry an actress ... You'll always be in that kind of a position ...

GENNADI. The theater is a ...

BETSY. Place of intrigues.

GENNADI. Betsy. The soubrette. A wonderful role. A big role. Understand? If you want, I'll give it to Chudnovskaya.

BETSY. If you please! (*She grabs the script.*)

GENNADI. Jacques Paganel, a Frenchman. An accent. An Imperialist. Suzdaltsev-Vladimirsky. Captain Hatteras—Chernobaev. A most appetizing little role.

HATTERAS. In a fat pig's eye, appetizing! Two pages!

GENNADI. In the first place not two, but six; and in the second, remember what our great Shakespeare said: "There is no such thing as a bad role, only cruddy actors who spoil everything you give them." Lord Glenarvan. Well, I'll play that myself. I will work for you, Vasily Arturych. The Arab Tohonga, a lover. Sokolenko. Passepartout, a servant . . . Oh, damn! . . . Is Staritsyn sick?

METELKIN. He is, Gennadi Panfilych.

GENNADI. That's bad, that's bad. Hm . . . Um, there isn't anyone else . . . Metelkin, you'll have to do it.

METELKIN. But I'm supposed to do the staging, Gennadi Panfilych.

GENNADI. Metelkin! I don't recognize you, old comrade!

METELKIN. All right, Gennadi Panfilych.

GENNADI. Well, now the main role. The rascal Kiri-Kuki, Sizi-Buzi's master of ceremonies. By all rights this should be Varrava Apollonovich Morromekhov's. Who is there who doesn't know Varrava! He's the public's favorite! Modesty, honor, simplicity! A man of the old Shchepkin school! The other day he was offered an award—People's National Artist of the Soviet Union. Varrava declined! Why should I have this, he said? Varrava Apollonovich! (*Voices: "He's not here! He's not here!"*) Why not? Call him immediately! What's the trouble?

METELKIN (*intimately*). He's at the Forty-fourth Precinct Station, Gennadi Panfilych.

GENNADI. What do you mean the Forty-fourth Precinct? How did he land there?

METELKIN. He was having dinner at the "Prague" yesterday with some admirers of his talent. Well, a row started.

GENNADI. A row started? What kind of thing is that? We have a special play production, everyone's at his post—and a row started!

Can he be an actor? Can he? He's a tramp, not an actor! That's what he is! How many times have I begged him . . . Drink, Varrava, but drink with restraint.

METELKIN. They called on the telephone, they'll let him out toward evening.

GENNADI. What good is he to me this evening? What the hell! . . . Savva will be here today, Savva is leaving for the Crimea! I need him this instant or not at all! And aren't you a fine one? "In the Forty-fourth."

METELKIN. For God's sake, Gennadi Panfilych! Was I the one who got him drunk?

GENNADI. To hell with everything! There'll be no rehearsal, there won't be any play either! I'm closing the theater! I can't work surrounded by the bourgeoisie and alcoholics! Go away, all of you! (*Movement.*) Stop! Where are you going! Back!

LIDIA. Gennadi! Don't be upset! It's dangerous for you to get all upset.

LIKKI-TIKKI. Gennadi! Let one of the students read the part.

GENNADI. What's wrong with you? Are you making fun of me? All they know how to do is ruin their tails. Everything's on my shoulders, everything crashes down on me! . . . National Artist! . . . He's an international drunkard!

DYMOGATSKY. Gennadi Panfilych!

GENNADI. Leave me alone, all of you! Leave me! Let the idealist Gennadi, who dreamed of a renaissance of the theater, die, like a homeless dog, on the volcano.

DYMOGATSKY. If the play is going to perish, allow me, I'll play Kiri-Kuki. I know all the roles by heart.

GENNADI. What's wrong with you? For goodness sake! Replace Morremekhov! . . . (*A pause.*) Have you ever acted?

DYMOGATSKY. I've acted at performances in country houses.

GENNADI. Country houses? (*A pause.*) Very well, we'll risk it. Let all see how old Gennadi saves the play. The role of the rascal Kiri-Kuki will be performed by the author himself.

SIZI-BUZI. Well, that knocks off all the roles.

LIDIA. There was no reason to get so hysterical.

GENNADI (*from the notebook*). So: Arabs, innumerable hordes of red natives—all of the student actors will be busy. (*A hum of noise.*) English sailors—the choir. A talking parrot . . . hm . . . well, that's Metelkin, naturally. Try it, my little friend. Likui Isaich! I'll ask you to get busy with the music right away—exoticism.

Likui Isaich. Say no more, I already understand. Men, hop to it—into the orchestra pit! (*The musicians go to the orchestra pit.*)

Gennadi. Everybody to make-up! Vasily Arturich, please come to my dressing room!

Sizi-Buzi. Wardrobe!

Lidia. Hairdresser!

The actors disperse, running.

Metelkin. Volodya, start up!

The backdrop goes up and reveals a row of mirrors with dazzling light bulbs. Hairdressers *appear. The actors sit down and begin to makeup and dress.*

Likki-Tikki (*from the notebook*). Shut up when I'm talking to you! Ma . . . ma . . . Give me some white feathers!

Sizi-Buzi. Fedoseev, I need a crown!

Ki-Kum. And I always get the pale blue, do-good role. What luck!

Sizi-Buzi. And you heard what Shakespeare said: "There are no pale blue roles, but there are red ones." Hey, you Fascists! Am I going to get a crown or not?

Metelkin (*flies through the storm*). Volodya! . . .

Conductor (*in the orchestra*). And where's the French horn? Sick? I saw her yesterday in the store, she was buying stockings. This is really ridiculous! Without a knife! (*A voice: "What without a knife?"*) She's cut my throat without a knife. I just can't understand musicians like her!

Gennadi (*from his dressing room*). Do I have to wait a hundred years for my pants? Wardrobe! Pants with big checks.

Metelkin (*on stage*). Volodya! Give me the backdrop!

A backdrop creeps down—a Gothic cathedral—into which there is sewn a piece of the Kremlin's Facet Chamber with some boyars in it. This covers the mirrors.

Volodka, what the hell! Just what are you putting down anyway? Not Gothic—exotic! Let's have the ocean and some blue sky!

The backdrop goes up, reveals the mirrors. Beside them—an uproar; wigs on wigstands!

LIKKI-TIKKI. The tricot's ripped again. That cheapskate Gennadi!

SIZI-BUZI. A regime of economy, sir.

Making a gloomy noise, the ocean descends. The instruments are being tuned up in the orchestra. The mirrors disappear. A bank of burning overhead lights and some sort of pulleys are let down.

METELKIN. To the left with the volcano! Move it to the left!

CONDUCTOR. Overture number seventeen. Get your music ready.

METELKIN. Ready actors? (*Voices: "Ready!"*) Volodya! *Curtain!*

The overall curtain closes and covers the stage.

ACT I

METELKIN (*in the parting of the curtain*). Ready! Likui Isaich, begin! (*He disappears.*)

A gong strikes.

LADY MUSICIAN with a French horn (*appears in the parting of the curtain. She is late and very upset*).

CONDUCTOR (*lowers his baton, the music pours forth*). Ah! It's you? Very glad to see you. Why are you so early? Oh, you have on new stockings? Well, congratulations, you've already been fined. To the orchestra, if you please.

> *The* Musician *descends into the orchestra. The overture is renewed. With its last bar the curtain opens. There is magic on stage—a sun is burning, flashing, and flooding the tropical island. On the branches there are monkeys, parrots are flying about.* Sizi-Buzi's *wigwam at the foot of the volcano is surrounded by a wicket fence. The ocean in the background.* Sizi-Buzi *is sitting on a throne surrounded by odalisques from the harem. Beside him, wearing white feathers, stand the glittering* Likki-Tikki, Tohonga, *and a row of Arabs carrying lances.*

SIZI-BUZI. Ay-ay-ay! Could I have believed that my faithful native subjects would be capable of a crime against their legal sovereign? I don't believe my majestic ears ... Where are the criminals?

LIKKI-TIKKI. In the dungeon, Sovereign Ruler. I put Kiri-Kuki in with them.

SIZI-BUZI. Why?

LIKKI-TIKKI. It was his idea. So that the natives wouldn't guess about his treachery.

266

Sɪzɪ-Buzɪ. Ah, that's clever!

Lɪᴋᴋɪ-Tɪᴋᴋɪ. Do you wish to see the culprits, Your Majesty?

Sɪzɪ-Buzɪ. Present them, brave general.

Lɪᴋᴋɪ-Tɪᴋᴋɪ. Hey! Tohonga! Get those loafers out of the dungeon!

The Arabs open the trapdoor and push out Ki-Kum, Farra-Teytey, *and* Kiri-Kuki.

Tᴀʜᴏɴɢᴀ. Come out to be judged by the Sovereign!

Sɪzɪ-Buzɪ. Ay-ay-ay! Well, hello, you dear bastards!

Kɪʀɪ-Kuᴋɪ. I wish you health, Your Majesty!

Ki-Kum *and* Farra-Teytey *are surprised.*

Lɪᴋᴋɪ-Tɪᴋᴋɪ. Do you want me to interrogate them, Your Majesty?

Sɪzɪ-Buzɪ. Interrogate them, you dear brave man.

Lɪᴋᴋɪ-Tɪᴋᴋɪ. Well now, you dandies, what were you talking about by the cornstalks?

Kɪ-Kuᴍ. We weren't talking about anything.

Lɪᴋᴋɪ-Tɪᴋᴋɪ. Oh, so that's how it is? Don't you blink your eyes! Were you talking?

Fᴀʀʀᴀ-Tᴇʏᴛᴇʏ. No.

Lɪᴋᴋɪ-Tɪᴋᴋɪ. Shut up when you're being spoken to! Were you talking? Answer when you're asked!

Sɪzɪ-Buzɪ. Ay-yay-yay! What stubborn ones they are! If you are going to hold it all in, the god Vaydua will punish you in the next world.

Kɪ-Kuᴍ. We no longer believe in the god Vaydua. We live too rottenly. He doesn't exist. Otherwise he would have interceded for us.

Sɪzɪ-Buzɪ. Oh! Get them further away from me! If lightning strikes them, it might catch me too.

Lɪᴋᴋɪ-Tɪᴋᴋɪ. Obviously, we won't get any sense out of them. Kiri, you tell it.

Kɪ-Kuᴍ. Be brave, Arab brother, keep silent.

Kɪʀɪ-Kuᴋɪ. Sorry, I'm not your brother.

Kɪ-Kuᴍ. What?

Kɪʀɪ-Kuᴋɪ. Your Highness! Horrors, horrors! But I'm so exhausted from the dungeon that I cannot speak. Tohonga, give me a swallow of firewater to strengthen me. (Tohonga *gives* Kiri-Kuki *a flask*.) Ooh, that's good! (Ki-Kum *and* Farra-Teytey *are amazed*.) And so, Your Highness, long ago I started to notice that there was unrest in the minds of your subjects. Oppressed by the thought of what might happen to our precious island, if this unrest should assume destructive proportions, I decided to resort to craft . . .

KI-KUM. What? Kiri . . .

FARRA-TEYTEY. So that's it! He's a provocateur! It's all clear!

LIKKI-TIKKI. Shut up!

KIRI-KUKI. These two fellows have been the objects of my attention for a long time. This morning I sat down by them and started talking. So we talk a bit and I ask, "Why are you so sad, fellows? Do you have such a bad life?"

FARRA-TEYTEY. Ki, we're in the hands of a traitor. Just you wait, you stinking snake!

KIRI-KUKI. Your Majesty, protect your devoted Kiri from the attacks of state criminals.

LIKKI-TIKKI. Shut up!

SIZI-BUZI. Continue, clever one.

KIRI-KUKI. And what do you think, Your Majesty. Horrors, horrors! It's terrifying even to say it . . . So I say to them—what's wrong with you, brothers, why are you so nervous? Why this secrecy among your own people? What do you mean, they say, you mean you are our people? You're a white Arab, you're part of Sizi-Buzi's entourage, what do you have in common with us— poor native slaves? Well, at this point I spin them a three-mile-long cock-and-bull story. I just look like an Arab, but in my soul I'm with them, with the red natives . . .

KI-KUM. Oh, is there any limit to human baseness on earth!

KIRI-KUKI. . . . and that long ago, moved by the aspirations of the native people, I had decided . . . it's terrifying to utter it, Your Majesty . . . and I ask them: "Well, how about it, would you follow me in that case?"—and just imagine, they answer: "We'd follow."

SIZI-BUZI. Where are you, celestial lightning?! There isn't no celestial lightning.

KIRI-KUKI. And at that point many of the people started coming up and sympathizing with the cause . . . I was absolutely horrified by the things that were being cooked up on our island . . . But I don't let on and I shout: "Horrors, horrors! Down with the tyrant Sizi-Buzi, I shout, and his gang of white Janissaries!" And what do you think, they started repeating after me . . . Down with them! Down with them! Well, then the guards ran up when they heard the shouting, as I had ordered, and grabbed us all.

Sɪzɪ-Buzɪ. And that's the truth?

Kɪ-Kᴜᴍ. Yes, that's the truth. And never before has truth emerged from lips more vile than the lips of this man.

Kɪʀɪ-Kᴜᴋɪ. You see what kind he is, Your Majesty?

Lɪᴋᴋɪ-Tɪᴋᴋɪ. Shut his mouth!

Kɪ-Kᴜᴍ (*breaking away*). Listen, you leech!

Sɪzɪ-Buzɪ. Leech? You're calling me a leech?

Kɪ-Kᴜᴍ. Yes, you! How did you get on that throne? Why do you rule innumerable hordes of native slaves with a few hundred armed loafers? . . .

Lɪᴋᴋɪ-Tɪᴋᴋɪ. Shut him up.

Tohonga *shuts* Ki-Kum's *mouth.*

Fᴀʀʀᴀ-Tᴇʏᴛᴇʏ. Thousands of natives, a crushed, obedient people crawls along the burning earth, sowing maize, finding pearls for you, and gathering turtle eggs. They work from the rise to the setting of the sun god.

Lɪᴋᴋɪ-Tɪᴋᴋɪ. Shut that one up too!

Kɪʀɪ-Kᴜᴋɪ. Horrors, horrors, Your Majesty.

They shut Farra-Teytey's *mouth.*

Kɪ-Kᴜᴍ (*breaks loose*). And you sell it all to the Europeans and sit around drinking! Where is justice? Natives! Do you hear us? . . .

The Arabs *shut his mouth tight.*

Fᴀʀʀᴀ-Tᴇʏᴛᴇʏ (*breaking loose*). Villain!

Kɪʀɪ-Kᴜᴋɪ. I am amazed at your long-suffering patience, Your Majesty.

Sɪzɪ-Buzɪ. What am I supposed to do, cuff stotten in my ears? Tfu!

Tuff scotten. This is a difficult script. Cotton in my ears . . . Shut up, you good-for-nothing!

FARRA-TEYTEY. But tremble, villain! The volcano Muanganam has been silent until now, but it is already glowing with an ominous flame. Look, look!

A cloud hides the sun, and an ominous reflection appears over the volcano.

SIZI-BUZI. Tfu, tfu! Knock on wood—and tomorrow's Friday, our sabbath! Don't you dare call down misfortune on us, you atheist!

The cloud lifts, it gets light. They shut Farra-Teytey's *and* Ki-Kum's *mouths tight.*

KIRI-KUKI. Your Majesty, you can see for yourself what sort of characters I've uncovered.

SIZI-BUZI. Thank you, Kiri, my faithful minister. You will receive a reward.

KIRI-KUKI. Oh, I do not work for rewards, Your Majesty. The consciousness of duty fulfilled is my sweetest reward. (*Softly.*) I did a good job on that! (*Aloud.*) Apropos of rewards. Your Excellency. For a while I shouldn't be seen by the natives. Have it be announced that I am in the dungeon.

SIZI-BUZI. That's a clever idea. Good! What should I do with them now?

KIRI-KUKI. Hank them on a palm tree, naturally, as a lesson for all the others.

SIZI-BUZI. That's an idea. Read the sentence.

KIRI-KUKI. For their attempt at revolt against the legal ruler of this island . . . and may the gods prolong his radiant reign without darkness . . . Sizi-Buzi the Second . . .

The director makes a sign, fanfares in the orchestra. The Arabs run up to get on guard.

the natives Ki-Kum and Farra-Teytey are condemned . . . (*drum roll*) to forfeiture of all their rights, confiscation of their property . . . where is your property located? Hey, grab that one's rag!

KI-KUM. You son of a bitch! . . .

KIRI-KUKI. Shut him up! . . . and to hanging on a palm tree, feet up!

SIZI-BUZI. Don't forget the "but considering the extenuating . . ."

KIRI-KUKI. Oh, Your Majesty, you are spoiling them with these "but considering the extenuatings . . ."

SIZI-BUZI. I don't want to give these bastards cause to reproach me for cruelty.

KIRI-KUKI. How could they reproach you while hanging from a palm tree? They'd hang there quietly . . . But considering the extenuating circumstances, they will not be deprived of their rights, they are to be hung with all rights and in the generally accepted manner—heads up.

> Ki-Kum and Farra-Teytey *break loose from the hands of the* Arabs *and run up the cliff.*

KI-KUM (*to* Farra). We have nothing to lose! Better death in the waves than a noose! Follow me!

FARRA-TEYTEY. Down with the tyrant!

> *They throw themselves into the ocean, a heavy splash from off-stage.*

SIZI-BUZI. Oh!

KIRI-KUKI. Why didn't you idiots hold them?!

LIKKI-TIKKI. Catch them!

> *The Arabs run off.*

KIRI-KUKI. To the canoes!

TOHONGA. To the canoes! (*He shoots an arrow from the cliff. Everyone runs out. Sizi too.*)

PASSEPARTOUT (*off-stage*). Europeans, make your entrance! Volodka! Why didn't you let the ship down? Ooh, stagehands, you devils!

> *The director makes a sign. The* sailors (*off-stage, they sing with the orchestra*): "O'er the seas . . . O'er the seas . . . Here today . . . Tomorrow there . . ."[6] *From the sky a ship de-*

6. Refrain from a popular song during the Revolution: "You're handsome, sailor boy,/ You're twenty years of age."

scends on ropes; on it are the Lord, Lady, Paganel, Passepartout, Hatteras, Sailors. *All are wearing costumes taken from Jules Vernes illustrations.*

SAILORS (*sing*). Oh, it's a long way to Tipperrary . . .

A cannon shot.

Land! Land! Hurrah! Hurrah!

LADY. Lord Edward, land! Oh, how happy I am!

LORD. Oh, yes. I see. Captain, put us ashore.

HATTERAS. Lower the gangplank! You gawkers! Hey! You in the bell-bottomed trousers, you're crawling to the gangplank like a flea! You no-good, rotten lazybones, may the fever knock you flat on your . . .

LADY. Oh, my lord, the way he curses!

PAGANEL. How can you curse in the presence of madame, Monsieur Hatteras.

HATTERAS. A thousand pardons, lady, I didn't notice you. Let down the gangplank, my little angels, let it down, little cherubims, I'm speaking English to you! Tram-ta-rum-ta-rum . . . (*He swears noiselessly.*)

The Sailors *lower the gangplank, all go ashore.*

LADY. What a wonderful place! Lord Edward, it seems to me that this island is uninhabited.

PAGANEL. Madame is right. The island is uninhabited. I swear by the Champs-Elysées, I was the first to notice it.

LADY. *Excuse, Monsieur Paganel,* I was the first to shout "uninhabited."

LORD. The lady is correct. Captain, give me the flag! (*He jams the English flag into the ground.*) Yes, an English island!

PAGANEL. Passepartout! The flag! (*He jams the French flag into the ground.*) *Oui,* a French island.

LORD. How is this act to be understood, sir?

PAGANEL. Understand it as you wish, monsieur.

LORD. You are a guest on my yacht, sir, and I do not understand you. I cannot permit the island to sit around waiting for just any vagabond to claim it.

PAGANEL. I cannot permit that either.

PASSEPARTOUT. I beg your pardon, gentlemen. A small piece of advice: divide the island.

LORD. Agreed. Yes.

PAGANEL. *Oui.* (Sizi *and all the rest of the group appear.*) Oh, *voilà!* Look, look!

LORD. This island is uninhabited. Who are you?

KIRI-KUKI. Allow me to congratulate Your Excellency on the occasion of your arrival on our esteemed island.

LORD. You live here?

KIRI-KUKI. Precisely so. We are registered on this island.

LORD. Take down the flags! Who rules the island?

SIZI-BUZI (*taking his place on the throne*). I, by the mercy of the gods and the spirit of Vaydua. (*Fanfares.*) I, Sizi-Buzi the Second, rule here. There are my guards, faithful Arabs and their leader, Likki-Tikki.

KIRI-KUKI. Allow me to introduce myself. I am Kiri-Kuki, Master of Ceremonies at His Majesty's court.

LORD. But where's the court?

KIRI-KUKI. Right here, please look, the wigwam on the volcano, and beside it the little picket-fence. This *is* the court.

LADY. Oh, what an amusing tribe we have discovered!

SIZI-BUZI. And who might you be, dear guests?

LORD. I . . . (*music in the orchestra*) . . . am Edward Glenarvan, owner of Malcolm Castle. With me are Lady Glenarvan, and Hatteras, my Captain, and his crew.

PAGANEL. I . . . (*the orchestra plays the "Marseillaise"*) . . . am Jacques Eliasine Maria Paganel, Secretary of the Geographical Society. With me is my servant . . .

PASSEPARTOUT. Passepartout.

SIZI-BUZI. My heart is glad to have such distinguished guests.

LORD. Put the folding chairs here.

The sailors put the chairs down. The Europeans sit down.

Where are your people?

SIZI-BUZI. My people are red natives. They live there, far away.

LORD. Are there many of them?

Sizi-Buzi. Oh yes, many . . . One . . . two . . . fifteen . . . and many other hordes besides.

Paganel. How interesting! (*He writes it down.*)

Lord. You rule, and they work?

Sizi-Buzi. Yes, my dear friend, that's the way it is.

Lord. Oh, that's very intelligent! Are they good people?

Kiri-Kuki. The most enchanting little people, Your Excellency! Just now, two of them were brought here . . . but never mind about that.

Lord. Is the island rich?

Sizi-Buzi. Glory to the gods, we live and do not complain. On our island we have maize, rice, turtles, elephants, parrots, and last year pearls were discovered.

Lady. Pearls? Oh, that's extremely interesting!

Paganel. Oh, yes.

Lord. Pearls? You say, pearls? And do you get many of them?

Sizi-Buzi. Not many, my dear friend. About eighteen thousand pounds a year.

Lord.
Lady.
Paganel. } *How* much?
Hatteras.

Sizi-Buzi. Why are you so surprised, oh distinguished foreigners?

Lord. It's nothing. And where do you put these pearls?

Sizi-Buzi. They are sold.

Lord. To whom?

Lady. They're sold!

Lord. Madam, I must ask you to be quiet.

Sizi-Buzi. A German came here once.

Paganel. This German is everywhere.

Lord. And how much did he pay you?

Sizi-Buzi. Five hundred yards of calico, twenty barrels of beer, one missionary, and, besides that, he gave Kiri-Kuki some pants . . .

Kiri-Kuki. These are the pants here.

Sizi-Buzi. And as a gift in parting he gave me five hundred of his money bills—I papered the walls of my wigwam with them.

LORD. And he got eighteen thousand pounds of pearls?

SIZI-BUZI. And he carried them away.

KIRI-KUKI. Your Majesty, I told you we sold it too cheap.

PAGANEL. The swindler!

KIRI-KUKI. I told you, Your Majesty.

SIZI-BUZI. Could he really have done old Sizi wrong? Why, he promised to come back and visit us in his puffing launch.

HATTERAS. And when he returns in that launch you should send him back to Europe. May his keel turn up! (*To* Sizi.) And you're a fine one, you old deformity! And if he shows up here again, and you don't throw him into the sea with a rusty anchor around his feet, I'll . . .

LORD. Captain, calm down.

HATTERAS. But I can't, Your Excellency. These Arabs . . . God!

LORD (*softly*). Sir . . . What a chance this is! Eh? Do you want to?! . . .

PAGANEL. *Certainement.* Of course. *Oui.*

LORD. Go halves?

PAGANEL. Go halves.

LORD (*aloud*). Well, here's what we'll do . . . Do you have any pearls right now?

SIZI-BUZI. Right now, my dear friend, we don't. We will in three months, in spring.

LADY. What are they like? Can you show me a sample?

SIZI-BUZI. Yes, I can. Tohonga! Bring the pearl I use to hammer nails with from the wigwam!

Tohonga *carries out a pearl of supernatural proportions.*

TOHONGA. Here.

KIRI-KUKI. *Voilà.*

LADY. Oh, I'm going to be sick.

PAGANEL. The Cathedral of Notre Dame!

HATTERAS. Eighteen thousand pounds like that? Like that?

SIZI-BUZI. No, the others were bigger.

KIRI-KUKI. Much bigger, Your Excellency.

HATTERAS. I cannot . . .

LORD. Well, here's what we'll do. In brief. We have to sail back to Europe right now. Please understand, King, that you had a swindler here.

SIZI-BUZI. Oh! Oh! The spirit of Vaydua will punish him.

HATTERAS. Don't hold your breath.

LORD. Captain, I'll thank you not to interrupt me. So! I will buy all of your pearls. And not only those which you get in the spring, but all that you manage to find in the next ten years. I will pay you . . .

PAGANEL. Going halves with me.

LORD. Yes, going halves with Monsieur Jacques Paganel . . . Have you ever seen a pound sterling?

SIZI-BUZI. No, my dear friend, what is that?

LORD. It's a convenient thing. Wherever you are on the globe, in a word, this piece of paper . . . here is one. Wherever you present it, you will receive a pile of calico, heaps of tobacco, trousers, and as much firewater as you wish.

HATTERAS. And not that stinking swindler's beer . . .

LORD. . . . But rum! Rum!

SIZI-BUZI. May the gods bless you, foreigners.

LORD. Listen. I will give you a thousand such notes. And you can wrap your island in calico as in a skirt. I will give you one hundred barrels of cognac, which burns like straw if you touch a match to it; I will give you one thousand yards of calico, a thousand, do you understand? One hundred . . . one hundred . . . ten times one hundred. Fifty tins of sardines . . . What else would you like?

SIZI-BUZI. Nothing else. You are a magnanimous foreigner.

HATTERAS. And for my part, I will give you a pipe on the condition that when I come next time, that son-of-a-bitch German will be hanging on a tree here like a rotten banana.

KIRI-KUKI. And a suitcase for me, Your Excellency.

LORD. All right. I'll pay you for all this right now, in advance, you understand?

SIZI-BUZI. I love you, foreigner!

LORD. I love you, too, but you're getting spit all over me. Kiss M. Paganel.

PAGANEL. *Merci,* I had a kiss the day before yesterday, and that's enough for me.

LORD. You sign here.

SIZI-BUZI. My dear friend, I spent a month on the liquidation of illiteracy, but I've forgotten everything. I remember the "S." It looks like a snake. But all the rest flew out of my head.

KIRI-KUKI. Allow me, lord. Here, please. KEE, E KEE, KIRI-KUKI.

LADY. Oh, are you literate? (*Softly.*) He's not bad at all, this Arab. (*Aloud.*) Who taught you?

KIRI-KUKI. Foreigners who dropped by, madam.

LORD (*reads*). Kiri-Kuki and . . . a suitcase. What's this?

KIRI-KUKI. I was just reminding you. Don't forget about the suitcase, Your Excellency.

LORD. Oh! Give him the suitcase with shiny straps.

Passepartout *gives him the suitcase.*

KIRI-KUKI. How lovely! Can I believe my blue eyes! Oh, oh! No, I'm unworthy of such a suitcase. Allow me to embrace you, lord.

The Lord *declines;* Kiri *embraces the* Lady.

LADY. Oh, such impertinence!

LORD. Well, there's no need of that. And so, take this . . . (*He gives him thick wads of money.*) These are the pounds sterling. But remember: you must be honest! In three months I will come back for the pearls. If the German shows up, kick him out! Don't be crooks! Otherwise I'll get angry.

PAGANEL. Me too. We'll start a war.

SIZI-BUZI. Ah, why threaten Old Sizi? He won't deceive you.

LORD. Well, there's a good fellow! Sailors, give him the calico and sardines, roll out the rum!

HATTERAS. Get the rum! Tum-te-tum . . .

SAILORS. Hey! Hey! (*They throw out goods, roll out barrels.*)

SIZI-BUZI. Thank you. I will give you the pearl. There!

LADY. *Merci!* Oh, it's a miracle! A miracle!

KIRI-KUKI. Tohonga! Catch a parrot for the lady!

TOHONGA. Right away! (*A flock of parrots flies out.* Tohonga *catches an enormous one, and presents it.*) Here.

KIRI-KUKI. Allow me, madam, to present you with this parrot as a remembrance. A nice decoration for your drawing room in Europe.

LIKKI-TIKKI. He's clever, the wretch!

PAGANEL. *Diable!* A gallant native!

LADY. It's charming, M. Paganel! *Merci! Merci!* Does it talk?

KIRI-KUKI. Of course!

HATTERAS. It's the first time in my life I've seen one like this. (*To the parrot.*) Oh, why don't you drop dead!

PARROT. Why don't you drop dead yourself?

General amazement.

HATTERAS. Who are you talking to? You tailless Satan!

PARROT. You're Satan yourself!

HATTERAS. I'll fix you!

LADY. What are you doing, Captain? Don't you dare insult my bird! Polly's a fool!

PARROT. A fool yourself!

LADY. Oh!

LORD. Knock it off, Metelkin!

PARROT. Yes, sir, Gennadi Panfilych.

HATTERAS. Lord, the sun is setting. It's time to go. There are reefs around the island.

LORD. Raise the sails, captain.

HATTERAS. Yes, sir. On board, men!

The Sailors *go onto the ship, the sails are unfurled.*

LORD. Goodbye!

SIZI-BUZI. So long!

LADY. Passepartout! Get the parrot!

PASSEPARTOUT. Yes, my lady.

PAGANEL. *Au revoir!*

HATTERAS. Raise the gangplank! Tum-te-tum!

PARROT. Mothah Mothah, Mothah . . .

HATTERAS. Ooh, I'll have you fried in the galley! Tie his beak with some rope! Head out of the bay!

They raise the anchor. The ship begins to move away. The sun sets in the ocean.

SAILORS (*growing fainter*). "O'er the seas, o'er the seas . . ."
PARROT (*sings*). "Here today, there tomorrow."

SIZI-BUZI. They've gone! They were good foreigners!
KIRI-KUKI. Your Majesty, may I congratulate you on a profitable deal.
LIKKI-TIKKI. And I, you—on the suitcase! You know how to beg, you son of a devil!
KIRI-KUKI. You know, Likki, I think that foreign woman fell in love with me.
LIKKI-TIKKI. Well, of course. She never saw anybody as handsome as you.
SIZI-BUZI. Kiri, take the money and hide it.
KIRI-KUKI. Yes, Your Majesty. (*He puts the money in the suitcase.*) What do you want done with the other things?
SIZI-BUZI. Put them in my storerooms. Give the Arabs a cup of foreign firewater each.
ARABS. Thank you very much, Your Majesty.
SIZI-BUZI. You're good men!
ARABS. We're glad to be of service, Your Majesty.
SIZI-BUZI. Good, just shut up.

Tohonga breaks open a barrel. Like a blue flame, it spurts into the twilight.

Now *this* I understand!
LIKKI-TIKKI. Your Majesty, you should announce some favor for the natives too.
SIZI-BUZI. Favor? You think so? Well, why not? Inform them that I forgive them for the revolt. And I forgive those two cutthroats who drowned. I'm not angry at them.
KIRI-KUKI. O Kind Sovereign! (*Softly.*) However, I'd like to know for sure whether they drowned.

Sızı-Buzı. I designate this evening as a holiday for all my courtiers and my faithful guards, and when the orb of night rises . . . (*a mysterious moon rises*) . . . let the odalisques from my harem entertain us with dance.

The Director *gives a sign and the orchestra furiously plays Franz Liszt's* Second Rhapsody. *The Odalisques begin the dance. Happiest of all,* Kiri-Kuki *dances with his suitcase. The curtain closes and covers the stage.*

Passepartout (*in the break in the curtain, waves his hand and the music ceases*). *Entr'acte.*

Light in the theater.

ACT II

Scene one

Rolls of catastrophe *from the orchestra. The curtain opens. On stage nothing but darkness except for an ominous glow over the volcano.*

Kiri-Kuki (*with a small lamp*). Oh! Who's here? Come toward me! Toward me! Who is it? General, is that you?

Likki-Tikki (*with a small lamp*). It's me! It's me! Is that you, Kiri?

Kiri-Kuki. It's me! It's me! What an uproar! Did you get out in one piece?

Likki-Tikki. As you see. Thanks to the gods!

Kiri-Kuki. Tell me, did Sizi-Buzi perish?

Likki-Tikki. Yes, he did.

Kiri-Kuki. How many times did I tell the old man, get your wig-wam off that damned primus stove! No, he wouldn't listen. "The gods won't allow it!" . . . Just see how they didn't allow it! . . . Who else perished?

Likki-Tikki. The whole harem and half of our Arabs. Everyone who was on guard duty.

Kiri-Kuki. That's just great!

Likki-Tikki. What's going to happen now, I can't make my brains function!

Kiri-Kuki. No, dear general, in fact at this point it is quite necessary to make them function!

Likki-Tikki. Well, go ahead, function quickly!

KIRI-KUKI. Hold it ... Let's sit down ... Ooh!

LIKKI-TIKKI. What?

KIRI-KUKI. I think I threw my leg out of joint. Ooh! . . . And so . . . First of all, let us analyze what's happened. What has happened is . . .

LIKKI-TIKKI. An eruption.

KIRI-KUKI. Hold it, don't interrupt! An eruption! Yes, the lava has flowed out and buried the king's wigwam. And here we are left without a ruler.

LIKKI-TIKKI. And without one half of our guards.

KIRI-KUKI. Yes, it's terrible, but it's a fact. The question arises, what will happen now on this island?

LIKKI-TIKKI. What?

KIRI-KUKI. I'm asking *you*—what?

LIKKI-TIKKI. I don't know.

KIRI-KUKI. But I know. There'll be a revolt.

LIKKI-TIKKI. Really?

KIRI-KUKI. Take it easy. You know perfectly well what state our good native population is in, and now when they learn that the ruler is no longer with us, they'll go completely beserk . . .

LIKKI-TIKKI. Impossible!

KIRI-KUKI. "Impossible!" . . . What's wrong with you—you're like a child, really! . . . Ay, look, more fire! . . . I hope it doesn't pour over here!

LIKKI-TIKKI. No, it's already quieting down.

KIRI-KUKI. Well, brother, I haven't been inside there. The devil only knows if it is quieting down or not . . . Let's go down some just in case . . . (*They run down.*) It's safer here. And so, the question arises, what must be done to avoid the horrors of a revolt and anarchy?

LIKKI-TIKKI. I don't know.

KIRI-KUKI. Well, I know. We must choose a new leader immediately.

LIKKI-TIKKI. Aha! I see! But who?

KIRI-KUKI. Me.

LIKKI-TIKKI. You?! Are you in your right mind?

KIRI-KUKI. No matter what happens, I'm always in my right mind.

LIKKI-TIKKI. You—the ruler! . . . Listen, that's impertinence!

KIRI-KUKI. Quiet, you don't understand anything. Listen to me carefully: did those two devils drown for certain?

LIKKI-TIKKI. Ki-Kum and Farra-Teytey?

KIRI-KUKI. Yes, of course.

LIKKI-TIKKI. I think I saw their heads disappear under the water.

KIRI-KUKI. Praise the gods! Only those two characters could prevent the execution of my plan—which I consider brilliant.

LIKKI-TIKKI. Kiri, you are insolent! Who are you that you should worm your way into being a ruler? It should sooner be me—the chief of the guards . . .

KIRI-KUKI. What can you do? Just what can you do? You only know how to holler commands, nothing more! An intelligent man is needed!

LIKKI-TIKKI. And I'm not intelligent? Shut up, when . . .

KIRI-KUKI. You are a man of average intellect, but one of genius is needed.

LIKKI-TIKKI. You are the one of genius?

KIRI-KUKI. Don't argue. Ay! . . . You hear that?

Noise off-stage.

LIKKI-TIKKI. Well, naturally, they've woken up, the devils!

KIRI-KUKI. Yes, they've woken up, and if you don't want them to toss you and the rest of your guards into the drink, you'd better listen to me. In brief! I will become the ruler. Give me an answer, do you wish to remain chief of the guards or not?

LIKKI-TIKKI. This is unheard of! I—Likki-Tikki, a general, am going to become chief of the guards for some upstart rascal! . . .

KIRI-KUKI. Oh, so that's the way it is! May you croak like a dog without the absolution of the church even! Bear in mind the fact that I will still execute my plan. I'll go over to the natives' side, and I'll still become ruler. Because there's no one to govern this island except me. And you're going to be feeding the crabs in the Bay of Blue Tranquility! Goodbye! I have no time!

LIKKI-TIKKI. Stop, you bastard! I agree.

KIRI-KUKI. Aha, that's another matter.

LIKKI-TIKKI. What am I supposed to do?

KIRI-KUKI. Gather the surviving Arabs and keep their mouths shut tight. No matter what happens! Understand? Shut up!

LIKKI-TIKKI. O.K. I'll see what comes of this . . . Tohonga! Tohonga! Where are you?

TOHONGA (*enters*). Here I am, general.

LIKKI-TIKKI. Call everyone who survived here!

TOHONGA. Yes, general!

> *The noise of a huge crowd. First separately, then in crowds, natives carrying red flags appear. The flame trembles, and the entire stage is illuminated by a mystical light from it.*

KIRI-KUKI (*hopping up on an empty rum barrel*). Hey! Hey! Natives, over here! Over here!

NATIVES. Who's calling? What happened? An eruption? Who? What? Why?

> Tohonga *leads the guards on stage carrying white lanterns.*

KIRI-KUKI. I am calling! It is I! Kiri-Kuki, friend of the native population! Come here! (*He raises his lantern over his head.*)

FIRST NATIVE. An eruption!

KIRI-KUKI. Yes! An eruption! Come here! Listen, everyone, listen to what I'm going to tell you!

NATIVES. Who's that talking? Who's talking? Who?

KIRI-KUKI. It's me talking—Kiri! Friend of the native population!

NATIVES. Listen! Listen!

KIRI-KUKI. Quiet, my friends. You're going to find out what has happened right now . . .

> *Silence falls over the group.*

Tonight, while our former tsar Sizi-Buzi the Second . . .

> *The orchestra sounds a fanfare.*

ARABS. May the gods preserve him! . . .

LIKKI-TIKKI. You shut up!

KIRI-KUKI (*makes desperate gestures from the barrel and the fanfares fall silent, the Arabs too*). There's no reason for the gods to preserve him! And they never preserved him! And there was no reason for the gods to preserve a tyrant who tortured his people!

The Natives *utter sounds of surprise.*

Kiri-Kuki. And so, when Sizi, having drunk his fill of firewater was sleeping peacefully in his harem on the side of the volcano, Muanganam, which had rested in silence for three hundred years, suddenly opened its fiery maw and erupted streams of lava, which wiped from the face of the earth not only Sizi-Buzi himself, but also his harem and half of his guards. Obviously the limit to divine patience, as set down in the Book of Life, had been reached, and by the will of Vaydua the tyrant was no more ...

A roar.

Likki-Tikki. Oh, what an elegant swine!
Kiri-Kuki. Brothers! I, Kiri-Kuki, an Arab by birth, but a native in spirit, I support you! You are free, natives! Shout hurrah together with me. Hurrah!
Natives (*at first softly, then louder*). Hurrah! Hurrah! Hurrah!
Director (*gets up and makes signs*). Hurrah! Hurrah! Hurrah!
Natives. Hurrah! Hurrah! Hurrah!

The roar quiets down.

Kiri-Kuki. There will be no more oppression on this island, there will be no stinging lashes from the Arab overseers, there will be no slavery. You are the masters of your own island now, you are the rulers yourselves! Oh, natives!
Second Native. Why is he saying that, brothers? Why is an Arab from the entourage rejoicing for us? What's going on?
First Native. That's Kiri-Kuki.
Third Native. Who? Who?

A roar.

Likki-Tikki. I said nothing would come out of this fine game! We should get the hell out!
Fourth Native. That's Kiri!
Kiri-Kuki. Yes, it's I. Who among you, my beloved natives, shouted: "Why is an Arab rejoicing together with us?" Oh, oh, oh! There

is sorrow in my heart from such a question! Who does not know Kiri? Who is there who did not hear him any longer ago than yesterday at the cornstalks.

FIRST NATIVE. Yes, yes, we heard him!

NATIVES. We heard!

FIRST NATIVE. Where are Ki-Kum and Farra-Teytey?

KIRI-KUKI. Quiet! Listen to what I did, I, Kiri-Kuki, true friend of the native population! Yesterday I was grabbed by the guards along with the other natives Ki-Kum and Farra-Teytey . . .

THIRD NATIVE. Where are they? Why are you alone?

KIRI-KUKI. Listen, listen! We were thrown into the dungeon, then brought here to the foot of Sizi's throne, and here certain death stared us in the face. I was witness to how poor Ki and Farra were sentenced to be hanged. Horrors, horrors!

THIRD NATIVE. And you?

KIRI-KUKI. Me? It was much worse for me. The old tyrant decided that for me, an Arab who had betrayed him, death in the noose was too light a punishment. I was cast back into the underground and left there for a day so that an execution unheard of in its cruelty could be devised for me. There, sitting in the damp bowels of the earth I heard it when the valorous Ki-Kum asd Farra-Teytey tore themselves out of the arms of the executioners, threw themselves into the ocean from Muanganam and swam off. May the god Vaydua protect them in the tumultuous abyss!

LIKKI-TIKKI (*softly*). Oh boy, and if they manage to swim out, oh my god, my god!

FIRST NATIVE. God protect Ki and Farra! Long live Kiri-Kuki, friend of the native people!

NATIVES. Long live Kiri! Long live Kiri! Praise to the gods!

KIRI-KUKI. Dear friends, now the question arises, what are we to do? Can our flourishing island be left without a ruler? Can the horror of leaderlessness and anarchy really be threatening us?

NATIVES. He's right, Kiri-Kuki! He's right!

KIRI-KUKI. My friends, I propose that right here, without leaving this place, we choose a man to whom we can entrust the fate of our island and all its riches without fear. He must be an honest and truthful man, my friends! He must be just and merciful; but, my friends, he must also be educated so that he can conduct relations with the Europeans who so often visit our fertile island. Who is it to be, my friends? . . .

NATIVES. That's *you*, Kiri-Kuki!

KIRI-KUKI. Yes, it's me! That is, *no!* Not for anything! I am unworthy of this honor!

NATIVES. Kiri, you don't dare refuse! Kiri! You cannot abandon us at such a hard moment! You are the only educated man on the island!

KIRI-KUKI. No! No!

LIKKI-TIKKI. The devil! (*Softly.*) Kiri! What are you fooling around for?

KIRI-KUKI (*softly*). Get away, you blockhead! (*Loudly.*) Can it be that I will have to take upon myself this terrible burden and responsibility? Can it really be for me to do?! All right, I agree.

NATIVES (*in thunderous voices*). Hurrah! Long live Kiri-Kuki the First, friend of the native population!

KIRI-KUKI. Oh, my dear ones, tears of heartfelt emotion becloud my eyes! All right, dear natives, I will apply all my efforts to make sure that you do not regret your choice. And as a sign that I am with you heart and soul, I am taking off my Arab dress and putting on your charming native colors . . . (*He takes off his headdress and puts on crimson native feathers.*)

The Natives *rejoice. Music.*

I Kiri-Kuki the First, announce my first decree. As a sign of joy, our dear island, which in the time of Sizi-Buzi bore the name of Native Island, I am renaming Crimson Island.

The Natives *rejoice.*

Now the question arises what are we to do with the remainder of Sizi-Buzi's guards? There they are!

Likki-Tikki *and the* Guards *are amazed.*

NATIVES. Into the water with them!

TOHONGA (*to* Likki). General, you hear?

LIKKI-TIKKI. The traitor ...

NATIVES. Into the ocean!

KIRI-KUKI. No! Hear me out, my faithful subjects! Who is going to defend our island in case of an attack by other tribes? To whom, finally, will we entrust the protection of myself? The life of a man who, it is clear, is so essential to the island? My friends, I propose that if they repent, they be forgiven, their former service to the tyrant be forgotten, and they be taken into our service. (*To* Likki.) Answer, oh criminal general, do you agree to repent and serve the native people and me in truth and faith?

Likki-Tikki *is silent.*

KIRI-KUKI. Answer when you're talked to, you clod!

LIKKI-TIKKI (*softly*). You told me to keep quiet ...

KIRI-KUKI. I recommend that you be a little more aware of the circumstances.

LIKKI-TIKKI. I agree, O Ruler!

KIRI-KUKI. Will you serve?

LIKKI-TIKKI. Yes sir, Your Majesty.

KIRI-KUKI. You won't go against me and the people?

LIKKI-TIKKI. Never, Your Majesty!

KIRI-KUKI. Atta' boy, you are a faithful old man!

LIKKI-TIKKI. Glad to be of service, Your Majesty.

KIRI-KUKI. Well, you shout louder than anyone else anyway. (*To* Arabs.) Do you agree?

ARABS. We agree, Your Majesty!

KIRI-KUKI. I forgive you, and as a sign of mercy I rename you as the People's Deserving Arabs.

ARABS. We thank you humbly, Your Majesty!

KIRI-KUKI. Oh, goddamn it! Those drum rolls will break my eardrums. Tell them to keep quiet!

LIKKI-TIKKI. Keep quiet!

KIRI-KUKI. Redress them in our native color!

LIKKI-TIKKI. Yes sir, Your Majesty!

KIRI-KUKI. Please, no shouting! Keep quiet!

LIKKI-TIKKI. Yes, sir . . . (*He claps his hands—instantaneously the feathers fall off the* Arabs *and crimson ones grow up on their heads. Their lanterns, instead of white, begin to burn pink.*)
KIRI-KUKI. There, native people, there are your guards!
NATIVES. Hurrah!
LIKKI-TIKKI. Ceremonial march!

> *The* Director *waves his baton.*

Forward . . . march!

> *The orchestra plays a march. The* Arabs *go past* Kiri-Kuki *in a ceremonial march step. Innumerable hordes of* Natives *wave little lanterns.*

KIRI-KUKI. Health to the guards!
ARABS. Yr . . . . . . ealth . . . Your Majesty!

> Likki-Tikki *marching out of the column, stands beside* Kiri.

KIRI-KUKI. Did you see that?
LIKKI-TIKKI. You really are a genius! Now I see!
KIRI-KUKI. You're so right!

CURTAIN

SCENE TWO

KIRI-KUKI'S *royal wigwam.*

KIRI-KUKI. Only three days have passed since I've been running this damned island, and still my head is spinning because of those pearls!
LIKKI-TIKKI (*taking a bite of something*). It's your own fault!
KIRI-KUKI. Why, may I ask?

LIKKI-TIKKI. You fed them such damned stories, now pay the piper. (*Ironically.*) Friend of the native population! (*He chews.*) Who was it that quacked: we'll have our fill of everything, our fill of rice and corn . . . and firewater. Everything is for and everything from you. You are your own masters. Remember how you told them that? Well, so now they're being their own masters.

KIRI-KUKI. The most monstrous thing is this demand not to give up the pearls to the English. A fine how do you do! How can I not give them up when they paid money for them?!

LIKKI-TIKKI. And firewater. So it looks like you'll have to give the pearls to the English!

KIRI-KUKI. But they're serious about not wanting to give them up. We'll go ahead and find them, they say, but let's keep them for ourselves. My flesh creeps at the thought that that fat physiognomy with the red side whiskers will appear on his ship. The question arises, what am I going to do? Oh, it's good fortune that those two instigators drowned . . .

LIKKI-TIKKI (*chewing*). Yes . . .

KIRI-KUKI. What did you say?

LIKKI-TIKKI. I said "yes."

KIRI-KUKI. "Yes." What good is "yes"? All you can do is moo. You'd better give some advice.

LIKKI-TIKKI. Giving advice is not my specialty. What is my job? *To guard you* and I guard you. But you go ahead and rule as you like.

KIRI-KUKI. You're really a big help!

LIKKI-TIKKI. Under the late Sizi-Buzi now, things were good!

KIRI-KUKI. How, may I ask?

LIKKI-TIKKI. Under Sizi they gave up the pearls without a fuss. There was order, that's what was good!

KIRI-KUKI. We have to establish order now too.

LIKKI-TIKKI. Now it's hard, my dear ruler. You've spoiled them too much.

KIRI-KUKI. Well, there's no reason to whine. That won't help anything!

TOHONGA (*enters*). Greetings to you, O Ruler!

KIRI-KUKI. Thank you. What have you to say, my dear fellow?

TOHONGA. The natives have come again. They wish an audience with Your Eminence.

KIRI-KUKI. Again? It's a punishment, I swear! You just drive them ... here, into my study.

TOHONGA. I obey, O Ruler. (*He exits.*) Come in!

First, Second, *and* Third Natives *enter.*

NATIVES. Greetings to you, Kiri, our ruler and friend, and may the gods protect you!

KIRI-KUKI. Ah! And may they protect you too. Very glad to see you. I have really missed you. Why, you haven't been here since morning.

NATIVES. May the gods protect Likki-Tikki, the brave general of the People's Guards.

LIKKI-TIKKI. And you, and you.

FIRST NATIVE. Are you having something to eat, bold Likki?

LIKKI-TIKKI. No, I'm dancing.

SECOND NATIVE. Our brave Likki loves to joke.

KIRI-KUKI. Yes, he always was a jolly sort. Incidentally, general, I think that you could talk with my dear subjects more amiably. (Likki *mumbles.*) Squat down here, my dear friends. (*The Natives sit down.*) So as not to lose precious time, explain, my doves, what has brought you to my wigwam at the hour when the sun god is highest in the heavens, when not only rulers, but simple mortals as well, exhausted by picking corn, are resting in their wigwams? (*Softly.*) They don't understand my hints, the devils!

FIRST NATIVE. We have come to inform you of joyous news.

KIRI-KUKI. I am joyous already, without even knowing what it is.

THIRD NATIVE. We came to tell you that the pearl hunting was extremely successful today. We dragged up fifteen pearls, the smallest of which was the size of my fist.

KIRI-KUKI. I am in ecstasy! But I am struck only by one thing— why haven't you brought them to my wigwam immediately as I told you yesterday morning?

FIRST NATIVE. Oh, Kiri-Ruler! The people are very disturbed about these pearls and sent us to you to find out what you intend to do with them.

KIRI-KUKI. My dear friends, it's too hot right now to repeat the same thing ten times. Nevertheless, I will repeat it for you the eleventh time—the pearls must be brought to my wigwam, and when we have stored up eighteen thousand pounds, the Englishman will come and take them with him.

SECOND NATIVE. Kiri! The people do not want to give the pearls to the Englishman.

KIRI-KUKI. Nevertheless, it will be necessary to give them up. Sizi received full payment for them and sold them to that Englishman.

THIRD NATIVE. Kiri, do you know what the people were chattering about at the bay during the dive today?

LIKKI-TIKKI (*through his teeth*). There, there . . . there are the fruits of . . . They wouldn't have chattered under Sizi! . . .

FIRST NATIVE. What are you saying, bodyguard?

LIKKI-TIKKI. Nothing, never mind. I'm singing a song.

KIRI-KUKI. General, it's bad for your health to sing when it's so hot.

LIKKI-TIKKI. I'll be silent, silent.

KIRI-KUKI. What were they chattering about?

THIRD NATIVE. They chattered that our Kiri, may the gods prolong his life, is acting badly in insisting on giving the pearls up.

KIRI-KUKI. My dear friends, do you understand your native language? The Englishman will come with cannon, and the document was signed by me.

FIRST NATIVE. Kiri, friend of the people, acted frivolously in signing the document.

KIRI-KUKI. Don't you find, my dear friend, that it is awkward for a simple native to thus comment on the ruler of the island?

FIRST NATIVE. I said it in love.

KIRI-KUKI. And I am telling you, in love, may you . . . be protected by the gods, that the pearls must be brought here.

SECOND NATIVE. The native people will not do it.

KIRI-KUKI. And I say they will.

NATIVES. No, they won't.

KIRI-KUKI. Yes, they will.

NATIVES. No, they won't.

KIRI-KUKI. Tohonga!

TOHONGA. What is it?

KIRI-KUKI. Give me some firewater! (*He drinks, shouts.*) They will!

FIRST NATIVE. Kiri, if you're going to shout so awfully, a vein in your neck might burst.

KIRI-KUKI. No, I don't have the strength to discuss it with you any more. So I will be forced to act otherwise. General! Take careful measures to see that the pearl catch is brought here immediately. I am going in, and I will stretch out on the mats, so that my exhausted limbs may rest if only a little.

LIKKI-TIKKI. So you're turning this thing over to me?

KIRI-KUKI. Yes. (*He disappears.*)

LIKKI-TIKKI. Yes, sir. (*He begins to roll up his sleeves.*)

FIRST NATIVE. What do you intend to do, brave chief?

LIKKI-TIKKI. I intend to smash you in the teeth, and for that I am rolling up my sleeves.

FIRST NATIVE. Do I really believe my ears? Dear friends, did you hear? He intends to smash me in the teeth! Me, a free native! . . . He, the chief of our guards, smash me in the teeth! . . .

SECOND and THIRD NATIVES. Oh, ho, ho! Ha, ha!

LIKKI-TIKKI (*smashes the* First Native *in the teeth. The* Second *and* Third Natives *sit down on the ground in horror*). The pearls will be *here*. Here! Here!

SECOND and THIRD NATIVES. Guards!

LIKKI-TIKKI. Call the sentries in here.

TOHONGA. Hey! . . . (*The* Arabs *run in.*)

LIKKI-TIKKI. Take these good-for-nothings into the dungeon!

SECOND and THIRD NATIVES. What? What . . . us?

A terrible noise off-stage, a crowd of Natives *appears. Behind them are* Ki-Kum *and* Farra-Teytey.

NATIVES. Let us in, let us in!

TOHONGA. Stop, stop! Where are you going?

LIKKI-TIKKI. What's the meaning of this? Get back! How dare you stick your noses in the ruler's wigwam uninvited?

FOURTH NATIVE. No, Likki, you stop that stuff! No more wigwams! We've brought great news! Friends, here!

SECOND and THIRD NATIVES. Guards! . . .

FIRST NATIVE. Friends, do you know what happened? ... He ... He ...

LIKKI-TIKKI. About the pearls again? I'll show you what it means not to obey your legal ruler, chosen by yourselves! Hey!

FOURTH NATIVE. No, this is not a matter of pearls! More interesting events have occurred. Where's Kiri?

NATIVES. Kiri! Kiri!

LIKKI-TIKKI. What the hell are you doing! Stop that yawping! Hey, Tohonga! Push them back!

FOURTH NATIVE. Pay no attention!

NATIVES. Kiri! Kiri!

KIRI-KUKI (*comes out*). What's going on?

NATIVES (*agitated*). There he is! There he is! There he is! Ah-ah!

KIRI-KUKI. Yes, here he is. Hello, my dear friends. How many of you there are. Charming!

FOURTH NATIVE. We've brought you news, Kiri! Yes!

KIRI-KUKI. My friends, I have already heard the news today. Besides, I want to sleep. But, still, what is it?

FOURTH NATIVE. Today, when the second party of divers dove into the bay to search for pearls ... what do you think they brought out besides pearls, Kiri?

KIRI-KUKI. Very interesting! Crabs, probably, or some scroungy necklace lost by some native girl swimming. But, really, this news is not significant enough to burst into the ruler's wigwam in a crowd!

FOURTH NATIVE. No, Kiri, it wasn't crabs we dragged out! We dragged out two utterly exhausted men ... Look! Move aside, my friends!

The Natives *move apart, and* Ki *and* Farra *walk out. Absolute silence sets in.*

KIRI-KUKI (*falling from the throne*). God-*damn!*

LIKKI-TIKKI. I had a feeling this would happen! Now the fun begins. (*To* Kiri.) I wonder what you're going to do now?

KI-KUM. You reign, Kiri? You recognize us?

KIRI-KUKI (*looking at them closely*). No ... hm ... no, I don't.

FARRA-TEYTEY. Ah, the scoundrel, the scoundrel!

KIRI-KUKI. How dare you speak to the ruler like that? (*To* Likki, *softly*.) Get the guards ready, there's going to be a scandal in a minute.

LIKKI-TIKKI. I know, I already know. Tohonga! Tohonga!

KI-KUM (*blocking his road*). Wait, wait! Back, my friend!

FARRA-TEYTEY. What, you don't recognize us?

KIRI-KUKI. A familiar face . . . but I don't recall where I've seen your honest, open physiognomy and ideological eyes . . . Maybe in a dream?

FARRA-TEYTEY. You bastard! The last time you saw us was right here the day of Sizi-Buzi's trial of us. (*To* Likki.) And you too, executioner!

LIKKI-TIKKI. Why, I don't deny it in the least, I recognized you right away, you trouble-making scum!

KIRI-KUKI. Bah! But where were my eyes! No, really, I have to get some glasses, I'm getting nearsighted. Oh, what happiness! Praise be to the immortal gods!

KI-KUM. Son of a bitch!

KIRI-KUKI. I don't understand you, dear sweet Ki-Kum! Why, the Lord be with you! Why are you hurling yourself against me? Can you have forgotten how we suffered together in the underground dungeon? Right here where your honorable feet are standing now.

KI-KUM. And you, blind people, ignorant folk! Whom did you choose as your leader?

KIRI-KUKI. Yes, whom? That is the question, as the great Hamlet cried out . . . Likki, prepare your arrows!

LIKKI-TIKKI. Don't drag it out, better begin the scrap now. Tohonga! Tohonga! Give me my spear!

KI-KUM. Whom? A bastard the likes of whom the world has not seen since the day it was founded by the great gods. A provocateur, a scoundrel, and an upstart.

KIRI-KUKI. Just explain one thing to me: how did you get out?

FARRA-TEYTEY. We swam for three days in sight of the island, getting worn out from thirst, and when we no longer had strength to fight with death, we swam out into the bay—where our faithful brothers dragged us out.

KI-KUM. Brothers, this good-for-nothing who has decked himself out in your feathers read our death sentences to us himself, on this very spot. Do you understand, this dishonest crook tricked us and you at the cornfields that time by pretending to be a friend of the people and a revolutionary. He, he, Tsar Sizi's gendarme!

KIRI-KUKI. Oy, oy! . . . What's going to happen!

NATIVES. Traitor!

KI-KUM. Death to him!

FARRA-TEYTEY. And death to the infamous oppressor Likki-Tikki!

LIKKI-TIKKI. No! I won't give up easily, brothers!

FIRST and FOURTH NATIVES. Death to them!

KI-KUM. Surrender, scoundrel!

NATIVES. Surrender!

LIKKI-TIKKI. Guards, forward!

> Director *makes a sign—a horn is heard.* Arabs *with spears run out on stage. A flurry of activity.*

KI-KUM. Oh, so, brother natives! To arms! To arms! Arm yourselves with bows and spears! Those that have none with stones! Everyone forward! Kill the miserable snake who crawled onto the throne!

NATIVES (*scatter with shouts*). To arms!

FARRA-TEYTEY. To arms!

LIKKI-TIKKI. You see that, friend of the people? Tohonga, lock the gates! Everyone to the palisade! Guards, in rank!

> *The* Arabs *rush to the palisade.*

KIRI-KUKI. Likki, dear fellow, try to hold them back, good man, so that we can manage to escape to the canoes. To arms, my faithful guardsmen! To arms! (*He rushes into his wigwam and runs out carrying his suitcase.*)

LIKKI-TIKKI. Oh, do you think a suitcase is a weapon? Please go that way, to the palisade. You must set an example for the guardsmen with your own bravery!

KIRI-KUKI. I'd rather set them an example of my personal bravery from here . . . Lord, what a battle! . . . from the wigwam . . .

LIKKI-TIKKI. You pitiful coward! You're the cause of . . .

NATIVES (*off-stage*). Here, comrades, over here! Death to the traitor Kiri-Kuki, a reward for his head!

KIRI-KUKI. You hear what they're yelling? Oy, horrors, horrors!

LIKKI-TIKKI. Well, don't hang around here, despicable slime! Tohonga, are the gates locked?

TOHONGA. Yes, sir, general.

LIKKI-TIKKI. Guards, fire on the attacking natives in volleys! . . .

> First Native *suddenly appears on the palisade.*

Fire!

> *The* Arabs *loose their arrows.*

FIRST NATIVE (*with an arrow in his chest*). I'm dying! (*He disappears behind the palisade.*)

> *The glass in one wigwam window flies out with a crash.*

KIRI-KUKI. Oy, what's that?

LIKKI-TIKKI. That's the first present for you—friend of the people! A rock through the window. Arabs, don't falter! Fire! The ruler and the commander-in-chief are with you. (*To* Kiri-Kuki.) Good-for-nothing! Don't you dare reveal your cowardice to the guards.

KIRI-KUKI. My dear Likki, I'm no specialist on military affairs. It's your turn now, and I'll go into the wigwam and think over the plan of further action. All the more so since the doctor strictly forbade me to get upset.

NATIVES (*off-stage*). Hurrah!

> *A cloud of native arrows flies onto the stage.*

FIRST ARAB. Oh, I'm dying.

LIKKI-TIKKI. Encourage the guards with some speech of attack.

> *A second wigwam window flies out.*

KIRI-KUKI. Guards! Every man for himself! (*He opens his suitcase, hides in it, and crawls out in the suitcase.*)

LIKKI-TIKKI. Scoundrel!

> *Arrows fly.*

CURTAIN

ACT III

Scene one

Lord Glenarvan's *luxurious drawing room, décor in the style of the eighteen-sixties. Evening. The drawing room windows open onto the embankment.*
The Lady *is singing a romance, accompanying herself on the piano. The* Lord *and* Paganel *are playing chess, and* Hatteras *is watching.*

Lord. Bravo, bravo! You have never been in better voice than to-night, my dear! (*He applauds.*)
Paganel. Bravo, bravo, madame!
Hatteras. Bravo!
Parrot (*in a cage*). Bravo! Bravo!
Paganel. Check.
Lord. I move here.
Paganel. Check.
Lord. I move here.
Paganel. Check and . . .
Lord. Dammit! I concede, sir.
Hatteras. You should have moved your pawn, sir.
Lord. And then what?
Hatteras. And then your bishop here . . .
Lord. And then what?
Hatteras. And then . . . hm.
Parrot. Moron!
Hatteras. My lord, I tell you that damned bird must have its head yanked off. He makes life impossible.
Lady. What are you saying, captain. I will never allow such a

thing! My dear one, I will never part with you! My little Polly! Polly!

LORD. Will you have a rematch?

PAGANEL. With pleasure, monsieur.

LADY. Oh, it's already five o'clock. Passepartout! Betsy!

Passepartout *and* Betsy *look out from two opposite doors.*

PASSEPARTOUT. ⎫
BETSY. ⎬ What do you wish, madam?
⎭

LADY. Serve tea.

PASSEPARTOUT. ⎫ Yes, my lady. (*They disappear and return with tea*
BETSY. ⎭ *and crumpets.*)

LORD. No, no matter what you say, after one travels for a long time and then returns home, the smoke of one's country seems pleasant to one, even from a distance.

PAGANEL. Oh yes, of course. It is extremely pleasant to be your guest, my dear lord. I am very obliged to you! Very!

LORD. My pleasure!

PAGANEL. I am quite obliged to Lady Glenarvan too. (*He bows.*)

LADY. Quite my pleasure.

PAGANEL. And to you too, brave captain.

HATTERAS. Yes, yes.

PAGANEL (*to* Betsy, *mechanically*). And to you ... er, that is, no ... Everyone.

LORD. No, in my opinion there is no better place than Europe.

PAGANEL. No, definitely!

HATTERAS. It is wonderful.

LADY. What is it that you like so much about Europe, gentlemen? I cannot understand it.

LORD. What do you mean "what"? You amaze me, my lady! It's comfortable, quiet and clean. No disturbances.

LADY. I disagree, disturbances are so nice. In my opinion what we have is hellish boredom.

LORD. My lady! From whom am I hearing such things? Can one speak like that of one's own English home? Hellish boredom? A man's home is a temple—you shouldn't forget that either, my lady.

LADY. Oh, no, no! It's far better travelling. Polly, do you remember your island?

Parrot puffs out his feathers.

LADY. Polly, was it better on the island? Ah? Wasn't it? Do you want to go back to your island again?

PARROT. Quoi . . . Quoi . . .

LORD. Apropos of the island. We got an excellent buy, didn't we, esteemed sir. Don't you think?

PAGANEL. Enchanting . . . Check . . .

LADY. And I still can't get the amazing pearls out of my mind's eye. When will we go back for them? I can hardly wait.

LORD. In a month.

LADY. Polly, do you hear, in a month? We'll go together . . . You will see your native shores again . . . Oh, how I would like to know what's happening there now. Oh, far-off, mysterious island . . . it glitters like a piece of white sugar on the blue silk sea. Gentlemen, do you remember the cresting waves?

LORD. Quite well, thank you.

PASSEPARTOUT. They were most excellent waves, Your Lordship.

LORD. Passepartout, leave. None of us gentlemen is interested in your opinion.

PASSEPARTOUT. Yes sir, Your Lordship. (*He exits.*)

LADY (*dreamily*). Well, it's still terribly boring here . . . My soul is wasting away . . . I thirst for some unexpected adventures.

LORD. I'm having no luck today. I cannot bear unexpected things.

A harsh ring of the bell.

LADY. Betsy, see who it is.

BETSY (*runs through the drawing room, then returns, walking backwards in terror*). Aie!

LORD. What is wrong?

BETSY. There . . . There . . .

LADY. Betsy! I simply cannot understand such tricks. What is wrong?

HATTERAS. What is this deviltry? Look!

A surprised Passepartout *appears. The door opens and in*

walk Likki, Kiri, *and* Tohonga. Kiri *is carrying his suit-case and his face is bandaged as if he had a toothache.* Likki *is limping.*

Kiri-Kuki. *Bon soir,* Your Lordship.

Lord. What does this mean? Who are you?

Kiri-Kuki. My lord, you see before you the unfortunate Kiri-Kuki, from the island.

Lady. It is he!

Paganel. I swear by the *Étoile,* it's the savages.

Kiri-Kuki. Precisely so, Monsieur Paganel. And this is the valorous general Likki and his adjutant Tohonga.

Lord. Allow me to ask, to what I owe ...

Betsy. My God, who are they, Passepartout?

Passepartout. Shut up, you'll find out in a minute.

Kiri-Kuki. He, he ... well, we sat and sat there on our island ... we got bored ... so, we thought, let's take a trip around Europe ... take news to the Lord. The weather, as if on purpose, is capital. We took our canoes and set off.

Lord (*amazed*). Very, very glad to see ...

Paganel. *Diable!* Savages come calling!

Lady. Remember, when we were on the island I said that he was extremely gallant. This is infinitely kind. Please sit down.

Kiri-Kuki. *Merci* ... Sit down, Tohonga, the Lord is a kind man ...

Lady. What's happened to you?

Kiri-Kuki. He bumped himself.

Lady. Poor fellow. What against?

Kiri-Kuki. Against the volcano, Your Esteemed Ladyship.

Lady. Really? You were probably drinking firewater?

Kiri-Kuki. What are you saying, Your Ladyship, what are you saying, what has drink to do with it! ...

Lord. I'm very happy that you came to pay a call on me, of course, but still I supposed that you would be sitting on your island and hunting for pearls.

Kiri-Kuki. Oh, Your Lordship! ...

Lady. How is that kind man, the fat one—the king? I've forgotten his name.

KIRI-KUKI. His name? ... Oh yes! Of course, Sizi-Buzi, madam ... Of course, he sends his regards, madam ...

LIKKI-TIKKI (*softly*). Don't hold it back, you damned liar! Better tell the whole truth.

KIRI-KUKI. You see, madam, he departed this life.

PAGANEL. What do you mean "departed"? Did he die somewhat?

LIKKI-TIKKI. What somewhat is there about it? The old man completely kicked the bucket.

LORD. Oh, so that's it! So ... so ...

KIRI-KUKI. Oh, Your Lordship!

LORD. Well, what happened? Get it all out.

KIRI-KUKI. Horrors, horrors! But allow me to relate everything in order, my dear Lord.

LORD. I'm listening!

KIRI-KUKI. A calamity struck, my dear lord.

LORD. Oh!

KIRI-KUKI. Did Your Lordship deign to note the volcano when you were on our island?

LORD. I don't remember.

KIRI-KUKI. What Your Lordship? The huge volcano. Like this— the king's wigwam here, and behind it a volcano of incredible proportions—Muanganam.

LORD. So?

KIRI-KUKI. A most colossal one ... a hole in the top.

LORD. The details be damned!

KIRI-KUKI. Yes ... so ... therefore, the volcano ... oh, ho, ho ...

LORD. Well?

HATTERAS. What are you doing, visitor, making sport of us, or what? Permit me, my dear lord, I'll slam him in the back of the head to make the words hop out of him more quickly.

LIKKI-TIKKI. Tell it, you devil!

KIRI-KUKI. Oh, I get so upset ... So here's the wigwam, and that's the volcano ... And then one fine night, right after your departure, there was the greatest eruption, Your Lordship, and both the wigwam and the Sovereign Ruler were covered over by lava.

LADY. Oh, how interesting.

Kiri-Kuki. Thus our Sovereign Ruler, Sizi-Buzi the Second, perished.

Lord. He alone?

Kiri-Kuki. And his harem with him—and half of the Arab guard.

Lord. I see. Then who is governing the island now?

Kiri-Kuki. Alas! Alas! You see before you, my lord, the unfortunate ruler of the Crimson Island—Kiri-Kuki the First .

Lady. What? You are the tsar? Oh, how interesting!

Lord. Ah, but why did you come here, to Europe? You should be on the island, hunting the pearls.

Kiri-Kuki. Alas, Your Lordship! Now I cannot even show my face on the island!

Likki-Tikki. Especially since there's a plague there.

All. What, plague!

Kiri-Kuki. Horrors! Horrors! After Sizi perished, moved by a desire to save our native island from anarchy and the horrors of leaderlessness , I accepted the offer of the best part of our native people to become their ruler, but Ki-Kum and Farra-Teytey, two vagrants who had been condemned for criminal and state offenses and had then slipped out of the sacred hands of justice, incited the native hordes to rebellion. I personally stood at the head of our guards, setting an example of bravery for them . . .

Likki-Tikki. Oh, the bastard!

Kiri-Kuki. . . . but our efforts came to naught. The crushing, numberless hordes of rebelling slaves attacked the wigwam, and we barely escaped with the remainder of the guards. Horrors! Horrors!

Lord. Oh, dammit! But *whose* hands is the island in *now?*

Kiri-Kuki. In the hands of villains—Ki-Kum and Farra-Teytey.

Lord. What! A fine bargain we made, dear sir.

Paganel. I am quite shaken. But won't they give us the pearls?

Lord. Oh, yes.

Lady. What, the pearls will be lost? . . .

Betsy. God, how her eyes flared! How greedy can she get?

Passepartout. Shut up!

Kiri-Kuki. Alas, dear sirs! It all started because of them. The gods witness that I wanted to fulfill our obligations to you honorably.

But the natives declared that they wouldn't give up the pearls for anything!

LADY. What? The pearls? For which we paid money? My lord, you will not allow this! They must be punished!

LORD. Oh, yes.

PAGANEL. Oh, no! I don't agree! This is called highway . . . how is it . . . robbery . . . I swear it by my aunt's flannel pantaloons!

LORD. Where is the rest of the guard?

KIRI-KUKI. Here, Your Lordship!

LIKKI-TIKKI. Men, come in!

Arabs carrying spears and shields burst in through all of the windows and doors. Lady and Betsy jump aside with screams.

LORD.
PAGANEL. } Oh, dammit!
HATTERAS.

LIKKI-TIKKI. Ten-*hut!*

PAGANEL. Oh, dammit!

LORD. And you all came to see me?

ARABS (*deafeningly*). Yes, sir, Your Lordship!

LORD (*in horror*). Thank you.

ARABS. You're welcome, Your Lordship!

LORD (*mocking the Lady*). Oh, I'm bored! I love all kinds of unexpected adventures so much! Damn them to hell! Tell me, isn't this an adventure!

ARABS.
PARROT. } Yes, sir, Your Lordship.

LADY. Oh God, they shout so!

LORD. Have them immediat . . .

LIKKI-TIKKI. Keep *qui*-et!

ARABS. We are quiet, Your Lordship!

KIRI-KUKI. There, my dear lord. And they're all I have left. Like a strange, incredible dream! Horrors! My hair stands on end at the sight of the remainder of my valorous guard, who defended their legal ruler honorably. I am so worn out and exhausted that I would drink a glass of rum with pleasure!

Lord *and* Paganel *in exhaustion lower themselves into armchairs facing each other.*

LADY. Betsy! Betsy! Give His Majesty some cognac.

BETSY. Yes, m'am. (*She brings the cognac.*)

Kiri-Kuki *drinks up.*

LORD (*coming to his senses*). Would you please explain, Your Majesty, how long did this gang come for? . . . The guard, that is.

LIKKI-TIKKI. Forever.

LORD. } What!
PAGANEL. }

HATTERAS. Oh, go to hell!

KIRI-KUKI. Sorry, my lord, sorry. Don't rush, brave commander-in-chief. No, my lord, we came only temporarily, in hope that you would give us military and material help so that we can return to our island.

LORD. Ah, I see. In that case, let's go right now. Captain!

KIRI-KUKI. Alas and alack! As I already had the honor to inform Your Lordship, there is a plague on the island now. And until it relents, there is no reason to even think of penetrating to the island.

LORD. It gets harder and harder!

PAGANEL. *Peste!*

KIRI-KUKI. *Oui, la peste.* After our battles with the natives, there were heaps of corpses on the island, and this catastrophic and noxious plague resulted from the decomposition of the aforementioned corpses.

LORD. But please, who is going to keep this whole company? Do you have any money? Provisions?

KIRI-KUKI. Oh, oh, oh! What provisions could we have, my lord! We have to thank the gods that we got out in one piece.

LORD. What? The result is that I have to feed this entire band and—what is most important—for an unspecified length of time? We made a profitable deal indeed, Monsieur Paganel.

PAGANEL. Oh, yes.

KIRI-KUKI. My dear lord! I appeal to your better feelings! To the feelings of a gentleman and a citizen. And besides that, esteemed lord, I assure you that you will get nothing from the island unless some power delivers us to it again.

LORD (*to* Paganel). What do you say to that, Monsieur Paganel?

PAGANEL (*intimately*). The Arab tsar is right. We'll have to take in this whole company and support them. But when the plague is over you send the ship to the island, deliver this Kiri-Kuki. He's a very sensible Arab, and we'll get all of the pearls. I swear by the Opéra Comique, there's no other way out.

HATTERAS. I'm ready to bet a Washington dollar against a Polish mark that the Frenchman is right!

LORD. We'll go halves to feed them?

PAGANEL. Agreed.

LORD. Yes. Your hand.

PAGANEL. Besides, we can make them work here so that they don't eat our bread for nothing.

LORD. Yes. You are very clever. So: I accept the entire company.

KIRI-KUKI. Oh, noble heart! There, in the sky, sir, you will receive reward for your beneficence!

LORD. I would prefer to receive it here.

KIRI-KUKI. Faithful guardsmen! The lord is taking you all in!

ARABS. We thank you humbly, Your Lordship!

LORD. Quiet. No shouting. But I want to announce that you are going to work and conduct yourselves properly here. First of all, be so kind as to put your weapons away.

LIKKI-TIKKI. What?!

LADY. Oh yes! Oh yes! Edward! I won't be at ease for a moment as long as they're carrying those horrid long spears around!

LIKKI-TIKKI. Kiri! Do you hear? He wants to take our weapons away. Allow me to report that that is impossible, Your Lordship! Judge for yourself, what the hell kind of guard it will be if you take its weapons away! How are we going to pacify the island then, may I ask?

KIRI-KUKI. Please don't argue.

LIKKI-TIKKI. What's wrong with you, are you joking?

HATTERAS. Oho, ho, ho . . . Your Lordship. Shut up!

A murmur among the Arabs.

LORD. Captain, get some sailors in here!

TOHONGA. So this is a friendly visit.

PARROT. Give it to him, give it!

Conductor *suddenly appears on the podium. Light flares on in the orchestra.*

HATTERAS. Call the ship's company in here! Tram, ta-ra, rum. Passapartout!

PASSEPARTOUT. Immediately, captain!

Horns in the orchestra, then a march. Feet marching in time are heard.

LADY. Edward! Edward! I beg you earnestly not to shoot! It's frightful! Betsy! Betsy! Where is my eau-de-cologne?

BETSY. Immediately, madame!

KIRI-KUKI. Men, settle down, what are you doing? General, take them away!

The walls burst open and ranks of armed Sailors *appear.*

TOHONGA. So look there—we came visiting! Force breaks even a straw. Thrown down your spears, dear *citoyens!*

ARABS. Oh, ho, ho! . . .

HATTERAS. One!

The sound of a horn.

LADY. I implore you not to shoot .

PAGANEL. Europe does not like revolt. Throw down your weapons. Or we're going to go piff-paff . . .

HATTERAS. Two!

The Arabs *throw down their spears.*

PAGANEL. Excellent!

LADY. Thank God.

LORD. But no! Why did you create a scandal as soon as you arrived.

You are going to be punished. You will go without hot food for a whole week and you will get only rice.

Arabs moan.

LORD. And for you, general, I announce this punishment—because instead of talking sense into their heads you permitted yourself to countermand my order—take him to the guardhouse for the whole time they are here.

LIKKI-TIKKI. Your Excellency, for what reason? (*To* Kiri.) Well, thanks a lot, you hairy devil!

KIRI-KUKI. I told you not to protest.

Two Sailors lead *Likki* away.

HATTERAS. And now, please! March!

The Sailors *form a convoy for the* Arabs.

TOHONGA. Just what we fools deserve!

PARROT. Just what you fools deserve!

KIRI-KUKI. You acted quite correctly, Your Lordship. If they are kept in the fear of God . . .

LORD. You are a conscientious ruler. I see that now.

PAGANEL. Oh, he understands, the white Arab does!

KIRI-KUKI. Your Lordship, how could I not understand? I've been to Europe, thank God!

LORD. You will remain here to live. You'll be my guest.

KIRI-KUKI. Very happy to. Very happy. (*To* Passepartout.) A glass of rum!

PASSEPARTOUT. Immediately!

KIRI-KUKI. *Votre santé!* Madame! And so, allow me to propose a toast. To the health of His Lordship, Edward Glenarvan, and to his enchanting wife as well!

LADY. Really, he is amazingly gallant! Betsy! Get me a handkerchief. Betsy! Oh, how inattentive you are.

BETSY (*to herself*). What an affected clown! (*Aloud.*) Here you are, Your Ladyship.

KIRI-KUKI. To the pacification of the island and the safe return of their lost goods to Lord Glenarvan and Monsier Paganel! Hurrah!

PAGANEL. The savage could really be a diplomat. Sir, I swear by the Palais Royal, you must pronounce an answering toast.

LORD. Yes! (*He makes a sign to the orchestra.*) I drink to the safe return to the island of its lawful ruler, Kiri-Kuki the First!

Music.

KIRI-KUKI (*ecstatically*). Hurrah!

PARROT. Hurrah! Hurrah! Hurrah!

CURTAIN

SCENE TWO

BETSY *is taking cups out of the cupboard.* KIRI, *wearing European clothes, sneaks up behind* BETSY *and covers her eyes with his hands.*

BETSY. Oh! (*She drops a cup and breaks it.*)

KIRI-KUKI. Guess, sweetie, who is it?

BETSY (*tearing loose*). It's not hard to tell the author of a stupid joke. Please leave me alone, sir.

KIRI-KUKI. My sweetie, you will not be erring in the least if you call me "Your Majesty."

BETSY. Your Majesty! Keep your hands off me!

KIRI-KUKI. Quiet, you!

BETSY. I'm tired of being pestered by you, sir from the island! And besides, who's going to answer for Her Ladyship's broken cup?

KIRI-KUKI. *You* are going to answer for the cup.

BETSY. What?

KIRI-KUKI. What are you so surprised about? You smashed it!

BETSY. Well! Do you know what a scoundrel you are, sir?

KIRI-KUKI. How dare you! You've forgotten with whom you are speaking, Betsy!

BETSY. No, I haven't. It seems to me that I'm speaking to a suspicious upstart.

KIRI-KUKI. Oh, so that's the way it is? Words like that to the Sovereign Ruler of Crimson Island! Well, you'll pay for that, my dear little pussycat.

BETSY. I'm not afraid of you. And not only am I not afraid—I despise you! You live with His Lordship in a posh set-up while your comrades suffer in the stone quarries! You have behaved meanly! . . .

KIRI-KUKI. . . . Your Majesty . . .

BETSY. . . . meanly, Your Majesty . . .

KIRI-KUKI. So, so, so . . . Lady Glenarvan has a nice little maid, what can one say? Well, listen to this, my dear, I noticed a long time ago that you and Tohonga have some sort of suspicious relation. Yes, yes, there's no reason to bug your eyes out. They're blue, incidentally . . . yes, blue . . . I saw him carry the garbage pail out of the quarry one day, and you gave him an absolutely huge piece of bread and ham. Besides that, one day I saw you whispering at the door of the lock-up . . . And I'll be not Kiri-Kuki the First, but the biggest bum around if his hand was not resting on your waist. Incidentally, it's an enchanting waist . . .

BETSY. That's a lie!

KIRI-KUKI. Please don't blush. On the other hand, yes, go ahead and blush again. You are extraordinarily pretty when your skin turns pink . . . Bravo! Bravo! Well, my little flirt, here are my conditions: if you kiss me five times . . . no, six, not five . . . I will not inform anyone about your other shenanigans.

BETSY. Get away from me, you good-for-nothing!

KIRI-KUKI. Wait, wait, wait!

LADY (*enters abruptly*). Oh!

KIRI-KUKI. Hm . . . now where was I? Yes, the broken cup . . . It's no use for you to run away, my dear Betsy, trying to conceal your crime. That's very bad! One shouldn't break the dishes! . . .

BETSY. Oh, you base man!

LADY. What does this scene mean, Your Majesty? Chasing after maids. That doesn't quite suit your position . . .

KIRI-KUKI. Forgive me, Your Esteemed Ladyship, this esteemed *femme de chambre* has cracked one of your cups, and when I wanted to expose her for this, she rushed to escape from me . . .

LADY. What? My cup? My favorite cup! The Marie Antoinette blue cup? . . . Oh! . . .

BETSY. Madam . . .

LADY. How dare you interrupt me? Your behavior is intolerable! No matter what you do, you're always smashing and breaking things!

BETSY. Madam, allow me . . .

LADY. No! She's arguing about it too! She wants to get me upset too! It's monstrous! Where are my smelling salts? . . . Ah! . . .

KIRI-KUKI. Betsy! You should be ashamed! You are getting your kind mistress all upset! Horrors! Horrors!

BETSY. Scoundrel!

KIRI-KUKI. You see, my lady!

LADY. The cup of my patience runneth over! This is unheard of! I cannot bear this fishwife in my home any more. Out! Get out this instant! Using His Lordship's absence to insult me in my own home without punishment! Oh, Your Majesty! Would you please remove her!

KIRI-KUKI (*to* Betsy). How dare you! Shut up! (*Softly, to her.*) Well, you're a fool too! You should have listened to me. (*Aloud.*) Ay-yay-ay! . . .

BETSY. What, you're sacking me?

LADY. Yes, be so good as to leave this house immediately!

BETSY. Oh, so that's the way it is? This is the reward for five years of faithful service . . . For getting up in the middle of the night to answer your ring . . . for fixing your hair and sewing your hems, for . . . for countless scenes with your caprices and fake hysterics . . .

LADY. What? Fake hysterics? . . . Your Majesty, do you hear?

KIRI-KUKI (*aloud*). Betsy! How dare you! Horrors, horrors! (*Softly, also to her.*) Fool, fool, fool!

BETSY. I refuse to listen to you, you base person!

LADY. Here is your passport. You are due ten shillings. For the broken cup I am deducting ten shillings. Therefore, sir, how much do you calculate she is due?

KIRI-KUKI. Just a second. Zero from zero is zero. One from one . . . therefore two zeroes. Zero plus zero equals zero. Nothing is due, Your Ladyship.

LADY. Yes. I'll ask you to pack your things and leave the house.

KIRI-KUKI. And you are not holding her responsible for the broken cup, madame?

LADY. No, I wish to repay her foul act with magnanimity.

KIRI-KUKI. The heart of an angel! (*Softly, to* Betsy.) Idiot! You should have kissed me!

BETSY (*softly, with fury*). Bastard!

LADY. Out!

BETSY. Thanks! Thanks!

LADY. Shut up!

PARROT. I shut up ... shut up ...

> Betsy *exits, sobbing.*

KIRI-KUKI. He ... he ... he ... very well done! ... How you ...

LADY. Yes, yes, yes ... Now, sir, I would like very much to have a little chat with you ...

KIRI-KUKI (*softly*). Well, I'm done for! *Je suis perdu!* (*Aloud.*) About what? With pleasure ... he, he, he ...

LADY. Would you please explain to me the meaning of that little *mise-en-scene* which I interrupted?

KIRI-KUKI. Why I've already reported, Your Ladyship ... the little cup ... there, you see, the pieces ... Horrors, horrors! ...

PARROT (*with a nasal twang*). If you don't kiss me right now, dear Betsy ...

LADY. Oh, oh-ho ... Thank you, thank you, Polly, my faithful friend! (*She takes off her slipper and hits* Kiri *on the cheek.*) Take that, you vile skirt-chaser!

KIRI-KUKI. So, put that down in the account book! Just what I saw in those cards I dreamed of last night, a true premonition of a slap in the face! My dear lady, that goddamn bird is lying!

LADY. Oh no! My Polly never lies. (*She hits him on the other cheek.*)

KIRI-KUKI. Oh. I told myself, Kiri, don't get mixed up with ladies! (*Aloud.*) Milady! Come to your senses! Horrors, horrors, horrors!

LADY. You have forgotten what a sacrifice I made for you—a common, vile savage! I, the wife of Lord Edward Glenarvan. Why you *are* nothing but a savage!

KIRI-KUKI. Yes, a downright savage.

LADY. Oh, how unhappy I am! Forgetting shame, I entrusted my honor to this cheap Romeo, this Don Juan—I betrayed my husband!

KIRI-KUKI. My lady, my dear, I implore you! His Lordship could come back any moment. (*Softly*.) Uh-oh, and today's the thirteenth. There's going to be a scandal!

LADY. I handed the tender flower of my love . . .

KIRI-KUKI. Sh! Someone will hear. Hit me if you must, but don't jab the heel into my eyeball. I beg of you!

LADY. What did you see in her, what?

KIRI-KUKI. Really! What did I see in her? (*Giggling artificially*.) It's quite comical! . . . Here, here, on the cheek, but not in the teeth! *Merci*. You have an iron hand, madame.

LADY. Vulgar red cheeks! A pug nose!

KIRI-KUKI. Horrors, horrors, horrors! Yes! My blood freezes in my veins at the mere sight of her disgusting physiognomy, and you say "kiss!" (*Softly*.) But no! Enough! Arab women are simpler. The fastest way would be to give her a good rap in the mouth. (*Aloud*.) My adored one! My enchantment! That sly thing tricked me, I swear to you by all the saints!

LADY. Oh you good-for-nothing!

KIRI-KUKI. They'll hear! My lady! (*Falling to his knees*.) My lady, I assure you that from this moment on I will never even look at another woman!

LADY. You swear it!

KIRI-KUKI. May I not see the joyful day of my return to my throne on the island, may I not ascend . . . (*Softly*.) If someone walks in right now, there is going to be quite a scene . . .

LADY. Kiss me, you good-for-nothing!

KIRI-KUKI. With pleasure, my lady, but perhaps it would be better some other time. I'm afraid that somebody might come in . . .

LADY. Again! Again! . . .

> Kiri *kisses her. The door opens and the* Lord *and* Paganel *enter.*

PAGANEL. Oh!

LORD. My lady!

KIRI-KUKI. Well, they've swooped down! I knew it! . . . Where was it I stopped now? . . . I wanted to point out . . . and who knows what I wanted to point out . . . Yes. What? I'm going to get it now, it would seem . . .

LORD. Vasily Arturich . . . I must ask you to delete this scene . . . Ha, ha . . . No . . . I don't like this scene . . .

KIRI-KUKI. But my dear lord, it just seems that way to you . . .

LORD. I'm sorry, Vasily Arturich, you didn't hear me . . . I must ask you to remove this scene . . .

KIRI-KUKI. But why, Gennadi Panfilych . . . The love intrigue in the play . . .

LORD. What can I say . . . it's done with talent, but, you know . . . Savva Lukich . . . he's a stern old man . . . he'll latch onto that—pornography . . . he's wild on the subject of pornography . . .

KIRI-KUKI. Well, if that's the way it is . . . (*He takes out one notebook.*)

LADY. Gennadi, in my opinion, you are making a mistake. This is one of the best scenes in the play . . .

LORD. I know, my lady . . . Oh phooey, Lida . . . in your opinion, the best scene is always the one where there's kissing . . . The theater, my dear, is a temple . . . I will not allow a *Zoya's Apartment* in my theater!

LADY. I am sur-prised . . .

PAGANEL (*intimately to* Kiri). Gennadi is as jealous as a devil. Don't be surprised.

LORD. Don't argue, my lady.

LADY. I don't understand . . . (*She crosses out something in the notebook. Intimately to* Kiri.) Don't be upset, dear author, your play is charming, and I am sure that you will not lose the kiss. Although, maybe it won't be on the stage . . . (*She makes eyes at him.*)

KIRI-KUKI. Harrumph . . .

PROMPTER (*from his booth*). Cross it out, Gennadi Panfilych?

LORD. Cross it out. Please continue.

PROMPTER. From where?

LORD. From "the fine weather."

PROMPTER (*stentorianly*). It's fine weather . . .

PAGANEL. It's fine weather, milady. And may I make so bold as to propose accompanying you on a short ride around the neighborhood by carriage . . .

LADY. With great pleasure. All the more so that I've been upset today. I dismissed my maid Betsy, my lord . . . She had become quite intolerable . . .

LORD. Well, so what, my dear, we'll find another.

LADY. And would Your Majesty like to go?

KIRI-KUKI. *Avec plaisir, madame.* Your arm . . .

PAGANEL. The savage has become positively charming here in Europe.

LORD. Passepartout! Have the horses brought around. We'll ride along the esplanade in the moonlight.

PASSEPARTOUT. Yes, sir.

> *All exit. For a while the stage is empty. One can hear an orchestra playing in the distance, on the esplanade. Betsy appears carrying a small bundle.*

BETSY. Well, I have my bundle with me. All of my poor belongings are packed in it. Where will I go? Whom can I turn to? Farewell, castle, the evil mistress has sacked me and a black abyss has opened up before me. There's only one thing left for me to do—go throw myself from the embankment into the ocean . . .

TOHONGA (*suddenly appears at the window*). Betsy! Betsy!

BETSY. Oh my God! Is that you, Tohonga?

TOHONGA. It is I, my dear, it is I. (*He climbs in the window.*) Are you alone?

BETSY (*sadly*). Yes.

TOHONGA (*embraces her*). Oh my golden-haired Betsy, how happy I am that I have found you. I must have a talk with you. But what's this? Your face in tears? You've been crying? What's wrong, my dear? Confess, don't torture my heart.

BETSY. Oh, Tohonga, Lady Glenarvan has just driven me out of the house. Here's my bundle. I have to leave the castle now.

TOHONGA. What? For good?

BETSY. Yes, for good. There's nowhere for me to turn.

TOHONGA. But why?

BETSY. That Kiri-Kuki has been forcing his attentions on me for a long time. Today he hugged me, and I broke a cup, and now . . .

TOHONGA. Oh, what a scoundrel! Well, just you wait, you "friend of the natives"! Just you wait, you vile rogue and cheat! You led us into the lord's stone quarries! Some day, the hour of retribution will come!

BETSY. Yes, poor Tohonga. Now there's no one to give you bread. You will languish in the quarry . . . until they take you to the island to fight with the natives. And there perhaps, you will lay down your head. And I . . . I . . . will find shelter in the waves of the ocean.

TOHONGA. Don't you dare say such horrible things. Everything that happens is always for the best. Glory to the gods! Listen, are we alone?

BETSY. Yes, no one is home.

TOHONGA. Do you love me?

BETSY. Yes. I love you, Tohonga!

TOHONGA. Oh, how happy I am to hear these words! (*He embraces her.*)

BETSY. Beside you, I forget all of my miseries . . . You return my strength to me.

TOHONGA. Listen, my beloved. Would you agree to share a bitter fate with me?

BETSY. Oh, yes!

TOHONGA. Then here's what we'll do; let's run away to the island.

BETSY. But how? . . . I don't understand . . .

TOHONGA. I no longer have the strength to go hungry under the lashes of Glenarvan's foremen in the quarries. And lately a plan has matured in my mind. I saw a fine steam-powered boat by the embankment. When the moon goes down, and the night becomes black, I will break off the lock and go out to sea. It would be a million times better to risk crossing the ocean in a fragile nut-shell, than to drag out my life as a slave here.

BETSY. But the natives will kill you!

TOHONGA. No, I'm convinced that they won't touch me. They're a kind people, and I am guilty of only one thing in regard to them—

that I went against them when I served in the guard. But I was blind. And now, when I have felt what slavery means with my own skin, I understand everything . . .

BETSY. Oh, how risky everything you want to do is, but how attractive too!

TOHONGA. I'll repent my sins before the natives, they'll forgive me. We'll build a wigwam, I'll marry you and we'll have a fine life in my native land, where there is no stone quarry and no Lady Glenarvan.

BETSY. But what will I do in a foreign land? Oh, Tohonga! I'm terrified . . . the island is alien to me, you know!

TOHONGA. Oh, you'll get used to it in a hurry. What a sun there, what a sky! There the nights are black and the stars are like diamonds! There the ocean murmurs all night, splashing on shores which are not enclosed in esplanades . . . It's so warm there that at night you can sleep on the bare earth! Betsy, let's flee. Let's flee, Betsy!

BETSY. Oh, let whatever will happen, happen! I agree!

TOHONGA. Oh, my charmer! (*He embraces her.*)

LIKKI-TIKKI (*ragged and horrible looking, suddenly appears in the window*). Where is that steam launch?

BETSY. Oh!

TOHONGA. We've been overheard! Who's that? Who? Oh, gods! It's Likki-Tikki! You overheard us?

LIKKI-TIKKI. Of course!

TOHONGA (*pulls out a knife*). Then die! You won't carry my secret out of this room, and you won't hinder my escape! (*He attacks Likki with the knife.*)

BETSY. Tohonga! Come to your senses, what are you doing?

TOHONGA. Don't get in my way, he'll do us in!

LIKKI-TIKKI (*takes away the knife*). You go to hell with your knife! Attacking people like a bandit! Madame! Get your fiancé away from me!

TOHONGA. What do you want from us, brave Likki?

LIKKI-TIKKI. First of all I need for you not to be an idiot. Sit down, I wish you were at the bottom of the sea!

TOHONGA. Can you really be a traitor, Likki! Oh, all is lost!

LIKKI-TIKKI. No, he's gone completely out of his mind. Will you sit down or not? Shut up! . . . You'll sit down? Sit down when you're being talked to!

BETSY. What do you intend to do with him? I'll scream if you cause him any harm!

LIKKI-TIKKI. Well, you too now? Shut up! Sit down! Pardon, madam!

Tohonga *and* Betsy *sit down in terror.*

LIKKI-TIKKI. Tell me, where's the launch?

BETSY. Tell him, tell him, Tohonga.

TOHONGA. But if you say just one word, Likki . . . just one word . . .

LIKKI-TIKKI. Shut up when you're being talked to! . . . Where's the launch?

TOHONGA. Under the window.

LIKKI-TIKKI. So. Is there any wood?

TOHONGA. Enough.

LIKKI-TIKKI. So. Well. And you've thought about the risk you're taking by going out into the open sea with a woman who doesn't know how to do anything but iron skirts? Well, suppose a storm begins? A gale? And if there's not enough fuel? And the pursuit? How are you going to get out of that, accompanied by a young creature who has done nothing all her life except pleat mobcaps?

TOHONGA. Yes, Likki, you're right. But what are you leading up to?

LIKKI-TIKKI. To the fact that you're a pig!

BETSY. Why are you insulting him?

LIKKI-TIKKI. Because he didn't think about the others. About the fact that languishing along with him in the stone quarry was his immediate chief and friend who had often fought shoulder to shoulder with him.

TOHONGA. Likki! If only I had known you had such good intentions!

LIKKI-TIKKI. In a word, I'm going with you!

TOHONGA (*throws himself on* Likki's *neck*). Likki!

LIKKI-TIKKI. Get the hell away! What am I, a woman, really! . . .

TOHONGA. Likki, wait! But have you thought about how the natives will receive you?

LIKKI-TIKKI. I have. Don't worry. I won't make you think for me . . . So, there's no time to lose! Not a second! Provisions?

TOHONGA. Nothing, Likki.

LIKKI-TIKKI (*looking out the window*). The moon's going down . . . It's time! (*He lights a lamp, and takes a tablecloth from the table.*) Open the cupboard! (Tohonga *opens it.*) What is there to eat?

TOHONGA. It's full, Likki.

LIKKI-TIKKI. Give it here . . . on the other hand, no . . . it'll take too long this way. Lock it. (Tohonga *locks it.*) Crawl out the window. I'll shove it out to you.

TOHONGA. Oh, Likki, with you along we won't perish! (*He climbs out the window.*)

LIKKI-TIKKI (*takes the cupboard and shoves the whole thing out to* Tohonga). Load it onto the boat . . . Where are His Lordship's weapons?

BETSY. Here in the cabinet.

LIKKI-TIKKI. So. (*He takes the cabinet and shoves it out the window to* Tohonga.) Careful, it's the weapons!

BETSY. My God, how strong you are! . . . But what will His Lordship say?

LIKKI-TIKKI. Shut up! . . . pardon, mademoiselle. What will *he* say? *He* is a good-for-nothing thief. The one pearl that he took from the island is worth more than all of this rubbish, five times as much. Take this! (*He throws a chair, table, carpet and paintings out the window to* Tohonga.)

BETSY. You . . . you are a remarkable man!

LIKKI-TIKKI. Keep quiet . . . when you're . . . h'mm . . . what else . . . is there we shouldn't forget.

PARROT. We shouldn't forget.

LIKKI-TIKKI. Ah, old friend! You won't remain here either. Grab this Tohonga! (*He hands* Tohonga *the cage with the* Parrot *in it through the window.*) Don't forget to take the barrel of rain water under the window.

TOHONGA. Yes, yes . . .

LIKKI-TIKKI. Madame, if you please. (*He takes* Betsy *and hands her through the window.*)

BETSY. Oh!

LIKKI-TIKKI. Keep quiet when you're being talked . . . oh yes . . . now a note . . .

> *He writes a note and pins it to the wall with a knife. There isn't a single object left in the room except the solitary lamp burning on the wall. Likki takes it down and goes out the window with it. The stage is in darkness. Voices are heard off-stage.*)

BETSY. You've loaded it so heavily that it's going to capsize.

LIKKI-TIKKI. Shut up . . . when you're being . . . Sit down on the piano, madame. Like this. Wait a minute, we'll turn it around. (*The piano strings crash.*) There . . .

TOHONGA. The lamp, don't break the lamp . . .

LIKKI-TIKKI. Start 'er up . . . (*The pounding of the engine in the launch is heard.*

PARROT (*gradually growing softer, sings*).
> O'er the seas . . .
> O'er the seas . . .

A pause. Then voices.

LORD. Why is it so dark?

LADY. That no good Betsy! She couldn't even light the lamp. Oh, that maid! Why, I ordered her to wait until I returned.

HATTERAS. It's as dark as the inside of a . . . barrel.

LORD. Light a lamp.

PASSEPARTOUT. Yes, sir. (*All enter.*) Sir, there aren't any lamps here. I don't understand.

PAGANEL. Passepartout, you're a little drunk.

PASSEPARTOUT. M'sieur, I haven't had anything to drink . . .

LADY. I'm afraid of bumping into a chair . . .

HATTERAS. Well, bring a lamp from the next room. The arm chair seems to have disappeared into the earth.

PASSEPARTOUT. Right away. (*He enters with a lamp in his hand.*)

LORD. What's this?

PAGANEL. Well!

LADY. What's the meaning of this?

PASSEPARTOUT. Sir, you've had burglars in your house!

LADY. Betsy! Betsy!

HATTERAS. Hold it! A note. (*He takes the note down.*)

LORD. Give it to me . . .

KIRI-KUKI. It's Tohonga! This is the work of the Arabs. Ay, ay, ay! Horrors, horrors, horrors!

LORD (*reads*). "Thank you for the stone quarries . . . and for the foreman's lashes . . . come to the island, we'll cut your heads off . . . regards to that bastard Kiri. (Signed) Likki and Tohonga."

KIRI-KUKI. My god!

PAGANEL. I swear . . . I don't even know what to swear by, this is stunning!

LORD. Wait, there's a P.S. here. Dammit, I don't understand anything! It's written in old orthography.[7] Ah! "Regards from Betsy and the parrot."

LADY. The hussy! Oh! . . . I feel ill! . . . ill . . .

HATTERAS. The main thing is that the room's been wiped as clean as the plate of a hungry bo'sun. May they choke on it! I've never seen neater work. They didn't take all of this away in a cart! The savages, may the sea wipe them out! But what did they leave in? (*He rushes to the window.*) Bah! The launch is gone! Everything's clear! Sir! The devils have made off in your launch!

LORD (*enraged, grabs* Passepartout *by the throat*). You good-for-nothing! You should have been keeping a look-out! A look-out!

PASSEPARTOUT (*with the lamp*). Help! Monsieur Paganel, help, how am I to blame?

PAGANEL. Monsieur, I will ask you to release my servant.

Passepartout *disappears after putting the lamp on the table.*

LORD (*rushes at* Kiri). And you, you Devil Majesty! Thank you, thank you for this whole gang you've brought to my home. I'll fix you . . . I'll fix you . . .

KIRI-KUKI. My dear lord! Please, how am I to blame? I . . . (*He hides behind the* Lady's *skirt.*)

LADY. What's wrong with you? What's the reason? What is His Majesty guilty of?

7. After the 1917 Revolution the old alphabet was simplified.

LORD. Shut up! Don't you intercede. "Oh, I'm bored! Oh, I thirst for adventures! Oh, oh! ..."

PAGANEL. My dear lord, be calm. We must assess the situation and take measures immediately.

LORD. Yes, you're right. Not a bad purchase! No pearls, no furniture, and now we're going to have to conquer that damned island!

KIRI-KUKI. Your Excellency!

LORD. Shut up! (Kiri *hides.*) Now we'll assess the situation. (*He thinks.*) Hey—Captain Hatteras!

HATTERAS. Yes, my lord!

LORD. The ship and crew! Arm all of the Arabs with spears! We're attacking the island, I'll ignore the plague!

PAGANEL. Quite right. Europe cannot allow thievery. Where is my *sac-de-voyage?* My lord, I assure you we will get the pearls and your things back.

HATTERAS. Yes, sir. (*He blows his whistle.*) Crew, ta-ra-ta-tam-ta-tam ...

> *A ship carrying* Sailors *appears in the background. It is all covered with electric lights.*

LADY. Lord! I'll go with you! I want to see them catch that good-for-nothing thief Betsy with my own eyes!

LORD. Very well, get dressed.

> *A bustle.*

PASSEPARTOUT (*runs in, upset*). My lord! My lord! My lord!

LORD. What other vile thing has happened in my home?

PASSEPARTOUT. Savva Lukich has arrived!

> *The curious voices of the* Musicians *immediately start to pour out of the orchestra.*

PROMPTER (*from his box*). Gennadi Panfilovich, Savva Lukich!

LORD. Metelkin! Have the parrot croak something a little nicer. And don't curse so much ... Say something sloganistic ...

PASSEPARTOUT. Yes, sir, Gennadi Panfilych. (*He hides behind the* Parrot.)

LORD. My lord! Finally! We've been waiting and waiting and waiting for you! Hello, precious Savva Lukich!

SAVVA (*enters*). He, he . . . excuse me for being late . . . held up on business, business. Hello, hello . . .

LORD. Now, Savva Lukich, allow me to introduce my wife—*une grande coquette* . . . And this gentleman is Jules Verne . . . the author . . . A most terrific talent . . . ideological profundity of soul . . . a radiant personality. In our times, Savva Lukich, authors like him are worth their weight in gold. They ought to be paid a double honorarium, if we judged things by their essence . . . (*Softly, to* Kiri.) That was a joke.

SAVVA. Very, very glad to meet you . . . What strange hair you have, young man . . .

KIRI-KUKI. I'm wearing make-up, Savva Lukich.

SAVVA. What? You act yourself?

LORD. Precisely so, Savva Lukich. He spared nothing for this performance. Varrava Apollonovich fell ill . . . and the author agreed to play the role for him. Kiri is an upstart.

SAVVA. So . . . so . . . one can see that right away . . . Well, what are you doing, please continue.

LORD. A little tea, perhaps, Savva Lukich?

SAVVA. No, why, better during the *entr'acte* . . .

LORD. Yes, sir. Allow me to give you a copy of the play . . .

SAVVA. How nice, a parrot!

LORD. I bought it especially for this play, Savva Lukich.

SAVVA. Was it expensive?

LORD. Seven hundred . . . five hundred fifty rubles, Savva Lukich, it talks. No other theater has one, but we do!

SAVVA. Speak. Hello, Polly!

PARROT. Hello, Savva Lukich, proletarians of all countries, unite. Handshaking has been abolished.

SAVVA (*falls down in terror, almost crosses himself*). I surrender!

LORD. Metelkin, you fool! God, what a blockhead!

SAVVA. What is this? I don't understand . . .

> He looks into the Parrot's *cage.* Passepartout *runs around to the other side.*

LORD. Don't overdo it, Metelkin!

PASSEPARTOUT. Yes, sir, Gennadi Panfilych.

SAVVA. A really nice thing! I am going to recommend one for every theater under my supervision. And now, continue . . . where had you stopped?

LORD. We're heading for the uninhabited island now, Savva Lukich. Capitalists. To subdue the natives who have revolted. On a ship. Where would you like to watch from? The parterre? The loges? Or perhaps here on stage, from the tea table?

SAVVA. No, let me come on the ship with you, old man that I am . . . I'd like to go sailing in my old age.

LORD. Welcome! Ladies and gentlemen! Please continue! (*He claps his hands.*)

HATTERAS. The ship is ready, my lord!

LORD. Get the Arabs out here!

HATTERAS. Yes, my lord! (*He whistles.*)

> *The walls crash down and ranks of* Arabs *appear carrying spears.*

LORD. Hello, Arabs!

ARABS (*deafeningly*). Your health, Your Excellency!

SAVVA. Very good! May I say it? Hello, Arabs!

ARABS. Hello, Savva Lukich!

> Savva *is impressed.*

LORDS. Arabs. Your chief has committed despicable treason. He has just robbed my castle and fled to the island with the aim of going over to the natives. Tohonga and my former maid fled with him. We must give them and some natives a proper punishment. Your Tsar Kiri-Kuki the First will be our leader, and I will assist.

ARABS. Glad to be of service, Your Excellency.

LORD. Your Majesty, try to show them an example of personal bravery.

KIRI-KUKI. Yes, sir. Well, I've put my foot in it again, damn me!

LADY. Kiri, my dear, don't be depressed. I'm thinking of you, and I'm certain that you will emerge the victor.

KIRI-KUKI. Oh, go away, for Christ's sake! Where is my suitcase?
PASSEPARTOUT. Here, Your Majesty! Oho, what a heavy one!
KIRI-KUKI. It contains seventy-two pounds of written appeals to my people, who have gone astray.
LORD. To the ship! Raise the gangplank! Savva Lukich, this way. Don't hit your leg on the gangplank.

> *All go onto the ship. On the way* Paganel *throws the* Parrot *out the window.*

LORD. Forward, and death to the natives! Death to Likki and Tohonga!
SAILORS. Death to them!
HATTERAS. Head out of the bay!

> *The* Conductor *waves his baton. The ochestra begins, "Oh, it's a long, long way to Tipperary." The* Lord *threatens the* Conductor *behind* Savva Lukich's *back. The orchestra instantaneously changes the tune and plays, "We all came from the common people . . ."*[8]

KIRI-KUKI. Gennadi Panfilych, what are you doing? English soldiers can't sing that!
LORD (*threatens him with his fist*). Shut up, ill-fated one!

> *The ship starts to move away.*

SAVVA (*standing in a prominent place on the ship*). An excellent little finale for the third act .

CURTAIN

8. From the second stanza of a revolutionary song entitled "Warszawianka": "Boldly, comrades, all in step."

ACT IV

THE ISLAND. KIRI-KUKI's *former wigwam has been decorated with a red flag.*

SECOND NATIVE (*running in*). A ship on the horizon! A ship! Comrades! Ki-Kum! Farra-Teytey! A ship! A ship!

KI-KUM (*runs out of the wigwam*). Where's this ship? Yes, there it is, really! . . .

FARRA-TEYTEY. A ship! European! That's not a canoe.

SECOND NATIVE. Isn't that the enemy? Maybe it's the Englishman coming for the pearls?

FARRA-TEYTEY. Possibly. Well, here's what we'll do, my friend, muster the native warriors here. Anything can happen.

SECOND NATIVE. There's one thing I don't understand . . . That can't be the lord's ship. It's much too small!

NATIVES. A ship! A ship!

FARRA-TEYTEY. My friends! It's possible that our enemies are on that ship . . . the treacherous sea could bring us anything . . . Are your weapons in order?

NATIVES. O, Farra! We're ready!

KI-KUM. I don't understand any of this. Some sort of bundles, and there's a woman sitting on top.

NATIVES (*crowding closer*). Yes, it's a woman! A woman!

KI-KUM. A white one . . .

THIRD NATIVE. If I didn't know that Likki-Tikki was in Europe right now, I would swear that's him on the stern!

SECOND NATIVE. And that other one in the stern is the spitting image of Tohonga!

NATIVES. What kind of nonsense are you babbling, how could Tohonga turn up in a little boat? . . .

326

FARRA-TEYTEY. Prepare your arrows!

NATIVES. We're ready.

KI-KUM. By god! As much like Likki as two drops of water!

FARRA-TEYTEY. Really, what's wrong with you?! One thing is for sure—that female is sitting on some sort of black box that has white teeth . . .

NATIVES. And a parrot . . . Likki! No, it's not Likki! . . . It is! It isn't! . . . What the devil?!

KI-KUM. It is Likki.

The launch comes into the bay; and Likki, Tohonga, *and* Betsy *jump out.*

NATIVES. Likki-Tikki!

LIKKI-TIKKI. Quite right. You don't have to howl like that. Shut up when . . . Likki! . . . Why are your eyes bugging out like you've never seen me before?

KI-KUM. Listen, you white Arab, throw down your weapons right now and surrender to the people! We are going to try you! . . .

FARRA-TEYTEY. Throw down your weapons!

LIKKI-TIKKI. Why are you shouting like that, my brothers? . . . And why should I throw down my weapon? . . . It might come in handy . . .

KI-KUM. Hands up!

Liki, Tohonga, *and* Betsy *raise their hands. They are searched.*

BETSY. Oh, Tohonga, I'm afraid. What will they do with us?

TOHONGA. Don't be afraid, my dear. They'll understand. We'll explain everything to them right now. Likki will tell them.

LIKKI-TIKKI. Right now. Hm . . . Get away from me! I can't talk when fifty men are panting in my face.

KI-KUM. But if you get it into your head to touch any of the natives, just you . . .

LIKKI-TIKKI. Shut up when . . . I'm still not so much of an idiot that I'd touch any of you . . . There's just one of me, and there are fifty of you!

KI-KUM. Why did you come?

LIKKI-TIKKI. That's just what I want to explain. Where's the native whom I cracked in the teeth?

FARRA-TEYTEY. He was killed by your Arabs during the siege . . .

LIKKI-TIKKI. A pity. May the gods clasp him to the heavenly bosom and the spirit of the unseen Vaydua repose in him in the lands of righteousness!

KI-KUM. Amen. Amen. But what's going on? Answer without any sly tricks.

LIKKI-TIKKI. I am capable of knocking a man's teeth out, but I have never descended to sly tricks. Everyone here can confirm that.

THIRD NATIVE. That's true.

LIKKI-TIKKI. So, he died. I ask his forgiveness posthumously—and your forgiveness too. I ask forgiveness for working in the service of the tyrant Sizi-Buzi and for being in his hands—which I did out of blindness and a poor education . . . How is that?

BETSY. True, true, brave Likki! Go on.

TOHONGA. Go on, Likki, they'll understand.

LIKKI-TIKKI. I was the instrument of oppression. I am a soldier, and I didn't realize what I was doing . . . Secondly, that . . . hm . . . that, secondly? . . . I ask the forgiveness of the native people for having been deceived by the upstart Kiri-Kuki, and going against the people and cracking them in the teeth, and also for having been the cause of many deaths.

NATIVES. He's repenting! Do you hear?

LIKKI-TIKKI. Yes, I repent. You can try me. I don't care about that.

TOHONGA. And tell them about me too.

LIKKI-TIKKI. And my adjutant . . . Tohonga . . . repents the same things.

TOHONGA. Yes.

KI-KUM. Who is the white woman?

TOHONGA. Don't be afraid, Betsy . . . I'll tell them right now . . . This is the Lord's maid. She was driven out. She is my beloved, I am going to marry her. She has never caused anyone any harm because she has a good heart. Accept her and don't hurt her. Even if you kill me.

KI-KUM. The native people do not kill women who are not guilty of anything.

LIKKI-TIKKI. ⎱ Yes.
TOHONGA. ⎰

BETSY. Yes, I can confirm that.

FARRA-TEYTEY. Likki, Likki! We have been deceived too often. Who can guarantee that there is not treachery behind your words?

LIKKI-TIKKI. I assure you there is no treachery.

FARRA-TEYTEY. Who will guarantee it?

LIKKI-TIKKI. What's wrong with all of you—guarantee, not guarantee?! Shut up when . . .

FARRA-TEYTEY. What, you are still shouting at me?

LIKKI-TIKKI. Well, why are you finding fault? Such is my habit. I'm too old to change my character in five minutes. Don't find fault so much.

KI-KUM. That's true, that's true.

LIKKI-TIKKI. Try to understand that in Europe I felt on my own skin everything that Sizi-Buzi subjected you to here I have taken everything into consideration, and I won't change sides any more. Slavery taught me that. I swear it!

TOHONGA. Me too!

FARRA-TEYTEY. And will you prove this to the native people?

TOHONGA. Yes.

LIKKI-TIKKI. Yes, And even sooner than I would like. Look on the horizon . . .

SECOND NATIVE. Heavy smoke! . . .

LIKKI-TIKKI. Yes, smoke . . . That is ominous smoke! Hey! Who is your tsar now?

NATIVES. We don't have a tsar now and never will again!

LIKKI-TIKKI. Well, who governs you?

NATIVES. They do, the ones we elect.

LIKKI-TIKKI. Just what I thought. Greetings to you, O Ruler! Ki, order that cupboard opened . . .

FARRA-TEYTEY. Be careful, Ki!

LIKKI-TIKKI. You should be ashamed! I am old and I have sworn.

KI-KUM. Weapons! Weapons! Rifles!

LIKKI-TIKKI. Yes, they're English rifles. I brought them to you as a gift, and you're going to need them very soon! . . .

SECOND NATIVE (*up on a palm tree*). A ship on the horizon!

LIKKI-TIKKI (*in a thunderous voice*). Listen, natives! That is Lord Glenarvan's ship. He is coming here to the island. Arabs are on board, armed to the teeth—plus a crew of sailors. They're coming to wipe you out, to set the good-for-nothing Kiri on the throne and rob you. And I, Likki-Tikki, the general who has come over to your side, have come to you in order to help you repulse them. And I'd like to see how you would do it without me—the most artful commander on all the islands of the ocean! Pick up the weapons! Pick them up!

FARRA-TEYTEY. Ah, now we believe you! You were evil and horrible, Likki-Tikki, but you have made up for your sins! Should we forgive him, my people?

NATIVES. Forgive him!

KI-KUM. Likki and Tohonga, in the name of the people you are forgiven!

LIKKI-TIKKI. Thank you, you won't regret it.

FARRA-TEYTEY. To arms, brothers! Obey Likki! Obey him!

The Natives *pick up the rifles instantaneously. A horn can be heard.*

LIKKI-TIKKI. Is there a plague here?

KI-KUM. It's almost over.

LIKKI-TIKKI. Do you have even one unburied body?

KI-KUM. Oh yes.

LIKKI-TIKKI. Well, here's what you do! Now, you'll dip your arrows in the plague poison. Only be careful not to infect yourselves. The plague is the only thing that the greedy Europeans are afraid of. Understand?

KI-KUM. Oh, Likki! You really are a great commander! Obey him, obey!

SECOND NATIVE (*on the palm*). It's getting close. The ship!

FARRA-TEYTEY. Brothers! Poison your arrows and bullets!

The process of arming themselves causes a tremendously frightening bustle. The whole island is covered with a cloud of spears.

LIKKI-TIKKI. Hide! . . . Behind the rocks, behind the bushes! (*He blows a small horn.*)

TOHONGA. Obey orders! Hide!

Everyone hides and the stage is empty. Ominous music is heard and the ship enters the bay. First to come off is Savva Lukich, carrying a copy of the play in his hands—he sits down on the former throne so that he rules over the island.

LORD. My lady, please do not lean overboard.

HATTERAS. Crew! Listen! . . . Lower the gangplank! . . . tram-tam-tam!

LORD. Well, now, Your Majesty, try to stand at the front of your army. Now you have an opportunity to get back your throne—and my pearls.

PAGANEL. Oh, yes! We are bored by the rebelliousness of your people. I swear by the French Republic!

KIRI-KUKI (*with his suitcase*). Yes, sir, Your Excell . . . oty . . . phooey, dammit, how did I get into this fix! . . . And when my kind people plant an arrow in my belly it'll be great fun! And why did I get mixed up in this business?!

LADY. Oh, don't subject His Majesty to danger!

LORD. Lady, your intercession is beginning to seem strange to me. What does it mean? An Arab tsar! What's wrong with you?

KIRI-KUKI. I'm going, I'm going, most esteemed lord. I'm going, but my legs are buckling under me from bravery and impatience! Oho-ho! . . . Well, dear Arabs, don't give in!

HATTERAS. Arabs, forward!

Arabs go down gangplank to the sounds of military march.

KIRI-KUKI. I, Your Majesty, will go behind you—so that no one decides to run away . . . why, they're such people . . .

LADY. Oh, it's not enough that you're a liar, it turns out you're a coward too! I despise you!

KIRI-KUKI. I really need that now—when my life is hanging by a hair!

LADY. Everything between us is over!

Kiri *goes off behind the* Arabs *onto the island. The* Sailors *fire from the deck. The* Arabs *march with their spears forward. A pause. And suddenly* Likki *appears carrying a revolver in his hand.*

LIKKI-TIKKI (*menacingly*). Where are you going, you spawn of a pike?!

ARABS (*in horror*). The general! . . .

LIKKI-TIKKI. Yes, it's I. Likki-Tikki, nicknamed "the Intrepid" here on the island! Where are you going?

ARABS (*in complete confusion*). Likki . . . we were . . . we are insignificant people . . . of course . . . (*A ho-humming.*)

LIKKI-TIKKI. Shut up when you're being talked to! . . .

PAGANEL. I swear by a bottle of Arpège, they are in confusion! My lord! . . .

LORD (*with a telescope*). Captain Hatteras, take measures.

HATTERAS. (*into his speaking-trumpet*). Forward, a hundred thousand devils and one. Forward!

LIKKI-TIKKI. Get back! . . . when you're being talked to!

ARABS. Gracious! What's going on! . . . (*Confusion.*)

HATTERAS. Forward!

LIKKI-TIKKI. Back!

NATIVES (*off-stage*). Hurrah! . . . for General Likki!

KI-KUM and FARRA-TEYTEY (*appear on stage*). Likki! Good man! Hurrah! Likki! . . . Don't be afraid, the whole island is with you!

ARABS (*fall down in an instant as if cut with the shout*). We surrender!

LIKKI-TIKKI. March to the natives!

ARABS. Yes, sir, Your Excellency! (*They disappear from the stage.*)

NATIVES (*utter a thunderous cry*). Hurrah! . . .

Kiri-Kuki *is left on the island with his suitcase.*

KIRI-KUKI. Your Highness! (*Desperately.*) Help! Help! Your Highness! . . . help me! . . . they've abandoned me to the whim of fate! Horrors! Horrors! Horrors!

LIKKI-TIKKI (*ominously*). A-ah! There he is! I've been waiting for this moment for a long, long time. Shut up, you scoundrel, the moment of your death has arrived!

KIRI-KUKI. Dear, golden-haired Likki! I surrender! Or, rather, I had already surrendered a long time ago! The pluperfect! I had surrendered! O, Likki! Will you really kill your unhappy Kiri-Kuki who had always loved you with a tender love?

LIKKI-TIKKI. Oh, you base scoundrel!

PAGANEL. My lord! They have fled, and the native tsar has been captured!

LADY. Oh, my lord! You must deliver him!

PASSEPARTOUT. The native tsar has been caught red-handed!

LORD. Captain! Captain!

HATTERAS. Crew, to arms!

They aim a cannon at Likki; Likki *grabs* Kiri *and uses him as a shield.*

KIRI-KUKI. Your Highness, dear lord! What are you doing? Don't shoot! You'll hit me!

LADY (*grabbing* Hatteras *by the arm*). Oh, you'll kill him! Don't shoot!

LORD. My lady! What is the meaning of this? I'm beginning to suspect you.

KIRI-KUKI. Quite right, Your Excellency. I'll tell you a secret—just don't shoot!

LADY. Oh, you miserable beast! (*She faints.*)

LIKKI-TIKKI. Well, I've really seen bastards . . .

LORD. I am dishonored! (*He takes out a pistol and shoots himself.*)

PASSEPARTOUT. The lord has shot himself.

PAGANEL. My God! What's happening on this damned island! May I be cursed three times for getting mixed up with these pearls and this trip!

LIKKI-TIKKI. Hey, natives! Everyone over here!

The Natives, Arabs *come out in hordes covering the stage.*

KI-KUM. ⎫
FARRA-TEYTEY. ⎬ Everyone over here!

LIKKI-TIKKI. Listen, you Europeans! (*Silence on the ship.*) You see that the attempt to conquer the island with the help of . . . but I'm no orator, the devils would gobble me up! . . . Ki, you tell them!

KI-KUM. Listen, Europeans. The attempt to conquer the island with the help of blind, deceived Arabs has been an utter failure. The Arabs have thrown themselves on our mercy as victors. They have been forgiven and have entered our army. And now before you is a firm and united people which is going to defend its homeland, life, and freedom!

NATIVES (*loudly*). That's right, that's right, Ki!

FARRA-TEYTEY. Listen, Europeans! Your attempts to capture the riches of the island will get nowhere, because numberless and politically aware hordes of natives will not give them to you.

KI-KUM. You will never see the pearls! They belong to the free native population, and to no one else!

KIRI-KUKI. Quite right! That's correct, how correct it is! I surmised the same, Ki.

KI-KUM. Shut up, you trash. Your case is still ahead.

KIRI-KUKI. I'm as quiet as a fish on ice.

KI-KUM. And this is the last of talking you'll get. Before you are a thousand bows, and the arrows in them have been poisoned with the plague.

PAGANEL. What—the plague?! Damn!

FARRA-TEYTEY. The last of the talking. If you don't leave the island this minute we will fire a volley at you and none of your long-range cannons will help you . . . Perhaps you'll kill a few of us, but your ship will be poisoned. You will carry the infection in your bodies to far-off Europe and burning like a bonfire you will envelop it from one side to the other. We'll wait one minute . . .

HATTERAS. Damn this campaign! I thought I would be fighting with arrows and bombs, but not with the plague.

PAGANEL. Yes, you're right. I retreat on all counts. To hell with the pearls and dubious profits!

PASSEPARTOUT. Monsieur! The crew is upset . . . Another minute and mutiny will flare! Let me give you some advice: you must return to Europe. The sailors don't want to fight the natives.

PAGANÈL. Captain, homeward!
HATTERAS. Get out of the bay!

The anchor is raised with a thunderous noise, and the ship starts to leave. The Sailors *sing: "O'er the seas . . . o'er the seas . . ."*[9]

LADY (*stands by the side, melancholy*). Oh, I'm unhappy! I lost everything in one instant . . . the pearls, my husband, and my lover . . . what am I to do?
PAGANEL. Madame, you should blame yourself as you look at your husband's body. Public opinion in Europe will destroy you.
SAILORS. "O'er the seas . . . o'er the seas . . ." (*Keeps getting further away and softer. The ship disappears.*)

The sun sets.

KI-KUM (*on the cliff*). Brother natives! Congratulations! All of our trials are over. No further danger threatens Crimson Island. Shout for joy: Hurrah!
EVERYONE. Hurrah!!!!!
KI-KUM. Stand aside!

All stand aside and Kiri *is revealed, with his suitcase.*

KIRI-KUKI. I thought I would be forgotten in the general celebration. Alas, no! Obviously I haven't drunk my cup to the bottom!
FARRA-TEYTEY. What are we going to do with this good-for-nothing?
LIKKI-TIKKI. Kill him. And that's not bad enough.
KI-KUM. What shall we do with him?
NATIVES. What shall we do?
KIRI-KUKI. Just forgive me—nothing else! Can it be that native hearts have a proclivity for blind vengeance? Can it be that you, dear rulers Ki-Kum and Farra-Teytey, do not understand that you cannot darken such a colossal native day of celebration by spilling blood, even if it were that of a guilty man?
LIKKI-TIKKI. You can be hanged—we won't spill one drop of blood.
KI-KUM. As you wanted to hang me and Farra-Teytey . . .

9. From "A Sailor's Song"—popular at the time of the Revolution.

KIRI-KUKI. Oh precious Ki! Don't be vindictive! Oh, native people! Do you know what I have in the suitcase?

FARRA-TEYTEY. What, you good-for-nothing?

KIRI-KUKI. Two pounds sterling—the same ones that the late lord gave Sizi—for the pearls. As you see, I honestly preserved this national treasure without concealing a penny.

KI-KUM. Put it into the national treasury!

LIKKI-TIKKI. Confess that you saved it to keep for yourself!

KIRI-KUKI. But I didn't keep it for myself! Ah, Likki, why are you destroying a man. Horrors, horrors, horrors!

LIKKI-TIKKI. Get out of my sight! Well—to the pigs with you then! Forgive him, brothers! I don't want to dirty my hands.

KI-KUM. Should we forgive him—because of our victory and the celebration?

NATIVES and ARABS. Forgive him!

FARRA-TEYTEY. Get up. You heard—the people have forgiven you.

KIRI-KUKI. O gods, bless you for your magnanimity! What a load has been removed from my soul! But I'm a little sorry to lose the pounds sterling. However, a man's life—even if it's a base one—is dearer than any pounds sterling. Allow me to take part in the celebration now!

The moon rises.

KI-KUM. Natives. There she is—the goddess of the night—she pours out her light on the island, which has survived many trials! . . . Let us meet her joyously!

Numberless torches flare up. A huge chorus sings to the orchestra's playing:
        The trials are done,
        The sea grows calm—
        Long live Crimson Island—
        The finest of all lands!

KIRI-KUKI. The play is over.

The torches and moon disappear, and there is full light on stage.

EPILOGUE

General noise and commotion begins. The NATIVES *disperse. Onto the stage pour: the late* LORD, *the* LADY, PAGANEL, HATTERAS; SAILORS *flit here and there . . .* PASSEPARTOUT *. . .* SAVVA LUKICH *alone is motionless; he sits on the throne above the crowd. He has a gloomy and deeply thoughtful expression. All eyes are turned to him.*

LORD. Ahem . . . well, what have you got to say about our little play, Savva Lukich?

Dead silence.

SAVVA. It's banned.

A groan spreads through the entire troupe. The heads of stunned musicians pop up out of the orchestra. Out of the box comes the Prompter.

KIRI-KUKI (*feverishly*). What?! . . .

LORD (*growing pale*). What did you say, Savva Lukich? I think I mis-heard you.

SAVVA. No. You didn't mis-hear. Its performance is banned.

LIKKI-TIKKI. There's an ideological one for you! Congratulations on the big profits, Gennadi Panfilych!

LORD. Savva Lukich! Perhaps you will set forth some of your considerations? . . . Incidentally, wouldn't you like a . . .

SAVVA. I will have some . . . *merci* . . . but the play won't go on . . . he-he.

LORD. Passepartout! A glass of tea for Savva Lukich!

PASSEPARTOUT. Right away, Gennadi Panfilych. (*He serves the tea.*)

SAVVA. *Merci, merci.* And you, Gennadi Panfilych?

LORD. I already had a bite earlier.

Dead silence.

LIKKI-TIKKI. You only get what you pay for. Heh, heh, heh.

PASSEPARTOUT. The cadres are asking if they can take off their make-up, Gennadi Panfilych.

LORD (*in a hissing voice*). I'll take off their make-up—I'll take it off for them . . .

PASSEPARTOUT. Yes, sir, Gennadi Panfilych! . . . (*He disappears.*)

Suddenly Sizi *appears, wearing street clothes, but still in the Tsar's make-up and wearing a crown on his head.*

SIZI-BUZI. Comrade Author, I have come to see you . . . allow me to introduce myself, Sunduchkov. It's a very nice play . . . remarkable . . . it smells of Shakespeare—even at a distance. I have a good nose, sir, I've been on the stage for twenty-five years. I used to be in the Crimea with the late Anton Pavlovich Chekhov. . . . Incidentally, you look like him in the daylight *en face*. But, sir, you can't do such things to tsars . . . Well, what did you do? . . . He disappears after the first act . . .

KIRI-KUKI (*looks dully*). He's killed . . .

SIZI-BUZI. I understand. That's what a tsar should get. I would kill them all myself. Thank God I'm a conscientious person and there have only been working people in my family—none of those high-class ones . . . Kill him—but in Act Two! . . .

LIKKI-TIKKI. What kind of habit is it you have, Anempodist, making fun of people? You see for yourself, the man has been killed.

SIZI-BUZI. What does that mean?

LIKKI-TIKKI. Well, Savva has scratched the play.

SIZI-BUZI. A-ah! So, so . . . So! I understand! I understand perfectly! Can you treat tsars like that? No matter what sort of Arab he might be, he is still the Lord's anointed . . .

LORD. Anempodist! You will oblige me very much if you shut up for a minute.

SIZI-BUZI. I am silent. I am silent in the face of the law. *Dura lex . . . dura.*

PARROT. *Dura!* fool . . .

SIZI-BUZI. That's not me, Gennada Panfilych, that's the seven-hundred-ruble parrot.

LORD. Metelkin! No jokes! Savva Lukich! I hope that your decision is not final.

SAVVA. Yes, it is final! . . . I like to drink tea at work . . . you've no doubt had some at the Central Union.[10]

LORD. Central . . . union . . . yes . . Savva Lukich.

KIRI-KUKI (*suddenly*). The attic! So, this must mean back to the attic again! Dry oatmeal and a primus stove . . . torn sheets . . .

SAVVA. Harrumph . . . sorry, are you speaking to me? I'm a little deaf in one ear . . . what did you say, sir?

Dead silence.

KIRI-KUKI. The laundry woman sneers every day when you pay money for washing your underwear? . . . At night the stars look through a smashed window and there's no way of getting a new one put in! . . . For six months, for six months I burned up and froze, I met the dawn on Plyushchikh Street with a pen in my hands and an empty stomach! . . . And the storms howl, iron leaves whistle . . . and I have no galoshes . . .

LORD. Vasily Arturych!

SAVVA. I don't quite understand . . . where is this coming from?

KIRI-KUKI. This? This is from here! From me! From the depths of my heart! . . . here . . . *The Crimson Island!* Oh, my *Crimson Island!*

LORD. Vasily Arturych, some tea . . . a monologue . . . it's a monologue, Savva Lukich, a monologue from the fourth act!

SAVVA. So . . . So . . . but I don't recall.

KIRI-KUKI. Six months . . . six months . . . I ran around to editors, I haunted their thresholds, I wrote reports on fires . . . for three rubles seventy-five kopeks . . . and how did I get my honorarium? With no hat, at the doorsill . . . (*He takes off his wig.*) Pay me please . . . give me an advance of three rubles. Soon I'll finish . . . *The Crimson Island* . . . and then this ominous old man appears . . .

SAVVA. Sorry, of whom are you speaking?

10. There were many groups and "unions" of writers during the twenties. The all-embracing Union of Soviet Writers was not founded until 1932.

KIRI-KUKI. . . . and with one swoop, one scratch of a pen he kills me . . . well, here's my chest, pierce it with a pencil . . .

LORD. What are you doing, you unhappy person? . . . some tea! . . .

KIRI-KUKI. Oh, I have nothing to lose! . . .

BETSY.⎫
LADY. ⎬ Poor, poor fellow, calm down! . . . Vasily Arturych! . . .

LORD. You have nothing to lose, but I do! Brothers, take him into the men's room! . . . The theater—is a temple! . . . Passepartout! Passepartout!

Likki-Tikki, Sizi-Buzi, *and* Passepartout *lead* Kiri *away.*

BETSY. Vasily Arturych! . . . Calm down . . . everything will be all right . . . What's wrong with you?

KIRI-KUKI (*tearing loose*). And who are the judges? Because of their old age, their hostility to free life is inflexible. They get their opinions out of forgotten newspapers from the time of Kolchak and the winning of the Crimea![11]

LORD. He'll get me into trouble yet! Sergei Sergeich, I'll be along. . . . Brothers, take him away!

LADY. My dear, calm down, I will kiss you!

BETSY. Me too! (*They all lead* Kiri *out.*)

SAVVA. What is the meaning of this?

LORD. He was wounded in the head on the Polish front . . . he has utterly incredible talent . . . but a born idiot . . . intellect, ideology . . . he has already been in the booby-hatch once! . . . The theater is a temple! Pay no attention, Savva Lukich! This isn't the first day of our acquaintance, is it, Savva Lukich? Savva Lukich— fifteen thousand rubles! Three months of work! . . . Tell me— what's wrong with it? . . . Nothing on earth is beyond repair! . . . No!

SAVVA. It is a counter-revolutionary play![12]

LORD. Savva Lukich! Have some fear of Go . . . what am I saying! . . . have some fear . . . of whom . . . I don't know . . . don't be afraid

11. This speech is a quotation of lines 339–42 of Griboedov's *Woe from Wit,* with the substitution of Kolchak (a White general) to bring it up to date.

12. The Russian is not "counter-revolutionary," but "changing landmarks." For the explanation of this term see the introduction to this play.

of anyone . . . A counter-revolutionary play? In my theater? . . .

SIZI-BUZI (*enters*). We put him to bed . . . a pillow below, Valerian drops above . . . Lidia Ivannovna is with him.

LORD. Alone?

SIZI-BUZI. Don't worry, Adelaida's there.

LORD. Savva Lukich! In my temple? . . . Ha, ha, ha . . . Why, the author of the comedy *Days of the Turbins* came to me, do you know, and offered it to me! How do you like that? But when I looked over that thing, my heart started to thump . . . out of indignation. What, I say, to whom did you bring this? . . .

SIZI-BUZI. Absolutely right! I was there then. Why did you bring this? . . . To where have you brought it? . . . From where did you bring it? . . .

LORD. Anempodist!

SIZI-BUZI. I'm silent. (*Softly.*) I offered him a thousand rubles myself.

LORD. Savva Lukich! What's the trouble? I wouldn't allow a counter-revolutionary play in this theater if I were to be shot with a cannon! What's the trouble? . . .

SAVVA. The ending.

General murmuring.

LORD. Absolutely right! My God! I kept thinking, I kept feeling that there was something lacking in the play! But what it was never occurred to me! Well, of course, it's the ending! Savva Lukich, you are pure gold for the theater! I swear to you! I keep saying it on every street corner, we need men like you in the U.S.S.R.! Need them desperately! What's the trouble with the ending?

SAVVA. My goodness, Gennadi Panfilych! How is it you did not guess it yourself? I don't understand. I am surprised by you . . .

LORD. Quite right, how is it I didn't guess, old jackass that I am— sixty years old?!

SAVVA. The sailors—who are they anyway?

LORD. The proletariat, Savva Lukich, may I turn sour if it's not the proletariat!

SAVVA. Well, how can it be? During the time when the liberated natives are celebrating, they remain . . .

LORD. . . . in slavery, Savva Lukich, in slavery! Oy, I'm a cretin!

SIZI-BUZI. I won't argue about that! No, sir!

LORD. Anempodist!

SAVVA. And what about international revolution and solidarity? . . .

LORD. Where are they, Savva Lukich? Oy, oy, me! Metelkin! If you arrange an international revolution within five minutes—understand? . . . I'll cover you with gold! . . .

PASSEPARTOUT. International, Gennadi Panfilych?

LORD. International.

PASSEPARTOUT. You shall have it, Gennadi Panfilych!

LORD. Fly! . . . Savva Lukich! . . . We'll have an ending with an international revolution right now . . .

SAVVA. But perhaps Comrade Author does not wish an international revolution?

LORD. Who? The author? Not wish it? I'd just like to see the man who doesn't desire an international revolution! (*To the parterre.*) Perhaps someone doesn't want it? . . . Raise your hand! . . .

SIZI-BUZI. Who's against it? He, he! Ob-viously the majority, Savva Lukich!

LORD (*emotionally*). People like that don't get into my theater. The cashier doesn't give characters like that tickets, no sir . . . Anempodist, it'll be better if I myself ask the author to add some lines for you in the first act—so that you don't get things mixed up now!

SIZI-BUZI. Thanks a lot for that!

LORD. Everyone on stage! Everyone!

PASSEPARTOUT. Volodya! Everyone up for the variant!

LORD. Likui Isaich, an international one! . . .

CONDUCTOR. Say no more, Gennadi Panfilych, I finished half an hour ago, and I haven't dismissed the orchestra.

LORD. Let's have the author!

Betsy *and the* Lady *lead in* Kiri *holding him under the arms.*

LORD (*in a hissing whisper*). We're about to play a variant of the finale . . . improvise an international revolution, the sailors must take part. If the play is dear to you . . .

KIRI-KUKI. Ah! I understand . . . I understand . . .

LADY. We'll all help you.

BETSY. Yes ... yes ...

A gong sounds and the moon flares up in the sky, instantaneously torches burst into flame in the natives' hands. The stage is lighted in red.

PROMPTER. There she is ... the goddess of the night ...

KI-KUM. ... the moon! Let us greet it with celebration! ...

The Chorus *sings with the orchestra: "Long live Crimson Island—/ The finest of all lands! ..."*

SECOND NATIVE. There are lights out at sea!

KIRI-KUKI. Wait! Quiet! There are lights out at sea!

KI-KUM. What does this mean? The ship is returning? Likki, be at the ready!

LIKKI-TIKKI. I'm always ready!

The ship enters the bay, lighted in red. On deck stand ranks of Sailors; *in their hands are crimson banners with the inscription "Long live the Crimson Island!" In front of them is* Passepartout.

PASSEPARTOUT. Comrades! When going out to sea, the crew of the yacht "Duncan" mutinied against the oppressor-capitalists! ... After a terrible battle the crew threw Paganel, Lady Glenarvan, and Captain Hatteras into the sea. I assumed command. The revolutionary English sailors wish me to convey to the native people that from this day forth no one will make any attacks on its freedom and honor ... Brothers, we greet the natives! ...

BETSY (*on the cliff*). Oh, how happy I am, Passepartout, that you've finally been freed from the oppression of the Lord too. Long live free English sailors! Long live Passepartout!

NATIVES. Long live Re-vo-lu-tion-ar-y En-glish sai-lors! ... Hurrah! Hurrah! Hurrah!

PARROT. Hurrah! Hurrah! Hurrah!

Savva stands and applauds. Thunderous music.

LORD. Louder! Louder! Oy, oy, oy! ...

CHORUS (*sings with the orchestra*).
So there's our logical conclusion:
It doesn't matter whether it's this way or that!—
In the finale
(*a soprano*)
we will conquer ...
(*basses*)
ideologically.
We close our performance!

Immediate silence. Kiri-Kuki puts his fingers in his ears.

SIZI-BUZI (*appears*). Maybe the tsar could at least stand over on the side? Maybe he didn't perish during the eruption, but hid and later repented.

LORD. Anempodist! Out!

SIZI-BUZI. I'm disappearing ... go to hell, my soul,[13] and be a prisoner there for all eternity. (*He is illuminated by a hellish light, falls through the trapdoor.*)

LORD. Savva Lukich! Savva Lukich! Savva Lu ... Did you hear them play that? Did you hear them sing? ... Savva Lukich! The theater—it is a temple! ...

Dead silence.

SAVVA. This play is ... (*a pause*) ... passed for public performance.

LORD (*in a howl*). Savva Lukich! ...

A thunderous outburst of rapture, an absolutely terrifying uproar. The backdrop goes up. Flashing lights and mirrors appear, wigs on wig stands.

ALL. Hurrah! Thank *God!* ... congratulations! ... *Bravo!* ... *Bravo!* ...

LIKKI-TIKKI. Hairdressers! ...

SIZI-BUZI (*rises up out of the trapdoor at the very back of the stage*). Patience?

13. From "go to hell," a quotation from the last speech in Alexander P. Sumarokov's play *The False Dmitri* (1771). The speech is made by Dmitri as he commits suicide.

PAGANEL. Hey, they really did a smashing finale!

HATTERAS. Where are my pants?

LORD. Vasily Arturych! Get up! . . . You're being congratulated!

KIRI-KUKI. I don't want to hear anything . . . nothing . . . I've been murdered . . .

LORD. Come to your senses, Vasily Arturych! The play has been passed.

BETSY. ⎱ Vasily Arturych, dear Jules Verne! It's all over!
LADY. ⎰ Congratulations! Congratulations!

KIRI-KUKI. What? . . . Who? . . .

LORD. ⎫
BETSY. ⎬ Congratulations! It passed!
LADY. ⎭

KIRI-KUKI. What do you mean passed? . . . Oh, my *Crimson Island!* Oh, my *Crimson Island!*

SAVVA. Well, thank you, young man! You've comforted me . . . comforted, I tell you frankly! And thanks for the ship . . . You will go far, young man! Very far . . . that is my prediction for you . . .

LORD. A terrific talent—I told you so!

SAVVA. Of course, I'm still banning your little play for all other cities . . . it's impossible . . . a play like that to be suddenly passed for everywhere![14]

LORD. Naturally! Naturally, Savva Lukich! One can't give them such plays. Could one, really? They haven't grown up to ones like this yet, Savva Lukich! (*Softly, to* Kiri.) Well, no, we won't give this to the provincials for them to try to understand . . . We'll control it ourselves. Incidentally, Vasily Arturych, so as to keep things tighter—don't you drop by any other theaters, you go straight home and beddy-bye! And I gave you five hundred rubles there, here's another thousand now—to keep an even number . . . And you just give me a little receipt . . . there, now . . . *Merci!* He, he!

BETSY. What an inspired face he has! . . .

SIZI-BUZI. Give me a thousand rubles and mine'll be inspired too. I was buried in Act One . . .

---

14. This restriction was one which the censors imposed on Bulgakov's *The Days of the Turbins.*

KIRI-KUKI (*dully*). Money ... Ten-ruble notes ...

PARROT. Ten-ruble notes! Ten-ruble notes!

KIRI-KUKI. And ... the attic, sixteen square yards and moonlight in place of a blanket ... Oh, you, my blind windows, miserly and pale dawn! ... Ten-ruble notes! ... Who wrote *The Crimson Island?* I—Dymogatsky, Jules Verne. Down with the fires on Meshchansky Street ... the stray dogs ... Long live the sun ... the ocean ... *The Crimson Island!*

Dead silence.

SIZI-BUZI. And monologues like that he doesn't write in the play!

ALL. Shhh ...

KIRI-KUKI. Who wrote *The Crimson Island?*

LORD. You did, you Vasily Arturych ... You forgive me if I was too hard on you ... Yes, yes ... Old Gennadi is hot tempered.

SAVVA. An attractive young man! I was like that myself once! It was during War Communism ... but now ...

KIRI-KUKI. And the reporters, the reviewers! ... Oy ... so ... is Jules Verne at home? No, he's sleeping, or he's busy, he's writing ... don't bother him! ... Drop by later ... His flaming heart does not fit into sixteen square yards; he needs the broad, free earth ...[15]

LADY. How interesting he is! ...

CONDUCTOR. The orchestra congratulates you, Vasily Arturych.

KIRI-KUKI. *Merci* ... Thanks, *danke sehr*. Comrades, I invite you to visit me, in my new apartment, the apartment of the dramatist Dymogatsky-Jules Verne, on the first floor—with red caviar ... I want music! ...

CONDUCTOR. Say no more, I already understand ...

The orchestra plays from "The Barber of Seville."

KIRI-KUKI (*to the* Lord). Well, my signor? Has inspiration been given to me? What do you think? ... What, my signor? ...

LORD. It has, it has, Vasily Arturych ... it has, it has! ... Who has it if not you?

---

15. A parodistic paraphrase of some famous lines spoken in Chekhov's story "Gooseberries," lines which were Chekhov's answer to Tolstoy's question and story "How Much Land Does A Man Need?"

KIRI-KUKI. How glorious our Lord in Zion . . . Oh it's a long way to Tipperary . . .

SAVVA. What's that about?

PASSEPARTOUT. He's gone mad over the money . . . that's not hard! . . . A thousand rubles! Gennadi Panfilych! The cashier wants to know if it's been passed. Can she sell tickets?

LORD. She can, she must, she should, certainly, immediately!

Music.

May the box offices sell from nine to nine! . . . Today, tomorrow, every day! . . .

KIRI-KUKI. And forevermore!

LORD. Take Oedipus out. *The Crimson Island* is playing! Metelkin, give us some light and the announcements!

PASSEPARTOUT. Yes, Gennadi Panfilych!

The fiery letters: "The Crimson Island—Today and Every Day" flare up on the ship, the volcano, and in the audience.

KIRI-KUKI. Today, always, and forever after!

SAVVA. Amen!

THE END

A CABAL
OF HYPOCRITES

MOLIÈRE

Rien ne manque à sa gloire,
Il manquait à la nôtre.

INTRODUCTION

IN OCTOBER OF 1929, eight months after *The Days of the Turbins* was banned, Bulgakov began work on a new play.[1] *A Cabal of Hypocrites (Molière)* was written during a period of great personal persecution—two months after finishing it Bulgakov wrote his letter to Stalin. Despite, or perhaps, because of the sufferings, both public and private, which he endured during this period, Bulgakov wrote a play about the glamorous court of the Sun King and the sad fate of his favorite playwright.

Bulgakov read the play to Leonidov in January of 1930, and he informed Stanislavsky that the play was interesting but that the theater had decided not to "push it through now" due to the need for contemporary plays. Sometime in February or March *A Cabal of Hypocrites* was rejected for reasons of censorship. Stanislavsky was still interested in the play and privately expressed the hope that Bulgakov would not give it to another theater. Despite the first rejection by the censorship, the theater assumed that the play could be rewritten so that it could pass the censors.

In 1931 *A Cabal of Hypocrites* was finally put in MXAT's repertory, but rehearsals were few and widely spaced. In the autumn of 1932 the play was accepted for production, but again no work was begun on it. In 1933 there were a few rehearsals, and sets were even being made, but Stanislavsky felt that the theater would not be able to stage it by the end of the year. Finally, in 1934, work began in earnest. The play which Bulgakov had given to the theater in 1930 was not put into production for four years.[2] By the time MXAT got around to actually working on the play, Bulgakov had written *Adam and Eve, Half-mad Jourdain, Bliss,* and an adaptation of *Dead Souls,* and Part One of *The Master and Margarita.* In October of 1934 he started work on the play *Last Days.* One can understand Bulgakov's desire to see *A Cabal of Hypocrites* produced with all possible speed. It was a strain for the author to immerse himself in the story of Molière again after having been involved with so many other projects in the interim. Given all of these circumstances, it is little wonder that Bulgakov was bitter about what occurred *after* work was finally started.

When Stanislavsky began work on a play, it was usual for him to meet with the directors and the set designers to discuss their general ideas about the production. N. M. Gorchakov was director of *A Cabal of Hypocrites,* Bulgakov the assistant director, and Stanislavsky himself served as production manager. A date was set for the first meeting, but on the night before, Stanislavsky called up Gorchakov and asked him to come to his apartment to discuss the play separately. By this time[3] the roles had been assigned, but there had been no rehearsals. This *sub rosa* colloquy was convened so that Stanislavsky could express dissatisfaction with the play. He disliked the picture presented of Molière, because Molière was not revealed as the great genius he was. Stanislavsky praised the way the play's action was developed, the vivid portrayal of the people and events surrounding Molière, but he insisted that it was a "great minus in the play" that Molière was not shown in all his glory as a writer. Stanislavsky came to the main point of this private meeting:

S. Don't you think it's necessary to work some more with the author on the text before the rehearsals begin?

G. I'm afraid to even think of it, Konstantin Sergeevich, Mikhail Afanasievich has suffered so much waiting for the rehearsal of this play that any remark about the text literally makes him start to shake. Maybe when he sees that the rehearsals have begun he will calm down some and it will be easier to make him agree about revising the text.

S. For me the question is not of revising the text, but in making the whole figure of Molière stand on two legs. . . . It's all written with just black colors. I understand that if we say that to Bulgakov he will take the play away from us and give it to another theater, and our troupe will again accuse us of not having a repertoire. It is a very complicated situation. I called you to consult.[4]

Stanislavsky went on to point out, correctly, that in not one scene do Molière or his ideas triumph. He then told Gorchakov not to rehearse the whole play, but only certain essential moments; in listing these essential scenes he left out the death scene. Gorchakov wondered at this, and Stanislavsky replied that although Molière does not really fight against his enemies the death scene is one half of an act long—therefore the death itself is sheer sentimentality: "Mikhail Afanasievich, I hope, will see that and want to change the last act."

At the end of this unusual "group discussion" Stanislavsky told Gorchakov to come with *only* the set designer the next day and to put off the meeting with Bulgakov until the first rehearsal: "Otherwise I fear that I will start to quarrel with Mikhail Afanasievich about the play's defects. He will get upset and won't do anything for us."

Rehearsals began, but Gorchakov had problems in using Stanislavsky's "new method"—rehearsing only certain parts of the play. (The obvious aim of this was to prevent the actors from learning the lines until after Bulgakov had rewritten the play as Stanislavsky wanted it.) The actors did not like the change in rehearsal method, and Bulgakov asserted that *all* of the scenes were important and tied together "by an unbreakable chain, by the logic of events and emotions."

Stanislavsky was ill for many weeks and unable to come to rehearsals until April 17, 1934—three months after work had begun. The company ran through the play for him (leaving out the last act). He said they had played well, but added: "There was something I didn't get from you. Perhaps it wasn't really said in the play itself. I did not see Molière—the man of immense talent." "Perhaps" rings falsely—both Gorchakov and Stanislavsky knew that Stanislavsky was convinced of this "defect" before he saw the run-through.

The protocol of this rehearsal is endlessly fascinating. One hears Ivan Vasilievich of *Theatrical Novel* in Stanislavsky's every phrase. During the course of the rehearsal Bulgakov and Stanislavsky duelled verbally. Bulgakov's mockery surfaced from time to time, but Stanislavsky either ignored it or, obtusely, never noticed it. For example, Stanislavsky complained that Molière is involved in too much action and that Bulgakov should write some scenes in which

Molière creates: "Whatever you want—a play, a role, a lampoon." Bulgakov answered: "I don't seem to recall that he wrote lampoons." Bulgakov maintained that Molière's genius is shown in the way he acts in the scene from *Le Malade imaginaire* at the end of the play. Then Stanislavsky objected to Molière's fights in every act, and Bulgakov pointed out that Molière had a "hot temper," and that at any rate in those days such things happened constantly. Finally, Bulgakov, obviously quite irritated by all of this criticism so late in the day, said: "I fear that my author's work on the play is over, and its future fate is in the hands of the actors...." But Stanislavsky did not give up so easily; he went on and on—saying that the play shows the bourgeois side of Molière, that this is not the Molière he remembered from school, etc. At the end of the exercise Stanislavsky said that he would like more "underwater reefs" of Molière's life revealed in the play, "... if, of course, Mikhail Afanaisevich is agreed wtih me." Bulgakov immediately replied, "There is little agreement," and continued to defend his views. Stanisvlasky repeated over and over that "one must have the courage to admit one's mistakes" and that "one should correct them as soon as one becomes aware of them." Bulgakov's weary answer was, "These corrections will drag on for five years, Konstantin Sergeevich, I have no more strength." The final exchange between the director and the author at this rehearsal seems almost friendly—Stanislavsky said, "Mikhail Afanasievich, I will try at the rehearsals, with the actors playing, to show you what else it is I want from you in the figure of Molière." Bulgakov answered: "I think that will be the most proper method of working with the author, Konstantin Sergeevich."

The next day when Stanislavsky was ready to show Bulgakov what sort of Molière he wanted the three main actors were out sick, and consequently the *Molière* scenes could not be rehearsed. This reminds one of the passage in *Theatrical Novel* which describes how actors "suddenly" get sick when they do not want to go through Ivan Vasilievich's ridiculous exercises. And one wonders what the statistical probabilities are for all three of the actors getting sick on the same day. Interestingly enough, a week and a half later, when the next attempt to show Bulgakov what Molière should be like was scheduled, Bulgakov himself got sick. But Stanislavsky went on with the rehearsal anyway—and had a copy of the transcript sent to Bulgakov.

Reading this protocol, one is struck by the sycophantic way in which the actors ecstatically respond to Stanislavsky's every suggestion, and by the ingenuous way Stanislavsky made such comments as: "I'm very sorry that Bulgakov is not at the rehearsal. If he saw your faces he would understand better what we expect of him." This remark is, of course, said with full cognizance of the fact that Bulgakov is going to read it a few hours later. Stanislavsky has the actors doing actual scenes from Molière's *Don Juan*—to show how the genius of Molière affects the actors themselves. When they finished Stanislavsky was pleased: "Now that's the atmosphere of Molière's house. Flights of genius, and sighs of love behind the screen." At this point in the transcript Bulgakov was probably rather annoyed—but the worst was still ahead. Next to receive Stanislavsky's attention was the role of Molière himself. Stanislavsky made major changes in its characterization. He told Stanitsyn (the actor playing Molière) that Molière's flattery of the king was not the important thing—when in fact it was an essential fact in Bulgakov's characterization.

Stanislavsky suggested several new scenes, such as Molière writing lines from *L'École des femmes*. At the end of the rehearsal Stanitsyn assured Stanislavsky that he would try to convince Bulgakov to rewrite the scene so that Molière is "creating" at his desk. Stanislavsky's last words were: "Wonderful, you all talk to Bulgakov, tell him about our rehearsal. It is quite vexing that he did not see it, did not *experience* it together with us."

The minutes run fifteen long pages in Gorchakov's book, so only a few examples have been cited here. There are many remarks which make it obvious that Stanislavsky did not understand (or perhaps did not want to understand) Bulgakov's play in the slightest. Stanislavsky's attraction to the mustiest clichés of the biographical drama is somewhat surprising.

A few hours after the rehearsal took place Bulgakov read the transcript—so carefully calculated by Stanislavsky to force the author to rewrite his play. We do not have to speculate about the precise degree of wrath aroused in Bulgakov by this record—we *know* from the following letter he wrote to Gorchakov:

> Having received today the extract from the minutes of the rehearsal of *Molière* on the 17th of April of this year, and having acquainted myself with it, I inform you that in view of the total destruction of my artistic intent and the attempt to compose another play in place of the play which the theater accepted, I categorically refuse to make any changes in the play *Molière,* a fact which I am simultaneously informing Konstantin Sergeevich.[5]

Rehearsals went on nevertheless, both at Stanislavsky's home and at the theater. Eventually all of the sets, costumes, and music were finished, and still Stanislavky would not give permission for the general rehearsals. Stanislavsky asked Gorchakov once again to try to persuade Bulgakov to rewrite the play. When Bulgakov again refused, Stanislavsky verbally washed his hands of the project, saying: "Release the play on your own responsibility. I will not undertake to answer for it, not having seen it on stage and not being sure of the play. Do everything that's possible, the things about which we talked so often." At this point it would seem that Nemirovich-Danchenko took over. He directed rehearsals in 1936 on January 4, 16, 20, and 29. On February 15 *A Cabal of Hypocrites* —entitled *Molière*—was premièred by the authority of Nemirovich-Danchenko.

The reviews were negative. Like Stanislavsky the reviewers wanted a Molière who showed his genius at every turn, not one who suffered family tragedies. The March 9, 1936 issue of *Pravda* contained an attack on the play entitled "External Glitter and False Content"—which could almost have been written by Stanislavsky himself so similar were the criticisms. The play was cut from the repertory after seven performances as a direct result of this review— in spite of the fact that it was very successful at the box office.

Stanislavsky regarded *A Cabal of Hypocrites* as a biographical drama, which shows a certain literary insensitivity on his part.[6] Bulgakov, who had done extensive research on Molière, both for the play and for the biography, certainly knew his facts. In his play, however, names of real persons are changed, and fictitious characters and events are added. Actual events described one way in the biography are given a completely different coloration in the play. Stanislavsky was ill informed about Molière and his life if he actually believed that the Archbishop of Paris was named Charron,[7] that a Moirron or Rivale had ever been in Molière's troupe,[8] or that Molière died on stage.[9] As for the Cabal itself, its real name was the Compagnie du Saint Sacrement. This group did secretly ban *Tartuffe*, but there exist no implications that they were one-tenth as powerful as Bulgakov's *Kabala*. *Tartuffe* was banned by the king for a short time, but then he lifted the ban and gave Molière permission to play it. Bulgakov changed dates in the play so that the ban occurs near Molière's death, when in actuality it occurred long before. As for the threatening d'Orsini—no such person is mentioned by Molière scholars, or by Bulgakov himself in his biography.

Since Bulgakov knew the facts of Molière's life, and since he wrote a biography based on those facts, one must conclude that he did not write—or intend to write—a historically accurate biographical play about Molière. This is not to say that the play is not historically accurate in other respects. Bulgakov tried to convey accurately the atmosphere of France under Louis XIV. The character of Louis himself seems to be represented accurately, as is that of Molière's wife Armande and his *registre*, La Grange. As for Molière himself, some aspects of his character seem to conform to the historical view —his temperament was an impulsive and inflammable one, he was a hypochondriac, and he did flatter the king. But the historical Molière suffered no persecutions to compare with Bulgakov's pitiful playwright.

Creative writers are seldom inclined to submit wholly to historical facts, but that does not explain why Bulgakov should change the events and people around Molière so drastically. In *A Cabal of Hypocrites* Molière is unaware of his own genius—he is a "simple man" who happens to be an artist. This is one of Bulgakov's constant themes: the freedom of the artist against the demands of society. Molière represents any artist who has had to bend to the demands of a despot in order to have his work played or published, in other words, in order to exist. Bulgakov's Molière bends willingly, accepting the fact that he must compromise if he wants his plays to live. He does not regret the vast amounts of flattery and self-abasement required of him by the king—until the king crushes him in the name of morality. Then and only then is he bitter. All his compromising was to no end. Molière's revenge is that his fame is greater than that of the Sun King; his works live on, but Louis lives only in history books. This is the reason for the epigraph to *A Cabal of Hypocrites:*

> *Rien ne manque à sa gloire,*
> *Il manquait à la nôtre.*

NOTES

1. Soviet editions of the play erroneously date it 1930–36. Page three of Bulgakov's *Zapisnaja kniga 1929–30* (Lenin Library, *Otdel rukopisej,* M10837/ No. 5) is headed *"Mol'er Material* oktjabr' 1929."

2. Bulgakov gave his friend Popov a typescript inscribed on January 28, 1934, noting it was a direct copy from the one given to the censors. It is now in the Lenin Library *Otdel Rukopisej,* Fond 218/ Karton 1268/ Ed. xran. 10.

3. N. Gorčakov, *Režisserskie uroki Stanislavskogo* (M. 1951), p. 532. This book by Gorchakov is the source of the account below. However, there is some doubt about his reliability, and the reader should bear in mind the fact that even what purport to be direct quotations from the minutes of rehearsals may be fabrications, or at least distortions designed to make Stanislavsky (who is officially regarded as a saint of the theater) look good at a time when he was showing signs of senility.

4. Gorčakov, p. 533.

5. M. Bulgakov, *P'esy* (M., 1962), p. 473. This letter is quoted by several Soviet scholars, but the year is never given. Certain details in Gorchakov's account (such as the fact that it was three months after work began) make it possible to deduce that it is from 1934.

6. One might argue that Stanislavsky, aware of the purges that were already beginning, was being careful. According to his friends Bulgakov

didn't think this was the case. Of course, it was nothing new for Stanislavsky to have views of a play which differed sharply from those of the author. Recall Chekhov's dissatisfaction with the way his plays were treated.

7. Archbishop Péréfixe had been Louis XIV's tutor. For his real-life role see R. Fernandez, *La Vie de Molière* (Paris, 1929), pp. 156–57.

8. They are not mentioned anywhere in the exhaustive study by Madeleine Jurgens, *Cent ans de recherches sur Molière, sur sa famille et sur les comediens de sa troupe* (Paris, 1963). Other names are, of course, real: Béjart, La Grange, and Du Croisy. Moirron does have a prototype in the real Michel Baron. If one compares Bulgakov's account of Baron and the magical musical instrument in his biography [Bulgakov, *Žizn' gospodina de Mol'era* (M. 1962), pp. 170–73] to Moirron in the play, one sees clearly Bulgakov's distortion of facts to suit his purpose.

9. For the account of Molière's death, as quoted from the *Registre* of La Grange, see Henry Trollope, *The Life of Molière* (London, 1905), pp. 542ff.

Cast of Characters

Jean Baptiste Poquelin de Molière, renowned dramatist and actor.

Madeleine Béjart
Armande Béjart de Molière } actresses.

Mariette Rivale, an actress.

Charles Varlet de La Grange, an actor, nicknamed the "Registre."

Zacharie Moirron, a renowned actor and lover.

Philbert Du Croisy, an actor.

Jean-Jacques Bouton, the lamplighter and Molière's servant.

Louis XIV, the king of France.

Marquis d'Orsini, a duelist, nicknamed "One-Eye, Start Praying!"

Marquis de Charron, archbishop of Paris.

Marquis de Lessac, a gambler.

The Honest Cobbler, the king's jester.

A Charlatan with a harpsichord.

An Unknown Woman wearing a mask.

Father Barthèlemy, an itinerant preacher.

Brother Force
Brother Fidelity } Members of the Cabal of the Holy Writ.

Renée, Molière's decrepit governess.

Prompter.

Members of the Cabal of the Holy Writ wearing masks and black cloaks. Courtiers. Musketeers and Others.

The setting is Paris, in the age of Louis XIV.

ACT I

Behind the curtain *the extremely hollow rolling laughter of a thousand people can be heard. The curtain opens—the stage represents the theater* Palais Royal. *Heavy curtains. A green poster on which there are coats of arms and a design. On it in large letters is:* "LES COMEDIENS DE MONSIEUR ..." *followed by some small words. A mirror. Armchairs. Costumes. At the junction of two dressing rooms, by the curtain which separates them, is a harpsichord of huge dimensions. In the second dressing room there is a crucifix of rather large dimensions before which a holy lamp is burning.*

In the first dressing room the door is on the left; there is a multitude of tallow candles (they obviously have not spared the light). But in the second dressing room there is only one lantern with a colored glass shade on the table.

On absolutely everything—both on objects and on people (except La Grange*)—there is the mark of an extraordinary event, of alarm and anxiety.*

La Grange, *who is not in the play, is sitting in the dressing room sunk in thought. He is wearing a dark cloak. He is young, handsome, and important looking. The lantern casts a mysterious light on his face.*

In the first dressing room Bouton, *with his back to us, has glued himself to a crack in the curtain. And even from his back it is apparent that the spectacle inspires him with a feeling of extreme curiosity. The* Charlatan's *mug is sticking through the door. The* Charlatan *puts his hand to his ear and listens.*

Bursts of laughter are heard, then a final roll of guffaws. Bouton *grabs some sort of ropes, and the sounds disappear. After a moment* Molière *appears from the split in the curtain and runs*

down the little stairs to the dressing room. CHARLATAN *humbly disappears.*
MOLIÈRE *is wearing an exaggerated wig and caricature helmet. In his hands is a broadsword.* MOLIÈRE *is made up as Sganarelle[1]— a lilac nose with a wart. He looks funny.* MOLIÈRE *is holding his chest with his left hand like a man who has a bad heart. The make-up is floating off his face.*

MOLIÈRE (*throwing off the cloak, catching his breath*). Some water!
BOUTON. Immediately. (*Gives him a glass.*)
MOLIÈRE. Phew! (*He drinks, listens with frightened eyes.*)

The door is flung open, Du Croisy *runs in made up as Polichenelle, his eyes thrown back.*

DU CROISY. The king is applauding! (*He disappears.*)
PROMPTER (*in the parting of the curtain*). The king is applauding!
MOLIÈRE. Give me a towel! (*He wipes off his forehead, worries.*)
MADELEINE (*appears made-up in the parting of the curtain*). Quickly! The king is applauding!
MOLIÈRE (*upset*). Yes, yes, I hear. Immediately. (*He crosses himself at the curtain.*) Holy Virgin, Holy Virgin! (*To Bouton.*) Open the whole stage!

First Bouton *raises the curtain separating us from the stage, and then the huge main curtain separating the stage from the theater where the audience sits. And now only the stage is visible to us—from the side. It is raised over the dressing rooms, which are empty. Tallow candles burn brightly in the chandeliers. The audience is not visible; only the closest gilded loge is visible—but it is empty. One can only sense the mysterious, alert dark blueness of the barely darkened hall.* Charlatan's *face appears momentarily in the door.* Molière *goes up onto the stage so that we see him in profile. He goes up to the ramp in a catlike walk, as if sneaking up —he bends his neck, the feathers of his hat brush the floor. At his appearance one unseen man in the theater begins to*

1. A character in Molière's play *Sganarelle* (1660).

*applaud, and after this there is thunderous applause from
the theater. Then silence.*

MOLIÈRE. Your . . . Majesty . . . Your Majesty . . . Most Radiant Sovereign . . . (*He pronounces the first words almost stuttering—in
real life he does stutter a little—but then his speech evens out, and
from his opening words it is clear that on stage he is first rate.
The richness of his intonations, expressions, and gestures is inexhaustible. His smile easily infects.*) The actors of the Troupe de
Monsieur, your most faithful and submissive servants, have asked
me to thank you for the unparalleled honor which you have done
us by visiting our theater . . . And now, Sire . . . there is nothing
more I can tell you.

Slight laughter ripples and dies out in the audience.

Muse, my Muse, oh sly Thalia!
Every evening, hearing your shout,
By the candles of the Palais Royal
I put on the wig of Sganarelle.
Bowing to each by rank, and even lower,
Is something I must do! The parterre pays its 30 sous!
Oh Sire, for the amusement of Paris (*Pause.*)
I often talk as if my head's on loose.

Laughter goes through the audience.

But today, oh Muse of comedy,
You should rush to my aid.
Oh, is it easy, is it easy in an *intermezzo*
To amuse the Sun of France? . . .

Applause thunders in the audience.

BOUTON. Oh, what a mind! He thought to call him the Sun.
CHARLATAN (*enviously*). When did he compose that poem?
BOUTON (*haughtily*). Never. Impromptu.
CHARLATAN. Is that even thinkable?
BOUTON. Not for you, it isn't.
MOLIÈRE (*sharply changing intonation*).

You carry the royal burden for us.
I am a comedian, an insignificant role,
But I am famous just for having acted in your time,
Louis! . . . The Great! . . .
   (*He raises his voice.*) French!!!
     (*He shouts.*) King!!! . . .
(*He throws his hat into the air.*)

Something unimaginable begins to happen in the theater. Roars: "Long live the king!" The flame of candles starts to diminish. Bouton and Charlatan wave their hats, they shout, but their words are inaudible. The broken signals of Guards' trumpets pierce through the roar. La Grange stands motionlessly by his fire, his hat off. The ovation ends, and silence descends.

Louis' Voice (*from the blueness*). Thank you, Monsieur de Molière.
Molière. Your ever-obedient servants ask you to watch one more amusing *intermezzo,* if we have not bored you.
Louis' Voice. Oh, with pleasure, Monsieur de Molière!
Molière (*shouts*). Curtain!

The main curtain covers the audience hall, and immediately music begins on that side of the curtain. Bouton also closes the curtain which separates us from the stage, and it disappears. Charlatan's face vanishes.

Molière (*appearing in the dressing room, mutters*). *He* bought them! . . . I'll kill him, I'll cut his throat!
Bouton. Whose throat would he like to cut in this hour of triumph?
Molière (*grabs Bouton by the neck*). Yours!
Bouton (*shouts*). I'm being strangled at a command performance!

La Grange makes a movement by the fire, but again becomes motionless. At the shout Madeleine and Rivale run in —the latter almost completely naked because she was changing. Both actresses grab Molière by the pants, dragging him away from Bouton, during which he kicks at them. Finally

they tear Molière *away along with a piece of* Bouton's *shirt.*
Molière *manages to fall into an armchair.*

MADELEINE. You're out of your mind! They can hear in the theater.
MOLIÈRE. Let them!
RIVALE. Monsieur Molière! (*She closes* Molière's *mouth.*)

The amazed Charlatan *peeks in through the door.*

BOUTON (*looking in the mirror, he feels his torn shirt*). Adroitly
done, just fine. (*To* Moliére.) What is this all about?
MOLIÈRE. This good-for-nothing . . . I don't understand why I keep
a sadist in my company. We've played it forty times, everything
was in order; but in the king's presence a candle fell into the
chandelier—tallow dripped onto the parquetry.
BOUTON. Maître, you yourself were making funny flourishes, and
you knocked over that candle with your broadsword.
MOLIÈRE. You're lying, you loafer!

La Grange *puts his head in his hands and weeps softly.*

RIVALE. He's right. You caught the candle with your sword.
MOLIÈRE. They're laughing in the theater. The king is surprised . . .
BOUTON. The king is the most cultured person in France, and he did
not notice any candle.
MOLIÈRE. So I knocked it over? Me? Hm . . . In that case, why was
I screaming at you?
BOUTON. I am at a loss to say, sir.
MOLIÈRE. I seem to have torn your shirt.

Bouton *laughs convulsively.*

RIVALE. God, look how I'm dressed! (*She grabs a shirt and covering
herself with it, she flies away.*)
DU CROISY (*has appeared in the parting of the curtain with a lantern.*) Miss Béjart, entrance, entrance, entrance . . . (*He disappears.*)
MADELEINE. I'm coming. (*She runs off.*)
MOLIÈRE (*to* Bouton). Take this shirt.

BOUTON. Thank you. (*He takes off his shirt and pants, adroitly puts one leg in* Molière's *pants with the lace trimming.*)

MOLIÈRE. Eh . . . eh . . . eh . . . And why those pants?

BOUTON. Maître, you must agree that it would be the height of poor taste to combine such a marvelous shirt with these disgusting pants. Just have a look—why these pants are a disgrace. (*He puts on the shirt too.*) Maître, in the pocket I have discovered two silver coins of insignificant worth. What do you wish me to do with them?

MOLIÈRE. Indeed. I suppose, you swindler, that it would be best to give them to a museum. (*He straightens his make-up.*)

BOUTON. Me too. I'll give them to one. (*He puts the money away.*) Well, I'll go snuff the candles. (*He arms himself with the candle snuffer.*)

MOLIÈRE. When you're on stage please don't bug out your eyes at the king.

BOUTON. Who are you saying that to, maître? I am also cultured, because I am a Frenchman by descent.

MOLIÈRE. You are a Frenchman by descent and a blockhead by profession.

BOUTON. By profession you are a great actor—and by nature a surly boor. (*He vanishes.*)

MOLIÈRE. I committed some kind of sin, and the Lord inflicted him on me at Limoges.

CHARLATAN. Monsieur Director! Monsieur Director!

MOLIÈRE. Yes, yes, I'll be with you. Now listen, sir. If you will excuse me for my frankness—this is a second-rate trick. But the parterre public will love it. I'll let you into the *entr'acte* for a week. But still, how do you do it?

CHARLATAN. It's a secret, Monsieur Director.

MOLIÈRE. Well, I'll find out. Play a few chords, but do it softly.

Smiling mysteriously, Charlatan *approaches the harpsichord, sits down on the stool at some distance from the harpsichord, makes movements in the air as if playing, and the keys of the harpsichord go down, the harpsichord plays softly.*

MOLIÈRE. Damn! (*He rushes to the harpsichord trying to catch hold of invisible wires.*)

Charlatan *smiles mysteriously.*

Well, all right. You'll get some money. There's a spring somewhere, right?

CHARLATAN. Does the harpsichord remain at the theater overnight?

MOLIÈRE. Well, of course. You can't drag it home with you.

Charlatan *bows and exits.*

DU CROISY (*looks out holding a lantern and a book*). Monsieur de Molière! (*He vanishes.*)

MOLIÈRE. Yes. (*He vanishes, and soon after his disappearance a rumble of laughter is heard.*)

The portière leading into the dressing room with the green lantern moves aside and Armande *appears. Her facial features are beautiful and reminiscent of* Madeleine. *She is seventeen. She tries to slip past* La Grange.

LA GRANGE. Stop!

ARMANDE. Oh, it's you, dear *régistre*. Why are you hiding here like a mouse! I was looking at the king! But I'm in a hurry.

LA GRANGE. You'll have time. He's on stage. Why do you call me *régistre?* Maybe I don't like a nickname like that.

ARMANDE. Dear Monsieur La Grange! The entire troupe respects you and your manuscript record. But, if you like, I'll stop calling you that.

LA GRANGE. I have been waiting for you.

ARMANDE. Why?

LA GRANGE. Today is the seventeenth, and there—I've put a little black cross in the register.

ARMANDE. Did something happen then or did someone in the troupe die?

LA GRANGE. It is an evil, black evening which I have marked. Refuse him.

ARMANDE. Monsieur La Grange, who gave you the right to interfere in my affairs?

LA GRANGE. Evil words. I implore you, don't marry him!

ARMANDE. Ah, you are in love with me?

Music is heard hollowly behind the curtain.

LA GRANGE. No, I don't like you.

ARMANDE. Let me by, sir.

LA GRANGE. No. You don't have any right to marry him. You are so young! I appeal to your better feelings!

ARMANDE. I swear, everyone in the troupe has lost his senses. What business is this of yours?

LA GRANGE. I cannot tell you, but it is a great sin.

ARMANDE. Ah, the gossip about my sister? I've heard it. Nonsense! And even if they did have an affair, what do I care? (*She makes an attempt to push* La Grange *aside and get past.*)

LA GRANGE. Stop! Refuse him. No? Well I'll run you through then! (*He takes out his sword.*)

ARMANDE. You crazy murderer! I . . .

LA GRANGE. What's driving you to unhappiness? Why you don't love him. You're a little girl, but he . . .

ARMANDE. No, I love him.

LA GRANGE. Refuse him.

ARMANDE. *Régistre,* I cannot. I am having a liaison with him and . . . (*She whispers in* La Grange's *ear.*)

LA GRANGE (*puts away his sword*). Go on, I won't hold you any longer.

ARMANDE (*passing by*). You are a man of violence. Because you threatened me, you will be repugnant to me.

LA GRANGE (*upset*). Forgive me, I wanted to save you. Forgive me. (*He wraps himself in his cloak and exits, taking his lantern.*)

ARMANDE (*in* Molière's *dressing room*). Monstrous, monstrous!

MOLIÈRE (*appears*). Ah! . . .

ARMANDE. Maître, everyone is against me!

MOLIÈRE (*embraces her, and at the same instant* Bouton *appears*). Oh dammit! (*To* Bouton.) Listen—go check the candles in the parterre.

BOUTON. I've just come from there.

MOLIÈRE. Then listen—go to the buffet woman and bring me a decanter of wine.

BOUTON. I bought it already. There it is.

MOLIÈRE (*softly*). Then listen—simply get the hell out of here and go somewhere else.

BOUTON. You should have started with that right off. (*He goes.*) Eh, he, he . . . (*From the door.*) Maître, tell me, please, how old are you?

MOLIÈRE. What is that supposed to mean?

BOUTON. The Cavalry Guards asked me.

MOLIÈRE. Get out!

Bouton *exits.*

(*Locking the door after him.*) Kiss me.

ARMANDE (*hangs on his neck*). That nose, you've still got the nose on. I can't get under it.

Molière *takes off the nose and wig, kisses* Armande.

(*She whispers to him.*) You know, I . . . (*She whispers something in his ear.*)

MOLIÈRE. My little girl . . . (*Thinks.*) Now it's not frightening. I have decided. (*He leads her up to the crucifix.*) Swear that you love me.

ARMANDE. I do, I do, I do.

MOLIÈRE. You won't deceive me? Do you see, I already have wrinkles, I'm beginning to get gray. I'm surrounded by enemies, and shame would kill me . . .

ARMANDE. No, no! How can you say that?

MOLIÈRE. I want to live another lifetime! With you! But don't worry, I'll pay for it, I will pay. I will create you! You will become the star, a great actress! That is my dream and no doubt it will be so. But remember, if you don't keep your oath, you will deprive me of everything.

ARMANDE. I don't see the wrinkles on your face. You are so bold and so great that you cannot have wrinkles. You are Jean . . .

MOLIÈRE. I am Baptiste . . .

ARMANDE. You are Molière! (*She kisses him.*)

MOLIÈRE (*laughs, then says triumphantly*). Tomorrow we will be married. True, I will have to suffer much because of it . . .

> *The distant rumble of applause is heard. Someone knocks at the door.*

Oh, what a life!

> *The knock is repeated.*

We will not be able to meet at home, at Madeleine's today. So here's what we'll do: when the theater lights are put out, come to the side door in the garden and wait for me; I'll lead you in here. There is no moon.

> *The knocking turns into pounding.*

BOUTON (*howls on the other side of the door*). Maître . . . Maître . . .

> Molière *opens the door. Enter* Bouton, La Grange, *and* One-Eye—*the latter wearing the uniform of the Black Musketeers and a slanting black bandage over his face.*

ONE-EYE. Monsieur de Molière?

MOLIÈRE. Your most obedient servant.

ONE-EYE. The king has ordered me to pay you for his seat in the theater—thirty sous. (*He hands him the money on a pillow.*)

> Molière *kisses the coins.*

ONE-EYE. But in view of the fact that you labored for the king more than required by the program, he also ordered me to give you something extra for the ticket—because of the poem which you composed and recited to the king. Here are 5000 livres. (*He hands him a bag.*)

MOLIÈRE. Oh, my king! (*To La Grange.*) Five hundred livres for me, and divide the rest equally among the actors of the theater and pass it out to them.

LA GRANGE. I thank you in the name of the actors. (*He takes the bag and exits.*)

In the distance a military victory march flies though the air.

MOLIÈRE. Excuse me, sir. The king is leaving. (*He runs out.*)

ONE-EYE (*to* Armande). Mademoiselle, I am very happy that chance ... ha ... ha ... has given me the opportunity ... Captain d'Orsini of the Black Musketeers.

ARMANDE (*sitting down*). Armande Béjart. Are you the renowned swordsman who can run anyone through?

ONE-EYE. Ha, ha ... Without doubt, mademoiselle, you act in this troupe?

BOUTON. It's started. Oh, my frivolous maître!

ONE-EYE (*looking at the lace on* Bouton's *pants in amazement*). Did you say something to me, my dear fellow?

BOUTON. No, sir.

ONE-EYE. You apparently have the habit of talking to yourself.

BOUTON. Precisely so, sir. You know, once I talked to myself in a dream.

ONE-EYE. What are you saying?

BOUTON. I swear to God. And, just imagine it, what a curious ...

ONE-EYE. What kind of devil is he? Start praying ... (*To* Armande.) Mademoiselle, your face ...

BOUTON (*interrupting*). I screamed wildly in the dream. The eight best doctors in Limoges treated me ...

ONE-EYE. And they helped you, I hope?

BOUTON. No, sir. They bled me eight times in three days, after which I laid down and remained motionless, taking the last sacrament constantly.

ONE-EYE (*sadly*). You are an eccentric, my dear fellow. Start praying ... (*To* Armande.) I flatter myself, mademoiselle ... Who is he?

ARMANDE. Oh, sir, that's the candle snuffer, Jean-Jacques Bouton.

ONE-EYE (*with a note of reproach*). My dear man, some other time I'll be glad to hear about how you howled in your sleep.

Molière *enters.*

I am your obedient servant. I must hurry to overtake the king.

One-Eye *exits.*

ARMANDE. Goodbye, maître.

MOLIÈRE (*seeing her off*). There is no moon; I will be waiting. (*To Bouton.*) Ask Mademoiselle Madeleine Béjart in to see me. Put out the lights. Go home.

Bouton *exits.* Molière *changes clothes.* Madeleine *enters, her make-up off.*

MOLIÈRE. Madeleine, there is a very important matter.

Madeleine *grabs her heart, sits down.*

I want to get married.

MADELEINE (*in a dead voice*). To whom?

MOLIÈRE. Your sister.

MADELEINE. I implore you, tell me you are joking.

MOLIÈRE. I assure you I am not.

The lights in the theater begin going out.

MADELEINE. And I?

MOLIÈRE. What do you mean, Madeleine, we are tied by the closest friendship; you are a faithful comrade, but there has been no love between us for a long time . . .

MADELEINE. Do you remember how you were in prison twenty years ago? Who brought you food?

MOLIÈRE. You did.

MADELEINE. And who has been taking care of you for twenty years?

MOLIÈRE. You have, you.

MADELEINE. No one drives away a dog who has guarded the house all its life. But you, Molière, you can do it. You are a terrible man, Molière, I am afraid of you.

MOLIÈRE. Don't torment me. Passion has taken possession of me.

MADELEINE (*suddenly gets down on her knees, crawls over to* Molière). Well? Change your decision anyway, Molière. Let's behave as if this conversation had never taken place. Well? Let's go home, you'll light a candle, I will come to you . . . You will read me the third act of *Tartuffe*. All right? (*Stammeringly.*) In my opinion it is a work of genius . . . And if you need someone with whom to consult, whom will you have, Molière? Why she's just a little girl . . . You know, Jean Baptiste, you've gotten old; there—your temple is gray . . . You love a hot water bottle for warmth. I'll fix everything up for you . . . Imagine, the candle is burning . . . We'll light a fire in the fireplace, and everything will be wonderful. And if . . . if you really cannot . . . oh, I know you . . . Look at Rivale . . . Is she really so bad? What a body! . . . Well? I won't say a word . . .

MOLIÈRE. Come to your senses. What are you saying? What role are you assuming? (*He sadly wipes off sweat.*)

MADELEINE (*standing up, in a fury*). Anyone you want, only not Armande! Oh, I curse the day I brought her to Paris!

MOLIÈRE. Quiet, Madeleine, quiet. I beg of you. (*In a whisper.*) I have to marry her . . . It's too late. It's my duty. Do you understand?

MADELEINE. Oh, so that's it. God, my God! (*Pause.*) I won't fight any more, I haven't the strength. I'll let you go. (*Pause.*) Molière, I'm sorry for you.

MOLIÈRE. You won't deny me your friendship?

MADELEINE. Don't come near me, I implore you! (*Pause.*) So . . . I am leaving the troupe.

MOLIÈRE. You're taking revenge?

MADELEINE. God is my witness, no. Today was my last performance. I am tired . . . (*She smiles.*) I will be going to church often.

MOLIÈRE. You are adamant. The theater will give you a pension. You've earned it.

MADELEINE. Yes . . .

MOLIÈRE. When your grief eases, I believe that you'll make up and see me again.

MADELEINE. No.

MOLIÈRE. Don't you want to see Armande either?

MADELEINE. I will see Armande. Armande must know nothing. Understand? Nothing.

MOLIÈRE. Yes . . .

The lights go out everywhere.

(*He lights a lantern.*) It's late, let's go, I'll take you home.

MADELEINE. No, thank you, that's not necessary. Let me sit here in your room for a few minutes ...

MOLIÈRE. But you ...

MADELEINE. I'll leave soon, don't worry. Go on.

MOLIÈRE (*wraps himself in a cloak*). Farewell. (*He exits.*)

> Madeleine *sits by the holy lamp, thinks, mutters. The light of a lantern appears through the light in the curtain.* La Grange *enters.*

LA GRANGE (*in a solemn voice*). Who has stayed in the theater after the performance. Who's here. Is it you, Mademoiselle Béjart? It's happened, yes? I know.

MADELEINE. I am thinking, *régistre*.

Pause.

LA GRANGE. And you didn't have the strength to confess to him?

MADELEINE. It's too late. I can't tell him now. It's better for me to be unhappy alone, and not all three of us. (*Pause.*) You are a knight, Varlet, and I told the secret to you alone.

LA GRANGE. Mademoiselle Béjart, I am proud of your trust. I attempted to stop her, but I did not succeed. No one will ever know. Let us go, I will accompany you.

MADELEINE. No, thank you, I want to think alone. (*She gets up.*) Varlet (*she smiles*), I have left the stage today. Farewell. (*She goes.*)

LA GRANGE. And you still don't want me to accompany you?

MADELEINE. No. Continue your rounds. (*She vanishes.*)

LA GRANGE (*reaches the place where he was sitting in the beginning. He stands the lantern on the table, is illuminated by the green light, opens his book, speaks, and writes*). February seventeenth. A command performance. As a sign of this honor I am drawing in a lily. After the performance I found Madeleine Béjart in the dark, suffering. She has left the stage ... (*He puts the pen down.*) The reason? There has been a terrible event in the theater—Jean Baptiste Poquelin de Molière, not knowing that Armande is not the sister—but the daughter—of Mademoiselle Madeleine Béjart, has married her. . . . This cannot be written down, but as a sign of the horror, I will put in a black cross. And none of our descendants will ever guess. An end to the seventeenth. (*He takes the lantern and exits.*)

For some time there is darkness and silence, then light appears in the cracks of the harpsichord, a musical sound is heard in its hinges. The top raises up, and out of the harpsichord steps Moirron, *eyes darting around like a thief's. He is a boy of about fifteen with an unusually handsome, spoiled, and exhausted face. He is ragged, dirty.*

MOIRRON. They've gone, they've gone. May you all go to hell, devils, demons . . . (*He snivels.*) I'm an unlucky lad, a dirty . . . I haven't slept for two days . . . I never get to sleep . . . (*He begins to sob, sets up a lantern, falls to the floor, falls asleep.*)

A pause. Then the light of a small lantern flows in, and stealthily Molière *leads* Armande *in. She is wearing a dark cloak.* Armande *shrieks.* Moirron *wakes up instantly; there is horror on his face, he trembles.*

MOLIÈRE (*menacingly*). Confess, who are you?

MOIRRON. Monsieur Director, don't stab me, I'm not a thief; I am Zacharie, the unfortunate Moirron . . .

MOLIÈRE (*bursting into laughter*). I understand! Ah, the damned Charlatan!

CURTAIN

ACT II

THE KING'S RECEPTION ROOM. *A multitude of lights everywhere. A white staircase leads somewhere unknown. At a card table the* MARQUIS DE LESSAC *is playing cards with* LOUIS. *A crowd of* COURTIERS *dressed in extraordinary luxury is watching* LESSAC. *There is a heap of gold in front of him; gold coins are lying on the carpet too. Sweat is pouring from* LESSAC's *face. Only* LOUIS *is seated, all the rest are standing. All are without hats.* LOUIS *is wearing the uniform of a White Musketeer, a dashingly creased hat with a white feather in it, a medallion cross on his chest, gold spurs, a sword.* ONE-EYE *is standing behind the table playing the king's hand. Also standing right beside him is a* MUSKETEER *with a musket who never takes his eyes off* LOUIS.

LESSAC. Three knaves, three kings.
LOUIS What is it, please.
ONE-EYE (*suddenly*). Beg pardon, Sire. These are marked cards, I swear it. Start praying!

The Courtiers *freeze. A pause.*

LOUIS. You came to play against me with marked cards?
LESSAC. Yes, precisely so, Your Majesty. The impoverishment of my estate . . .
LOUIS (*to* One-Eye). Tell me, Marquis, according to the rules of card playing, what should I do in such a peculiar case as this?
ONE-EYE. Sire, you may strike him in the face with a candleholder. That is the first thing . . .
LOUIS. What an unpleasant rule! (*Taking up a candelabra.*) This candleholder weighs fifteen pounds . . . I suppose one should use a light one.

ONE-EYE. Allow me.

LOUIS. No, don't bother. And second, you say ...

COURTIERS (*in a chorus, with rage*). Curse him like a dog!

LOUIS. Ah, fine. Be so kind, send for that fellow—where is he?

> *The* Courtiers *rush in various directions. Voices: "The cobbler! The king wants the Honest Cobbler!"*

(*To* Lessac.) And tell me, how is it done?

LESSAC. With the fingernail, Your Majesty. For example, I put little zeroes on the queens.

LOUIS (*with curiosity*). And on the knaves?

LESSAC. Slanting crosses, Sire.

LOUIS. Extremely interesting. And how does the law view such actions?

LESSAC (*having thought a little*). Negatively, Your Majesty.

LOUIS (*sympathetically*). And what can be done to you for this?

LESSAC (*having thought a little*). I could be put in a dungeon.

HONEST COBBLER (*enters with a lot of noise*). I'm coming, I'm running, I'm flying, I've arrived. Here I am. Hello, Your Majesty, Great Monarch, what has happened? Who must I curse?

LOUIS. Honest cobbler, the Marquis here sat down to play me using marked cards.

HONEST COBBLER (*crushed, to* Lessac). Why you ... Why what were you? ... Why have you gone nuts or what? ... Why at the market they smash your mug in for that kind of trick.—Did I give him a good going over, Your Highness?

LOUIS. Thank you.

HONEST COBBLER. Can I have an apple?

LOUIS. Please do. Marquis de Lessac, take your winnings.

> Lessac *crams his pockets with gold.*

HONEST COBBLER (*upset*). Your Majesty, what is this ... are you laughing?!

LOUIS (*into space*). Duke, if it is not too much trouble for you, put the Marquis de Lessac in the dungeon for one month. Give him a candle and a deck of cards while he's there—let him draw little crosses and zeroes on it. Then pack him off to his estate—along with the money. (*To* Lessac.) Get it in order. And one other thing —don't ever play cards again; I have a premonition that you will not be so lucky the next time.

LESSAC. Oh, Sire . . .

A voice: "Guard!" Lessac is led away.

HONEST COBBLER. Fly out of the palace!

ONE-EYE. The s-scoundrel!

The room servants bustle about, and as if out of the earth a table appears in front of Louis, *on it a place setting for one.*

CHARRON (*rises up near the fireplace*). Your Majesty, allow me to introduce you to an itinerant preacher, Father Barthèlemy.

LOUIS (*starting to eat*). I love all of my subjects, including itinerants. Introduce him to me, archbishop.

Strange singing is heard while he is still outside the door. The door opens and Father Barthèlemy *appears. He is barefoot, in rags. There is a rope tied around his waist; his eyes are insane.*

BARTHÈLEMY (*dances a jig, sings*). We are fools of Christ.

Everyone is surprised except Louis. Brother Fidelity (*a somberly pious face with a long nose, wearing dark clothes*) *comes out of the crowd of* Courtiers *and sidles up to* Charron.

ONE-EYE (*looking at* Barthèlemy, *softly*). Start praying—you ghastly . . .

BARTHÈLEMY. Most Glorious Ruler in the world! I have come to you to inform you that the Anti-Christ has appeared in your realm.

The Courtiers' *faces look stupefied.*

This atheist, this poisonous worm that is gnawing away at the base of your throne bears the name Jean Baptiste Molière. Burn him on the square along with his blasphemous work *Tartuffe.* The whole world of true sons of the Church demands this.

At the word "demands" Brother Fidelity *grabs his head.*
Charron's *face changes.*

Louis. Demands? From whom does it demand this?
Barthèlemy. From you, Sire.
Louis. From me? Archbishop, they are demanding something of
me now.
Charron. Forgive me, Sire. He's obviously out of his mind today.
And I didn't know. It's my fault.
Louis (*into space*). Duke, if it is not too much trouble for you, put
Father Barthèlemy in the dungeon for three months.
Barthèlemy (*shouts*). It is because of the Anti-Christ that I'm
suffering.

Commotion—and Father Barthèlemy *disappears as if he
were never there.* Louis *eats.*

Louis. Archbishop, approach me. I wish to speak privately with you.

The whole crowd of Courtiers *retreats onto the staircase.
The* Musketeer *retreats, and* Louis *is alone with* Charron.

Is he a fool, half-mad?
Charron (*firmly*). Yes, Your Majesty, he is half-mad; but he has
the heart of a true servant of God.
Louis. Archbishop, do you find this Molière dangerous?
Charron (*firmly*). Sire, he is Satan.
Louis. Hm. This means you share Barthèlemy's opinion?
Charron. Yes, Sire, I share it. Sire, hear me out. Nothing has dark-
ened your cloudless and victorious reign, nor will it be darkened
as long as you love . . .
Louis. Whom?
Charron. God.
Louis (*taking off his hat*). I love Him.
Charron (*raising his hand*). He is there, you are on earth, and there
is no one else.
Louis. Yes.
Charron. Sire, there are no limits to your power and there never
will be as long as the light of religion rests upon your realm.

Louis. I love religion.

Charron. So, Sire, together with the blissfully insane Barthèlemy I ask you to intercede for it.

Louis. You find that he has offended religion?

Charron. Yes, Sire.

Louis. The presumptuous actor is talented. Very well, archbishop, I will intercede for it . . . But . . . (*lowering his voice*), I will try to reform him. He can magnify the glory of my reign. But if he does one more presumptuous thing, I will punish him. (*Pause.*) That blissfully insane one of yours, does he love the king?

Charron. Yes, Sire.

Louis. Archbishop, let the monk out after three days, but make sure he knows that when conversing with the king of France it is forbidden to utter the word "demand."

Charron. May God bless you, Sire, and may He bring your punishing hand down on the atheist.

A voice: "Your Majesty's servant, Monsieur de Molière."

Louis. Invite him in.

Molière (*enters, bows to Louis at a distance, walks past the* Courtiers *who display intense attention. He has grown much older; his face is sick and gray*). Sire!

Louis. Monsieur de Molière, I am having dinner, you have no objections?

Molière. Oh, Sire!

Louis. And will you have some with me? (*Into space.*) A chair, dishes.

Molière (*turning pale*). Your Majesty, I cannot accept this honor. Allow me not to.

A chair appears, and Molière *sits on the very edge.*

Louis. How do you like chicken?

Molière. My favorite dish, Sire. (*Imploringly.*) Allow me to stand.

Louis. Go ahead and eat. How is my godchild?

Molière. To my great sorrow, Sire, the baby has died.

Louis. And the second one?

Molière. My children do not live long, Sire.

LOUIS. One should not get depressed.

MOLIÈRE. Your Majesty, never before in France has there been an occasion when anyone dined with you. I am worried . . .

LOUIS. France, Monsieur de Molière, is sitting in a chair in front of you. It is eating chicken, and it is not worried.

MOLIÈRE. Oh, Sire, you are the only one in the whole world who can say such a thing.

LOUIS. Tell me, what present will your talented pen make to the king in the near future?

MOLIÈRE. Sire . . . Something which can . . . serve . . . (*He gets agitated.*)

LOUIS. You write wittily. But one must realize that there are themes which must be touched with caution. And agree, in your *Tartuffe* you were incautious. Men of the cloth must be respected. I hope that my writer cannot be an atheist.

MOLIÈRE (*frightened*). My goodness, no . . . Your Majesty . . .

LOUIS. Since I am firmly convinced that in the future your work will take the correct path, I am giving you permission to stage your play *Tartuffe* in the Palais Royal.

MOLIÈRE (*a strange state coming over him*). I love you, my king! (*Agitated.*) Where is Archbishop Charron? Do you hear? Do you hear?

> Louis *stands up. A voice: "The king has finished his dinner."*

LOUIS (*to* Molière). Today you are going to get my bed ready for me.

> Molière *grabs two candelabras from the table and walks ahead.* Louis *follows him and—as if a wind were blowing— everyone in front of him moves aside.*

MOLIÈRE (*shouts in a monotone*). Make way for the king! Make way for the king! (*Going up the staircase, shouts into emptiness.*) Look, archbishop, you can't touch me! Make way for the king!

> *Trumpets blast up above.*

Tartuffe has been allowed! (*He disappears with* Louis.)

All of the courtiers exit and only Charron *and* Brother Fidelity *are left, both black.*

CHARRON (*by the staircase*). No. The king will not reform you. Almighty God, arm me and lead me in the footsteps of the atheist so that I can get him! (*Pause.*) And he will fall from this staircase! (*Pause.*) Approach me, Brother Fidelity.

Brother Fidelity *approaches* Charron.

Brother Fidelity, what did you do that for? You sent me a half-mad man. I believed you when you said he would make an impression on the king.

BROTHER FIDELITY. Who could know he would utter the word "demand"?

CHARRON. Demand!

BROTHER FIDELITY. Demand!! (*Pause.*)

CHARRON. Did you find the woman?

BROTHER FIDELITY. Yes, archbishop, everything is ready. She sent a note and will bring him.

CHARRON. Will he come?

BROTHER FIDELITY. For the woman? Oh, rest assured of that!

One-Eye *appears at the top of the staircase.* Charron *and* Brother Fidelity *disappear.*

ONE-EYE (*is merry in this loneliness*). The priest caught the Anti-Christ—he caught three months in the dungeon! Ah, God in Heaven, start pr . . .

HONEST COBBLER (*appearing from under the staircase*). Are you "Start Praying?"

ONE-EYE. Well, let's say I am. You can simply call me Marquis d'Orsini. What do you want?

HONEST COBBLER. I have a note for you.

ONE-EYE. From whom?

HONEST COBBLER. Who knows? I met her in the park, and she was wearing a mask.

ONE-EYE (*reading the note*). Hm, what sort of woman was she?

HONEST COBBLER (*studying the note*). Of loose behavior, I imagine.

ONE-EYE. Why?

HONEST COBBLER. Because she writes notes.

ONE-EYE. Idiot.

HONEST COBBLER. What are you barking about?

ONE-EYE. Did she have a good figure?

HONEST COBBLER. Well, you'll find that out for yourself.

ONE-EYE. You're right. (*He exits thoughtfully.*)

The lights begin to go out, and like ghosts dark Musketeers appear at the doors. A drawn-out voice from the top of the stairs: "The king is sleeping!" Another voice, in the distance: "The king is sleeping!" A third voice in the underground, mysteriously: "The king is sleeping!"

HONEST COBBLER. I'll go to sleep too.

He lies down on the card table, wraps himself in a crested portière so that only his monstrous boots stick out. The palace floats away into the darkness and disappears . . . and Molière's apartment rises up. Daytime. The harpsichord is open. Moirron, dressed up luxuriously, a very handsome man of about twenty-two, is playing tenderly. Armande is sitting in an armchair listening, without taking her eyes off him. Moirron finishes playing.

MOIRRON. What do you think of the way I play, mama?

ARMANDE. Monsieur Moirron, I have already asked you not to call me "mama."

MOIRRON. First of all, madame, I am not Moirron, but Monsieur de Moirron. That's what! He, he. Ho, ho.

ARMANDE. And I suppose that you got your title by sitting at the harpsichord.

MOIRRON. Let's forget the harpsichord. It has been covered with the dust of oblivion. That was long ago. *Now* I am a renowned actor whom Paris applauds. He, he. Ho, ho.

ARMANDE. And I advise you not to forget that you are obliged to my husband for that. He dragged you out of the harpsichord by your dirty ear.

MOIRRON. Not by the ear, but by my feet—which were no less dirty.

Father is a decent sort, no doubt about that, but he's as jealous as
Satan, and he has a terrible personality.

ARMANDE. I can congratulate my husband. He's adopted an amazingly brazen son.

MOIRRON. True, I am somewhat brazen, it is so. Such is my personality . . . But I am an actor! No actor in Paris is my equal! (*He
gets excessively merry, like a person who is just asking for bad
luck.*)

ARMANDE. Oh, what impudence! And Molière?

MOIRRON. What can I say? . . . There are three of us: the maître
and I . . .

ARMANDE. And who is the third?

MOIRRON. You, mama. You, my renowned actress. You, Psyche.
(*Softly accompanies himself, declaims.*) Spring in the forest . . .
Amour flies . . .[2]

ARMANDE (*hollowly*). Move away from me.

MOIRRON (*with his left arm he embraces* Armande, *with his right
hand accompanies*). How graceful your figure . . . My hero
Amour . . .

ARMANDE. Carries a quiver . . . Threatens with an arrow . . . (*Nervously.*) Where is Bouton?

MOIRRON. Don't be afraid, your faithful servant is at the market.

ARMANDE (*declaims*). The Goddess Venus sent love. Cling to me,
my love, make my blood foam. (*Shudders, closes her eyes.*) Good-
for-nothing. (*Nervously.*) Where is Renée?

MOIRRON. The old woman is in the kitchen. Mama, let's go into
my room.

ARMANDE. Not for anything, I swear by the Holy Virgin.

MOIRRON. Let's go to my room.

ARMANDE. You are the most dangerous man in Paris. May the hour
be cursed when they dug you out of the harpsichord.

MOIRRON. Mama, let's go . . .

ARMANDE. I swear by the Virgin, no. (*She stands up.*) I won't go!
(*She goes, disappears behind the door with* Moirron.)

---

2. Lines from Molière's *Psyché,* a ballet written in collaboration with La
Fontaine, Corneille, and others.

Moirron *locks the door with a key.*

ARMANDE. Why are you locking the door, why? (*Hollowly.*) You will ruin me!

A pause. Bouton *enters with a basket full of vegetables, carrot tails sticking out.*

BOUTON (*listens, puts the basket on the floor*). Strange! (*He takes off his shoes, sneaks to the door, listens.*) Oh, the thief! . . . But, gentlemen, I have no business here . . . I haven't seen anything, I haven't heard anything, and I don't know anything . . . King of Heaven, here he comes! (*He hides, leaving the basket and shoes on the floor.*)

Molière *enters, puts down his cane and hat, looks at the shoes in a puzzled way.*

MOLIÈRE. Armande!

In a moment the key turns in the lock. Molière *rushes through the door. Behind the door* Armande *screams, noise behind the door, then* Moirron *runs out holding his wig in his hand.*

MOIRRON. How dare you?!

MOLIÈRE (*running out after him*). Scoundrel! (*Catching his breath.*) I don't believe it, I don't believe my eyes! (*He lowers himself into a chair. The key turns in the lock.*)

ARMANDE (*behind the door*). Jean Baptiste, come to your senses!

Bouton *peeks through the door and vanishes.*

MOLIÈRE (*threatens toward the door with his fist*). So you ate my bread, and in return for that you have dishonored me?

MOIRRON. You dared to strike me! Be careful! (*He takes the handle of his sword in his hand.*)

MOLIÈRE. Get your hand off that immediately, you damned snake!

MOIRRON. I challenge you.

MOLIÈRE. Me! (*Pause.*) Get out of my house!

MOIRRON. You are crazy, that's what, father. A perfect Sganarelle.

MOLIÈRE. You honorless tramp! I have sheltered you, but I will fling you back into the abyss too. You will play at country fairs. Zacharie Moirron, from this date on you will not serve in the Palais Royal troupe. Go.

MOIRRON. What, you're kicking me out of the troupe?

MOLIÈRE. Go away, you adopted thief.

ARMANDE (*behind the door, desperately*). Molière!

MOIRRON (*losing control*). Father, you're imagining things—we were rehearsing *Psyche* . . . Don't you know your own text? . . . Why are you wrecking my life?

MOLIÈRE. Go away, or I really will run you through with my sword.

MOIRRON. So be it. (*Pause.*) It would be highly interesting to know just who is going to play Don Juan? Maybe La Grange? Ho, ho! (*Pause.*) But be careful, Monsieur de Molière, that you don't repent your insanity. (*Pause.*) I know your secret, Monsieur Molière.

Molière *bursts out laughing.*

Have you forgotten Madame Madeleine Béjart? Yes? She is near death . . . She keeps praying . . . And, dear sir, there is a king in France.

MOLIÈRE. You despicable, yellow-mouthed liar, what are you babbling about?

MOIRRON. Babbling? I will go straight from here to the archbishop.

MOLIÈRE (*laughs*). Well, thanks for the betrayal. Now I know you. But bear in mind the fact that until what you just said my heart might still have softened, but after that—never! Be off, you pitiful fool!

MOIRRON (*from the door*). You damned Sganarelle!

Molière *grabs a pistol from the wall, and Moirron disappears.*

MOLIÈRE (*shakes the door, then talks into the keyhole*). Woman of the streets.

Armande *loudly bursts out crying behind the door.*

Bouton!

Bouton *enters in his socks.*

BOUTON. Sir, I . . .

MOLIÈRE. Pimp!

BOUTON. Sir . . .

MOLIÈRE. What are your shoes doing here?!

BOUTON. Sir, it's . . .

MOLIÈRE. You're lying, I can see by your eyes that you're lying!

BOUTON. Sir, in order to lie, one must at least say something. But I still haven't said anything. I took off my shoes because . . . Do you see the nails? Shoes with heel plates on them, may they be damned . . . I was making such a racket with my feet, do you see; and they were rehearsing and they locked the door to get away from me.

ARMANDE (*behind the door*). Yes!

MOLIÈRE. What is the purpose of the vegetables?

BOUTON. Well, in general the vegetables play no role. They're irrelevant. I just brought them from the market. (*He puts on his shoes.*)

MOLIÈRE. Armande!

Silence.

(*He talks into the keyhole.*) What's wrong with you, do you want to kill me? I have a weak heart . . .

BOUTON (*through the keyhole*). What's wrong with you, do you want to kill him? . . . He has a weak heart . . .

MOLIÈRE. Get out! (*He kicks the basket.* Bouton *disappears.*) Armande . . . (*He sits down on a little bench by the door.*) Have just a little more patience, I will soon free you. I don't want to die in loneliness . . . Armande . . .

Armande *comes out, her eyes tear-stained.*

And can you swear?

ARMANDE. I swear it.

MOLIÈRE. Tell me something.

ARMANDE (*wiping her nose*). A playwright such as you, and at home, at home . . . I don't understand how you can harbor such thoughts. How? What have you done? A scandal all over Paris. Why did you kick Moirron out?

MOLIÈRE. Yes, true. Terrible shame. But you know he *is* a good-for-nothing, a little snake . . . Oh a depraved, depraved lad, and I am afraid for him. He really will start gadding around Paris in desperation, and I struck him . . . Oh, how unpleasant!

ARMANDE. Bring Moirron back, bring him back.

MOLIÈRE. Let him walk around for a day, then I'll bring him back.

CURTAIN

ACT III

A STONE CELLAR *lit by a three-candled chandelier. A table covered with red cloth, on it a book and some sort of manuscripts. At the table sit the* Members of the Cabal of the Holy Writ *wearing masks;* Charron, *without a mask, sits separately in an armchair.*

The door opens, and two gloomy-looking men in black lead in Moirron *with his hands tied and a blindfold over his eyes. They untie his hands and remove the blindfold.*

MOIRRON. Where have I been brought?

CHARRON. That makes no difference, my son. Now, repeat your denunciation in the presence of these honorable brethren.

Moirron is silent.

BROTHER FORCE. Are you a deaf-mute?

MOIRRON. Ahem . . . I . . . Holy Archbishop . . . I didn't hear it very well at the time and . . . I think it would be best if I didn't say anything.

CHARRON. My son, it appears that you slandered Monsieur de Molière to me this morning.

Moirron is silent.

BROTHER FORCE. Answer the archbishop, you graceful piece of garbage.

Silence.

CHARRON. My son, it is with sorrow that I see you have slandered him.

BROTHER FORCE. Lying is harmful, dear actor. It will be necessary to put you in the dungeon, pretty boy, where you will feed the bedbugs for a long time to come. And we are going to move this case along anyway.

MOIRRON (*hoarsely*). I did not slander anyone.

BROTHER FORCE. Don't make me lose my patience—tell us!

Moirron is silent.

Hey!

Two men of even more unpleasant appearance than those who led in Moirron *come out of the doors.*

(*Looking at* Moirron's *shoes.*) You have nice shoes, but there are even nicer ones. (*To the torturers.*) Bring the Spanish boot here.

MOIRRON. You don't have to do that. Several years ago, as a little boy, I began sitting in the Charlatan's harpsichord.

BROTHER FORCE. Why should you get in there?

MOIRRON. I played an inside keyboard. It was a trick, as if it were a harpsichord that played itself.

BROTHER FORCE. Well, then what?

MOIRRON. In the harpsichord . . . No, I can't, Holy Father! I was drunk this morning; I have forgotten what I told you . . .

BROTHER FORCE. This is the last time I will ask you not to stop!

MOIRRON. And . . . at night I heard a voice say that Monsieur de Molière . . . married not the sister of Madeleine Béjart . . . but her daughter . . .

BROTHER FORCE. So whose voice was it?

MOIRRON. I think that I must have imagined it.

BROTHER FORCE. Well then, whose voice did you imagine?

MOIRRON. The actor La Grange.

CHARRON. All right, that's enough, thank you, my friend. You have done your duty honorably. Do not reproach yourself. Every faithful subject of the king and son of the Church should consider it an honor to inform about crimes of which he is aware.

BROTHER FORCE. He's not a bad fellow. At first a didn't like him, but now I see that he's a good Catholic.

CHARRON (*to* Moirron). My friend, you will spend a day or two in quarters where you will be fed and treated well, and then you will go to the king with me.

They blindfold Moirron, *tie his hands, and lead him away.*

And now, brothers, we will have another outsider here, and I will ask Brother Fidelity to talk to him, because he knows my voice.

A knock on the door. Charron *pushes his hood over his face and disappears in the half-darkness.* Brother Fidelity *goes to open the door. An* Unknown Woman *wearing a mask appears, leading* One-Eye *by the arm. His eyes are covered with a scarf.*

ONE-EYE. Enchantress, when will you finally allow me to remove the blindfold? You could have relied on my word. Start praying— it feels damp in your apartment.

UNKNOWN WOMAN in the mask. One more little step, marquis. There . . . Take it off. (*She hides.*)

ONE-EYE (*removes the blindfold, looks around*). Ah! Start praying! (*He instantly snatches out his sword with his right hand, a pistol with his left, and stands with his back to the wall, showing he is very experienced. Pause.*) The tips of swords are sticking out under the cloaks of some of you. A large group of you may kill me, but I warn you that I'll take three of you out of this hole feet first. I am called "Start Praying!" Don't move! Where's the trash that enticed me into this trap?

UNKNOWN WOMAN in the mask (*from the darkness*). I'm here, marquis, but I'm not trash at all . . .

BROTHER FORCE. Fie, marquis, a lady . . .

BROTHER FIDELITY. Please be at ease, no one wishes to attack you.

BROTHER FORCE. Marquis, put away your pistol, it looks like an eye with a hole in it, and it spoils the conversation.

ONE-EYE. Where am I?

BROTHER FIDELITY. In the catacomb of the church.

ONE-EYE. I demand to be let out of here!

BROTHER FIDELITY. The door will be opened any time you wish.

ONE-EYE. In that case why entice me in here. First of all tell me one thing—is this a plot against the king's life?

BROTHER FIDELITY. God forgive you, marquis. The men here are fervent admirers of the king. You are at a secret session of the Cabal of the Holy Writ.

ONE-EYE. Bah! Cabal! I didn't believe that it really existed. What need does it have of me? (*He puts the pistol away.*)

BROTHER FIDELITY. Have a seat, marquis, please.

ONE-EYE. Thanks. (*He sits down.*)

BROTHER FIDELITY. We grieve for you, marquis.

MEMBERS OF THE CABAL (*in a chorus*). We grieve!

ONE-EYE. Well I don't like it when people grieve. Explain your business.

BROTHER FIDELITY. Marquis, we wished to warn you that you are being laughed at at the court.

ONE-EYE. That is a mistake. I am called "Start Praying!"

BROTHER FIDELITY. Who in France does not know of your incomparable skill? That is precisely why they are whispering behind your back.

ONE-EYE (*pounding his sword on the table*). His name!

The Members of the Cabal *cross themselves.*

BROTHER FORCE. Why make such noise, marquis?

BROTHER FIDELITY. The whole court is whispering.

ONE-EYE. Tell me, or I'll lose my patience!

BROTHER FIDELITY. Do you know the basest play of a certain Jean Baptiste Molière, one entitled *Tartuffe?*

ONE-EYE. I don't go to the Palais Royal, but I've heard of it.

BROTHER FIDELITY. In this play the atheist-comedien has sneered at religion and at its servants.

ONE-EYE. What a good-for-nothing!

BROTHER FIDELITY. But it isn't only religion that Molière has offended. Since he hates high society, he has cursed it too. Perhaps you know the play *Don Juan?*

ONE-EYE. I've heard of that too. But what relation is there between d'Orsini and a clown at the Palais Royal?

BROTHER FIDELITY. We have totally accurate information that this scribbler used you, marquis, as the model for his hero, Don Juan.

ONE-EYE (*putting his sword away*). What kind of person is this Don Juan?

BROTHER FORCE. An atheist, a good-for-nothing, a murderer, and, forgive me, marquis, a debaucher of women.

ONE-EYE (*his face changing*). So. I thank you.

BROTHER FIDELITY (*taking a manuscript from the table*). Perhaps you would like to familiarize yourself with the material?

ONE-EYE. No thank you, I'm not interested. Tell me, is there perhaps someone among those present who considers that there is some basis for showing d'Orsini to be so depraved?

BROTHER FIDELITY. Brothers, is there anyone?

Complete denial by the Members of the Cabal.

No one. And so, you can see the kind of motives by which we were guided when we invited you to this secret session in such a strange manner. The men here, marquis, are from your circle; and you yourself can understand how unpleasant it is for us . . .

ONE-EYE. Absolutely. I thank you.

BROTHER FIDELITY. Esteemed marquis, we rely on your keeping what has been said today between us, just as we assume that no one will know that we have troubled you.

ONE-EYE. Don't worry, sir. Where is the woman who brought me?

UNKNOWN WOMAN in the mask (*comes out*). Here I am.

ONE-EYE (*gloomily*). I beg your pardon, madame.

UNKNOWN WOMAN. God will pardon you, marquis, and I pardon you. Please come with me; I will take you to the place where we met. If you will allow it, we will cover your eyes again, because this honored society does not wish anyone to know the way to the place of its sessions.

ONE-EYE. Well, if it is so essential . . .

One-Eye's *eyes are covered, and the* Unknown Woman *leads him away. The door closes.*

CHARRON (*taking off his hood and coming out of the dark*). The session of the Cabal of the Holy Writ is closed. Let us pray, brothers.

MEMBERS OF THE CABAL (*stand and sing softly*). *Laudamus tibi, Domine, rex aeternae gloriae* . . .

. . . An immense cathedral. The archbishop's small con-
fessional; in it there are candles. Two dark figures walk
past, a hoarse whisper is heard: "Have you seen Tartuffe?
Have you seen Tartuffe?*"* Armande *and* La Grange *ap-*
pear, they are leading Madeleine *by the arm. She is gray, ill.*

MADELEINE. Thank you, Armande. Thank you, too, Varlet, my devoted friend.

The organ begins to play.

LA GRANGE. We'll wait for you here. Here is the archbishop's door.

Madeleine *crosses herself, and stepping softly she enters the*
confessional. Armande *and* La Grange *wrap themselves in*
dark cloaks, sit on a bench, and the darkness swallows
them up.

CHARRON (*rises up in the confessional*). Come closer, my daughter.
You are Madeleine Béjart?

The organ falls silent.

I have learned that you are one of the most pious daughters of
this cathedral, and you are dear to my heart. I decided to hear your
confession myself.

MADELEINE. What an honor for me, sinner that I am. (*She kisses*
Charron's *hands.*)

CHARRON (*blessing* Madeleine, *he covers her head with the veil*).
Are you ill, poor woman?

MADELEINE. I am, Holy Father.

CHARRON (*sorrowfully*). What's wrong, do you want to leave this
world?

MADELEINE. I want to leave this world.

The organ high up above.

CHARRON. What illness do you have?

MADELEINE. The doctors say that my blood has been ruined, and I
see the Devil and I am afraid of him.

CHARRON. Poor woman! What are you doing to save yourself from
the Devil?

MADELEINE. I pray.

The organ falls silent.

CHARRON. For that the Lord will raise you up to love you.

MADELEINE. And He won't forget me?

CHARRON. No. How have you sinned, tell me.

MADELEINE. I sinned all my life, Father. I was a great debauchée, I lied, for many years I was an actress and seduced everyone.

CHARRON. What especially burdensome sin do you remember?

MADELEINE. I don't remember any, Holy Father.

CHARRON (*sadly*). People are insane. You will arrive with a red-hot nail in your heart, and when you get *there*, there will no longer be anyone to take it out. Never! Do you understand the meaning of the word "never"?

MADELEINE (*thinks a little*). I do. (*She gets frightened.*) Oh, I am afraid.

CHARRON. And you will see the fires, and between them . . .

MADELEINE. . . . the sentry walks and walks . . .

CHARRON. . . . and he whispers . . . why didn't you leave your sin behind, why did you bring it with you?

MADELEINE. And I will wring my hands, I will cry out to God.

The organ sounds.

CHARRON. But the Lord will not hear you then. And you will hang in chains, and you will put your legs down into the fire . . . And that is what it will be forever. Do you understand the word "forever"?

MADELEINE. I'm afraid to. If I understood, I would die right now. (*She cries out weakly.*) I understand. And if I leave it here?

CHARRON. You will have eternal life.

Children's voices begin to sing.

MADELEINE (*feels around with her hands, as if in the dark*). Where are you, Holy Father?

CHARRON (*hollowly*). I am here . . . I am here! . . .

MADELEINE. I do want eternal life. (*She whispers passionately.*) Long, long ago I lived with two men, and I begot a daughter,

Armande, and all my life I was tormented by not knowing whose she was . . .

CHARRON. Ah, you poor woman . . .

MADELEINE. I gave birth to her in the provinces. And when she grew up I brought her to Paris and passed her off as my sister. And *he,* overwhelmed by passion, came together with her; and I didn't tell him anything, so as not to make him unhappy too. Because of me he has perhaps committed a mortal sin, and cast me into Hell. I want to fly up to the eternal life.

CHARRON. And I, the archbishop, by the power invested in me, absolve and release you.

MADELEINE (*crying from rapture*). Now I can fly?

The organ.

CHARRON. Fly, fly.

The organ falls silent.

Is your daughter here? Call her in, I will forgive her unwitting sin too.

MADELEINE (*coming out of the confessional*). Armande, Armande, my sister, go, the archbishop will bless you too. I am happy! . . . I am happy! . . .

LA GRANGE. I'll put you in the carriage.

MADELEINE. And Armande?

LA GRANGE. I'll come back for her. (*He leads* Madeleine *away into the dark*.)

> Armande *enters the confessional.* Charron *crosses* Armande. *The organ begins to rumble.*

CHARRON. Tell me, do you know who was just in here?

ARMANDE (*is horrified, she suddenly understands everything*). No, no . . . She is my sister, my sister . . .

CHARRON. She is your mother. I forgive you. But run away from him this very day, run.

> *Crying out weakly,* Armande *falls forward and remains motionless on the threshold of the confessional.* Charron *disappears. The organ rumbles.*

LA GRANGE (*returns in the half-darkness*). Armande, don't you feel well?

Darkness. . . . Day. The king's reception room. Wearing a dark shirt decorated with gold, Louis sits at the table. Before him is a dark and exhausted Charron. *The* Honest Cobbler *is sitting on the floor repairing a shoe.*

CHARRON. She confirmed it in her deathbed confession to me, so then I didn't even consider it necessary to interrogate the actor La Grange, Your Majesty—so as not to spread this foul affair. And I have terminated the investigation. Your Majesty, Molière has besmirched his name with this crime. But how does Your Majesty wish to judge it.

LOUIS. I thank you, my archbishop. You have acted correctly. I consider the matter clarified. (*He rings, speaks into space.*) Summon the director of the theater Palais Royal, Monsieur de Molière, immediately. Remove the sentries from these rooms, I am going to talk to him alone. (*To* Charron.) Archbishop, send me this Moirron.

CHARRON. Immediately, Sire. (*Exits.*)

HONEST COBBLER. Great Monarch, is it true that no kingdom can exist without the acts of informers?

LOUIS. Keep quiet, jester, fix the shoe. Don't you like informers?

HONEST COBBLER. Well, what is there to like about them? Such a bastard, Your Majesty!

Moirron enters. His eyes are those of an animal brought to bay; he is frightened and looks as if he has slept in his clothes. Louis, whom he is seeing so closely for the first time, obviously produces a great impression on him.

LOUIS (*politely*). Zacharie Moirron?

MOIRRON. Yes, Your Majesty.

LOUIS. You were the one in the harpsichord?

MOIRRON. It was I, Sire.

LOUIS. Monsieur de Molière adopted you?

Moirron is silent.

I asked you a question.

MOIRRON. Yes.

LOUIS. He taught you the art of acting?

Moirron *is silent.*

I asked you a question.

MOIRRON. He did.

LOUIS. By what motive were you guided when you informed and wrote this denunciation addressed to the king? It says here, "desiring to further justice."

MOIRRON (*mechanically*). Yes, desiring . . .

LOUIS. Is it true that he hit you in the face?

MOIRRON. It is true.

LOUIS. Why?

MOIRRON. His wife was betraying him with me.

LOUIS. So. It will not be essential to report that at the interrogation. You can just say this: for personal reasons. How old are you?

MOIRRON. Twenty-three.

LOUIS. I have some good news to tell you. Your information has been confirmed by the investigation. What reward do you wish to receive from the king? Is it money you want?

MOIRRON (*shudders. Pause*). Your Majesty, allow me to work in the king's Théâtre Burgogne.

LOUIS. No. There is information that you are a poor actor. Impossible.

MOIRRON. I—a poor actor? . . . (*Naively.*) And the Théâtre du Marais?

LOUIS. No, again.

MOIRRON. But what am I to do?

LOUIS. Why do you need this dubious profession of acting? You are a man without a spot on your reputation. If you wish you could be taken into the king's service, in the secret police. Make an application using the king's name. It will be accepted. You may go.

Moirron *goes.*

HONEST COBBLER.. He ought to be hanged, hanged . . .

Louis. Jester! (*He rings.*) Monsieur de Molière!

No sooner has Moirron *disappeared behind the door than* La Grange *appears in the other door, leads in* Molière, *and immediately disappears.* Molière *looks strange: his collar is on crooked, his wig disheveled, his face leaden, his hands are shaking, his sword hangs crooked.*

Molière. Sire . . .

Louis. Why have you come with this guide when you were invited alone, and who is he?

Molière (*smiling with fear*). My faithful pupil, the actor de La Grange brought me. You see, I've had some sort of heart attack, and I could not get here alone . . . I hope that I haven't angered Your Majesty in any way? (*Pause.*) You see, I've been struck by misfortune . . . forgive me for the disorder in my dress. Madeleine Béjart passed away yesterday, and my wife Armande ran away from the house at the same time . . . She abandoned everything . . . Her dresses, imagine it . . . the chest of drawers . . . rings . . . and she left an insane note . . . (*He takes some sort of scrap out of his pocket, stutteringly smiles.*)

Louis. The Holy Archbishop turns out to be right. You are not only a dirty blasphemer of religion in your works, you are a criminal too—an atheist.

Molière *freezes.*

I inform you of my decision in the matter of your marriage: I forbid you to appear at court, I forbid you to play *Tartuffe.* Only so that your troupe will not die of hunger, I am allowing your light comedies to be played at the Palais Royal, but nothing else . . . And from this day you should beware of reminding me of your existence! I am depriving you of the king's patronage.

Molière. Your Majesty, why that's a calamity worse than the block . . . (*Pause.*) Why?!

Louis. Because of the shadow of a scandalous marriage which has been thrown across the king's name.

Molière (*falling into an armchair*). Forgive me . . . I cannot get up . . .

Louis. Go away. The audience is over. (*He exits.*)

La Grange (*glancing in through the door*). What happened?

Molière. The carriage . . . Take me away . . . Call . . .

> La Grange *disappears.*

Madeleine so that I can get her advice . . . but she is dead. What is this?

Honest Cobbler (*sympathetically*). What's happened to you? You don't believe in God, is that it? Eh . . . what a bind you've gotten into. Have an apple.

Molière (*takes the apple mechanically*). Thank you.

> Charron *enters and stops, looks at* Molière *for a long time.* Charron's *eyes glitter with satisfaction.*

(*At the sight of* Charron, Molière *begins to come to life—until this point he has been lying with his chest on the table. He raises himself up, his eyes start to sparkle.*) Ah, Holy Father! Are you satisfied? Was this for *Tartuffe?* I can understand why you have been so quick to take up arms in defense of religion. You are a good guesser, my Holy One. There's no argument about that. My friends sometimes say to me, "You should describe some swine of a monk." And so I depicted you. Because where could one get a better swine than you?

Charron. I grieve for you, because anyone who has taken that path will certainly be on the scaffold, my son.

Molière. Don't you call me your son—because I'm not the son of a devil. (*He takes out his sword.*)

Honest Cobbler. What are you barking about?

Charron (*glittering*). But you won't get as far as the scaffold. (*He looks back menacingly.*)

> And from the door comes One-Eye *with a cane.*

One-Eye (*approaches* Molière *silently and steps on his foot*). Sir, you pushed me and you have not excused yourself. You are a churl!

Molière (*mechanically*). Excuse me . . . (*With effort.*) You pushed me.

ONE-EYE. You are a liar!

MOLIÈRE. How dare you! What do you want of me?!

La Grange *enters at this moment.*

LA GRANGE (*his face changing*). Maître, leave right now, leave! (*Agitated.*) Marquis, Monsier de Molière is unwell.

ONE-EYE. I found him with a sword in his hand. He is well enough. (*To* Molière.) My name is d'Orsini. You, dear sir, are a horse's ass!

MOLIÈRE. I challenge you.

LA GRANGE (*in horror*). Leave. This is "Start Praying!"

CHARRON. Gentlemen, what are you doing in the king's reception room, oh . . .

MOLIÈRE. I challenge you!

ONE-EYE. Things are settled. I won't insult you any more. (*With menacing gaiety.*) May God judge me, great king! (*To* La Grange). You, sir, will be the witness. (*To* Molière.) Give him the instruction concerning your belongings. (*He takes out his sword, tests the tip.*) There are no instructions? (*He calls out in a drawling voice which is not loud.*) Start praying! (*He crosses the air with his sword.*)

CHARRON. Gentlemen, come to your senses! . . . Gentlemen! . . . (*He flies lightly up the staircase and watches the duel from there.*)

LA GRANGE. Cold-blooded murder!

HONEST COBBLER. People are chopping each other up in the king's reception room!

One-Eye *grabs the* Honest Cobbler *by the collar, and he shuts up.* One-Eye *rushes at* Molière; Molière, *waving him off with his sword, hides behind a table.* One-Eye *jumps up on the table.*

LA GRANGE. Throw away the sword, my teacher!

Molière *throws the sword away, falls to the floor.*

ONE-EYE. Pick up that sword!

LA GRANGE (*to* One-Eye). You cannot run through a man who doesn't have a sword in his hand.

ONE-EYE. I won't run him through. (*To* Molière.) Pick up the sword, you miserable coward!

MOLIÈRE. Don't insult me and don't beat me. Somehow there's something I don't understand. You see, I have a sick heart . . . and my wife has abandoned me . . . Her jewelled rings are lying around on the floor . . . she didn't even take her linen . . . calamity . . .

ONE-EYE. I understand none of this!

MOLIÈRE. I cannot comprehend why you have attacked me. Why, I have only seen you twice in my whole life. You brought the money? . . . But that was a long time ago. I am sick . . . please, don't touch me any more . . .

ONE-EYE. I will kill you after your next performance! (*He puts the sword in its scabbard.*)

MOLIÈRE. All right . . . all right . . . it makes no difference . . .

> *The* Honest Cobbler *suddenly tears away from his place and disappears.* La Grange *raises* Molière *from the floor, grabs the sword, and leads* Molière *out.* One-Eye *watches them go.*

CHARRON (*comes down from the staircase, his eyes burning. A pause*). Why didn't you run him through?

ONE-EYE. What business is it of yours? He threw his sword away.

CHARRON. You blockhead!

ONE-EYE. What?! You devil's priest!

CHARRON (*suddenly spits at* One-Eye). Tfui!

> One-Eye *is so startled that he replies by spitting at* Charron. *The door has opened and the agitated* Honest Cobbler *flies in,* Louis *following him. The two quarreling men are so carried away that they do not stop spitting right away. For a long while the four of them stand looking at each other dully.*

LOUIS. Excuse me for interrupting. (*He disappears, closing the door behind him.*)

CURTAIN

ACT IV

MOLIÈRE'S APARTMENT. *Evening. Candles in candelabras. Disorder. Manuscripts are scattered around.* MOLIÈRE *is sitting in a huge arm-chair wearing a nightcap, underwear, and bathrobe.* BOUTON *is in another chair. On the table are two swords and a pistol. On another table is supper with wine, toward which* BOUTON *moves close from time to time.*

Wearing a dark cloak, LA GRANGE *is walking back and forth, making some sort of noise between a moan and a hum.*

LA GRANGE. Oh, the harpsichord . . . the harpsichord . . .

MOLIÈRE. Stop it, La Grange. It's Fate which has come to my house and stolen everything from me.

BOUTON. That is the real truth. I have had a tragic fate too, I have. For example, I was selling pies in Limoges . . . Of course no one was buying them . . . I decided to become an actor, and I fell into your hands . . .

MOLIÈRE. Shut up, Bouton.

BOUTON. I'm shut up.

A bitter pause. Then one can hear the creaking on the stairs. The door opens and Moirron *walks in. He is not wearing a long coat, but some sort of dirty short jacket. He is ragged, unshaven, and half-drunk; he is carrying a lantern in his hand. Those who are sitting shade their eyes with their hands to see him. When they have recognized* Moirron, La Grange *grabs the pistol from the table,* Molière *hits* La Grange *on the arm,* La Grange *fires and hits the ceiling. Not at all surprised,* Moirron *looks apathetically at the spot where the shot has hit. Grabbing at whatever he can,* La

405

Grange *breaks a jar, attacks* Moirron, *knocks him to the floor, and starts to strangle him.*

LA GRANGE. Punish me, oh king, punish . . . (*Roaring.*) Judas!
MOLIÈRE (*like a martyr*). Bouton . . . Bouton . . . (Bouton *and he drag* La Grange *away from* Moirron. *To* La Grange.) Do you want to kill me—with all this shooting and racket . . . What more are you going to do. Do you want to commit a murder in my own apartment?

A pause.

LA GRANGE. Zacharie Moirron, do you know who I am, you cur?

Moirron *nods affirmatively.*

Wherever you go tonight—you should expect death. You won't see the dawn. (*He wraps himself in his cloak and falls silent.*)

Moirron *nods his head affirmatively to* La Grange, *gets down on his knees in front of* Molière *and bows down to the ground.*

MOLIÈRE. Why have you come here, son. My crime has been exposed, so what more can you get out of my house? What will you write to the king about? Or do you suspect that I am a counterfeiter too? Go ahead, search the shelves and closets, I give you my permission.

Moirron *bows down a second time.*

Tell me what you need without any bowing.
MOIRRON. My respected, my precious teacher, you think that I have come to ask forgiveness. No. I am here to reassure you: not later than midnight tonight I will hang myself under your windows, as a result of the fact that my life cannot continue. Here's the rope. (*He takes a rope out of his pocket.*) And here is the note: "I am going to Hell."
MOLIÈRE (*bitterly*). You've really reassured me.
BOUTON (*swallowing a mouthful of wine*). Yes, this is a very difficult situation. A certain philosopher said . . .

MOLIÈRE. Shut up, Bouton.

BOUTON. I am shut up.

MOIRRON. I came to be near you. But even if I remained alive I would not look at Madame Molière even once.

MOLIÈRE. You won't have to look at her, my son, because she has left, and I am alone forever. I have an unrestrained personality— that's why I do things first and think about them only later. And now, having thought and become wiser after what has happened, I forgive you and return you to my house. Come in.

Moirron *begins to cry.*

LA GRANGE (*opening his cloak*). Teacher, you are not a man, not a man. You are a rag that people use to wipe floors with.

MOLIÈRE (*to him*). Impudent puppy! Don't make judgments about things you don't understand. (*A pause. To* Moirron.) Get up, don't wear holes in your trousers.

A pause. Moirron *gets up. A pause.*

Where's your coat?

MOIRRON. I pawned it in a tavern.

MOLIÈRE. For how much?

Moirron *waves his hand.*

MOLIÈRE (*mutters*). That's swinishness—leaving satin coats in taverns. (*To* Bouton.) Redeem the coat. (*To* Moirron.) They say you wandered all over and even dropped in on the king.

MOIRRON (*beating his breast*). And the king said to me: join the secret police, the secret police . . . You are a bad actor, he said . . .

MOLIÈRE. Oh, human heart! The king was mistaken: you are an actor of the first rank, but you're no good for the secret police— you have an unsuitable heart. There's only one thing I regret— that I won't get to act with you very long. They've set the one-eyed dog on me, my son, the musketeer. The king has deprived me of his patronage, and it follows that they will run me through. I'll have to flee.

MOIRRON. My teacher, while I am alive, he won't manage to run you through, believe me! You know how I handle a sword.

LA GRANGE (*sticking his ear out of the cloak*). You handle a sword amazingly well, that's true. But before you go up against "Start Praying," you snivelling scum, you'd better buy yourself a funeral mass at the cathedral.

MOIRRON. I'll run him through from behind.

LA GRANGE. That's your kind of thing.

MOIRRON (*to* Molière). I will be at your side constantly, at home and on the street, night and day, that's why I came.

LA GRANGE. As a secret policeman.

MOLIÈRE (*to* La Grange). Why don't you stuff your mouth full of lace!

MOIRRON. Dear *régistre,* don't insult me, why insult someone who cannot answer you. I should not be touched—I am a man with a stain on his honor. And don't attack me tonight. You'll kill me, they'll hang you, and the Cabal will murder the defenseless maître.

MOLIÈRE. You've become considerably more intelligent since your disappearance from home.

MOIRRON (*to* La Grange). Bear in mind the fact that they have declared the maître an atheist for *Tartuffe.* I was in the Cabal's catacomb . . . It is above the law—that means we should expect anything.

MOLIÈRE. I know. (*He shudders.*) Did someone knock?

MOIRRON. No. (*To* La Grange.) Take the pistol and lantern, let's go stand guard.

> La Grange *and* Moirron *take arms and the lantern and exit. A pause.*

MOLIÈRE. The tyrant, the tyrant . . .

BOUTON. Who are you talking about, maître?

MOLIÈRE. About the king of France . . .

BOUTON. Shut up!

MOLIÈRE. About Louis the Great! The tyrant!

BOUTON. It's all over. We're both as good as hung.

MOLIÈRE. Oh, Bouton, I almost died of fright today. The golden idol, and, would you believe it, his eyes are emerald. My hands were covered with cold sweat. Everything has gone awry, askew, crushing me, and all I can comprehend is that he is crushing me! The idol!

BOUTON. We're both as good as hung, me included. Right beside each other on the square. You'll be hanging like this, and alongside—me. The innocently perished Jean-Jacques Bouton. Where am I? In the Kingdom of Heaven. I don't recognize the locale.

MOLIÈRE. All my life I licked his spurs, and I kept thinking just one thing: don't crush me. And now he's crushed me anyway. The tyrant!

BOUTON. And the drum beats on the square. The person who sticks his tongue out at the wrong time will have it hanging down to his waist.

MOLIÈRE. Why? Do you understand—I asked him this morning, why? I don't understand . . . I told him, Your Majesty, I hate such acts, I protest, I have been insulted, Your Majesty, allow me to explain . . . Please . . . perhaps I have flattered you too little? Perhaps I haven't crawled enough? . . . Your Majesty, where will you find another bootlicker like Molière? . . . But why was it, Bouton? Because of *Tartuffe*. Because of it I humiliated myself. I thought I would find an ally. I found one! Don't humiliate yourself, Bouton. I hate the king's tyranny!

BOUTON. Maître, they'll put up a monument to you. A girl by a fountain, and a stream of water gushing out of her mouth. You're a famous personality, but just shut up . . . May your tongue dry up and fall off . . . Why are you doing me in?

MOLIÈRE. What else do I have to do to prove that I am a worm? But, Your Majesty, I am a writer, I think, don't you know, I protest . . . she's not my daughter! (*To* Bouton.) Ask Madeleine Béjart in to see me, I want to ask her advice.

BOUTON. What's wrong with you, maître?

MOLIÈRE. Oh . . . she died . . . Why didn't you tell me the whole truth, my old woman? Or no, better yet, why, oh why didn't you teach me, why didn't you beat me? . . . Do you understand, you'll light a candle, she said, I will come to you . . . (*He is sad.*) The candles are burning, but she is not here . . . And I tore your shirt . . . Here's a louis d'or for your shirt.

BOUTON (*crybabyishly*). I'll call for someone . . . That was ten years ago, what's wrong with you . . .

MOLIÈRE. Pack everything. Tomorrow I will play for the last time and we will flee to England. How stupid! The wind blows across the sea, an alien language, but generally the problem isn't England, it's . . .

The door opens, and old Renée's *head appears.*

RENÉE. A nun has come for you out there.

MOLIÈRE (*frightened*). What? What sort of nun?

RENÉE. You were the one who wanted to give her the theater costumes to be laundered.

MOLIÈRE. Phooey, Renée, you old fool, how you scared me! Hey! The costumes! Tell her to come to the Palais Royal at the end of the performance tomorrow. You fool!

RENÉE. Why me? It was your own order.

MOLIÈRE. I didn't order anything.

Renée *disappears. A pause.*

Now, what other business is there? Oh yes, the shirt. Show me, where did I tear it?

BOUTON. Maître, lie down, for God's sake! What shirt?

Molière *suddenly jumps under the covers and hides his head under them.*

Almighty God, fix it so that no one hears what he has said. Let's apply some craft now. (*Unnaturally loudly and falsely, as if continuing a conversation.*) So what are you saying, dear sir? That our king is the very best, the most brilliant king in the whole world? For my part I have no objections. I subscribe to your opinion.

MOLIÈRE (*under the blanket*). No talent.

BOUTON. Be quiet. (*In a false voice.*) Yes, I was shouting, I am shouting, and I will continue to shout: long live the king!

Knocking on the window. Molière *sticks his head out from under the blanket anxiously.* Bouton *opens the window cautiously, and* Moirron, *upset, appears in the window with a lantern.*

MOIRRON. Who shouted? What happened?

BOUTON. Nothing happened. Why must something definitely have happened? I was chatting with Monsieur de Molière and I shouted, "Long live the king!" Doesn't Bouton even have the right to shout anything? So he shouts. "Long live the king!"

MOLIÈRE. God, what a talentless fool!

. . . The actors' dressing room in the Palais Royal. *And the old green poster hangs there as before, and* La Grange's *green lantern and the holy lamp by the crucifix are burning as before. But behind the curtain one can hear roaring and whistling.* Molière *is sitting in the armchair, wearing a skullcap, bathrobe, and make-up with a caricature nose.* Molière *is excited, in a strange state, as if drunk. Beside him, wearing doctor's costumes but without make-up are* La Grange *and* Du Croisy. *Caricature masks of doctors are lying around. The door opens and* Bouton *comes running in. At the beginning of the scene* Moirron *stands motionlessly at a distance, wearing a black cloak.*

MOLIÈRE. Well, is he dead?

BOUTON (*to* La Grange). They did it with a sword . . .

MOLIÈRE. I'll ask you to direct your remarks to the director of the Palais Royal, and not to the actors. I am still the boss of the last performance!

BOUTON (*to him*). Well, he is dead. He was struck in the heart with a sword.

MOLIÈRE. The Kingdom of Heaven be his. Well, what'll we do . . .

PROMPTER (*looking in the door*). What's going on?

LA GRANGE (*emphatically loudly*). What's going on? Musketeers have broken into the theater and killed the guard.

PROMPTER. Eh! . . . (*He disappears.*)

LA GRANGE. I, secretary of the theater, announce the following: the theater is full of ticketless musketeers and characters whom I do not know. I am helpless to restrain them, and I forbid the performance to be continued.

MOLIÈRE. But . . . but . . . but! . . . He forbids! Don't forget who you are! Compared to me you're a little boy; I have grey hair, that's what.

LA GRANGE (*in a whisper, to* Bouton). Has he been drinking?

BOUTON. Not a drop.

MOLIÈRE. What else did I want to say?

BOUTON. Precious Monsieur de Molière . . .

MOLIÈRE. Bouton! . . .

BOUTON. . . . go away! . . . I know, I have been with you for twenty years and all I have heard is "go away" or "shut up, Bouton!" And I have become used to it. You love me, maître, and in the name of that love I implore you on my knees—don't finish the performance —flee—the carriage is ready.

MOLIÈRE. Where did you get the idea that I love you? You're a babbler. No one loves me. They annoy me, they are persecuting me! And the archbishop's order not to bury me in the cemetery has been announced: so I suppose everyone will be inside the fence, but I will be on the edge, outside the fence. So keep this in mind—I don't need their cemetery, I spit on it! All my life you have hounded me, you are all my enemies!

DU CROISY. Have some fear of God, maître, we . . .

LA GRANGE (*to* Bouton). How can we act in such a state, how can we act?

Whistling and roaring behind the curtain.

There!

MOLIÈRE. A holiday it is! They've broken the chandeliers in the Palais Royal many times. The parterre is having some fun.

BOUTON (*ominously*). One-Eye is in the theater.

A pause.

MOLIÈRE (*quieted down*). And . . . (*Frightened.*) Where is Moirron? (*He rushes to* Moirron *and hides in his cloak.*)

Baring his teeth, Moirron *is silent, embraces* Molière.

DU CROISY (*in a whisper*). We must call a doctor.

Molière (*looking out from the cloak, timidly*). He cannot touch me on the stage, right? . . .

Silence. The door opens and Rivale *runs in. She is wearing a peculiar costume, half-naked as usual, with a doctor's hat on her head and eye-glasses like wheels.*

Rivale. The *entr'acte* can't be drawn out any longer. Either go on . . .

La Grange. He wants to go on, what should we do?

Rivale (*looks at* Molière *for a long time*). Go on.

Molière (*climbing out of the cloak*). Good girl! My brave old woman, come, I'll kiss you. Could you really start the last performance and not play it to the end? She understands. You've been acting with me for twelve years, and do you believe it, not once have I seen you dressed; you're always naked.

Rivale (*kisses him*). Eh, Jean Baptiste, the king will forgive you.

Molière (*cloudily*). He . . . Yes . . .

Rivale. Are you going to listen to me?

Molière (*having thought a bit*). I am. And I won't listen to them. (*Moving his leg somehow clumsily.*) They are fools. (*Suddenly he shudders and changes sharply.*) Forgive me, gentlemen, I allowed myself to be coarse. I can't understand how that popped out of me. I am upset. Try to understand my position. Monsieur du Croisy . . .

Du Croisy.
La Grange. } (*in a chorus*). We are not angry!
Bouton.

Rivale. Immediately after your last speech we will lower you through the trapdoor, we'll hide you in my dressing room until morning, and at dawn you will quit Paris. Agreed? Let's begin then.

Molière. Agreed. Let's have the last scene.

Du Croisy, La Grange, and Molière *grab their masks and disappear.* Molière *embraces* Rivale, *and she disappears.* Molière *takes off his dressing gown.* Bouton *opens the curtain separating us from the stage. On stage are a huge bed, a white statue, a dark portrait on the wall, a small table with a little bell. The chandeliers are blocked off with green screens and because of this there is comfy night lighting on stage. Candles are lit up in the prompter's box, the* Prompter *appears in it. The audience rumbles beyond the main curtain; from time to time ominous whistles break out. Sharply changed,* Molière *leaps into the bed with extraordinary ease, gets settled down, covers himself with the blanket.*

Molière (*to the* Prompter, *in a whisper*). Let's go!

A gong rings, the audience beyond the curtain quiets down. Gay, mysterious music starts up. Molière *starts to snore. The huge curtain falls with a rustle. It can be felt that the theater is overcrowded. In the close gilded loge some sort of gloomy faces crowd together. A thunderous roll of kettledrums in the music, and* La Grange *grows up out of the floor wearing an improbable nose and a black nightcap. He looks into* Molière's *face.*

Molière (*in terror*).
        What the devil! In my bedroom at night?
        Be so good as to get right out![3]

                Music.

La Grange.
        Don't shout so insolently,
        I am your therapist, Purgon!
Molière (*sits on his bed in terror*).
        Sorry. Who's that behind the screen?

The portrait on the wall tears apart, and out of it Du Croisy *sticks a drunken mug with a red nose, wearing doctors' eye-glasses and an oval hat.*

3. The company is putting on *Le Malade imaginaire*, but the lines in Bulgakov's version bear little if any relation to Molière's play. Except for the repetition of *bene, bene, bene, bene,* taken from one of the intermezzi, Bulgakov makes up and rhymes (in Russian) the speeches himself.

There's another one. (*To the portrait.*) I'm glad ...

Du Croisy (*in a drunken bass*).

    A delegate has come to you
    From the academy of venereologists.

Molière.

    Am I dreaming all this?! ...

The statue disintegrates, and out of it flies Rivale.

    What a bizarre occasion!

Rivale.   I am the permanent president
    Of the medical faculties.

In the audience: "Ha, ha, ha!" A monster grows up out of the floor—a doctor of implausible size.

Molière.   A doctor as tall as the first balcony.
    Servants. (*He rings.*) I'm going out of my mind!

Pillows explode on the bed, and Moirron *grows up at the head of the bed.*

Moirron.   And here I am—Diafoirus,
    The unforgettable Doctor Thomas!

A third, more distant curtain falls, and beyond it a choir of doctors and pharmacists grows up wearing strange and amusing masks.

Molière.   But to what do I owe this honor?
    Why, the hour is so late ...

Rivale.   We have come with news!

Chorus of Doctors (*roars*).

    You are being made a doctor!!

Rivale.   Who takes care of his stomach?

Moirron.   He who eats prunes by the fistful.

Rivale.   *Bene, bene, bene, bene!*

Chorus of Doctors.

    Novus doctor dignus est!

Du Croisy.   For example, let's say—lues? ...

Molière.   Seven years treatment if you catch that!

In the audience: "Ha, ha, ha!"

LA GRANGE. *Bravo, bravo, bravo, bravo,*
         A remarkable reply!
RIVALE.   He has great knowledge . . .
DU CROISY. And he swings from the shoulder!

Suddenly One-Eye *appears from the loge, sits on the edge of it, and freezes in an expectant pose.*

MOIRRON.
         And he'll get a degree in paradise . . .
CHORUS OF DOCTORS.
         A baccalaureate and a doctor's!
MOLIÈRE (*all of a sudden he falls ridiculously*). Send Madeleine to me! I need her advice . . . Help me! . . .

In the audience: "Ha, ha, ha!"

Parterre, don't laugh, just a moment, just a moment . . .

It quiets down. The music plays for a few more minutes, then breaks off. Confusion on the stage.

LA GRANGE (*taking off his mask near the front of the stage*). Ladies and gentlemen, Monsieur de Molière who is playing the role of Argan has taken a fall . . . (*Agitated.*) The performance cannot be finished.

Quiet. Then a shout from the loge: "Give us our money back!" Whistling and rumbling.

MOIRRON (*taking off his mask*). Who shouted about money? (*He takes out his sword, tests the tip.*)
BOUTON (*on stage, choking*). Who could shout such a thing?
MOIRRON (*pointing at the loge*). You, or you?

Quiet.

(*To* One-Eye.) You filthy animal!

Taking out his sword, One-Eye *comes onto the stage.*

MOIRRON (*like a cat, goes to meet him*). Come on, come on. Come here! (*When he gets even with* Molière, *he looks at him, sticks his sword into the floor, turns around and leaves the stage.*)

All of a sudden the Prompter *starts crying in the prompter's box.* One-Eye *looks at* Molière, *puts his sword in its scabbard and leaves the stage.*

LA GRANGE (*to* Bouton). Well drop the curtain!

The chorus recovers from its paralysis, the doctors and pharmacists rush to Molière, *surround him in a crowd and carry him off.* Bouton *finally drops the curtain, and this is followed by a roar in the audience.* Bouton *runs out after the group carrying* Molière.

LA GRANGE. Gentlemen, help me! (*He speaks through the opening in the curtain.*) Please, gentlemen . . . break it up . . . A misfortune has befallen us.

RIVALE (*through the other opening*). Gentlemen . . . Gentlemen . . .

The curtain bulges out, curious people try to climb up on stage.

DU CROISY (*through the third opening*). Gentlemen . . . Gentlemen . . .

LA GRANGE. Extinguish the lights!

Du Croisy *puts out the chandeliers, snuffing the candles with his sword. The roar in the audience quiets down somewhat.*

RIVALE (*through an opening*). Have some sympathy, gentlemen! . . . Break it up, gentlemen . . . The performance is over . . .

The last candle goes out, and the stage is plunged into darkness. Light comes out near the crucifix. The stage is open, dark, and empty. Not far from Molière's *mirror sits a dark hunched-up figure. Lantern light flows out onto the stage, a dark* La Grange *walks across.*

LA GRANGE (*in a solemn and severe voice*). Who is still here? Who's here?

BOUTON. It's I, Bouton.

LA GRANGE. Why don't you go to him?

BOUTON. I don't want to.

LA GRANGE (*comes to his own room, sits down, is illuminated by a green light, throws open the register, speaks, and writes*). "February seventeenth. It was the fourth performance of the play *Le Malade imaginaire* by Monsieur de Molière. At ten o'clock in the evening Monsieur de Molière, playing the role of Argan, fell down on the stage and was taken immediately, without confession, by unmerciful death." (*Pause.*) As a sign of this I am drawing the largest of black crosses. (*He thinks.*) What was the cause of this? What was it? How can I write it down? . . . The cause was the disfavor of the king and the black Cabal! . . . And thus I shall record it! (*He writes.*)

THE END

Date Due